Yale Agrarian Studies Series
JAMES C. SCOTT, *Series Editor*

The Agrarian Studies Series at Yale University Press seeks to publish outstanding and original interdisciplinary work on agriculture and rural society—for any period, in any location. Works of daring that question existing paradigms and fill abstract categories with the lived-experience of rural people are especially encouraged.
—James C. Scott, *Series Editor*

James C. Scott, *Seeing Like a State: How Certain Schemes to Improve the Human Condition Have Failed*

Brian Donahue, *The Great Meadow: Farmers and the Land in Colonial Concord*

J. Gary Taylor and Patricia J. Scharlin, *Smart Alliance: How a Global Corporation and Environmental Activists Transformed a Tarnished Brand*

Michael Goldman, *Imperial Nature: The World Bank and Struggles for Social Justice in the Age of Globalization*

Arvid Nelson, *Cold War Ecology: Forests, Farms, and People in the East German Landscape, 1945–1989*

Steve Striffler, *Chicken: The Dangerous Transformation of America's Favorite Food*

Parker Shipton, *The Nature of Entrustment: Intimacy, Exchange, and the Sacred in Africa*

Alissa Hamilton, *Squeezed: What You Don't Know About Orange Juice*

Parker Shipton, *Mortgaging the Ancestors: Ideologies of Attachment in Africa*

Bill Winders, *The Politics of Food Supply: U.S. Agricultural Policy in the World Economy*

James C. Scott, *The Art of Not Being Governed: An Anarchist History of Upland Southeast Asia*

Stephen K. Wegren, *Land Reform in Russia: Institutional Design and Behavioral Responses*

Benjamin R. Cohen, *Notes from the Ground: Science, Soil, and Society in the American Countryside*

Parker Shipton, *Credit Between Cultures: Farmers, Financiers, and Misunderstanding in Africa*

Paul Sillitoe, *From Land to Mouth: The Agricultural "Economy" of the Wola of the New Guinea Highlands*

Sara M. Gregg, *Managing the Mountains: Land Use Planning, the New Deal, and the Creation of a Federal Landscape in Appalachia*

Michael Dove, *The Banana Tree at the Gate: A History of Marginal Peoples and Global Markets in Borneo*

Patrick Barron, Rachael Diprose, and Michael Woolcock, *Contesting Development: Participatory Projects and Local Conflict Dynamics in Indonesia*

For a complete list of titles in the Yale Agrarian Studies Series, visit www.yalebooks.com.

The Banana Tree at the Gate

A History of Marginal Peoples
and Global Markets in Borneo

Michael R. Dove

Yale UNIVERSITY PRESS   NEW HAVEN & LONDON

Published with assistance from the Louis Stern Memorial Fund.

Yale University Press books may be purchased in quantity for educational, business, or promotional use. For information, please e-mail sales.press@yale.edu (U.S. office) or sales@yaleup.co.uk (U.K. office).

Set in Ehrhardt and TheSans types by Tseng Information Systems, Inc.

Printed in the United States of America.

Library of Congress Cataloging-in-Publication Data
Dove, Michael, 1949–
The banana tree at the gate : a history of marginal peoples and global markets in Borneo / Michael R. Dove.
p. cm. — (Yale agrarian studies series)
Includes bibliographical references and index.
ISBN 978-0-300-15321-7 (hardcover : alk. paper) 1. Marginality, Social—Borneo—History.
2. Markets—Social aspects—Borneo—History. I. Title. II. Series: Yale agrarian studies.
HN930.7.Z9M37 2011
306.3'49095983—dc22   2010015137

A catalogue record for this book is available from the British Library.

This paper meets the requirements of ANSI/NISO Z39.48-1992 (Permanence of Paper).

10 9 8 7 6 5 4 3 2 1

This work is dedicated to Carol Carpenter, who helped me start down the long path that led to this book.

Just what makes that little ol' ant,
Think he'll move that rubber tree plant.
Anyone knows an ant, can't
Move a rubber tree plant.
But he's got high hopes, he's got high hopes,
He's got high apple pie in the sky hopes.
—Sammy Cahn (1959)

Contents

Preface

When I first began fieldwork in Indonesian Borneo in 1974, in a longhouse of Kantu' Dayak located two weeks' travel upriver from the coast in West Kalimantan, I was greeted with questions and speculation as to whether I was one of the "Keling." This name subsumes a group of named individuals, including Kumang—the wife of Keling—and Laja and Ijau—their cousins—who are collectively called the *sebuah kana* (the fabled ones). (Richards [1981] translates these terms from the Iban as "spirit deities.") The Kantu' said that they once lived together *serumah* (in one longhouse) with the Keling, and at least one location on the nearby Mount Kedempai is identified as the site of one of their former settlements. The Keling are said to have looked like human beings, like the Kantu' themselves, but to have differed from the Kantu' in important ways: they kept fire in bronze vessels; they had yellow skin and wore yellow clothing; they could acquire valuable things without working for them; and they are said to have had other supernatural powers as well. The Kantu' claim that they copied their marital *adat* (customary law), especially that regarding the fetching of brides from wife-givers and the escorting of grooms to husband-takers, from the Keling. They say that the Keling helped the Kantu' in their historic wars with the Iban, but as the result of some dispute related to these wars—some say over competing claims to Iban trophy heads—the Keling left the Kantu'. Some say they went to Majapahit on Java, but before they left they made this promise: whenever the Kantu' need their help in war, they can be summoned by drum and/or war cry (see Sandin 1994 and Wadley 2004 for the Iban view of the Keling's role in war). The Keling are also supplicated in ritual and prayer on other occasions, most notably by the Kantu' when starting out on trading expeditions.

It is not unusual for anthropologists to be thus greeted in the field. Whenever an anthropologist or any other outsider enters a community, community members usually try to fit the newcomer into—so that he or she can thus be accommodated and explained by—existing social structures and world views. Sometimes this encompasses local visions of the past and even future, as in Anna Tsing's (1993) placement by her South Kalimantan mentor, Uma Adang, in a tale stretching back to the kingdom of Majapahit and forward to a new era of kings and peace (cf. Braginsky and Murtagh 2007 on Indo-Malay portrayals of foreigners).

I credit the people who thus try to make sense of the coming of anthropologists—Uma Adang kept asking Tsing, "What are you *really* here for?"—with more historical insight than is implied in the anthropologist's typical embarrassment at such moments. I suggest that anthropologists do not simply get fitted into local histories by our informants, but that we are already fitted in by our own histories. In my own case, the wider political, economic, and social currents that made it possible for me to work among the Kantu', which literally brought me to the doors of their longhouses, were bringing, or were soon to bring, other historic changes that would have far-reaching consequences for their lives. These changes included logging, plantation development, road building, transmigration, primary education, and, more generally, the ever-focusing gaze of the Indonesian state. In some sense therefore, my arrival among the Kantu' both heralded and personified these coming changes, of which I too was a product. But most crucial, these were not changes coming to a society that did not know change, and this is why my initial linkage to the Keling is important.

The Sanskrit origins of the term *Keling* lie far beyond Borneo in the ancient Kalinga kingdom of central-eastern India and its later namesake the seventh-century Kalingga kingdom in Indonesia. In the early modern era, *Keling* (or Kling) came to refer to traders from Coromandel on India's southeastern coast, who were central figures in the trade of Indian textiles for the valuable natural resources of the Indonesian archipelago. These Keling certainly sailed to and traded with people on Borneo's coasts, who were themselves trading with communities in the remoter interior; and some Indianized Hindu communities established kingdoms in the interior themselves, including in the interior of West Kalimantan. Indeed, the seventeenth-century court chronicle that I analyze in chapter 2, the *Hikayat Banjar*, lists "Keling" among the foreign traders who visited the kingdom, which was itself supposedly founded by a rich trader from Keling in India (Ras 1968). The earliest stone inscriptions in the entire Indonesian archipelago, which are found on seven stone pillars near Kutei in East Kalimantan, written in Sanskrit in the Pallava script of southern India and dating from around A.D. 400, further attest to the fact that the peoples of Borneo have been playing a role in the wider regional landscape for the better part of two millennia. The archaeological studies of Harrisson and O'Connor (1969, 1970) provide further evidence of the antiquity of Bornean commodity production and trade. The initial question of the Kantu' as to whether I was a Keling thus sprang directly from a particular economic and political history. Whereas linking me to a semimythical Indian community seemed fanciful to me, it would have made sense to most of Borneo's interior peoples. This was a historically informed assertion of the reality of the local experience of extra-local relations, a reality both ancient and ongoing. My book is an examination of this experience, focusing on the production and trade of commodities for global markets by Borneo's interior, tribal, swidden-cultivating peoples.

My interest in the way that Borneo's autochthonous peoples have historically participated in the global community runs against the grain of popular conceptions of this island and its peoples. These conceptions revolve around such quintessentially exotic, Orientalist phenomena as, for example, head-hunting, penis-pins, the orangutan, the Englishmen who became "rajahs" of Sarawak, and even the internationally renowned blockades of logging roads by Penan hunter-gatherers in the late 1980s and early 1990s. All of these foci of western interest are things that separate "us" from "them," not the reverse. Indeed, Borneo has long been an iconic site for the study and personal experience of the cultural as well as natural "other." This image is reflected in the wildly popular *Survivor: Borneo* 2000 television series, the nearly annual release of yet another personal account of traversing "wild" Borneo on foot, and the numerous popular accounts of living with Borneo's "headhunters." The more consequential but mundane economic interests that link us to them and our history to Borneo's history have received scant attention by comparison. That we are linked, as in the production in Borneo of commodities for global markets—including the rubber that American vehicles have run on for the better part of a century—has not been of interest.

But this is not a simple story about how even such distant and seemingly disparate members of the global community are really the same as us after all. The story is more complicated. The Bornean societies that are thus linked to us through participation in the global economic system are in many ways *not* like us: they are not simple peasants, for example; some of them were historically at one and the same time headhunters, shifting cultivators, and commodity producers; and they historically tried just as hard to stay out of the global system as to get into it. There is a conceptual welcoming niche for stories about people who are different; and there is another, revisionist niche for people who appear to be different but prove to be the same after all. But there is no niche for stories about people who are both the same and different, whose linkage to the global system is not straightforward (Ong and Collier 2005; Tsing 2005).

To tell this more complicated story, I have been obliged to depart from the traditional anthropological framework of a village-based ethnography. I do indeed draw on the several community-level studies that I have carried out in Kalimantan, including among the Kantu' Dayak and the Banjar, an Islamicized Dayak group in southern Borneo, but I also transcend them in time, space, and focus. I draw, for example, on both primary and secondary historical sources on the trade relations of Borneo and the rest of the archipelago; I analyze Malay court annals and native oral history; I examine colonial-era accounts of commodity production in both Southeast Asia and rubber's homeland in South America; I utilize contemporary accounts from parastatal plantations and primary data collected in government plantation offices on Java; and I weigh the evidence from native agro-ecology, social structure, economics, and cosmology. I analyze much local case-study material, but I also try to say something about the history of native society in Borneo as a whole.

This book is in part a historical work, and there is a general historical progression to the chapters from beginning to end, but it is not quite a historical ethnography, either. I do not strictly follow a linear historical narration, nor do I begin by telling the colonial story, then the developmental state story, and then the conservationist story. But these time frames emerge in the course of a more fractured narrative that pauses and deviates into Dutch-Banjar conversations over pepper, Promethean thefts of genetic material, tribal dreams, the way Dayak drew rubber into their agro-ecology, stories of rubber the wonder crop "killing the land," stories of "big gemstones and little men," and accounts of planter-worker mutual distrust. These micro-stories not only scatter the rudiments of the linear story but also travel back and forth in the same time frame.

The structure and scope of this work serve the additional purpose of forcing us away from a traditional vertical topography of opposition between central states and local communities. Ferguson (2006) believes that the waning of central-government authority and the waxing of other sorts of authority, especially transnational authority, pose new challenges for anthropology:

> Traditional leftist conceptions of progressive politics in the Third World . . . have almost always rested on one or another version of the vertical topography of power that I have described. "Local" people in "communities" and their "authentic" leaders and representatives who organize at the "grassroots," in this view, are locked in struggle with a repressive state representing . . . both imperial capitalism and the local dominant classes. . . . I do not mean to imply that this conception of the world is entirely wrong, or entirely irrelevant. But if, as I have suggested, transnational relations of power are no longer routed so centrally through the state, and if forms of governmentality increasingly exist that bypass states altogether, then political resistance needs to be reconceptualized in a parallel fashion.

My studies of the Dayak began early in the long and oppressive reign of Suharto, a reign that exemplified to many observers, including me, a stark Manichaean opposition between brutal central authority and oppressed, marginal minority populations. With the fall of Suharto and his regime in 1998, the situation has changed. As Lowe (2006) writes, "The effect Suharto's fall from power had on many of us, foreign scholar and Indonesian citizen alike, was that for the first time we were forced to think beyond good and evil." The Indonesianists Tsing (1999, 2005) and Li (2000, 2007) have been pioneers in moving anthropological analysis beyond a simple oppositional model of "bad state" and "good indigenous people" to the more nuanced realities of collaboration in many cases.

But the challenge posed by Lowe is complicated, because for over three decades, while foreign scholars thought about Indonesia in terms of good and evil, very few studied and wrote about it in such terms. The Suharto regime was extremely successful in suppressing outspoken scholarly critique (not to mention domestic critique, which was virtually eliminated by undisguised political intimidation) through the artful manipulation of research access, permission, funding, consulting opportunities, and other resources. I would therefore argue that Suharto's fall did not end the need for a discussion of the ills of an authoritarian central government but, rather, that it made it possible for the first time. This will not be a simple discussion. In response to McGlynn et al.'s (2007) decidedly negative retrospective of Suharto and his reign of fear, Henley (2009: 155) asks, rather startlingly, "Why not turn Nietzsche on his head, and ask: how much good has not also been done in the world out of fear?" So it quite likely will take scholars as long to come to grips with Suharto's legacy as it took him to build it.

My hope for this volume, therefore, is that it will contribute to painting a more complex picture of local resistance and state relations at the times and places where this is called for, while not forgetting, as the interior, minority groups of Kalimantan certainly have not, the times and places characterized by more starkly drawn lines of conflict and alliance.

Note on spelling: I have modernized the spelling of all Indonesian, Malay, Banjarese, Javanese, and Kantu' (Iban) terms.

Acknowledgments

I initially carried out field research on subsistence and cash-crop agriculture in Kalimantan between 1974 and 1976, with support from the National Science Foundation (Grant #GS-42605) and with sponsorship from the Indonesian Academy of Sciences (LIPI). I gathered additional data during six years of subsequent work based in Java between 1979 and 1985, making periodic field trips to Kalimantan with support from the Rockefeller and Ford Foundations and the East-West Center's Program on Environment and with sponsorship from Gadjah Mada University. I am deeply grateful to the national Institute for Plantation Education (LPP), which invited me to participate in its 1984–85 seminar on the conditions of estate agriculture in Indonesia. My first prolonged period of analysis and writing on the subject of this book was supported by fellowships from the East-West Center's Programs on Environment and Population (1989–1991) and by a visiting fellowship in Yale University's Program in Agrarian Studies (1991–1992). A subsequent series of short field trips to Java and Kalimantan, beginning in 1992, was supported by the Ford Foundation and the United Nations Development Programme. A collaborative regional study from 1993 to 2003 of sustainable resource use in Southeast Asia, which helped to place this project in context, was supported by the John D. and Catherine T. MacArthur Foundation, with sponsorship from Padjadjaran University and the State Ministry of National Development Planning, BAPPENAS.

Earlier versions of the chapters in this book were presented and/or published in the following places:

Chapter 1: An early version of part of this discussion was presented as "The Linked Ideologies of Smallholder and Estate Rubber in Southeast Asia," in the workshop "Ideologies of Plantation Agriculture," on 20 February 2004, Watson Institute, Brown University. Janet Sturgeon and Nick Menzies created a very stimulating environment for thinking through some of the ideas presented here.

Chapter 2: Earlier versions of this chapter were presented at the 91st annual meeting of the American Anthropological Association in San Francisco, 2–6 December 1992; the annual meeting of the American Institute of Biological Sciences (Society for Economic Botany) in Honolulu, 9–13 August 1992; and the Koninklijk Instituut voor Taal-, Land- en Volkenkunde's workshop "Man and Environment in Indonesia, 1500–1950," on 28 June 1996, which opened my eyes to the scope of historical approaches to Indonesia's environment. The input and feedback during and subsequent to this workshop from Peter Boomgaard, David Henley, Freek Colombijn, and Anthony Reid were invaluable. Harold C. Conklin at Yale and Barbara Andaya at the University of Hawaii also offered very useful comments. My papers from those meetings were published as "Political Ecology of Pepper in the Hikayat Banjar: The Historiography of Commodity Production in a Coastal Bornean Sultanate," in *Man and Environment in Indonesia, 1500–1950*, D. Henley and F. Colombijn, eds., Verhandelingen 178, Leiden: Koninklijk Instituut voor Taal-, Land- en Volkenkunde (1997); and "The 'Banana Tree at the Gate': Perceptions of Pepper Production in a Seventeenth Century Malay State," in *Economic Botany* 51 (4): 347–61 (1997).

Chapter 3: An earlier version of this chapter was presented at the XVII Pacific Science Congress in Honolulu on 30 May 1991. The convener of the congress, Jefferson Fox, offered me valuable comments on my analysis. Different versions of this paper were published as "The Transition from Native Forest Rubbers to *Hevea brasiliensis* (Euphorbiaceae) among Tribal Smallholders in Borneo" in *Economic Botany* 48 (4): 382–96 (1994); "The Impact of Cultivation on Peasant-State Relations in Forest Product Development" in *Society and Non-Timber Forest Products in Tropical Asia*, J. Fox, ed., East-West Center Occasional Paper No. 19, pp. 55–72 (1995); and "Political versus Techno-Economic Factors in the Development of Non-Timber Forest Products: Lessons from a Comparison of Natural and Cultivated Rubbers in Southeast Asia (and South America)" in *Society and Natural Resources* 8:193–208 (1995).

Chapter 4: An earlier version of this chapter was presented as "Indigenous Knowledge versus Jungli Thinking: The Case Study of Natural Rubber Production," in the workshop "Indigenous Environmental Knowledge and Its Transformations," 8–10 May 1997, Canterbury, UK. This was a path-breaking and extremely stimulating, critical assessment of the then-explosion of interest in indigenous knowledge. Different versions of this paper were published as "The Life-Cycle of Indigenous Knowledge, and the Case of Natural Rubber Production," in *Indigenous Environmental Knowledge and Its Transformations,* Roy F. Ellen, Peter Parkes, and Alan Bicker, eds., pp. 213–51, Amsterdam: Harwood (2000); and "Hybrid Histories and Indigenous Knowledge among Asian Rubber Smallholders," in *International Social Science Journal* 173:349–59 (2002). Roy F. Ellen and Arun Agrawal both made extremely helpful contributions to these earlier analyses.

Chapter 5: Earlier versions of this chapter were presented at the 90th annual meeting of the American Anthropological Association in Chicago on 23 November 1991; in Cornell University's Southeast Asia Program on 5 December 1991; in Yale University's Agrarian Studies Program on 11 September 1992; and in the University of Michigan's Department of Anthropology and School of Natural Resources and the Environment on 12 April 1995. I benefited from valuable insights from a number of colleagues in Yale's Agrarian Studies Program, especially David Nugent, Parker Shipton, K. Sivaramakrishnan, and James C. Scott. An earlier version of this paper was published as "Rice-Eating Rubber and People-Eating Governments: Peasant versus State Critiques of Rubber Development in Colonial Indonesia" in *Ethnohistory* 43 (1): 33–63 (1996).

Chapter 6: An earlier version of this chapter was presented in Yale University's Southeast Asia Program on 23 January 1991, at the invitation of Joe Errington. An earlier version was published as "Rubber and Swidden Agriculture in Borneo: A Sustainable Adaptation to the Ecology and Economy of the Tropical Forest" in *Economic Botany* 47 (2): 136–47 (1993). The long-time editor of this journal, Lawrence Kaplan, was of great help in editing and publishing not only this paper but also earlier drafts of chapters 2 and 3 as well.

Chapter 7: Earlier versions of this chapter were presented at the annual meeting of the International Association for the Study of Common Property in Washington, DC, on 19 September 1992, and the 92nd annual meeting of the American Anthropological Association in Washington, DC, on 19 November 1993. An earlier version was published as "Living Rubber, Dead Land, and Persisting Systems in Borneo: Indigenous Representations of Sustainability," in *Bijdragen* 154 (1): 20–54 (1998).

Chapter 8: Earlier versions of this chapter were presented as the Henry S. Graves Lecture at the Yale University School of Forestry and Environmental Studies on 12 December 1991; as the keynote address for the Fourth Annual Conference of the Northwest Regional Consortium for Southeast Asian Studies at the University of Oregon on 8 November 1991; and at the conference "Interactions of People and Forests in Kalimantan" at the New York Botanical Garden on 21 June 1991. Different versions of the paper from these meetings were published as "A Revisionist View of Tropical Deforestation and Development" in *Environmental Conservation* 20 (1): 17–24, 56 (1993); "Marketing the Rainforest: 'Green' Panacea or Red Herring?" in the East-West Center Issues Paper No. 13 (1994); and "So Far from Power, So Near to the Forest: A Structural Analysis of Gain and Blame in Tropical Forest Development" in *Borneo in Transition: People, Forests, Conservation, and Development*, C. Padoch and N. Peluso, eds., pp. 41–58, Kuala Lumpur: Oxford University Press (1996). Christine Padoch, Nancy Peluso, Lawrence Hamilton, and A. Terry Rambo all offered very useful critiques of this analysis.

Chapter 9: Earlier versions of this chapter were presented in Cornell University's Southeast Asia Program and Department of Rural Sociology on 14 November 1989, and in the conference "Agrarian Transformation in the Indonesian Uplands," organized by Tania Li at Dalhousie University on 14 May 1995. The latter was one of the most intensive and stimulating seminars in which I have ever participated, and much credit goes to it for the development of my thinking about planters and smallholders. The paper from this meeting was published as "Representations of the 'Other' by Others: The Ethnographic Challenge Posed by Planters' Views of Peasants in Indonesia," in *Transforming the Indonesian Uplands: Marginality, Power, and Production*, T. Li, ed., pp. 203–29, Amsterdam: Harwood (1999). Tania Li heroically and usefully pushed me to clarify my analysis of this material.

Yale University has provided a supportive and stimulating environment for the work on this book which is, indeed, very much a product of this wonderful institution. Early versions of the arguments presented here were presented in a number of different classes and seminars at Yale, including: "Seminar on Tropical Forest Resource-Use" (Spring 1998); "Agrarian Societies: Culture, Power, History, and Development" (Fall 1998, 1999, 2000); and "Society and Environment: Advanced Readings" (Spring 2007). The entire text was presented and discussed in "Leaves, Livelihoods, and Landscapes: Socioeconomics and Politics of Development across Borneo" (Fall 2008) and "Disaster, Degradation, Dystopia: Social Science Approaches to Environmental Perturbation and Change" (Fall 2008). The students in these classes were wonderful interlocutors. I am very grateful to my administrative assistant Laurie Bozzuto for keeping the world at bay; to a series of sterling research assistants, Caroline Simmonds, Yuliya Shmidt, and Katie Hawkes, for their heroic work on obscure library searches; to my excellent copy editor Kate Davis and to Jack Borrebach and Jaya Chatterjee at Yale University Press, and especially Executive Editor Jean Thomson Black, for making the publication of this book a joy; and finally to my mentors at Yale and two of the greatest modern scholars of Southeast Asia, Harold C. Conklin and James C. Scott, for gently insisting that I make this project a priority.

None of the aforementioned people or organizations necessarily agree with anything said in this volume, however, for which I am alone responsible.

PART I

Introduction

This first section of the book introduces the key concepts and themes that will occupy the chapters to come. I begin by introducing and then complicating the concept of the "smallholder" agriculturalist or commodity producer and reviewing the ancient history of commodity production for global markets in Borneo. I then discuss the concept of the "dual household economy," which is central to the entire book, comprising both a subsistence-oriented sector and a market-oriented sector; and I examine the implications of this dualism for the relationship of the local household to the extra-local society. The dual economy entails a particular pattern of daily labor, and I look at the way this pattern is determined by culture, by agronomy, and by the state and the parastatal estate sector. I argue that the legitimacy and viability of the estate sector depends upon its drawing an epistemological boundary between itself and the smallholder sector. The survival of the smallholder sector, in turn, depends upon the strategic manipulation of its own legibility and illegibility. Finally, I discuss some of the implications for this analysis of past scholarship on estates and smallholdings.

The Study of Smallholder Commodity Producers

Background

Angkol ari nya' beburong nebang kampung. Apai ari nya' nebas memudai. Inai ngau Bernai mutung getah kami dapi' Lubuk Kepaiyang. (Angkol that day sought omens to fell old forest [for a swidden]. Father that day slashed secondary forest [for a swidden]. Mother and [sister] Bernai tapped our rubber near the river bend Kepaiyang.)
—*Journal of Angkol, Longhouse Tikul Batu, West Kalimantan, Indonesia*

In these seemingly banal few sentences, written down in a daily journal kept by a former research assistant of mine, lies the key to an important thread in the history of globalization. These sentences illustrate the all-important division within the household between two fundamentally different types of production: one, swidden cultivation in this case, oriented toward meeting the household's subsistence needs; and the other, here rubber tapping, oriented toward meeting the household's market needs. They illustrate *the* central dynamic in the historic role of the tribal peoples of Borneo, and elsewhere, in the global economy.

Angkol is a Kantu', a member of an Ibanic-speaking tribe of Dayak who live in the northern and westerly headwaters of the Kapuas River in West Kalimantan, Indonesian Borneo (figure 1.1). Through most of the twentieth century the Kantu' met their subsistence food needs through the swidden cultivation of food crops;[1] and they met their market needs through the gathering of forest products, the cultivation of the pepper plant (*Piper nigrum* L. [Piperaceae]), and, in particular, cultivation of the Para rubber tree (*Hevea brasiliensis* [Willd. ex Adr. de Juss.] Müll.-Arg.). They accomplished this by dividing their lands and especially labor between subsistence- and market-oriented activities. They seasonally divided their time between the two types of work, and sometimes, as on the day narrated above, they

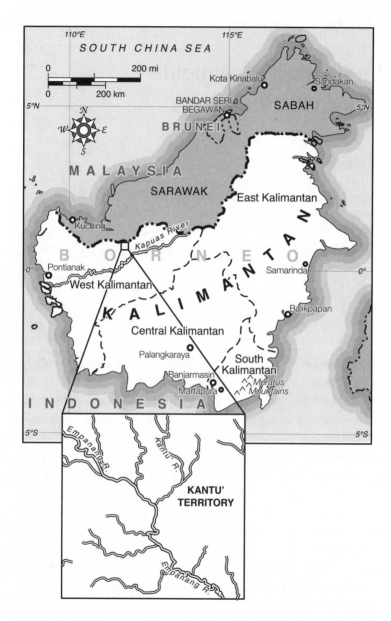

Figure 1.1. Kalimantan, Indonesia, showing the territories of the Kantu' in the west and the center of the Banjarese homeland at Banjarmasin in the southeast

divided the day and their household labor force in two. This routinized division of labor and other resources, this day-to-day differentiation of household production, has been documented all over the world throughout the modern era. It is central to understanding both the history of groups like the Kantu' and the political-economic history of the global trade in which they have participated.

Smallholders

I refer to the Kantu' and similar groups by the term *smallholder*.[2] In the bible of smallholder studies, Robert McC. Netting's "Smallholders, Householders" (1993: 2), smallholders are defined as "rural cultivators practicing intensive, permanent, diversified agriculture on relatively small farms in areas of dense population."[3] In fact, most of the groups to whom I apply the label "smallholder" practice *extensive* agriculture—including swidden cultivation—in regions of *low* population density. The rarity with which such groups have been called smallholders is due to a basic misunderstanding of their agricultural economies. As Netting (1993: 10) himself says: "Perhaps the most stubborn and pervasive myth about smallholders is that their physical isolation in rural areas, their simple technology, and their modicum of self-sufficiency remove them from dependency on a market and the mentality of maximization, greed, private property, and inequality that is thought to be the market's inevitable accompaniment." But as he continues, "In fact, smallholders do not normally live in isolation from larger networks of economic exchange or political organization" (Netting 1993: 15).[4] The myth of removal from the market is even more pronounced with tribal swidden cultivators like the Kantu', and yet their involvement in markets is an integral part of their history and identity.

In Indonesia *kebun rakyat* (people's holdings), or smallholdings, must be distinguished from *perkebunan besar* (big holdings), or plantations or estates, most of which are parastatal organizations, including both *Perusahaan Negara Perkebunan* and *Perusahaan Terbatas Perkebunan*, respectively government and semiprivate plantation corporations, as well as *pabrik gula*, semiprivate sugar mills. They are managed by a national cadre of professional managers, drawn mostly from Indonesia's dominant ethnic groups, mainly Javanese or Batak. These state and parastatal agricultural enterprises have for one half-century been among the most important forces affecting the social and physical environment in rural Indonesia, as their colonial predecessors were for the half-century before that. The rural peoples whose lives are most directly affected by these plantations are the local peasant and tribal communities whose land and/or labor is coveted by them. Disagreements over the terms of exchange of this land and labor have been the rule rather than the exception. These enterprises nonetheless escaped widespread critical attention until the late 1990s (but see Stoler 1985a: 7), when they were at the center of dramatic episodes of social, environmental, and economic violence, notably: (1) recurring outbreaks of ethnic violence in the vicinity of huge oil palm and rubber plantations in West Kalimantan; (2) the burning of plantation lands throughout Kalimantan by wildfires so great as to imperil human health in neighboring countries; and (3) the collapse at the national level of the crony capitalism to which these plantations were integral.

According to the long-prevailing development discourse in Indonesia regarding export crops, there is a presumption that forest-dwelling smallholders live outside the market and must be assisted into it. This is a remarkable premise, given that the involvement of the region's smallholders in production of commodities for global markets is ancient. It represents the active erasure of nearly two millennia of history, which is thus made "empty" (Benjamin 1969). It neatly reverses the smallholders' real problematic, which is not how to get into the market, but how to stay — partly — out of it. The development discourse also reverses the problematic for the plantation establishment. Rubber smallholders like the Kantu' not only dominate rubber production in Indonesia and Malaysia, but this dominance is the product of a century of direct competition with the estates. The estates held a commanding share of the region's rubber production during the industry's early years at the start of the twentieth century, and they have steadily lost ground to the smallholders ever since (figure 1.2). The smallholders — more primitive, less capitalized, less intensive, but more efficient and tenacious — have continually threatened the estates with their cut-rate competition. Smallholders held more than 84 percent of Indonesia's rubber acreage in 2004, and they produced more than 80 percent of its rubber (Government of Indonesia 2004: 1/table 1).[5] The smallholders' historical success has been attained without support from the successive central governments of Indonesia and often in spite of active government hindrance. Up to the present day, the Indonesian government has directed almost all of its technical, material, and regulatory support to the estate sector or to block-planting schemes that make the smallholders over in the image of the estates (for example, the

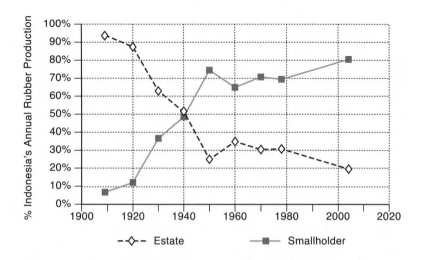

Figure 1.2. History of smallholder versus estate market share

"nucleus-estate" schemes; see p. 28). Almost the only attention that it has given to the smallholder sector has been punitive in nature.[6]

General analyses of smallholder agriculture are found in historical studies of Indonesian economics by Boeke (1953), Booth (1988), Lindblad (1988), and Pelzer (1978a). In the 1980s a plethora of pioneering studies came out on the contemporary economics of this sector, many from Colin Barlow and his colleagues, for example, Barlow and Jayasuriya (1984) and Barlow and Tomich (1991); followed by an equally pioneering groups of studies on their agro-forestry (de Foresta and Michon 1994; Mary and Michon 1987). More recent studies of this topic have focused on new topics, such as the ecology of smallholdings (for example, Lawrence 1996) or their political economy and ecology (for example, Cramb 2007; Li 2002; Wadley and Mertz 2005). Studies devoted to smallholder rubber in particular have been carried out by ACIAR (1985), Angelsen (1995), Barlow and Muharminto (1982), Cramb (1993), Gouyon, de Foresta, and Levang (1993), Joshi et al. (2003), Penot (2004), and Tomich (1991). Important recent studies of successful small-holder systems of production from beyond the region include Bassett (2006) on cotton in the northern Cote d'Ivoire, Brondizio (2008) on the açai palm of the Amazon, Grossman (1998) on bananas in the eastern Caribbean, and Sturgeon (2005) on opium and tea in the China/Thailand borderlands.

In addition to being a study of smallholders and estates, this book is a study of commodities and their production and circulation, which has become a subject of increasing interest within anthropology. The pioneering work in this area within anthropology is Mintz's (1985) study of sugar, followed by similar studies of cotton (Isaacman 2005), maize (McCann 2005), and other crops, all using a single crop as a prism to refract our vision of society. Whereas this work was deeply historical, other contributions have been less so (for example, Edelman and Haugerud 2005), reflecting a widespread vision of commoditization and even of globalization as contemporary phenomena, but this vision is belied by the relevant history in Southeast Asia.[7]

Historical Setting

The involvement of the land and people of the Indonesian archipelago in commodity production is not a modern phenomenon. Wolters (1967: 158, 159) suggests that Indonesian kingdoms were trading with India by the third century A.D. and probably earlier, that Indonesian ships were carrying foreign products—those from India and points west—to China in the fourth century, and that Indonesia developed a direct trade with China in its own products in the fifth century.[8] He says that Java's trade with China was well established by 430, and that between 430 and 473 there were twenty separate trade and diplomatic missions from western Indonesia to China (Wolters 1967: 152, 153). The archipelago may have initially been a way station in the trade between western Asia and China. In time, the traders and sailors in the archipelago began to substitute local products for the scarce and costly products from distant lands to the west, a process that Wolters (1967) claims underlay the development of the archipelago's China trade. Donkin (1999: 11) writes that as early as the fifth century, Indonesian merchants were passing off *Pinus merkusii* as frankincense (originally one of several species from the genus *Boswellia*, native to the Arabian Peninsula and North Africa) to the Chinese. Another example is "dragon's blood," the sap of the rattan *Daemonorops* Blume, spp., found in Sumatra and Borneo, which appears to have partially replaced in the China trade a similar product from Arabia (Hirth and Rockhill 1911: 197–98). This duplicitous trade by substitution eventually became a trade in local products in their own right. For example, India was the primary source of pepper for China and the rest of the world for the better part of a millennium, shipped through entrepôts in North Sumatra; but by the fifteenth century these Sumatran ports were growing pepper themselves. Extensive planting there in the sixteenth century began to threaten India's dominance, and Sumatra dominated global production from the seventeenth to nineteenth centuries (Bulbeck et al. 1998: 62, 69).

Sumatra was long a center of commodity trade and production within the archipelago. Another center, because of their natural wealth of spices (nutmeg, mace, and cloves), was the Banda and Moluccan islands in the eastern part of the archipelago.[9] Kalimantan, or Borneo (to use the term for the entire island), was historically prominent in the regional trade as a source of diamonds, gold, and a variety of forest products (see chapter 2). Java played a central role in regional trade for a millennium, based on the political clout of a succession of Javanese kingdoms and on the traditional rice surpluses of their fertile volcanic soils, which were traded for spices from the islands to the east and for pepper from Sumatra to the west (Meilink-Roelofsz 1962: 23, 105).[10] Mention must also be made of the great emporium of Malacca on the southern coast of the Malay Peninsula, which was founded around 1400 by a Sumatran prince fleeing an attack by the kingdom of Majapahit, and which dominated the region's trade until its fall to the Portuguese in 1511 (Ricklefs 2008: 21, 25). For a century, Malacca tied the archipelago into a trading network that reached westward to South Asia, the Middle East, Africa, and the Mediterranean, and northward and eastward to mainland Southeast Asia and East Asia, constituting "the greatest trading system in the world at this time" (Ricklefs 2008: 23). Malacca waned under the Portuguese, and with the entry of the Dutch to the archipelago and the union of competing Dutch firms in the United East India Company (the Vereenigde Oost-Indische Compagnie, or VOC) in 1602 (Ricklefs 2008: 29–30), the center of gravity shifted to Batavia on the northwest coast of Java, which the Dutch founded in 1619.

Prior to the arrival of the Europeans, the principal foreign actors in the archipelago's trade were India—of which the Keling have already been mentioned in the preface—and China. The Chinese first traded directly with the Moluccans for their spices in the fourteenth century (Meilink-Roelofsz 1962: 99, 158), although they had received Moluccan spices via Java for centuries before that (Ptak 1993), and much of our knowledge of the trading history of the region comes from Chinese port records (for example, Hirth and Rockhill 1911). The Portuguese came to the archipelago in the beginning of the sixteenth century with the policy goal, never attained, of establishing a spice trade route from Asia to Portugal via the Cape of Good Hope, which would cut out merchants from Asia and the Mediterranean (Meilink-Roelofsz 1962: 116–17, 134). The Portuguese were uninterested in the local, coastal trade, which was little affected by their presence (ibid.: 120, 136). This was not true of the Dutch and English who followed them, both of whom had much more interest in controlling commodity production and trade within the archipelago. The Americans were latecomers to this trade but eventually came to play a major role as well. Traders out of Salem, Massachusetts, shipped more pepper out of Sumatra than the Dutch or English did in the early 1800s (Bulbeck et al. 1998: 66), and American firms became major players in the colonial-era plantation cultivation of rubber in Sumatra (Stoler 1985a: 17–22).[11] By the outbreak of World War II, American firms were producing about one-fifth of Sumatra's rubber, and almost one-half of its exported rubber was going to the United States (Stoler 1985a: 21; Tucker 2007: 126). The interruption in supply occasioned by that war prompted an enormous American investment in research on synthetic rubber, second in magnitude only to the atomic bomb project (Tucker 2007: 137–38)[12]; and today the United States is still the major importer of rubber (34 percent of the total) from Indonesia (Government of Indonesia 2004: xxvi). Colonial and post-colonial political-economic relations reoriented the trading dynamics of the archipelago from an internal to an external focus: whereas much or even most of the archipelago's trade was internal in the days of Malacca, by 1914 this accounted for only 5–6 percent of the total (Ricklefs 2008: 186–87).

For over a millennium, the archipelago's trade focused on exotic goods, in particular aromatics,[13] initially based on tree resins and then later on spices.[14] The spice trade was pivotal in the early modern history of Europe. As Freedman (2008: 164) writes, "The great expeditions at the end of the fifteenth century, journeys that marked the beginning of Europe's global reach, were launched by the desire for spices." And among the spices, pepper was historically the most important (see my chapter 2). Pepper was the great boom product of international trade from the fifteenth to seventeenth centuries (Ricklefs 2008: 18) and played a pivotal role in the rise of the European colonial project. The dominant role of pepper and the other spices was waning by the eighteenth century,[15] however, even before colonialism reached its zenith (Freedman 2008: 3), to be replaced by more mundane goods, including oil and rubber for machinery, textiles—which surpassed pepper in importance by 1700 (Ricklefs 2008: 76)—and sugar and tea for the laboring masses, although Freedman (2008) and Mintz (1985: 80) note that sugar itself was considered to be a "spice" before it became transformed into a food item of mass consumption. Rubber in the late modern era was as pivotal as pepper in the early modern era: as Schultes (1987: 89) writes, "There can be little doubt that no other species has so drastically changed human life around the world in the short space of a century. The domestication of this tree literally altered the course of civilization."

The earliest methods of commodity production in the region involved—in the case of tree resins, saps, and other forest products—finding, gathering, and processing by interior tribal populations, who then passed on the final product as trade or tribute to coastal, native states involved in wider trade networks. The integration of coastal and interior populations into a single economic system extends back to the earliest trading state in the archipelago, Śrīvijaya in Sumatra (Wolters 2008: 96, 99).[16] More intensive and historically subsequent methods involved the cultivation of crops like pepper by smallholders working under the political authority of native states.[17] Colonial European intrusion into the region initially consisted of simply trying to monopolize the trade with these states. Dutch interest in controlling and monopolizing the valuable spice trade in eastern Indonesia, and in particular in excluding the English from this trade, led to a dramatic ratcheting up of the intensity of colonial involvement in that part of the archipelago early in the seventeenth century. This consisted of close control of natives and spices on certain islands and complete eradication of both, and thus the possibility for competing trade, on all others (Meilink-Roelofsz 1962: chap. 9). Another dramatic intensification of colonial control was the Dutch implementation of the *cultuurstel* (cultivation system) in 1830, which involved the compulsory sale of export crops to the colonial government at fixed prices, as a way of paying land taxes (Ricklefs 2008: 144, 145). Initially very remunerative, this system undermined food-crop production, and led to soil infertility, rice shortages, famines, peasant flight, and epidemics; and it was gradually dismantled in the second half of the nineteenth and beginning of the twentieth centuries (Ricklefs 2008: 149). One of the principal actions that the Dutch took to replace the *cultuurstel* was passage of the Agrarian Law of 1870, which opened up the East Indian agricultural sector to private entrepreneurs (Ricklefs 2008: 150). This prompted a flood of activity by individual planters, but they were largely replaced within a generation by corporations (Stoler 1985a: 16–17). The latter were responsible for the development of the huge, monospecific, industrialized estates that are seen as typifying export commodity production today but that, as this history attests, are actually relatively recent developments in the archipelago.[18] During the colonial era in Indonesia and Malaysia, rubber, for example, was cultivated by native smallholders with several acres, who did not live entirely off of their tapping; medium-holders of up to one hundred acres, often Chinese, who depended entirely on their tapping; and European-owned, heavily capitalized estates of more than one hundred acres (cf. Kato 1991: 155; Ooi 1959: 142–44).[19] The Japanese occupation during World War II seriously disrupted export-crop production by all producers large and small, and then in 1957 the national government confiscated all of the Dutch estates (Tucker 2007: 141). Although local "squatters" took over many of the estates in Sumatra after World War II (ibid.: 140), many if not most of the colonial-era estates have persisted to the present day as parastatal enterprises, in form and function much like their colonial-era forbears. The histories of Sumatra, Java, and Kalimantan are quite different in this regard: colonial estate sectors like the ones in Sumatra and Java never developed in Kalimantan, where, on the contrary, smallholder production dominated for most of the twentieth century (ibid.: 142; Dijkman 1961: 253).

Borneo has played an important role in the history of the archipelago's commodity trade (see chapter 2). Organized states on the island are ancient, as attested to by the stone pillars at Kutai mentioned in the preface, but throughout much of recorded history the island has fallen under the at-least-nominal orbit of some external power. For example, southern Borneo has been subject to political authorities based on Java; first to Majapahit, then Demak, then Japara, and then eventually to the Dutch (Meilink-Roelofsz 1962: 101). The Dutch began interceding in the trade of the coastal Bornean states early in the seventeenth century, but the island was a low priority for them until the arrival of the Englishman James Brooke in western Borneo in 1839 and the development of coal mines in southern and eastern Kalimantan beginning in 1846 (Ricklefs 2008: 169–70). The historic place of Borneo within wider political networks, in particular the asymmetry between its resource wealth and its subservience to external political powers, has persisted into modern times as part of a broader distinction between "inner" and "outer" Indonesia. Ricklefs (2008: 186) writes of this pattern as it developed early in the twentieth century:[20] "The outer islands were the areas of deeper Islamic commitment, greater entrepreneurial activity, more valuable export products, greater foreign investment, more recent Dutch subjugation and less population pressure. Java was the land of more uneven Islamisation, less entrepreneurship, declining value as a source of exports, less new economic development, longer and more fundamental colonial interference, and overpopulation. Such generalisations of course conceal much variety and many changes, but nevertheless the history of twentieth-century Indonesia was shaped to a considerable degree by this distinction." An important dimension of this distinction during the Suharto regime was a confiscatory pattern of development of natural resources—for example, timber, oil, export crops—in the outer islands at the expense of the local population and for the benefit of the Javanese-dominated regime in Jakarta. A related development was the relocation of hundreds of thousands of Javanese to the outer islands through government-sponsored transmigration projects.

These transmigrants, and spontaneous migrants as well from Madura, joined an older mixture in Borneo of Dayak, Malays, and Chinese. Chinese traders have been on the island since ancient times—a gravestone records the death of a Chinese Muslim in Brunei in 1264 (Ricklefs 2008: 4)—and large numbers came to the island in more recent times to cultivate pepper (Bulbeck et al. 1998: 68) or to mine gold (Jackson 1970).[21] The Malay population, enlarged through much of this history by Islamicized Dayak, has been settled since earliest recorded history along the island's coasts and rivers, where it specialized in trading, fishing, and agriculture. This population succeeded the ancient Indianized Hindu communities mentioned in the preface, who have disappeared as distinct entities. The Dayak population can be divided into the hunter-gatherer Penan and Punan, forest-product specialists who historically practiced little if any agriculture, and the rest of the Dayak, comprising culturally quite diverse groups, but all of whom, like the Kantu', lived—at least through most of the twentieth century—by swidden cultivation for subsistence and, for market purposes, the gathering of forest products and/or cultivation of export crops.

The Dual Economy of Subsistence and Market Production

A defining characteristic of the smallholders being discussed here is that production of commodities for global markets comprises only a part of their productive activities. They have dual or composite economies (Dove 1985a), which include both activities oriented toward food production for the subsistence of the household and activities oriented toward production of commodities for sale in the market to meet needs for cash and/or market goods.[22] The relationship between the "house economy" and the market, between more-monetized and less-monetized sectors, is one of the principal challenges to the smallholder economy. Since the work of Polanyi (1957) on the so-called double movement, it has been a central topic for economic anthropologists (Gudeman 1986; Gudeman and Rivera 1990; Mayer 2002; Parry and Bloch 1989; Shipton 1989); and it is one of the principal subjects of the present study. The evolution, persistence, and historical resilience of these dual economies—which de Janvry (1981: 37) erroneously called only a passing "phase in the development of capitalism in the periphery"—is a subject of special interest here.

In the case of the Kantu' of West Kalimantan, throughout most of the twentieth century they met their subsistence food needs by cultivating dry rice as well as some swamp rice and a wide variety of nonrice cultigens, including a second cereal, maize, a number of different cucurbits, and a number of different tubers, including cassava and sweet potato and, to a lesser extent, taro. Rice is the primary starch staple and the focus of each meal, supplemented with one or more of the nonrice cultigens as a "relish." When the rice crop fails to meet subsistence requirements, as it may several years in ten, the market crops are sold to buy rice; and if that is impossible, then cassava and other tubers become the starch staple for the duration of the famine period. Before the twentieth century, the Kantu' met their market needs primarily through the gathering of forest products, especially plant "exudates," including gums, resins, and, in particular, latexes (see chapter 3). During the twentieth century, they largely abandoned the gathering of native rubbers for the cultivation of the exotic Para rubber (*Hevea brasiliensis*) from the Amazon and, to a lesser extent, the older exotic black pepper (*Piper nigrum*). Malayic[23] groups like the Banjar in southern Borneo were involved in the cultivation of pepper as early as the fifteenth century (see chapter 2).

This combination of market-oriented agriculture and extensive, subsistence-oriented agriculture was long common in Southeast Asia (see Pelzer 1945, 1978b).[24] Other examples from Indonesia include swidden agriculture and rattans in East Kalimantan (Fried 2000; Lindblad 1988: 59–60; Peluso 1983a, 1983b; Tsing 1984; Weinstock 1983); swidden agriculture, coffee, and damar (resins) in Sumatra (Mary and Michon 1987; Michon et al. 2000); and sago palm and spices in the Moluccas (Ellen 1979, 2003).

Different Transactional Orders

The constituent parts of such dual economies—their subsistence versus market sectors—are not interchangeable. Rice and rubber, for example, cannot replace one another. Success or failure in one is not cause for abandonment in favor of the other.[25] There is complementarity between the subsistence and market spheres, based in part on their agro-ecology: thus, rubber tapping and swidden cultivation fit differently into calendars of labor use, times of plenty and want, ritual versus secular days, and even rain versus sunshine (see chapter 6). But equally important is the fact that the cultural niches constructed for rubber gardens versus food swiddens are fundamentally different; they belong to different "transactional orders" (see chapter 5). The subsistence, nonmonetized cultivation of swidden food crops—and especially rice, the cultivation of which is culturally valorized and ritualized—focuses more on the long-term reproduction of the social and cosmological order; whereas the monetized, market-oriented cultivation of rubber focuses more on the short-term maximization of individual benefit (Bloch and Parry 1989: 23–24, 25, 26). The two transactional orders occupy different places in the moral hierarchy, which leads to an asymmetry in their interaction. This is reflected in the Kantu' saying "If you have rice, you do not tap rubber." No one would ever have said, at least in the past, "If you have rubber, you do not cultivate rice."

The differences between the two transactional orders are fundamental to the relationship between the local society and wider market relations. For example, the Kantu' refer to the land that they put under rubber as "dead," in contrast to the "living" land that they keep under swidden cultivation (see chapter 7). This curious classification illuminates the important *lack* of local "fit" of cash crops. It has been commonly assumed that in order to be successful, commodity production must fit seamlessly into the smallholders' systems of food production; but this is in error. Thus, a historically successful crop like Para rubber does indeed "fit" into the local agro-ecology of production, but it does *not* fit into the local morality of production.

The challenge of smallholder commodity production is to open a door into wider relations of production that swings "out" but not "in." That is, the challenge is to establish access out to these wider market systems while simultaneously blocking untrammeled access back in to fragile community and household economies. This challenge is ill met when the local and extra-local economic systems have homogeneous and easily translatable structures of production. It is ill met when global market mechanisms can penetrate the local means of production, such as the allocation of land and labor (Kahn 1982). Given the likely power imbalances, the wider society can take greater advantage of this homogeneity and translatability than can the local community. The translatability of economic systems is not neutral, therefore it

serves the powerful more than the powerless (Scott 1998). Historic examples
of this include the way that colonial tobacco planters piggybacked their crop
on the labor of Sumatran swidden cultivators and the way that colonial as
well as post-colonial sugar planters piggybacked on the land and labor of
Javanese wet-rice cultivators (see chapter 7).

Legibility and Vulnerability

Illegibility and incommensurability, differences between local and
extra-local systems of production, act as a sort of "fire wall," protecting the
local community from the wider society.[26] This fire wall is literally a line
drawn within the household between the two systems of production—the
subsistence-oriented one and the market-oriented one. It is drawn in everyday life in the course of the daily allocation of land, labor, people, and other
resources to one sector versus the other, as illustrated by the passage from
Angkol's journal with which this chapter began. It is in part a line of legibility: part of the household, part of its decision making, remains illegible to
the wider society. Because subsistence production is less legible, it is less vulnerable; it may be more apt to be proscribed by the state, but it is harder for
the state to exploit, to take advantage of (Carpenter 1997, 2001; Scott 1998).
As Foucault ([1975] 1995: 200) has written, "Visibility is a trap"—although
in some circumstances, when invisibility fails to protect native resources,
they may seek visibility as an antidote.

This sort of dual involvement in both subsistence and market spheres
has not been supported by either colonial or post-colonial states in the region. There has been a marked policy preference, instead, for 100 percent
commitment by smallholders to *either* food production *or* production of
commodities, in the latter case typically as coolies on estates. One of the
signature examples of this was the British colonial policy in Malaya to encourage rice cultivation by ethnic Malays and discourage their cultivation
of rubber (Barlow and Drabble 1990: 197; Drabble 1979: 77; Kato 1991: 143;
Sundaram 1986: 61, 66).[27] Such policies had ideological premises, namely
that food production was the proper province of peasants and commodity
production was the proper province of Europeans or, in the post-colonial
era, state elites. As Geertz (1963: 48) writes of Indonesia, "The Dutch colonial period consists, from an economic point of view, of one long attempt
to bring Indonesia's crops into the modern world, but not her people." The
colonial Dutch scholar Boeke's (1953) work on "economic dualism" is one

of the most sustained exegeses of this thesis that the economy and indeed mentality of the Indo-Malay peasant was fundamentally different from that of the European planter.[28] The principles of this view continue to dominate commodity production, in spite of insightful critiques by the likes of van Leur ([1955] 1967: 226): as Barlow (1991: 97) writes, "Sixty years on, the dualism of Boeke (1931) still essentially persists, with only a slight movement towards an integration of traditional and modern sectors."

The attitude of the state toward peasants that can straddle the divide between food and cash-crop production is summed up in the ubiquitous criticism leveled at smallholders or estate workers: "They only work when they need money"—meaning that they are otherwise supported by their subsistence food crops. The degree of worker autonomy made possible by the presence of other resources is anathema to the state-supported plantation sector because it affects a basic dimension of power—who controls the mobilization of labor. For this reason, when estates in Kalimantan have to enter into production agreements with smallholders (for example, on nucleus-estate schemes), they prefer transmigrants from Java or Madura who do not have the range of alternative resources to rely on that locals do (Potter and Lee 1998).

The logic of the dual economy has an agro-ecological underpinning. Most of the chapters in this volume commence with a description and understanding of the local agro-ecological system. This is what structures the daily articulation of local practices to overarching political economies. The agro-ecology of Para rubber, for example, determines both the possibilities for smallholder production and the limits to state control. I don't leave ecology behind, a criticism that has been leveled at contemporary political-ecological work (Vayda and Walters 1999). Rather, the approach taken here is in the tradition of Steward (1977), one of the founders of environmental anthropology, who always tried to tie the ecology of particular systems of production to particular systems of social organization.

Practice and Discipline

The competitiveness of smallholder cultivation of a commodity like rubber is based on mundane, daily production practices. Consider, for example, those practices that allocate daily labor to rubber tapping as opposed to swidden food-crop cultivation. Rainfall, the cry of an omen bird, a sudden need for cash or trade goods, all may affect the decision on any given morning to allocate the labor of the household—or even the labor of individual members of the household—to the rubber grove as opposed to the swidden (see chapter 6). Multiplied over thousands of households and dozens of years, these quotidian agro-ecological practices have implications for national and international industries and economies.

This is why I began this chapter with the passage from Angkol's daily journal. My view of the daily household schedule mirrors Moore's (2005: 317) view of the household hut in his study of Kaerezians in eastern Zimbabwe:

> In my view, a humble hut, as much as colonial evictions and postcolonial villagization, constitutes an articulated *assemblage;* it gathers together nature and culture, labor and landscape, producing material and discursive consequences. I probed such consequential constellations to argue that agency and situated struggles *matter;* both inform, rather than script, landscapes entangled with power relations and geophysical substance. Administrative efforts to shepherd settlers into linear grids encountered the shoals of sedimented livelihoods linked to specific sites and environmental attributes such as springs, slope, and soil quality. For most Kaerezians, a home, or *musha,* mingled fields, huts, and pastoralism in ways that defied state spatial segregation of these zones.

Whereas Moore is talking about spatial discipline and resistance, I am talking, in part, about temporal discipline and resistance. Whereas Moore looks at how the Kaerezians configure the landscape in defiance of state views about settlement and rural society, I look at how groups like the Kantu' structure their time, as well as space, in defiance of state views about commodity production.

Practice

Over the past generation there has been a surge of academic interest in everyday practice (Bourdieu [1972] 1977; Ortner 1984: 148). In part in reaction to what was seen as an excessive tendency on the part of neo-Marxists to view communities and their inhabitants as the pawns of the capitalist world system (for example, Wallerstein 1974; Wolf 1982), scholars like Giddens (1979, 1984) sought to demonstrate how individual practice in fact helps to reproduce higher-order social structure. Giddens (1984: 141) attributes strongly defined structural properties to activity in microcontexts. He draws our attention to the importance of the routinized character of daily life, the structural constraints that daily routines encounter and reflect, and how such routines relate to the structural properties of larger collectivities (Giddens 1984: 24, 111). Giddens (1984: 2) sees social behavior as recursive: "In and through their activities agents reproduce the conditions that make these activities possible." In the case of rubber smallholders, given that their comparative advantage comes from keeping a foot in both subsistence and the market, how is the daily alteration of rubber tapping and swidden cultivation reproducing the larger structure of relations between smallholders, estates, and the state?

Giddens says that agents can "know" structures. He suggests that social structure has no existence independent of the knowledge that agents have about what they do in their day-to-day social activities. Following Giddens, to what extent are the smallholders themselves able to articulate the structural dimensions of their system of production? A number of examples of such articulation are presented in the chapters to follow, including the "death-bed" injunction against planting pepper in chapter 2, the belief that rubber "kills" the land in chapter 7, and the dream of the "rice-eating rubber" in chapter 5. The last-mentioned case occurred during the depression of the 1930s, when the increased pressures on capital further added to the competitive edge of the smallholders. Dayak smallholders became alarmed by the public retelling of a dream that their rubber trees were eating their rice, and some actually felled their rubber trees in response. The dream symbolized Dayak anxiety that the subsistence rice sector of their economy would be overwhelmed by the market-oriented rubber sector. It symbolized, at the same time as it enacted, their historic commitment to balancing the two sectors, thereby helping to preserve the sustainability of their dual economy. Such beliefs and practices are suggestive of Giddens's duality of structure, with the same elements simultaneously playing a role in social activity and social structure.

To recognize that everyday practice is constrained by but in turn constrains overarching structures is to see the "agency" in such practice, defined as "the socioculturally mediated capacity to act" (Ahearn 2001: 112). There has been a recent increase in interest in the subject of agency in anthropology, including in environmental anthropology (Brosius 1999a, 1999b; Dove et al. 2008), most obviously in such topics as environmental movements (for example, Escobar 1999). The history of smallholder competition with the state plantation sector is an exemplary case of the exertion of agency by peasant and tribal households and communities. Because this involves production of commodities for global markets, it also corrects the impression that globalization leads to the inevitable capitulation and loss of independence on the part of local people, like the tribal producers of Borneo (see chapter 10).

Staple Theory

The issue of agency in crop production is also raised by "staple theory," which posits that the character of different crops will necessarily lead to particular modes of production.[29] Chapter 2, for example, revolves around the attempt by native Banjar rulers in southeastern Borneo to forbid any involvement by their subjects in colonial pepper cultivation, based on their belief that such involvement would be inevitably injurious to their welfare and sovereignty; and chapter 5 analyzes the message of the tribal dream that production of rubber for the market posed an inherent threat to the traditional subsistence sector. In fact, rubber and pepper are quite different in this regard. The agronomy of pepper actually is less suited than that of many other crops to estate cultivation, and it was not part of the great private sector expansion of commodity-crop production that followed the passing of the colonial Dutch Agrarian Law in 1870 (Bulbeck et al. 1998: 91). However, pepper still seems, as reflected in the Banjar rulers' proscriptions, to be inherently more threatening to smallholders than a crop like rubber, to be more likely to expose them to external control and extraction. Rubber, in contrast, has more variable qualities as an export crop. Although some observers, like Brockway (1979: 164), have deemed rubber "the most satisfactory plantation crop in all of British-controlled Southeast Asia," this assessment ignores its suitability for smallholder cultivation. Precisely because of its suitability for smallholders, Paige (1975: 51) has more accurately called rubber "a marginal plantation crop," writing (1975: 354): "Rubber, unlike sugar, requires little or no estate processing and therefore no expensive industrial equipment, and although rubber can be harvested continuously, it actually benefits from neglect, so that peasant subsistence farmers can easily allow their trees to vegetate when the rubber price is low and harvest when it is high. Small holders are therefore formidable competitors in the world rubber market. . . . The rubber market is not subject to either cartelization or political control, and the competition from synthetics and fluctuation in industrial demand expose the rubber producers to market forces unknown to sugar producers."[30] As Paige implies, rubber is not merely suited to smallholder cultivation, it is suited to being part of a nonspecialized, low-intensity, composite system of smallholder production (cf. Kato 1991: 154–55). This suitability makes Para rubber far from the "most satisfactory" plantation crop, which is attested to by the history of fierce competition between estate and smallholder rubber cultivators in Southeast Asia.[31] On the other hand, in Para rubber's homeland in South America, smallholder production (although from wild as opposed to cultivated rubber) was historically structured in a manner far more inimical to the welfare of the participants than was the case in Southeast Asia.

Notwithstanding the successful history of rubber smallholder cultivation in Southeast Asia, the parastatal estate sector has historically considered estate cultivation to be the only proper mode of production for rubber. This sector has dismissed smallholder cultivation as "jungly," diseased, inefficient, anomalous, which is its own version of a staple theory. For the estate sector to recognize the viability of smallholder cultivation would be to recognize that its own mode of production is not the only one possible. The articulation of a staple theory can be partisan, therefore, insofar as it denies the historical contingency of a particular system of production. Noncontingency may be feared as well as asserted. When the Banjar kings uttered their staple theory—like warning against involvement in pepper cultivation—what they feared was the lack of contingency in such cultivation; they feared that a disempowering mode of production would inevitably attend pepper cultivation.

Government Discipline and Regulation

The idea that a particular pattern of discipline is inherent in the crops themselves must be seen in the context of the long history of efforts by political authorities in the region to impose such discipline. For many centuries, state control of many of the commodities discussed here was necessarily limited to their extraction via tribute or taxation. With the coming to the region of the colonial powers, such efforts were intensified and new avenues of control were developed, such as the infamous Dutch policy in the seventeenth century of literally erasing the spice-producing lands and people in eastern Indonesia that they could not control (Ricklefs 2008: 69–73),[32] and their effort early in the nineteenth century to insinuate their administrative reach into existing smallholder production through the *cultuurstel* (cultivation system). With the passage of the 1870 Agrarian Law, however, Dutch interest increasingly shifted toward promoting the development of large-scale, corporate estates and granting corporate concessions for those plants that could not be cultivated (for example, native rubbers; see chapter 3), and they adopted an increasingly punitive stance toward competing smallholders. In the early days of the Para rubber industry, ostensibly because the attraction of smallholders to rubber was thought to threaten food-crop production, an unsuccessful effort was made to restrict the spread of smallholder cultivation. Within a decade or two, as the smallholders demonstrated their ability to challenge the dominance of the estate sector, a concerted international effort was made to restrict their production and further expansion, via the Stevenson Restriction Scheme (also called the Stevenson Plan) and the International Rubber Regulation Agreement (IRRA), but these too were near-total failures (see chapter 5). Even the IRRA's alteration of the tax structure to favor rubber with lower water content simply led to the extraordinarily rapid spread of cast-iron "rubber mangles," which pressed the water out of the raw latex slabs, into even the remote interior of Borneo (see chapter 4).

Direct regulation of smallholder production has proved challenging for colonial and post-colonial state authorities alike. The everyday practices of smallholders have lain beyond the direct authority of the state for much of the colonial and post-colonial period. The smallholders' production techniques were to a great extent locally developed and alien in the eyes of the state. In the case of rubber—planting, spacing, weeding, tapping schedules—all were unfamiliar and incomprehensible to the state. And typically none of the smallholders' factors of production—land, labor, or technology—were allocated by means of market mechanisms. Orthodox market signals, such as price fluctuations, often did not result in the predicted response from smallholders. Smallholders not infrequently responded to decreases in the market price of rubber by *increasing* their production—the so-called inverse production curve—which was seen as perplexing and vexing by colonial governments. As a result, the state often had little leverage over smallholder production except (1) through usurious taxation of the smallholder product at the point of export, (2) by denying research and development resources to the smallholder sector, (3) by appropriating smallholdings and replacing them with estates, or (4) by coercing smallholders into government estate schemes.

Central governments in Indonesia have seen the lack of tractability of smallholder production as a reason in itself to suppress it; but from the opposite viewpoint, this is the *raison d'être* of smallholder production. The historic strength of this sector lies precisely in its *un*tractability to the state. This explains why the smallholder schemes sponsored by the Indonesian government over the past generation, notably the nucleus estates, are 100 percent transparent to and dependent upon the government and why they have by and large been failures. Foucault ([1975] 1995) argued that power forms its subject through everyday forms of discipline. This principle holds for the operation of estates but not the operation of smallholdings. In the smallholder case, the flexibility of the daily routine, its ongoing and ad hoc division between subsistence pursuits and cash-crops pursuits, is the very opposite of estate discipline. Whereas the estates are true totalizing systems, the smallholdings—as composite, hybrid systems—are literally the opposite. The firewall that smallholders build between their subsistence and market activities is designed precisely to frustrate evolution into a totalizing system of commodity production.

Epistemological Boundaries

One of the principal dimensions of the state effort to discipline commodity production in the region has consisted of the demarcation, establishment, and defense of a unique zone of state space: the plantation, estate, or concession. The predecessors to these state spaces were the forest concessions granted by the colonial governments to European entrepreneurs during the nineteenth-century boom in gathering forest rubbers, which privileged Europeans over the natives who had for centuries been involved in this industry (see chapter 3).[33] When the wild rubbers were supplanted by the exotic and cultivated *Hevea*, the scope for constructing a distinct state space of production was all the greater. New insights into these estate-like institutions of resource management have recently come from scholars influenced by post-structural studies as well as the history of science. An example is Hardin's (2002) work on concessions in Africa. Hardin (2002: 3) uses the term *concession* to refer to "a spatial unit of exploitation and development, also to a social process of relinquishment, acquisition, and consolidation of control." She continues (2002: 10): "The term 'concession' refers . . . to the territorial units allocated to actors for the extraction of wealth in the form of raw materials. More broadly, it refers to the social interaction through which a state can allocate territories or resources and social rights of exploitation. . . . Used from the eighteenth century to consolidate central government control over internal and outlying geographical areas, the notion of the concession worked to reinforce the totalizing nature of sovereign power, and then to extend that power through various mediating actors and codes or norms, across varied geographical and social contexts." This assessment of the way that state power operated through concessions is also applicable to colonial and post-colonial Southeast Asian estates.

Estate Isolation and Knowledge Production

Wolf (1982: 315) has characterized the plantation as an invader: "They [plantations] are in fact the outposts of one mode of production in the midst of other modes. The relation between the plantation and the forms of production predicated on these other modes is usually antagonistic. The plantation is an invader, and its successful expansion is the fruit of successful invasion." What the estates in colonial Indonesia and Malaysia invaded, and developed partly in opposition to, was the smallholder sector. The economic competitiveness of the smallholder sector, and the colonial state's difficulty in penetrating it, contributed to an implicit state commitment to develop a commodity production sector that was as different as possible from the smallholder sector. Establishing a dissimilarity with the smallholder sector was integral to the development of the state sector. If the smallholder sector was quintessentially local—local people, plants, and technology—then one of the principal ways for the state to distinguish its sector from smallholders was to decouple it from the local, which is a very modernist project (Hornborg 1996), by emphasizing the nonlocal, the exotic. This decoupling from the local makes estate production look like more of a heroic effort, in addition to having obvious political and economic advantages.

Brockway (1979: 164) captures the importance of delocalization to the concept of the estate: "Imported men, an imported plant, and imported quinine to control malaria all combined to make the Malay states an embodiment of the ideal colony, and to make rubber the most satisfactory plantation crop in all of British-controlled Southeast Asia." To import means to ignore, suppress, supplant the existing, the local. From colonial times to the present in Indonesia and Malaysia, the history of estate development is one of the erasure of preexisting environments and modes of production and their replacement with something completely different: a new topography, new biota, new labor regimes, even new microclimates. The compulsion of this logic is reflected in the common practice in Indonesia even today for parastatal rubber estates to clear productive rubber smallholdings, evict the owners, and plant in their place immature rubber and in-migrating workers of their own in nucleus-estate schemes. There can be no better example of the sense in which estate development is an epistemological as well as political, and not simply agronomic, project. This is further seen in the rare cases when an estate is unable to erase a smallholding in its way. The remaining un-erased smallholder rubber is termed a *daerah kantong* (enclave) on the resulting estate landscape (Soesaptono 1993), which reflects the estate's desire for a landscape primarily structured according to its views, on which incompatible spaces have the status of exceptions. Intrusive smallholdings are seen as threats to the estate's control over marketing (see chapter 9), and it is usually estate policy to erase enclaves by any means possible.

Central to the concept of the estate is construction of an epistemological boundary around it as a unique zone of knowledge production. The historic context for this was the Orientalist premise that the ways of knowing in European society and Oriental society are fundamentally different (Said 1978: 40). Accordingly, an important part of colonial rule consisted of imposing a European epistemology on local societies and environments in the colonies (Cohn 1996; Mitchell 1988). This task was not an easy one in alien and complex environments where preexisting native epistemologies were ancient, culturally embedded, and highly functional. One way that colonial powers dealt with this challenge was simply to change the environment, to create a blank slate. The colonial plantation regimes, by radically transforming the physical and social environments, could thereafter claim to be creating knowledge from scratch. By creating a completely new and alien environment, the colonial estate created for itself a landscape of which it might still be ignorant but on which it had, by default, a much more privileged position for future experimentation and construction of new regimes of knowledge. As the science historian Bonneuil (2001) astutely notes, it was not expert knowledge that made large-scale, totalizing development schemes like plantations possible, rather it was the reverse: that is, it was the creation of such schemes that made it possible for colonial and post-colonial authorities to create and then lay claim to expert knowledge. As he writes (2001: 271), "Geometrization, simplification, standardization, and discipline ensured not only the social order and legibility sought by the state but also the experimental order necessary to produce expert knowledge." This remaking of the landscape reversed the relative value of state versus local regimes of knowledge: whereas the existing resource landscape privileged local regimes of knowledge developed over time; the newly wrought, highly planned, more artificial landscape privileged the to-be-created knowledge regime of the estate.[34]

Estate Discoveries and Smallholder "Ignorance"

There are many possible ways that estate knowledge production could have potentially recognized the value of local knowledge systems, including imitation, hybridization, negotiation, and so on. But the premises of knowledge construction on estates, given their need to distinguish themselves from smallholders, required a discourse of discovery that erased and denied any such knowledge. Writing of the depredations of contemporary corporate mining in Kalimantan, Tsing (2000: 133) observes that the landscape is populated by multiple actors with multiple and competing histories, claims, and modes of production. Therefore, an extra-local corporate actor wanting to enter and dominate such a landscape "must continually erase old residents' rights [in order] to create wild and empty spaces where *discovering* resources, not stealing them, is possible. To do so, too, it must cover up the conditions of its own production." Obfuscating the reality of resource appropriation with a discourse of discovery and knowledge construction enhances the apparent justice and incontestability of resource claims. As Tsing (2000: 133) continues: "The lone prospector replaces swarming migrants and residents, searching the landscape. The excitement of scientific discovery replaces the violence of expropriation as local resource rights are extinguished and armed gangs enforce the interdependent negotiations of big companies and illegal miners, each leading the other to new sites and trading political and material assets as they form complementary players."

The history of plantation agriculture in the Indo-Malay region is of course replete with impressive scientific discoveries, but there are important lacunae in this history that illuminate the ideological context. The most famous example for the purpose of the current discussion is the commitment by the early managers of rubber estates in the region to clean weeding, meaning the removal of all natural vegetation from the ground under the rubber trees (see chapters 4 and 5). Managers favorably compared this practice with the smallholder practice of letting secondary growth come up among their rubber. Several decades of experience eventually demonstrated that clean weeding of rubber stands actually promoted erosion and disease and a less salubrious microclimate—which inhibited both latex flow and healing of tapping scars—and that the smallholder practice—which the estates eventually adopted in large part, although without attribution—was the correct one (see chapters 4 and 5). The enormous reluctance of the estates to learn from the smallholders in this and other respects reflects the explicit premise

that the estates were the producers of knowledge and the smallholders were its consumers, an asymmetry that has been integral to the very identity of the estates from colonial times to the present.

Far from being able to learn from smallholders, the estate sector and its government supporters have devoted themselves to a portrayal of the smallholder sector as driven by ignorance and greed. This depiction was already well established during the pre-*Hevea* era of exploitation of native rubbers. When a global boom in these native rubbers developed in the mid-nineteenth century, the British in the Malay Peninsula and the Dutch in the Indonesian archipelago quickly judged traditional local systems of exploitation to be overly exploitive and awarded exclusive concessions to European trading houses (see chapter 3). This pattern repeated itself after *Hevea* was introduced from the Amazon; smallholders followed estates in planting it, and, within the astonishing space of two decades, threatened the estates' market share. The rubber-producing colonies joined together in the 1920s and 1930s to try to restrict smallholder production (see chapter 5), on two ostensible grounds: first, that the smallholders were overexploiting their trees, which would destroy their productivity and lead to the spread of root disease, including to the European estates; and, second, that smallholder rubber production took land and labor away from food-crop production. The premises of these regulatory efforts were completely repudiated by subsequent field studies of smallholdings, however, and it became obvious to observers that they were actually designed to protect the less-efficient estate sector from smallholder competition. Thus, on the one hand there developed a smallholder practice of economically efficient and ecologically canny production, whereas on the other hand a reactive and deceptive state discourse developed regarding the need to regulate smallholder practices in order to protect natural resources and society.

Totalizing Schemes for Smallholder Development

The estate sector's self-privileging view of its own knowledge production, vis-à-vis that of the smallholder sector, has persisted with remarkably little change into the post-colonial era. This is reflected not only in the continued focus of state research and development on the estate sector but also in the character of the rare examples of state engagement with the smallholder sector. In the 1950s and 1960s leftist politics in Malaysia finally led to an effort by the government to develop the smallholder sector.

Two decades later in Indonesia, projections of decreasing oil and gas exports led the government and its international creditors like the World Bank to look at the export crop sector as an alternate source of foreign exchange. In planning the development of this sector, questions of equity raised by some of the international actors involved led to the allocation of some resources to the smallholder sector (Barlow 1990: 28–30, 30n; Penot 2004; Rudner 1976). Both Indonesia and Malaysia came up with similar models of small-holder development, which involved replacing the traditional smallholdings with something completely new: the Federal Land Development Authority (FELDA) schemes in Malaysia and the Perkebunan Inti Rakyat (People's Nucleus Estate schemes, abbreviated as either PIR in Indonesian or NES in English) of Indonesia (see chapter 9). Both exemplified totalizing, concession-like approaches to the development of rural people and resources. Both, but especially the Indonesian schemes, completely suppressed any recognition of smallholder knowledge. The nucleus-estate schemes consisted of smallholdings clustered around and selling their produce to a nucleus government estate. In the 1980s, some of these estates were developed in conjunction with transmigration schemes, based on the government's hope that such schemes would not only produce export crops but would also support the relocation of "surplus" population from Java to the outer islands, where they could help to promote regional development.

The contrast between these schemes and traditional smallholdings could not be greater. In the case of the Kantu', for example, when I first worked with them, the average smallholder owned five small rubber gardens, one hectare in size each, which were spread out over the household's holdings of more than fifty hectares of forest and exploited intermittently to meet market needs. In the case of smallholders on the nucleus estate, they typically hold two to three hectares of land, most of which is devoted to rubber or oil palm or some other commodity, with a fraction left for permanent food-cropping, a home garden, and a house site; and they are given a start-up food and cash allowance. The cost of the land, improvements, house, and start-up allowance is all borrowed from the estate, and the smallholders must work their holding intensively to repay their loans while also meeting their basic subsistence needs. The nucleus estate represents to the smallholders a completely new and alien biosocial environment, in which they are totally dependent on the state for their food, finances, housing, planting material, technology, and processing. The relationship between the smallholders and the central estate is reflected in their respective official labels, based on terms

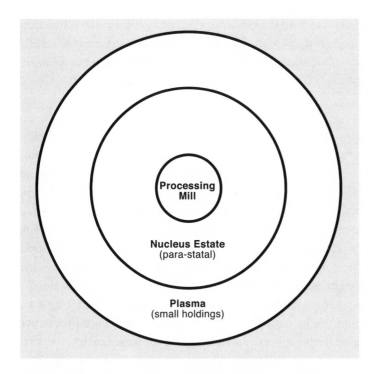

Figure 1.3. Schematic layout of nucleus estate and smallholdings

drawn from biology: the central estate, with its own plantings and a processing mill to which all produce must go, is the "inti" or nucleus and the
surrounding smallholdings are the "plasma"[35] (figure 1.3). An explicit goal
of nucleus-estate managers is to ensure the dependence of the smallholders
and the dominance of the nucleus not only in terms of politics, economics,
and technology but also in terms of the authority of the estate's regime of
knowledge (see chapter 9). The nucleus estate is spatially and ideologically
represented as the source of all direction and expertise for the surrounding
smallholdings. Both the spatial and mental maps of the nucleus estate reflect
an explicit privileging of estate knowledge: the smallholders are supposed to
learn from the central estate holding, not the reverse.[36]

The geographies of the nucleus estate and the smallholding reflect completely different resources, needs, and priorities. For example, whereas the
former emphasizes the tie of the smallholding to estate production, the
latter emphasizes the tie of smallholdings to swidden cultivation (see chapter 6); whereas the former emphasizes the smallholder's technological short-

comings and dependence on the estate, the latter emphasizes the differences between cash crops and swiddens and their complementary economics and ecology in the dual household economy; and whereas the former emphasizes production for the estate, the latter emphasizes production for household consumption.[37]

Indonesia's nucleus estates and Malaysia's FELDA schemes, both designed and supported with the help of multilateral international banks, epitomize high-modern, totalizing state projects (Scott 1998). They represent governance through sweeping reordering of the landscape, settlement pattern, daily household routine, and mobilization of land, labor, and capital. The schemes are explicitly designed to promote close surveillance of all stages of production, especially the marketing of the fruits of production. They are designed to ensure complete legibility of the smallholders to the estate, but not the reverse. As Bonneuil (2001: 269) writes, "Whereas the African village remained a social hieroglyph for the early colonial state, the planned-development schemes of the developmentalist era were major attempts to capture the peasantry into stable, legible, and more productive units that would make taxation, conscription, and 'enlightened' intervention easier." Such schemes resemble, indeed, the structure of the famous Panopticon of Jeremy Bentham (figure 1.4), which is their intellectual antecedent. Bentham (1791) coined the term for "a proposed form of prison of circular shape having cells built round and fully exposed towards a central 'well,' whence the warders could at all times observe the prisoners." Bentham's concept was recently popularized by Foucault ([1975] 1995), who used the concept of a panopticon in his work on governmentality, whereby modern states exert power not simply through the surveillance of the everyday lives of their subjects but through the more insidious structuring of the seemingly apolitical, day-to-day dimensions of these lives, through the "conduct of conduct" (Foucault 1991). This is achieved on the nucleus estates not through the insinuation of the state into pre-existing landscapes but through the erasure of these landscapes and construction of completely new ones, on which smallholder conduct is an explicit focus of management.[38]

Indonesia's nucleus estates illustrate not only the power of the totalizing schemes of the modern state, they also illustrate the limits to such power. The panopticon-like legibility of these schemes does not ensure that information flows freely.[39] These estates, and the parastatal estate sector as a whole, have a reputation for vigorously distorting the dissemination, even internally, of accurate information about smallholder participants as well as wage workers

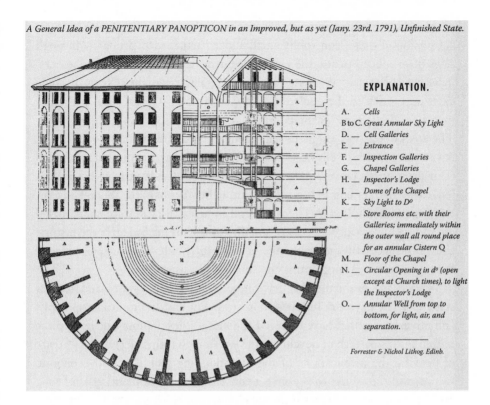

A General Idea of a PENITENTIARY PANOPTICON in an Improved, but as yet (Jany. 23rd. 1791), Unfinished State.

EXPLANATION.

A.   *Cells*
B to C. *Great Annular Sky Light*
D. __ *Cell Galleries*
E. __ *Entrance*
F. __ *Inspection Galleries*
G. __ *Chapel Galleries*
H. __ *Inspector's Lodge*
I. __ *Dome of the Chapel*
K. __ *Sky Light to D°*
L. __ *Store Rooms etc. with their*
     Galleries; immediately within
     the outer wall all round place
     for an annular Cistern Q
M.__ *Floor of the Chapel*
N. __ *Circular Opening in d° (open*
     except at Church times), to light
     the Inspector's Lodge
O. __ *Annular Well from top to*
     bottom, for light, air, and
     separation.

Forrester & Nichol Lithog. Edinb.

Figure 1.4. J. Bentham's plan of the Panopticon

(see chapter 9; Dove and Kammen 2001). These distortions both contribute to and are a function of systemic problems with the operation of these schemes. At one point the biggest smallholder tree-crop-development program in the world, the Indonesian government's block-planting schemes for smallholders largely failed, and those involving rubber were the worst of all (Tomich 1991: 250). Most smallholders, upward of 85 percent, were not even reached by these schemes (Joshi et al. 2003: 137; Penot 2007: 583; Tomich 1991: 250).[40] And for that small minority of smallholders who were reached, success was elusive. Virtually all of the nucleus-estate schemes have been plagued with serious agronomic and economic problems, which Barlow and Jayasuriya (1986: 652n) suggest are "inherent to the institutional structure of these schemes" (cf. Potter and Badcock 2004: 346). Thus, seedlings were distributed out of season, plants died, production fell short of targets, women were forced into prostitution to meet subsistence needs, loans were not repaid, and so on (see chapter 9). Most schemes have been beset with outright subversion of estate control by smallholder participants, primarily through sales of produce outside the estate, deemed illegal until the smallholders' loans have been paid off, as well as open refusal to repay these loans. In some cases opposition to the nucleus estates has taken on violent forms, whether involving disaffected participants or disenfranchised local communities. The areas of nucleus-estate development in West Kalimantan, for example, have been centers of ethnic violence since the Suharto regime was toppled (Davidson 2008; Dove 2006). Finally, the nucleus estates have been challenged by market competition from the lightly capitalized, more-efficient, traditional smallholdings. The fact that the nucleus estates were not modeled after these historically successful smallholdings but instead after the historically less-successful estates themselves reflects the absolute intransigence of the estate sector in confronting the smallholder sector.[41]

Given the problems that have beset the nucleus estates and related schemes, why have the Indonesian government and the multilateral banks and other bodies that have financed Indonesia's development been so committed to this pattern of development? As Tomich (1991: 262) writes, "Years of denying the implications of the disappointing technical and economic record, and the efforts to preserve a consensus on block planting after 1983 raise the questions of what interests really were being satisfied by the persistence of block planting projects." Tomich (ibid.: 262–63) acknowledges that such projects offer attractive rent-seeking opportunities but he believes that the problem is more fundamental than this: "Indonesian implementing agencies and international lenders share organizational interests in large expenditures for tree crop development. These mutual organizational interests are the primary explanation for continuation of the block planting strategy. Large-scale, expensive block planting projects are a way of 'moving' money that government agencies and foreign lenders find particularly satisfying. In this sense, the project bias and the plantation bias work together to reinforce arguments for large expenditures."

Concealment versus Discovery

Estate efforts to construct an epistemological boundary around commodity production have not gone uncontested by smallholders. This is reflected in the smallholders' tenacious development and defense of their own bounded space of production in the face of state opposition. It is also

reflected in more subtle efforts to manipulate these epistemological boundaries, which are subject to constant contestation by smallholders and estates
alike (table 1.1).

The Dutch Disease

When the nineteenth-century boom in gathering wild rubbers led
to the displacement of native gatherers by colonial concessions, in the space
of a generation the former switched from tapping native rubber in the forest
to cultivating exotic rubber on their own lands. The smallholders essentially
shifted their production across the boundary between nature and culture and
thereby obtained a measure of protection against appropriation by state elites
(see chapter 3). The strategic manipulation of the nature/culture boundary
is an ongoing theme in relations between estates and smallholders and is
an explicit focus of their contests. For example, when contemporary estate
operations encroach on smallholder lands in Indonesia and clear planted
trees, rattans, and so on, a standard reason given for rejecting any claims
for compensation by the local community is that these plants were seeded
by *tahi babi/burung* (the feces of wild pigs and birds—see page 92). Even
the cultivated status of Para rubber, the origins of which cannot be attributed to pigs and birds, is assailed by labeling it "jungle rubber"; such rubber is not uncommonly simply cut down by estates wanting to expand their
lands.[42] Tribal smallholders in Kalimantan have responded to such assaults,
and to the government disinterest in collecting data on smallholder production,[43] by raising public awareness of the existence of their rubber holdings
and the economic and political role that it plays in their lives—by making it
more legible, in short. Thus, a Dayak nongovernmental organization (NGO)
in Pontianak published the following assertion from a Dayak leader to the
vice-governor of the province: "Ada ratusan calon sarjana dari Simpang
Hulu. Mereka bukan karena perusahaan HPH atau HTI atau PIR melainkan karena karet. Jadi tidak ada alasan jika kami mau menerima HTI atau
PIR atau sejenisnya di Simpang Hulu." (There are hundreds of holders of
bachelor's degrees from Simpang Hulu. This [is] not because of logging concessions or pulp plantations or nucleus estates but rather because of [small-
holder] rubber. Thus there is no reason for us to accept pulp plantations or
nucleus estates in Simpang Hulu.) (IDRD 1994: 24)

Instead of defending resources by making them more legible, sometimes
the smallholder response is just the opposite. Thus, the historic Banjar kingdom characterized the vulnerability of its pepper-based wealth to the Dutch

Table 1.1. Historical Relations between Governments and Smallholder Producers of Export Commodities in Indonesia

DATE	ACTION	RESULT
1870	*Government* passes the Agrarian Act, claiming all fallow land as the state's, for granting to European estates, etc.*	*Smallholders* decide to plant more perennial crops in their fallowed fields.
1910–1913	*Government* restricts the gathering of native forest latexes by smallholders, to protect European concessions.	*Smallholders* decide to cultivate the exotic Para rubber instead.
1910–1930	*Smallholder* rubber producers outplant estates and increase their market share.	*Government* decides to protect the rubber estates.
1935–1944	*Government* imposes punitive export taxes on smallholder rubber producers to force a decrease in their production.	*Smallholders* increase the quantity and quality of their production to maintain a constant level of revenue.
1951–1983	*Smallholder* rubber producers increase their market share from 65 percent to 84 percent by expanding the area of cultivation.	*Government* focuses all capital and technical assistance on the rubber estates to minimize their loss of market share by increasing yields.
1980–2000	*Government* promotes nucleus-estate schemes to bring smallholder rubber production under estate control.	*Smallholder* rubber producers resist the loss of autonomy implicit in these schemes.
Present	*Government* supports conversion of rural lands to estate cultivation of oil palm, rubber, pulpwood, etc.	*Smallholders'* responses run the gamut of participation, co-optation, defense of own smallholdings, resistance, and rebellion.

The Agrarian Act of 1870 classified as state dominion any land not kept under constant cultivation (Sonius, 1981 xlvii).

as "the banana tree at the gate" (see chapter 2). This is a folk metaphor for a resource that is simply too attractive and vulnerable to others, just as a ripe banana in front of your house will be picked and eaten by someone passing by. The historic power of native, coastal kingdoms like Banjar was explicitly based on their ability to veil the wealth of the interior from the eyes of outsiders, thus enabling them to act as middlemen in the trade of everything from pepper to bird-of-paradise feathers.[44] For the interior peoples themselves, like the Kantu', the simple complexity of the natural environment, to be understood only by dint of long and intimate acquaintance, has played a similar veiling function from the days of the nineteenth century wild-rubber boom to the present, tempering the ability of outsiders to exploit their resources at will (see chapter 2). Even so, some resources are thought to attract so much outside attention as to be inherently problematic. Thus, among contemporary smallholder miners of alluvial diamonds in South Kalimantan, there is a saying: "Siapa yang mendapat batu besar, dia pasti susah nanti" (Whoever finds a big stone, he will eventually suffer [as a result]) (see chapter 8). Great riches, especially for the politically marginal, can be a curse rather than a blessing. In such cases, the answer may be to avoid the resource in question, as exemplified by the case of the Banjar rajahs' death-bed injunctions against planting pepper (see chapter 2). The Banjar court concluded, and correctly, that pepper cultivation was fatally attractive to the Dutch and so it should be shunned.

The idea that natural resources may be so rich as to pose a challenge to the well-being of society is well known as the "Dutch disease."[45] This refers to the thesis that the political economics of great national oil and mineral wealth are not conducive to the development of democratic government and civil society (for example, Ross 2001). The gist of this thesis, that resource abundance, not scarcity, is often at the root of conflict, has been used to critique contemporary neo-Malthusian views of conflict and state failure in the developing world (for example, Homer-Dixon 1991 and Kaplan 1994; critiqued by Richards 1996 and Fairhead 2001). The Dutch curse has also been used to critique the hegemonic development tenet that the way to develop marginal societies is to bring in more resources, because it raises the possibility that what such societies need is to have fewer resources taken away in the first place (see chapter 8). The history of smallholder commodity production in the Indo-Malay region is not a history of people lacking resources; rather, it is a history of people whose use of existing resources has been under constant assault by states and their elites.

Promethean Acts

This history of resource contest is illuminated by a case where it was more invented than real, namely the purported theft of rubber seeds from the Amazon by the Englishman Henry A. Wickham (see chapters 4 and 8). The rise of the Southeast Asia rubber industry to global dominance—and the consequent collapse of the Amazonian economy—purportedly dates to the collection of seventy thousand *Hevea* seeds by Wickham in 1870, their subsequent transportation to Kew Gardens in England for germination, and then their final dispersal to Britain's Asian colonies. To this day this action is widely interpreted as the theft of Brazil's premiere natural resource. The most interesting aspect of this story is that it is completely untrue. Wickham did not remove the seeds secretly from Brazil, there were no Brazilian laws against the export of rubber seeds in any case, and he was neither the first nor the last to remove rubber seeds from Brazil. From the standpoint of the colonial British, their estates, and their modern-day successors, what is important is the myth's trope of the heroic individual and the Promethean act of the theft, constituting a "clean break" with competing histories, uses, and actors.[46] Estate ideology emphasizes the complete erasure of existing environments and modes of production and their replacement with something totally different. This is what appeals in the myth of rubber theft, which is akin in this respect to the earlier-discussed trope of discovery. Just as discovery of cultivation practices suits the estate epistemology more than copying would, so does the theft of biogenetic resources suit it more than borrowing (or buying, etc.) would.

Ironically, the only real thefts in the case of rubber have been in the opposite direction, not to but *from* the estate sector. From the very beginning of the industry in Southeast Asia down to the present time, smallholders have appropriated biogenetic material from the estates, from the first Brazilian seeds or seedlings to the latest clones. As Tomich (1991: 257) writes, "Indeed, the first rubber seedlings planted by Indonesian smallholders probably were stolen from plantations. . . . In fact, smallholders are still stealing [clonal] rubber seedlings from projects." Such behavior is completely consistent with native traditions in the region. One commonly encounters in Dayak communities land races of hill rice with names like *padi belabok*, which translates as "rice [taken by] stealth," meaning stolen seed. When Dayak pass by a stand of crops that strike their fancy, they will take a handful of seeds or cuttings for later trial planting in their own fields. This combination of envy, curiosity, and experimentation has been one of the engines of the development of their highly diverse crop complexes.

A final area where the image of the heroic estate and hapless smallholder sector breaks down involves support by the state. From the inception of the rubber industry in Southeast Asia, the estate sector has both needed and received enormous state support to cope with agronomic challenges, market challenges, and competition from the smallholder sector. The most infamous example is the earlier-mentioned international programs in the 1920s and 1930s to restrict smallholder expansion (see chapter 5). The motivation for these programs was completely obfuscated, however, as is the case today regarding the use of government research and development monies. Such funds are focused solely on estate priorities, but this privileged treatment of the estate sector, its subsidization by public funds in effect, is naturalized by the official ignoring of the smallholder sector. If only one sector exists, then the direction of government funding to it cannot be problematic. The use of research and development funds for the smallholder sector was non-existent until the late 1970s and early 1980s, and even then it was restricted to smallholder development within the confines of parastatal nucleus estates.

Paradoxically, in spite of this historic focus of state assistance on estates versus smallholders, the accepted wisdom in government circles is that it is the latter and not former that need such assistance. The development of the nucleus-estate projects was officially justified on the grounds that smallholders could not develop without state assistance. Tomich (1991: 252) refers to this as "the strong conviction that smallholder rubber development would not occur without government planting projects."[47] Even their ability to respond to market signals is denied, given a "widely held belief that markets could not be relied on as institutions for smallholder tree crop development" (ibid.: 253). In fact, as Tomich (ibid.: 257) goes on to say, "The history of rubber in Southeast Asia suggests that, despite economic imperfections, smallholders planted massive areas of rubber without assistance or, more often, in the face of policies designed to discourage them." Indeed, "Unassisted planting, and not block planting schemes, accounts for more than half of the rubber planting in Indonesia" (ibid.: 258).

Studying Smallholders and Estates

One of the chief determinants of the way estates are conceived and constructed is the coexistence of a very successful smallholder sector. There has of course been a relationship of competition between smallholders and estates; but there is also a relationship of subsidization—not of the small-holders by the estates as might be expected but often just the opposite, either directly due to estates "piggybacking" on smallholder labor or indirectly through punitive regulatory regimes (see chapter 7). Of most importance perhaps, the coexistence of estates and smallholdings seems to have mutu-ally affected their very self-identity—which suggests that there are really not two separate systems of belief and practice but one. For both domestic and international audiences there is in fact but a single system, that of estate cul-tivation, with the smallholder sector being invisible.[48]

Scholars like Haenn (1999) and Sivaramakrishnan (2002) suggest that when we see two parties locked in a discourse of opposition, we should ask not just how they conflict but how they may be reproducing one another. It seems likely, for example, that if the widespread and highly successful alter-native mode of production of smallholders did not exist, there would have been less need to draw the boundary as clearly around estate knowledge pro-duction. The existence of smallholder production shows the estates' ways of organizing labor and resources to be neither natural nor inevitable but his-torically contingent—and the erasure of contingency is the object of myth-making (Barthes 1972: 142).

Large-scale colonial and post-colonial estate development schemes cre-ated an important venue for the production of academic knowledge about these systems of production, but this research has been quite narrow in character. As Bonneuil (2001: 261) writes, "Large-scale, prepackaged de-velopment schemes offer a particularly promising field—but one largely unexplored by historians of science and technology—for research into the relations among science, the state, and society from the colonial to the post-colonial periods." What Bonneuil says of historical studies also applies to social science and the humanities, where work on such schemes has been thin to nonexistent. Smallholders, estates, and estatelike schemes have re-ceived surprisingly little scholarly attention (Stoler 1985a: 7). In Indonesia, there were few if any social science studies of contemporary parastatal planta-tions during the more-than-three-decades-long reign of Suharto's so-called New Order regime, although such studies have started to appear during the post-Suharto era (for example, Harwell 2003; White 1999).[49] Given the fact that these enterprises represented perhaps the most significant mechanism for control of rural labor and natural resources during this period, this is an astonishing gap in research. There have been many more studies of Indonesia's colonial-era plantation agriculture, especially of its sugar industry (for example, Breman 1983, 1989; Elson 1979, 1984; Fasseur 1992; Knight 1980).[50] Of special relevance here are Stoler's (1985a, 1985b) studies of representations of protest on colonial plantations in Sumatra (cf. Breman 1989) and Geertz's ([1963] 1971) analysis of the relationship between sugar and rice cultivation in colonial Java. The comparative abundance of studies of the colonial era reflects the fact that the colonial estates are much more removed from current politics, and the risks attending its study, than the contemporary parastatal estates, which were key nodes of power during Suharto's repressive regime.

Bonneuil argues that large-scale development schemes stimulated the social scientific study of the indigenous systems of production that they replaced and/or competed with, by conditioning African farmers for lengthy and detailed questioning by social scientists (Bonneuil 2001: 279–80): "More generally, the work of dozens of agricultural scientists, demographers, rural economists, geographers, anthropologists, medical and nutrition scientists, and sociologists attached to settlement schemes proved decisive in the development of agronomy, rural economy, and economic anthropology. In the 1950s and 1960s, when quantitative analysis was fashionable and data collection painstaking, fieldwork research presupposed compliant Africans, ready to answer long series of questions and to accept intrusions into their lives." Bonneuil further claims that time studies of smallholder agriculture were stimulated both by the prevalence of such studies within large-scale agricultural projects and by the anthropologists' felt need to compare favorably the productivity of smallholders. This was indeed one of the reasons that I carried out my own studies of the inputs and outputs of Dayak swidden and rubber cultivation.

The study of large-scale, western-derived agricultural schemes may also have helped to create the conceptual space for the study of small-scale, local agriculture. The imagination of the former (following Tsing 2000) may have facilitated the imagination of the latter, and perhaps the reverse is also true. In order to be able to think of small-scale cultivation, one must be able to think of large-scale cultivation, and vice versa. The contrast involves not only scale, however, but also the way land, labor, and capital are mobilized. It is also, importantly, a distinction of locality. The idea of exotic state spaces helps to clarify the idea of indigenous nonstate spaces. As Bonneuil (2001: 280) writes, "Paradoxical and ironical as it may seem, decades of vertical technocratic intervention and cognitive penetration of agrarian societies through prepackaged development schemes have certainly been preconditions for the emergence of the present vast scholarship on indigenous knowledge and African farming systems." Bonneuil suggests, that is, that the creation of scientific knowledge within the boundaries of estates made the study of indigenous knowledge possible. This is similar to Hirtz's (2003) argument that it is modern means that have created indigeneity (see chapter 4).

A number of common themes run through the coming chapters. First, the long-term ability of groups like the Kantu' to simultaneously engage in both subsistence and market-oriented production has depended upon an ideological divide of their dual economy into two transactional orders, one of which is open and vulnerable to the market and one of which is protected from it. The success of this dual economy is tied to the agro-ecology of the crops involved. Some crops, like rubber, have an inherent agronomic predisposition toward smallholder versus estate cultivation, for example, whereas others, like pepper, are inherently more threatening to smallholder welfare. Second, the day-to-day agricultural practices of smallholders like the Kantu' have higher-order structural implications. There is a relationship between microlevel agricultural practice and macrolevel political economy. The key dimension in this relationship is the relative remove of smallholders from direct state control, which forces the state to try to discipline smallholder practices in other ways. Third, the vigor of smallholder cultivation has obliged colonial and post-colonial states to defend commodity production in estates on epistemological as opposed to economic grounds. Fourth, the importance of the epistemological boundaries between smallholders and estates is responsible for an estate discourse that obscures smallholder innovation at the same time as it emphasizes discovery and heroic individualism on the part of the estates. Fifth and finally, the historic competition between smallholders and estates has been so mutually influential that it is instructive to think of them in some contexts as part of a single structure.

PART II

The Challenges of the Colonial Trade in the Seventeenth to Nineteenth Centuries

This second section of the book takes up the story of the Bornean trade in the seventeenth to nineteenth centuries. The involvement of the island and its peoples in global trade dates back a millennium before that, but this is when European colonial intrusion into the trade system became much more intense. The colonial powers were not simply taking the place of regional traders like the Chinese nor competing with one another for trade monopolies, although they did both as well; they began to involve themselves in the local, on-ground details of commodity production and politics. In so doing, they challenged local societies as never before to respond to the realities of trade in a way that balanced their market needs, subsistence needs, and sovereignty. Chapters 2 and 3 both emphasize that, although these new pressures from the global political-economic system were often, perhaps typically, coercive, the local producers were keenly aware of this coercion and actively tried to resist and even respond in kind, sometimes successfully and sometimes not.

Chapter 2, which gives the book its title and sets the tone for the entire book, is an analysis of a seventeenth-century *hikayat* (chronicle) of the Malayic Banjar kingdom on the southeast coast of Borneo. The focus is on four passages in particular, in which successive rulers of the kingdom enjoin their subjects against the planting of pepper in commercial amounts for international trade and spell out all of the misfortunes that will visit them if they disobey. The aim of my analysis of the *Hikayat Banjar* is to retrieve and illuminate this native critique of linkages to international commodity markets. This critique is striking not least because it comes from the court of a kingdom that owed its very existence to regional and international trade. Indeed, closer examination shows that this is a critique not of all market-oriented production and trade but only that involving pepper. The implication, thus, is that different commodities and systems of production and trade have different political implications; and during the colonial Dutch era, the implications of pepper cultivation and trade were uniquely sinister. In order to avoid sinister outcomes, means of buffering the kingdom against the political-economic forces associated with this trade were needed. One such means involved decreasing the legibility, and thus vulnerability, of the local society to outsiders. Thus, the Banjar court likened itself and its pepper wealth to "the banana tree at one's gate," which is ripe for picking by any passerby, and which would be better off hidden from sight. The *Hikayat* offers an unusual case study in that the vulnerable party here is not a tribesman or peasant but a coastal native state. This state, moreover, has to manage not only a relationship with the colonial powers from across the sea, but also with the tribal producers of pepper and gatherers of forest products, who live upriver in the interior—and the two sets of relations are very different (Bronson 1977).

Chapter 3 is an analysis of the historic involvement of Borneo's tribespeople in gathering and trading native forest rubbers, in particular during the boom years of the mid-nineteenth century and their transition early in the twentieth century to the cultivation of the exotic *Hevea*. The analysis illustrates the important role played by forest products in the tribal economies; it shows how these communities were tied intimately into the dynamics of global markets; and it examines the ongoing, dialectical relationship between changes in the wider world and changes in the tribal production systems. The native forest rubbers were subject to a boom-bust cycle, which is characteristic of many tropical forest products (Homma 1992). The boom-bust cycles brought different actors and modes of production into and out of the picture, with the most rapacious typically holding sway at the peak of the booms. During nonboom periods (see Coomes and Barham 1997: 182), the native rubbers tended to be exploited less intensively and more sustainably as part of a composite household economy. As market booms waxed, collecting was taken over by more specialized, full-time actors employing less-sustainable methods. The booms invariably led to greater state intervention in resource exploitation, always with the justification of promoting the welfare of the local peoples and the protection of their resources but typically with ill results for both. There was a complementary relationship between gathering the native rubbers and swidden agriculture, which paved the way for the introduction of *Hevea*. This exotic, especially in the context of increasing state intervention, offered additional advantages. Most notably, *Hevea* had to be planted and it had to be cultivated. This moved tribal rubber production much further along the continuum from nature to culture, which was of great significance in the global economy, and which the tribespeople used to their advantage. This helps to explain the paradoxical historical fact that Southeast Asia became the world's leader in latex production based not on its own rich resource of native forest latexes but on an exotic from the Amazon. This "domestication" of their rubber industry by Borneo's tribespeople was a strategic response to the global economic system. The global system was not just expanding but was, therefore, actively being drawn into Borneo's tribal hinterlands, just as Borneo's societies were not simply being incorporated into but were aggressively engaging the global system.

CHAPTER 2

A Native Court's Warning about Involvement in Commodity Production

And let not our country plant pepper as an export-crop,
for the sake of making money.
— *King Ampu Jatmaka, Kingdom of Banjar*

Introduction

Whereas the records on the participation of indigenous Southeast Asian kingdoms in commodity production for colonial markets are very good, the records of how such kingdoms perceived this participation are scanty by comparison. This analysis is an attempt to interpret one such record.

The Pepper Injunction

There is a remarkable passage in the *Hikayat Banjar* in which its founder and ruler, King Ampu Jatmaka, issues an injunction against the cultivation of *sahang* or "black pepper":

And let not our country plant pepper as an export-crop, for the sake of making money, like Palembang and Jambi [two kingdoms in Sumatra]. Whenever a country cultivates pepper all food-stuffs will become expensive and anything planted will not grow well, because the vapours of pepper are hot. That will cause malice all over the country and even the government will fall into disorder. The rural people will become pretentious towards the townsfolk if pepper is grown for commercial purposes, for the sake of money. If people grow pepper it should be about four or five clumps per head, just enough for private consumption. Even four or five clumps per head will cause much vapour, owing to the great number of people involved, let alone if it is grown extensively as a crop; the country inevitably would be destroyed. (Ras 1968: 265–67)

This injunction is repeated further on in the *Hikayat*, in almost identical terms, by three subsequent rulers (ibid.: 331, 375, 443). This injunction is given added weight by the fact that in two of these cases, it is the ruler's last act before he disappears (ibid.: 331–32, 373–75). A modern transcriber of the chronicles notes that these multiple references are "completely stereotyped, yet the author [of the *Hikayat*] seems to attach great importance to them" (ibid.: 58)—an importance that is attested to by their repetition.

These passages in the *Hikayat Banjar* are not unique in the region. There is a similar passage in the *Hikayat Pocut Mohamat*, an eighteenth-century epic from Aceh, in North Sumatra (Drewes 1979: 166–67):[1]

> Marketing does not yield much profit, even if you grow pepper, my friends.
> If there is no rice in the country, nothing else will be of use.
> What is the use of a purple kerchief or a dagger with a hilt of pinch-beck [brass]?
> If there is no rice in the country, the standing of royalty will be lost.
> If there is nothing to eat, your children will starve, and you will have to sell all you possess.

Some of the region's rulers took concrete action against pepper. Reid (1993: 299–300) reports that early in the seventeenth century, the sultan of Aceh ordered the destruction of pepper vines in the vicinity of the capital, because their cultivation was leading to the neglect of food crops and to annual food shortages. Reid (ibid.) also reports that Banten in West Java "cut down its pepper vines around 1620 in the hope that this would encourage the Dutch and English to leave the sultanate in peace, though self-sufficiency must have been an additional reason"; and the sultan of Maguindanao in the Philippines told the Dutch in 1699 that he had forbidden the continued planting of pepper so that he could avoid conflict with foreign powers. Noorlander (1935: 4–5, 124–25, cited in Hudson 1967: 70) says that in the Banjar court itself, an isolationist faction sought to end the sultanate's foreign contacts by destroying the kingdom's pepper groves.[2] Meilink-Roelofsz (1962: 216) reports on an analogous case involving cloves in the Moluccas: a 1618 inquiry into a drop in clove production on Ternate and Tidore concluded that "The inhabitants of both Tidore and Ternate wanted to be rid of the Europeans—the Tidorese of the Spanish and the Ternatans of the Dutch—and that they felt their only chance of accomplishing this was by calling a temporary halt to clove production."[3]

The *Hikayat Banjar*

The "Story of Lambu Mangkurat and the Dynasty of the Kings of Banjar and Kota Waringin," more commonly known as the *Hikayat Banjar*, is the native, court-based chronicle of a coastal Malayic kingdom that existed in southeastern Borneo until 1860,[4] although the chronicle itself only covers the period up until 1661 (Ras 1968: 1, 3).[5] According to the foremost contemporary scholar of this *Hikayat*, J. J. Ras, it was written and rewritten over the period of about a century between the mid-sixteenth and mid-seventeenth centuries (ibid.:177–81, 196) by three or four separate chroniclers sitting in different courts at different times (ibid.).[6] Ras views the *Hikayat* not as history, but as historiography.[7] This is obviously the case with the four passages on pepper, since it is highly unlikely that four different rulers—two on their deathbeds—chose to repeat almost verbatim an injunction against pepper planting. Drawing on the work of A. Teeuw and Snouck Hurgronje, among others, Ras (ibid.: 16) writes, "Malay texts of this kind must be seen primarily as *functional documents*, not written with the aim of simply giving a historical account, but *composed for the sake of the king* and the dynasty to which he was taken to belong." Ras is critical of earlier scholars of chronicles such as the *Hikayat*, who saw them only as bad history and were interested only in separating fact from fiction. Instead, he sees the distinction between fact and fiction as historically interesting in its own right. Although he does not insist on the historical validity of the *Hikayat*, he does insist on its sociological and mythological validity. "We deny that the *Hikayat Banjar* is the product of one single author who collected epic materials in a haphazard way from various sources, borrowing from this text or tradition and that, and elaborated on these in order to provide a story suitable to serve as the legendary beginning of local history" (ibid.: 116).[8]

Following Ras, I regard the *Hikayat* as a chronicle produced by, and thus reflective of, the sixteenth- and seventeenth-century Banjarese kingdom. I regard the references to pepper cultivation, in particular, as deliberate and meaningful. As Snouck Hurgronje writes (1888, cited in Ras 1968: 15), "If one takes these myths and legends for what they are, one has in them precious sources of knowledge concerning the character of the people." These references to pepper cultivation thus represent a unique source of knowledge on commodity production in early modern Borneo. This production represented a critical element in the historic development of the Banjar kingdom, and the chronicle represents an indigenous articulation of this element.[9]

Background: Pepper Cultivation, Trade, and the Banjar Kingdom

In order to understand what message was being conveyed in the *Hikayat* about pepper, it is necessary to understand something of pepper cultivation, the history of its trade, its place in Banjar trade in particular, and its historic attraction to foreigners in general and the Dutch in particular.

Pepper Cultivation

Like many of Southeast Asia's export crops, much of the pepper that reaches global markets—and practically all of it in the case of Indonesia[10]—is cultivated not on estates or plantations but on smallholdings worked by local peasant and tribal communities, many of whom, at least traditionally, were otherwise dependent for their livelihoods upon swidden agriculture. A number of different observers have noted a similarity between pepper cultivation and swidden cultivation, based on the use of similar techniques to clear, burn, and plant on forested land, followed by a lengthy fallow. Thus, early in the nineteenth century Crawfurd (1820, 1:433) writes, "The land chosen for a pepper garden is a piece of forest land similar to that from which, after the felling and burning of the timber, a fugitive crop of mountain rice is taken"; and Suntharalingam (1963: 46) suggests that at the beginning of the eighteenth century, pepper was being cultivated in the hinterlands of the Banjar kingdom by "the shifting method of cultivation." Based on this similarity, it has been widely concluded that pepper fits easily into swidden systems—although this will be debated here (see chapter 7)—and that this has been one of its historic attractions (Andaya 1995: 171–73; Heidhues 1992: 101). Reid (1993: 33) suggests that this was central to the initial dissemination of pepper through the archipelago: "It spread in lightly populated areas of shifting cultivation, where pepper could be planted without necessarily foregoing staple food crops." Kathirithamby-Wells (1977: 16) writes, "Even after the introduction of pepper as an export product in west Sumatra . . . padi-growing continued on the same simple basis, alongside pepper cultivation which demanded a more settled form of agriculture. Often, *ladang* [swidden] lands, otherwise abandoned after a single crop of padi, were planted out with pepper which continued to occupy the plot for the next seven to ten years, until the vines declined."

There is, in fact, considerable evidence of a linkage between pepper cultivation and subsistence swidden cultivation: late in the nineteenth century

Figure 2.1. Kantu' pepper garden and adjoining secondary forest

Jacobs (1894) writes of "enrichment" planting of pepper in Acehnese rice swiddens in North Sumatra; and early in the twentieth century Jongejans (1918) writes that the location of swiddens in the Lampong region of South Sumatra was determined by the prospects for transforming them into pepper gardens. The historic association of pepper and swidden cultivation does not mean, however, that this was a beneficial one for the people involved.

An example of pepper cultivation by a contemporary group of swidden cultivators is that of the Kantu'.[11] The Kantu', at the time that I initially studied them, were cultivating pepper in tiny gardens cleared from the forest, which averaged 500 square meters in area and contained perhaps 225 plants (figure 2.1). Cultivation was intensive, at least by comparison with their swidden agriculture. De Waard (1989: 227) sums up this system by saying that pepper cultivation in Borneo "is characteristically associated with chemically poor soils, high inputs and high productivity"—which is reflected in the need to apply homemade manures like "burnt earth" (figure 2.2), mixture of earth and vegetation that has been burned together in a fire.

The Kantu' experience with pepper compared unfavorably with their cultivation of rubber, their other major cash crop. There are several reasons for this (see Schneider 1995: 31–32). The cost of the optimal inputs (factory

Figure 2.2. Kantu' man preparing "burnt earth" fertilizer

pesticides and fertilizers) is one reason; another is the impact of pepper cultivation on the land, which renders it useless for swidden cultivation.[12] Pepper is said to take all of the *lang-lemak* (fertility) from the soil, eliminate its *bau* (aroma), and make it *kusi* (barren). It was historically the only land use in the Kantu' territory that precipitated *belayang madang,* a grassland succession of *Imperata cylindrica.*[13] These impacts are reflected in the fact that while the Kantu' would ordinarily lend land to one another for the purpose of swidden-making, they would not lend land for pepper gardening.

Even more important than the consequences of pepper cultivation for land use are its consequences for labor use. Pepper requires comparatively great attention.[14] The Kantu' said of it, "Kebun lada nadai tau' leka' sekali'; asa belega' dibantun-ditupi', mati" (Pepper gardens cannot be ignored at all; if [you] momentarily stop weeding and caring for [it], [it] dies). Indeed, the Kantu' said, though perhaps not without hyperbole, "If you ignore pepper for even ten days, it will die" (compare to Padoch 1982: 113). This posed a problem for the Kantu' during the seasons of peak labor demand in their

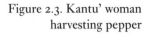

Figure 2.3. Kantu' woman
harvesting pepper

swiddens, namely planting, weeding, and harvesting. The Kantu' said only
a household that has adult children in it, which is capable of splitting up its
labor force, can cultivate pepper. The timing constraints of pepper cultivation have other consequences as well, with respect to the market. It takes a
minimum of three years for a pepper garden to start producing, so there is
a three-year time lag in the cultivator's response to market conditions (de
Waard 1964: 24). And once a crop of pepper has ripened, it must be harvested immediately and dried: pepper cannot be stored on the vine (figures
2.3, 2.4) (Padoch 1982: 113).[15] The time lag in initial production and the inability to delay harvesting place the pepper cultivator at the mercy of market
prices, which is not the case with rubber.[16] These factors themselves contribute to market volatility and extreme price swings (Bulbeck et al. 1998: 67;
Cramb 1993: 222; Wadley and Mertz 2005). More generally, they contribute
to the volatility and uncertainty that have characterized the pepper market
throughout history (Purseglove et al. 1981: 81).[17]

Figure 2.4. Pepper drying on the veranda of a Kantu' longhouse

History of the Pepper Trade

Black pepper is today the most important spice in the world in terms of usage and value, and it has been important in global trade since the first century A.D., when Pliny noted its availability in Roman markets (Bulbeck et al. 1998: 60).[18] China began to import pepper from India during the Tang dynasty (A.D. 618–907), and it was the most important item in trade between the Indian Ocean and the Mediterranean in the twelfth to fourteenth centuries (ibid.).

Black pepper is native to the Western Ghats of India (Burkill 1966, 2:1776). Burkill (ibid.: 1779) suggests that Hindu colonists migrating from India brought pepper to Indonesia between 100 B.C. and A.D. 600 (see also Crawfurd 1868: 191).[19] Wolters says that there is some evidence that western Indonesia may have been exporting pepper to China before A.D. 400: in a Chinese translation undertaken in A.D. 392 of the *Sutra of the Twelve Stages of the Buddha,* five maritime kingdoms are enumerated, and the account of one, called She-yeh—which has been plausibly identified as Java[20]—states, "This land produces long pepper and black pepper" (Wolters 1967: 66–67, 183). Hirth and Rockhill (1911: 223n2) suggest that the first Chinese author to mention pepper as a product of the East Indies was Chóu K'ü-feï, an assistant subprefect in Kui-lin, in his Sung topography, the *Ling-wai Tai-ta,* published in 1178. Pepper from a number of places in Java is mentioned in the *Chu-fan-chï* (literally, "A Description of Barbarous Peoples"), a trade handbook compiled in 1225 by the superintendent of maritime trade in Fu-chien, Chau Ju-kua. Indeed, it may be largely due to the trade in pepper that Chau Ju-kua ranks Shö-p'o, (Java) second after Ta-shï (the realm of the Arabs), of "all the wealthy foreign lands which have great store of precious and varied goods" for trade with China (ibid.: 23).[21] Marco Polo mentions black pepper as part of the "surpassing wealth" of Java at the end of the thirteenth century (Polo [1298] 1969: 241). Reid (1993: 12) suggests that Ming trading missions and territorial expansion early in the fifteenth century stimulated pepper production in Indonesia for trade to China (see also Bulbeck et al. 1998: 77).[22] By the early modern period, pepper was the most important Southeast Asian export by a factor of ten (Reid 1995: 100; see also Glamann 1958: 73). Bulbeck et al. (1998: 64) write that "Southeast Asian production reached a peak in about 1670, when it provided pepper for most of Europe and much of western Asia as well as China."

Up until the arrival of the Portuguese in the archipelago in 1509, almost all Indonesian pepper was being exported to China (ibid.: 71; Reid 1993: 144), whose pepper consumption was as high as in Europe at that time (Meilink-Roelofsz 1962: 76). But the role of increasing Chinese imports and consumption of Southeast Asian pepper in the fifteenth century was replaced by that of Europe in the sixteenth century (Glamann 1958: 75). Bulbeck et al. (1998: 60) write, "The passion to obtain pepper more cheaply and stop the flow of European silver and gold into Muslim hands to pay for it was one of the principal factors which propelled the Portuguese and Spanish on their voyages of discovery." As a result, by the middle of the sixteenth century, most of the region's much-expanded pepper production was going to Europe (ibid.: 83; see also Andaya 1993b: 43–45; Reid 1993: 144). Growing European consumption in the 1600s was met by establishment of new areas of cultivation, mainly in Sumatra and in southeastern Borneo around Banjarmasin (Bulbeck et al. 1998: 64), the latter being the area that figures in the *Hikayat Banjar.* The forces behind this expansion and redirection of the pepper trade to Europe

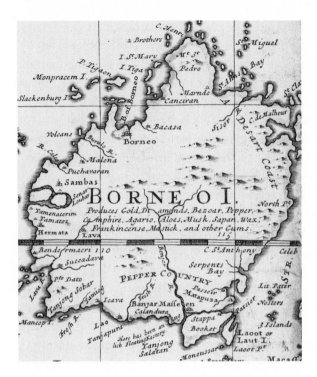

Figure 2.5.
Herman Moll's 1708
map of Southeast
Asia, highlighting
trade commodities
(detail). Courtesy of
Map Department,
Yale University
Library.

dominated both regional and global trade for three centuries. As Bulbeck et al. (ibid.: 69) write, "As a key item in the long-distance luxury trade of the fourteenth to seventeenth centuries, pepper's role in the building of an integrated global commercial system is difficult to exaggerate. It ensured that Southeast Asia enjoyed a trade boom in that period and became *uncomfortably* [emphasis added] tied to that world system."[23] The 1708 map of the region by Herman Moll (who was born in Holland or Germany but worked in England) shows the importance of pepper (along with other commodities) in European views of the landscape, including that of the Banjar region of southeastern Borneo (figure 2.5).

This history is reflected in pepper's terminology. The English term *pepper* derives from the Sanskrit name for one of India's pepper plants, *pippali* or *pippalī* (*Piper longum*) or "long pepper" (Monier-Williams 1899: 628). Crawfurd (1868: 188–89) suggests that this may be due to the historical precedence of India's long pepper in the trade to Greece and Rome, under the Greek term *peperi* or the Latin term *piper*. The Sanskrit name for "black or round pepper" (*Piper nigrum*) is *maricha* (ibid.: 790). Black pepper is called *miricha* and *mrica* in old and modern Javanese, respectively (Zoetmulder

1982, 1:1143; Horne 1974: 384); but it is called *lada* in Indonesian and Malay (Echols and Shadily 1992: 321; Wilkinson 1959, 2:636–37), Sundanese, and many of the languages of Sumatra and Borneo, as in the case of the earlier-mentioned Kantu' (Richards 1981: 174). Burkill (1966, 2:1776–77) suggests that *lada* was originally a term for peppers indigenous to the archipelago (for example, *Piper cubeba* L. and *Piper retrofactum* Vahl, both of which were ancient trade commodities and are still called by this term), and that it was adopted, in the aforementioned languages, for the exotic, adopted black pepper. The term used for black pepper in the *Hikayat*, is *sahang*, which is still used in contemporary Banjarese (Hapip 1977: 155), and is also, as *sahaŋ*, an old Javanese (Kawi) word (Ras 1968: 593; Wilkinson 1959, 2:999; Zoetmulder 1982, 2:1596).[24]

The Banjar Kingdom and Its Trade

The pepper trade mentioned in the *Hikayat Banjar* belonged to an ancient trading tradition both within Banjar and the archipelago as a whole. Borneo's role in this regional trade was initially indirect: whereas inscriptions like those at Kutai in eastern Borneo show external influences as early as the fifth century, there were no direct Borneo–China trade or political ties even in the sixth or seventh centuries (Wolters 1967: 175, 176). Rather, as Wolters (ibid.: 176) says, "Borneo's produce would have been re-exported through other and more important commercial centres in the region,[25] and from these centres it would have received in exchange trade goods and cultural influences."[26] Bornean toponyms begin to appear in Chinese literature in the ninth century (Hirth and Rockhill 1911: 158n1), and there are a number in Chau Ju-kua's thirteenth-century *Chu-fan-chi*, notably the dependency of *Shö-p'o* (Central Java) called *Tan-jung-wu-lo* or *Tan-chung-pu-lo* (ibid.: 83). Wheatley (1959: 12) identifies this place name as a transliteration of the *Tanjungpura* mentioned in fourteenth-century Majapahit court chronicles, and he notes that all authorities locate it in southern Borneo, and some locate it in the vicinity of modern Banjarmasin (see chapter 1, figure 1.1).[27] Ras (1968: 192–96) is among those who locate *Tanjungpura* in southeastern Borneo, based on his innovative analysis of the alteration of the region's coastline over the past two millennia as a result of sedimentation. Southern Borneo was trading gold, diamonds, foodstuffs, and junks to Majapahit in Java as early as the fourteenth century;[28] and the involvement of this part of the island in trading similar goods with Java and Malacca for Indian textiles was documented by the Portuguese observer Tomé Pires early in the sixteenth century (Meilink-Roelofsz 1962: 100; Ricklefs 2008: 23; Pires 1944). The first recorded European visits to Borneo date from the beginning of the sixteenth century (Crawfurd [1856] 1971: 63–65; Logan 1848b). Banjarmasin first appears on European maps at the end of the sixteenth century, and it was one of the first place names within Borneo to do so, reflecting its importance to European traders (Cleary and Eaton 1992: 42; Hudson 1967: 61n14).

According to the *Hikayat*, the Banjar kingdom was founded by a trader from Keling in India, who says on his deathbed: "In my heart I still take pride in considering myself as nothing but a prominent merchant" (Ras 1968: 229, 231, 267–68).[29] The importance of trade to the kingdom is reflected in the fact that the presence of foreign traders is cited throughout the *Hikayat* as a sign of a healthy kingdom. A typical line is, "The country was bustling and prosperous, and foreign traders also came in great numbers" (ibid.: 231, 335, 373). The participation of the large trading community in periodic dynastic conflicts is recounted in the *Hikayat* (ibid.: 413); and when the Banjar capital is periodically relocated — whether because of dynastic conflict or land accretion between it and the sea (ibid.: 192–96) — the relocation of the traders is explicitly mentioned as well (ibid.: 371, 405). The *Hikayat* variously describes the "foreign traders" as Acehnese, Balinese, Buginese, Biaju, Chinese, Johorese, Hollanders, Javanese, Madurese, Makassarese, Malaccans, Malay, Minangkabau, Patanis, Sumbawanese, and those from Bantan, Jambi, Gujerat, Keling, Macao, Palembang, and Tuban (ibid.: 263, 371, 431).

The Banjar kingdom's trade initially focused on forest products, the oldest trade goods of the archipelago.[30] Ras (1968: 189, 198) suggests that natural abundance in such products, coupled with navigable waterways for bringing them out to the coast,[31] were critical determinants of the development of the Banjar kingdom in southeastern Borneo. The importance and diversity of this trade is reflected in the rich, evocative lists that appear throughout the *Hikayat* of goods sent to other kingdoms as gifts or tribute (ibid.: 255, 305):[32]

> So Wiramartas was sent to the king of China [to ask for men able to make statues of bell metal], taking with him ten diamonds, forty pearls, forty emeralds, forty red corals, forty rubies, forty opals, forty loads of beeswax, forty bags of damar,[33] a thousand coils of rattan, a hundred gallons of honey, and ten orangutangs.

The mission [to request military assistance from Demak for a dynastic struggle] was entrusted to Patih Balit who took with him a gift of homage consisting of one thousand coils of rattan, one thousand dish-covers, ten loads of bees-wax, one thousand bags of hard damar, ten diamonds and ten loads of dragon's blood.[34]

The way that these lists are used to signify and summarize relations with other kingdoms testifies to the importance of forest products in the identity of Banjar.

These lists exclude certain items, notably subsistence tubers. Boom-gaard (2003) suggests that cultivated yams were found in Amuntai district of South Kalimantan in the late sixteenth century. And indeed, the *Hikayat* refers to various yams, *hubi* and *gumbili* (likely *Dioscorea esculenta* [Lour.] Burk. and *Dioscorea alata* L.), as well as taro, *kaladi* (*Colocasia esculenta* [L.] Schott.) being cultivated for personal use (Ras 1968: 374–75). Boomgaard also suggests that *gadung*, wild yams (*Dioscorea hispida* Dennst.), were being exploited in the same area in the seventeenth century and were being ex-ported to Java at the end of the eighteenth century (for example, in 1794, Banjarmasin exported 11,500 kilograms to Java), in a trade that continued until 1860. Given this volume of trade well into the eighteenth century, and given the prominent mention of yams as an important foodstuff in the *Hika-yat*, it seems likely that yams were also being exported during the period (six-teenth to seventeenth centuries) reported on in the *Hikayat*. If so, their omis-sion from the lists of trade/tribute goods is probably due to their banality. These lists emphasize the exchange of the exotic symbols of two poles: the center of empire, whether in Java or China, and the periphery of empire, in the forests of Borneo. As Tsing (1993: 272) writes, "The power of the things of empire extends from the center along lines of delegated authority, tribute, and trade; even the humblest iron daggers and china plates thus carry im-perial magic. Such objects promote royal power precisely because they are dispersed."

Whereas Banjar exported yams, it imported rice from Java, which was partly responsible for keeping it subservient to a succession of Javanese king-doms—Majapahit, Demak, and Mataram—until late in the seventeenth century (Suntharalingam 1963: 35).[35] This is obvious from the way that a gift to Demak, when Banjar sought its military assistance, was reciprocated (Ras 1968: 429): "A return gift was given [by the sultan of Demak] consisting of ten ship-loads of rice, as well as sugar, coco-nuts, tamarind, onions, garlic, salt and ten pieces of batik *kain* [cloth] to be used as clothing." Banjar's non-involvement in rice production verged on being an article of faith. The inhabitants of Nagara Daha, site of Banjar's second royal compound (*kraton*), when interviewed in 1824 reported that their ancestors had taken a vow to never plant rice (Ras 1968: 626).[36] The interviewer goes on to describe the majority of Nagara's population as "artisans," meaning smiths, gunsmiths, carpenters, and boat builders—not farmers.[37] Banjar's paradoxical import of one starch staple, rice, and its simultaneous export of another, yams, underlines its status as a kingdom committed to living from trade as opposed to primary production of foodstuffs.

Pepper was a relatively late addition to Banjar's exports. Lindblad (1988: 31) suggests that Hindu immigrants first brought pepper to Martapura, later one of the Banjar capitals, in the fifteenth century. A combination of factors at the beginning of the seventeenth century resulted in an efflorescence in the Banjar trade in pepper:[38] (1) the impact of the expansion of the Mataram Sultanate on the central and eastern Javanese ports of Jepara, Ceribon, Tuban, Madura, and Surabaya and the displacement of not just their trade but their traders to Banjar; (2) the monopolist policies of Aceh; (3) the international competition for Sumatran pepper; and (4) the Dutch closing of many other ports to traders of other nations (Hudson 1967: 66–68; Schrieke [1955] 1966: 60–61, 67). This growth in the pepper trade put Banjarmasin on the map. As Schrieke (ibid.: 29–30) writes,[39] "Southern Borneo was not by any means so important for Java in those days, because the only goods to be obtained there were forest products—such as damar, dragon's blood, wax, *myrabolans* [*sic*][40] for the batik industry, rattan and wicker work—which could also be imported from elsewhere, Palembang and Timor, for example. Banjarmasin in actuality became a center of importance only in the first part of the seventeenth century, when the amount of pepper grown was increasing every year thanks to the Chinese for whom the Bantam market was insufficient or inaccessible, overwhelmed by the European demand as it was."

Banjar Pepper and the Europeans

Banjar's pepper drew many traders to it, foremost amongst whom in the seventeenth to nineteenth centuries were the Dutch and English. In accordance with the prevailing colonial political-economic logic, both nations sought to monopolize this trade in Banjar, as they did elsewhere. The Dutch established a factory in Banjarmasin in 1606, destroyed the capital in 1612, and finally, after an English attempt to set up a factory in 1615, won initial concession of a monopoly on the pepper trade in 1635 (Suntharalingam 1963: 37, 38). Banjar granted the 1635 treaty because it needed Dutch help to protect it from the powerful Mataram sultanate in Central Java (ibid.: 35). But Banjar was able to conclude peace with Mataram just two years later, upon which they reneged on their agreement with the Dutch (ibid.: 37–38) and killed the entire staff of their trading post in 1638 (Lindblad 1988: 9). This was the pattern for the next two centuries, with the Dutch and the English undertaking short-lived ventures and following a pattern of in-and-out moves (ibid.: 8; Suntharalingam 1963: 37, 38). Cleary and Eaton (1992: 44) note that during the two centuries between 1615 and 1814, the Dutch and the English each concluded four separate formal agreements with Banjar regarding trade in general and pepper in particular. Dutch and English desires notwithstanding, the Banjar rulers were quite successful well into the colonial period in maintaining a free trade policy, even when they signed treaties to the contrary, and even when they were provoked. Suntharalingam (1963: 43) writes of Banjar's response to actions by the chief of the English trading mission that had led to open hostilities with Banjar at the beginning of the eighteenth century: "Despite Landen's [the English chief's] behaviour, the Sultan showed little animosity towards the British traders. Indeed, he appeared anxious that the English should continue trading in his dominions, as he realised that foreign trade was vital for the prosperity of the state. The Banjarmasin rulers adopted the policy of trying to encourage as many foreign nations to trade at Banjarmasin as possible, provided they did so peacefully." Indeed, during the seventeenth and first half of the eighteenth centuries, up until the Dutch imposed a monopolistic treaty and military presence in 1747, Banjarmasin was open to pepper traders from other countries more often than not (Bulbeck et al. 1998: 80, 82; Meilink-Roelofsz 1962: 262).[41] The treaty of 1847 did not sit well with the Banjarese, who rose against the Dutch in the Banjarmasin War of 1859–1863; in later years they allied themselves with the Dayak against the Dutch, and their last armed resistance only ended in 1906 (Ricklefs 2008: 169–70).

Interpreting Key Elements in the *Hikayat Banjar*

Given this background on historic and contemporary pepper cultivation, Ampu Jatmaka's speech in the *Hikayat Banjar* now can be examined in detail.

Jambi and Palembang

The first sentence of this passage runs as follows: "And let not our country plant pepper as an export-crop, for the sake of making money, like Palembang and Jambi." Sumatra was an early hub of trans-shipment to China of Indian pepper and was growing and trading its own pepper by the fifteenth century (Andaya 1993b: 43; 1995: 169).[42] By 1545 Jambi, in southern Sumatra, already was known to the Portuguese as a pepper producer (Andaya 1993a: 97; 1993b: 45). In 1615 English and Dutch ships first reached Jambi and established trading posts; and despite intermittent battles with one another, they were able by the second quarter of the century to displace both the Chinese and Portuguese from their dominant positions in Jambi's pepper trade (Andaya 1993a: 103; 1993b: 43–44, 45–46, 48, 53–55, 56). This pepper was cultivated in the upstream regions (Andaya 1993b: 17–18), from whence it was gathered and then traded to the foreigners under the auspices of the downstream state. This linkage of upriver and downriver in the pepper trade was initially very successful, and, coupled with the decline of other pepper-producing regions as a result of trade-related conflicts (Schrieke [1955] 1966: 55), it made Jambi into the second city of Sumatra (Andaya 1993a: 99). In time a market glut and precipitate price declines led to a breakdown in this linkage (ibid.: 104; Reid 1993). The relation of the European traders with the downriver half of the state became more problematic, and this made relations between upriver and downriver more problematic as well. It culminated by the end of the seventeenth century in rejection of pepper by the upriver people and the precipitate decline in political-economic importance of those downriver (Andaya 1993a: 109–12).

The dramatic rise and fall of Jambi and the factors that drove it were obviously seen as an object lesson by Banjar and other kingdoms in the region involved in pepper production. And Jambi was not an isolated case. Indeed, Thomas Stamford Raffles ([1817] 1978, 1:131), the British lieutenant governor of Java from 1811 to 1816, though not wholly objective where his Dutch predecessors were concerned, blames the "oppressive, unprincipled, and impolitic" policies of the Dutch for the disappearance of pepper cultivation from much of Java and Sumatra in the early nineteenth century.

Expensive Food, Poor Crops, Hot Vapors

The next line in the passage from the *Hikayat Banjar* is: "Whenever a country cultivates pepper all food-stuffs will become expensive and anything planted will not grow well, because the vapours of pepper are hot." Note, first, that this passage is specifically about pepper, not all cash crops. There are no warnings or proscriptions in the *Hikayat* against any other crops or commodities besides pepper, including forest products. This point is driven home by the other deathbed injunctions in the *Hikayat*, which actually contain preferred lists of crops to be planted instead of pepper: for example, "What people should definitely cultivate with energy is rice, maize, yams, taro and bananas" (Ras 1968: 331).

As regards the reference "food-stuffs will become expensive," in the case of Jambi, intensive involvement in pepper cultivation led to a greater reliance on imported rice (Andaya 1993b: 66). The reference to "expensive" here probably does not just allude to reliance on foodstuff markets, however, but to the conditions of this reliance, based on the flexibility versus inflexibility of one's agricultural strategy. As discussed earlier, the relatively long maturation period of pepper makes it harder for farmers to respond to short-term market fluctuations, and this inevitably means that they will often have to trade a crop that the market is not favoring (namely, pepper) for one that the market is favoring (for example, rice)—and make out less well in consequence (Andaya 1993a: 104; 1993b: 79). As a result, the farmers in Jambi developed a preference for shorter-maturation crops like rice, cotton, tobacco, and gambier (*Uncaria gambir* Roxb.) over pepper (Andaya 1993a: 114). By planting such crops, the farmers stood a better chance of getting foodstuffs—and cloth, which was the major trade good obtained with pepper[43]—on good terms.

The remaining portion of this line from the *Hikayat* states, "anything planted will not grow well, because the vapours of pepper are hot."[44] One reason that nothing else will grow well with pepper is its environmental impact. Pepper is one of Southeast Asia's most environmentally demanding export crops. Its cultivation is associated with erosion, loss of soil fertility, and grassland succession. On the one hand, pepper cultivation compares favorably with swidden cultivation of food crops because pepper gardens may be cultivated for eight to ten years in succession, whereas swiddens are normally cultivated for just one or at most two years. On the other hand, the longer cropping period in the pepper garden is only attained by the importation of nutrients/fertilizers from outside the garden, which thereby subsidize it. In addition, whereas a multiple-year forest fallow will restore the former swidden and permit its recultivation, this does not suffice in the case of the pepper garden. For these reasons, Brookfield et al. (1990: 497) blame pepper for the first sustained attack on the region's upland forests. One casualty of this attack is diminished land and resources for other crops to "grow well," just as the *Hikayat* suggests.

Malice and Government Disorder

The next sentence in the death-bed passage reads as follows: "That [pepper cultivation] will cause malice all over the country and even the government will fall into disorder." The cultivation of pepper in Jambi clearly led to ill will when involvement in the colonial trade obliged the down-river authority to intensify its exactions from upriver communities, and the latter's awareness of their own best interests led them to resist. This was perhaps an inevitable consequence of the collaboration of the native state with the colonial powers, given the latter's interest in a set of values probably antithetical to the moral economy. This refers to a community-based guarantee of basic subsistence to all members, which takes priority over all external claims (Scott 1976). Andaya (1993a: 119–20) writes, "The Jambi experience encapsulates a basic problem of many coastal rulers who found themselves caught up with a European power. Any alliance between them was bound to increase tensions as the Europeans attempted to manipulate or recast traditional upstream–downstream relations to attain specific commercial goals." The Europeans were interested in monopolizing the trade with the coastal powers to maximize their own profits.[45] This compelled coastal states like Jambi to resist granting the Europeans a monopoly while trying to preserve their own monopoly over trade with upriver communities. Similarly, Saleh (1976: 212–13) says that the Banjar aristocracy resisted Westerners' attempt to enforce a monopoly with them but sought to enforce their own monopoly with the upriver peasantry.[46]

Government disorder enters with this new system of values. Abandonment of the moral economy gave every faction in the coastal courts a self-interest in striking their own deals with both the European traders and the upriver producers; and of course the Europeans had even greater incentives to do the same. Hudson (1967: 70) writes, "It should not be imagined . . . that there was any sort of unity behind Banjar policy. The court was ridden by factionalism and regionalism, with individuals and policies contending to guide the kingdom. There were shifting 'internationalist' factions that sought to gain power with the support of one foreign power." Indeed, Saleh (1976: 215) interprets the *Hikayat*'s mention of hot "vapours" as a metaphor for "inter-family power rivalries, political intrigues, group conflicts and usurpations." European traders took advantage of these turbulent political waters to advance their own agendas, typically by tipping the balance of power in favor of one particular faction in exchange for a monopoly on the pepper trade.[47]

Rural Pretensions

The next line in the *Hikayat* reads, "The rural people will become pretentious towards the townsfolk if pepper is grown for commercial purposes, for the sake of money." The interpretation of this important line poses a number of pithy questions, beginning with this one: Who are the so-called "rural people"?

Definition of Sakai

There are four references to rural people in the *Hikayat*'s pepper passages. In two of these references, "rural people" is acceptably translated from *orang desa* in the original (Ras 1968: 330, 331, 374, 375): "Orang kota tiada diupamai oleh orang desa" (The rural population will not think highly of the townsfolk);[48] and "Maka orang kota tiada ditakuti oleh orang desa" (Thus the rural people will not fear the townsfolk anymore). But in the other two references, "rural people" is less clearly translated from *sakai* or *orang sakai*[49] (Ras 1968: 264–65, 330–31): "Orang sakai pun banyak barani pada orang kota" (The Sakai will become pretentious towards the townsfolk); and "Orang yang kaparak pada raja itu tiada ditakuti oleh sakai yang bersahang itu"[50] (The functionaries from the capital will not be respected by the Sakai who grow pepper).

The term *sakai* has the following meanings in Malay: "subject, dependent, of subject peoples in contrast to the ruling race, aborigines who do not speak Malay" (Wilkinson 1959, 2:1002). In his own glossary, Ras (1968: 593) translates *sakai* as "the tribal or rural people subjected to the rule of a political centre (*nagara*), and so in a certain way the opposite of *rakyat*." Ras (ibid.: 589) translates *rakyat* as "the (Malay) subordinates or subjects, i.e. the (male) members of the ruling race who were in principle entitled to attend the royal audience meetings on Saturdays, in contradistinction to the *sakai*, i.e. the (Dayak) tribal people subjected to Malay rule."[51] *Sakai* does not, thus, simply denote "rural people"; and it specifically does not denote Banjars.

The referent for *sakai* is the Dayak, therefore, who were distinguished from the Banjarese by religion, culture, and political marginality, as they still are today (Tsing 1993). Throughout the Malay-Indonesian Archipelago, forest products were gathered by non-Moslem peoples upstream, like the Dayak, who traded them to Moslem peoples downstream, like the Banjar (Andaya 1993a: 120). The initial role of the Dayak in the Banjar kingdom was to supply the kingdom with the interior forest products that were its chief trade goods up to the end of the sixteenth century (Hudson 1967: 67). The Dayak expanded on this role, when pepper was introduced, to become Banjar's first pepper cultivators. Hudson (ibid.: 56, 67) writes, "The historical evidence seems to indicate that pepper cultivation in the Hulu Sungai was in the hands of Dayak swidden agriculturalists until the closing decades of the seventeenth century." Pepper cultivation certainly would have been possible within the extensive, mobile,[52] low-density system of swidden cultivation that then prevailed; and the trade-based, nonagricultural Banjar kingdom would have had few alternatives in any case. As Reid (1993: 35) writes, "Pepper cultivation was . . . developed in a particularly sparsely populated region of seventeenth century Banjarmasin (southern Borneo) that had no previous tradition of pepper or even of intensive rice cultivation." The lack of a large in situ agricultural population available for pepper cultivation is reflected in the fact that slaves also played a significant role in this system:[53] Reid (1993: 35), citing Speelman ([1670] 1983: 112), writes that "One of Makassar's major exports to the region was 'male and female slaves fitted for labour in the pepper-gardens.'"[54] The use in the *Hikayat* of the term *sakai* as opposed to *rakyat* for the pepper growers also makes sense if one of its referents was non-Banjarese slaves, in addition to non-Banjarese tribesmen.

Dayak "Pretensions" and the Banjar Response

The *Hikayat* passage under discussion continues to say, "The rural people will become pretentious." The traditional Dayak role in the Banjar kingdom, as collectors of forest products, was critically important; and this importance would have been further enhanced by the Dayak's initial involvement in pepper cultivation—but the political power of this role was the site of an ongoing contest between Dayak and Banjar.[55] In a manner that typified the policy of coastal states (including Jambi) toward interior resource-producing populations all over the archipelago, Banjar sought to strengthen its negotiating position and weaken that of the Dayak by insulating them from contacts with other traders or outsiders (Hudson 1967: 55). As Vlekke (1961: 202) writes, perhaps reflecting historic Dutch views of Banjar, "The sultans of Banjarmasin feared nothing so much as direct contact between the Europeans and the Dayak, whom they cruelly exploited and oppressed." A similar account of the European view, nearly contemporaneous with the *Hikayat*, is as follows: "I have seen some of the former [inland inhabitants] come down the River to the port of Banjar Maseen in very ill-shap'd Praws; and bring down Gold Dust, Diamonds, Bezoar-stones, Rattans, and sundry other Merchandizes. The Bajareens will not suffer the Europeans to have any Acquaintance or Trade with them, but do purchase the goods from them, which they sell to us at a greater Price. And I do verily believe, that the many frightful Stories they tell us of those people's Barbarity and Cruelty, are only invented on purpose to deter us from having any Acquaintance or Commerce with them, which would be a great disadvantage to the latter; tho' some of these Reports may be true" (Beeckman [1718] 1973: 155). Hudson (1967: 65) suggests that some of the periodic relocations of the Banjar capital—for example, from Nagara to Banjarmasin—"may have been motivated at least partly by an attempt to minimize contacts between foreign merchants and the Dayak people of the interior who produced the export commodities." The contest between Banjar and Dayak would have intensified with the introduction of pepper and European traders to the scene, because trade agreements with the European powers would have obliged Banjar to structure its trade with the Dayak in terms ever less favorable to the latter.[56]

The principal expression of "pretension" by the Dayak was resistance of one sort or another. In East Kalimantan (Peluso 1983a),[57] as in Jambi (Andaya 1993a: 112; 1993b: 137), this resistance sometimes took the form of open aggression toward the coastal kingdom. However, in southeastern Kalimantan, although some Dayak groups, like the Ngaju, were both feared and used as mercenaries by the Banjars (Ras 1968: 22, 50, 52), open aggression appears to have been less common. Rather, the major response of these Dayak seems to have been passive resistance to pepper cultivation, perhaps coupled with flight from Banjar control, both of which responses also were documented in Jambi (Andaya 1993a: 102, 107–8, 114; 1993b: 136). Similar responses have been documented for other Dayak, at other times and places, with other cash crops (see chapter 5); and it is based on a strong cultural commitment to subsistence rice culture. Thus, Hudson (1967: 66) writes, "Although they [the Dayak in southeastern Borneo] were willing to collect forest products and grow a little pepper to trade for Chinese goods, they were not willing to allow these secondary pursuits to interfere with the primary task of rice cultivation."[58]

The Banjar response to the Dayak resistance to pepper cultivation was not heightened exactions and oppression, as happened in Jambi and in many other commodity-producing areas, but rather displacement of Dayak by Banjar. Hudson (ibid.: 67) writes, "As mere part-time cultivators, the Dayak were not able to meet the increasing export needs nor were they willing to give up their traditional way of life to become full-time commercial agriculturalists. The result was that elements of the Banjar-Malay population began to move inland from the coast and to displace the Dayak in the best interior pepper growing region which was in the upper Nagara drainage above Amuntai." The result was a replacement, during the seventeenth and eighteenth centuries, of part-time Dayak pepper producers, operating within the overall framework of a system of swidden agriculture, by full-time Banjar pepper producers, operating within a system of sedentary agriculture. Hudson (ibid.: 67–68) writes, "By the end of the eighteenth century, pepper was being cultivated in more or less permanent plots in the Hulu Sungai, and there were inland regional pockets with relatively high population densities, from which we may infer that Dayak, with their shifting cultivation, had given way to Banjar-Malay sedentary agriculturalists." This displacement of Dayak by Banjar was accompanied by Banjar slave raids, land acquisition, and coercive religious proselytizing in the Dayak regions (ibid.: 56).

Private Consumption

The next two lines in the *Hikayat* passage read, "If people grow pepper it should be about four or five clumps per head, just enough for private consumption. Even four or five clumps per head will cause much vapour, owing to the great number of people involved, let alone if it is grown extensively as a crop; the country inevitably would be destroyed." Given the famous lack of pepper consumption among its producers (Crawfurd 1868: 191), the phrase "private consumption" probably refers not to literal pepper consumption but more figuratively to the sale/trade of small amounts of pepper to meet limited household needs of "consumption" or subsistence. This interpretation is supported by the fact that this phrase is structurally opposed, within the overall passage on pepper, to the earlier injunction against planting pepper "as an export crop." Thus, we have first an injunction against planting as an export crop, followed by approval for planting to meet household consumption/subsistence needs. In the original Banjarese text, the reference to "export crop" is translated from *dagangan negri* (Ras 1968: 264). This term has a much narrower referent than just export or trade, however, which is a slightly misleading translation of it in this context. It more properly translates as "state trade," referring to the sort of state involvement in export that Jambi (for example) had in its collaboration with the European traders. This translation is supported by Saleh's (1976: 208) suggestion that "By the end of the seventeenth century pepper was being cultivated in all the regions of Banjar, mostly on the big appanage lands of the king, the royal family and the ruling class." Thus, two different types of pepper production and trade are distinguished in this passage: production and trade carried out by and on behalf of the state is enjoined, while production and trade oriented toward household consumption/subsistence is approved. This interpretation is consistent with the prior line enjoining the cultivation of pepper "for commercial purposes, for the sake of money": not all pepper cultivation is proscribed, and not all cultivation for market, just certain types. Thus, the *Hikayat* is urging a return to a different type of market-oriented economy, not to a mythical premarket natural economy (Roseberry 1991: 223), which indeed would have been a strange goal for a trading state like Banjar.

The Hikayat's ideal of growing "four or five clumps . . . for private consumption" resembles the traditional system of pepper cultivation in Sumatra. Andaya (1995: 185; citing Forbes [1885] 1989: 135) suggests that pepper cultivation in Jambi, before the sixteenth-to-seventeenth-century boom, involved cultivation of a few stakes[59] of *pohon wang* (money trees) to meet the household's periodic needs for cash or market goods. This means that pepper would have been just one part of a wider composite household economy, likely comprising a subsistence sector of swidden and perhaps also irrigated or swamp-based cultivation of rice, and a market-oriented sector of forest-product gathering and cultivation of export crops like pepper. This sort of economic setting—which still characterized much of the agricultural economy in outer Indonesia through the twentieth century—is indicated by the use of the phrase "money trees" for pepper, which makes sense only against a nonmonetary subsistence background. Hudson (1967: 67) suggests that this also characterized the initial system of pepper cultivation in Banjar: "The earliest commercial pepper was grown by Dayak as a part of the swidden complex, a situation that continued to the end of the seventeenth century in some interior regions." This Dayak system of pepper cultivation represents the one that is endorsed in the *Hikayat;* it is replaced, when sedentary Banjar cultivators displaced the Dayak, by the state-trade type of system that is enjoined in the *Hikayat*. The contest between these two systems, state-supported commodity production versus smallholder production, is a leitmotif of the history of commodity production in Indonesia and is reproduced today in the opposition between parastatal plantations and smallholders.

The opposition of "private consumption" to the market is further illuminated by a passage in the *Hikayat* that deals with foreign dress (Ras 1968: 265):

> The king of Nagara-Dipa once said, when all the dignitaries with their subordinates were sitting before him in the audience-hall, "People of Nagara-Dipa, let none of you dress like the Malays or the Hollanders or the Chinese or the Siamese or the Acehnese or the Makassarese or the Buginese. Do not imitate any of them. You should not even follow the old customs of dress from the time when we still lived in Keling, for that is no longer our country now. We have now set up a country of our own, following the ways and manners of Majapahit. Therefore we should all dress like the Javanese. According to the stories of olden times handed down by the elders, whenever the inhabitants of a country imitated the clothing of people from elsewhere, misery inevitably fell upon the country that had turned to foreign ways of dressing. 'Misery' means 'misfortune' and 'misfortune' means that there is much evil in such a country, either because there is much illness among the people or because the monsoons do not behave properly, that is, the north-east monsoon behaves like the south-west monsoon or the south-west monsoon behaves like the north-east monsoon, or there is much malice, or the king's instructions are not carried out because the common people do exactly as they themselves like. The coming of any of these country-wide ailments brings the country into a state of affliction."

The principal trade good given for pepper during the boom in the early modern era was cloth from India (Andaya 1995: 173–74).[60] Prior to this era, women in the pepper-producing regions had woven their own cloth; with the advent of pepper—and the cloth for which it could be traded—women shifted their labor from weaving to pepper cultivation (ibid.). There appears to be a general association in the region between the cessation of weaving and the initiation of market activity. For example, contemporary Kantu' women say that the labor that they put into rubber tapping, much of the output of which has been traded in recent times for sarongs and other ready-made clothing, had formerly been put into weaving. This process also worked in the opposite direction. Andaya (1993b: 135; 1995: 178) states that Jambi women took up weaving again when pepper prices fell and cloth prices rose; and Reid (1993: 301–2) tells us that a similar reversal took place in Banten, Java, Makassar, and among the Bugis. This turning away from foreign cloth and the mode of production that was necessary to obtain it is likely encoded in the *Hikayat*'s proscription of foreign attire. Reid (ibid.: 302) says that the proscription is an ideological reflection of the shift away from Indian cloth.

The Role and Meaning of the Historic Text

Given the foregoing line-by-line exegesis of the pepper passages in the *Hikayat*, what the text as a whole achieves can now be better assessed.

What the Text Does Not Say

The deathbed injunctions against planting pepper are illuminating both for what they say and what they don't say. The pepper passages discuss the division between ruling and subject populations, for example, but they do not discuss divisions within the court, despite the fact that the passages begin with the case of Jambi, where such divisions were an obvious problem. Saleh (1976: 210–11, 215) suggests that divisions within the court were also a problem for Banjar, as pepper made the aristocracy more powerful than the Banjar king himself: "The king could not take any action or measure without its [the court council's] permission or talk alone with foreigners." On the other hand, there is a remarkable amount of candor in the *Hikayat*, which is reflected in the fact that even if "government disorder" is not discussed in detail, at least it is mentioned. Even more impressive is the fact that it is *dagangan negri* (state trade) that is condemned and proscribed, and not the traditional smallholder cultivation, which represents a remarkable example of self-critique.

A second notable omission from the *Hikayat* is the failure to mention the Dutch in the pepper passages, despite the dominant role that they played — due to their interest in pepper — in the affairs of the Banjarese sultanate during the sixteenth to seventeenth centuries in which the *Hikayat* was written. Another notable omission is the failure to include pepper in any of the detailed lists of gifts, tribute, and trade that are presented in the *Hikayat* (Ras 1968: 255, 305, 325, 363, 427, 441), until its very end, after the Dutch bombardment of Banjarmasin, when a mission to the Mataram Sultanate is described (ibid.: 483): "They went to offer the diamond Misim together with a quantity of pepper, rattan, dish-covers and beeswax."

It seems highly unlikely that pepper was not actually present in gift, tribute, and trade shipments before this date, especially in the case of China, which had a strong appetite for pepper, and which received shipments of tribute described in the *Hikayat* (ibid.: 255). The fact that pepper only appears in these shipments after the reference to the Dutch associates pepper with the Dutch era. It suggests that pepper shipments took on a different meaning during the Dutch era. The Dutch indeed elevated pepper into something qualitatively different from all other trade commodities; and relations with the Dutch over pepper were qualitatively different from all other trading relations. This was a departure from the preceding millennium of Oriental trade in pepper. Pepper was *not* part of the trade of Banjar in this way before the coming of the Dutch. This new, politically charged interpretation of pepper is also supported by the fact that pepper first appears in a shipment of goods to Mataram intended to test its political intentions vis-à-vis Banjar.

The coming of the Dutch is described in the *Hikayat* as follows (ibid.: 465): "Then, about two years later [after the reigning rajah, Marhum Panambahan,[61] had recommended, but in vain, that they move the capital to a safer location], the Hollanders came. Four ships anchored south of Pulau Kambang and bombarded the town of Banjar. There was great consternation among the Banjarese." The most significant aspect of this passage is its location within the *Hikayat:* it follows all four of the major passages warning against the planting of pepper,[62] which thereby helps to preconfigure the coming of the Dutch and their problematic interest in pepper. This interpretation is supported by a metaphor that is used by Marhum Panambahan in his speech to the court two years before the bombardment by the Dutch, in which he recommends the relocation of the capital (ibid.: 463): "I propose that we move the capital to somewhere on the Mangapan river . . . for it is like a banana tree in front of one's gate, too many people take an interest in it. Since this place lies near the sea it is an easy prey for an enemy. We had better move elsewhere. At that time none of the *dipatis* [governors] was willing to move because it would give too much trouble." Predictably of course, since the purpose of the *Hikayat* is in part to glorify the wisdom of Banjar's rulers, the capital does indeed prove to be like "a banana tree in front of one's gate," and it is the Dutch who "take an interest in it" because of its pepper. The relationship of pepper to the kingdom, therefore, is like that of the banana tree to the household. The *Hikayat*'s injunctions against pepper cultivation thus represent a failed attempt to remove this "banana tree in front of one's gate."

This interpretation of the banana tree story is reinforced by a contemporary shamanic story from the Meratus Dayak living in the mountains above the historic Banjar territory (Tsing 1993: 77): "The Banjar king at Kayu Tangi built his palace in a grove of thorned bamboo, where it could not be seen by invaders. But the Dutch shelled the grove with pieces of silver. When people saw the silver, they cut down the bamboo to gather the money. Then the Dutch captured the palace, and the king was forced to disappear at the headwaters of the Barito river." Kayu Tangi, near Martapura, was the site of the fourth, and last, Banjar *kraton* (royal compound) and capital, although in fact it was Banjarmasin, the third capital, that the Dutch attacked in 1612, and it was Kayu Tangi to which the Banjarese fled (Ras 1968: 55, 77). Tsing (1993: 77) writes, "I don't know whether they [such stories] are 'true'; but some are telling parables of political relations in the region." And indeed, many of the elements that I have been discussing in the *Hikayat* are found in Tsing's story as well. The emphasis in Tsing's story on the desirability of not being seen is obviously analogous to the *Hikayat*'s passage on the banana tree in front of the gate: insofar as relations with the colonial powers were concerned, it was best to not attract attention. In both stories, economic activity draws what proves to be the fatal attention. In the *Hikayat* it is cultivation of a banana tree, read as a metaphor for pepper cultivation; and in Tsing's story, it is gathering of money from the Dutch, which can be read as responding to the economic opportunities — like expanded pepper cultivation — brought by the Dutch. In both cases, it is misreading of the risks of interaction with outsiders that leads to the native society's downfall.

What the Text Accomplishes — or Does Not

Implicit in the pepper injunctions in the *Hikayat* is the idea that at some earlier point in Banjar's history an alternate path of political-economic development was possible. The concept of having successive rulers tell their subjects not to plant pepper for state trade implies that there was a choice in the matter, that the Banjar people could have chosen to carry on a state pepper trade or not. This indigenous recognition of choice belies characterizations of the incorporation into the world system of local systems like the Banjar kingdom as a highly deterministic process, in which the global economic system is the active player and the local society is the passive subject. It is an assertion of agency in a globalizing world, something that resonates with the native peoples of Borneo to this day (Dove 2006). The *Hikayat* shows how clearly this process of incorporation and its possible ills and bene-

fits may be perceived by local society. One of the keys to this perception is
the local society's knowledge of the experiences of similar societies, in this
case those of Jambi and Palembang. The *Hikayat* reminds us that all such
societies will have been keen students of one another's experiences and will
have modified their own behavior accordingly, thereby constituting a process of incorporation of feedback that world-systems theorists have tended
to ignore.

The injunctions in the *Hikayat* notwithstanding, the state trade in pepper continued.[63] Why? The evidence that there was a difference of opinion
within the Banjar court in this matter would have been a factor. Moreover,
given such differences of opinion, the pressures from the Dutch to continue
the pepper trade would have been difficult to resist. Perhaps most important, however, the *Hikayat* may not have articulated this warning until it
was too late. The last rewriting of the *Hikayat* was carried out around 1663,
one-half century after the Dutch established their first trading post in the
Banjar capital, and nearly three decades after the first treaty that granted the
Dutch a monopoly on the pepper trade. Accordingly, it may be more useful
to see the pepper passages in the *Hikayat* not as a warning before the fact
but as an after-the-fact commentary or "damage control," as Koster (2005)
characterizes treatment of the Dutch in Peninsular Malay historiography.[64]
In that case, the more appropriate question is not Why did the Banjarese not
heed the warning? but rather Was the ex post facto analysis correct? And the
answer is yes.

CHAPTER 3

The Antecedent to Cultivating Exotic Rubber

Gathering Native Forest Rubbers

Sida' nenek-moyang bunga-bungas datai kito' ngega' jangkang ngau kubal.
(Our ancestors first came here looking for *gutta-percha* and India rubber.)
— *Kantu' elder*, speaking of his home in the Empanang river valley

Introduction

Chapter 2 examined the intensive, closely monitored, and politically contested cultivation of pepper in Borneo early in the seventeenth century. This chapter looks at the less-intensive and less-controlled, if still politically contentious, tradition of gathering forest products on the island, which persisted well into the twentieth century.[1] The juxtaposition of the two analyses shows that the history of commodity production and trade on Borneo is complex and does not follow an obvious evolutionary sequence. This historic trade in forest products is of interest for what it tells us about the politics of natural resource management and how these politics play into the adoption of *Hevea* and the spread of rubber cultivation in the twentieth century. As noted in the previous chapter, pepper's role on the regional stage in the fifteenth to seventeenth centuries was in some senses taken by natural rubber in the nineteenth to twentieth centuries. There are important differences in the modes of production of pepper and rubber, however; they did not fit into identical political-economic niches. In this sense, a closer precedent for *Hevea* was the gathering of Borneo's native rubbers.

The diffusion and adoption of *Hevea* early in the twentieth century among Indonesian smallholders, called "one of the most remarkable periods of development in the history of agriculture" (Allen and Donnithorne [1957] 1962 has been perceived as near miraculous, but there was in fact a historical logic to it. The few scholars who have examined this history look to comparatively recent events for its explanation. For example, Booth (1988: 205) attributes this development to the expansion of Indonesia's trade with Europe, before which, she concludes, the land and labor involved must have been "under-utilized." Cramb (1988: 107) suggests that the development of cash-cropping in Sarawak was stimulated by the exhaustion of primary forest at the end of the nineteenth and beginning of the twentieth centuries, leading to inadequate swidden harvests. Dillon (1985: 116) argues that the development of smallholder rubber cultivation in tandem with rice cultivation was due to the widespread abundance of land in Indonesia at that time. But none of these analyses ask whether there was any precedent for this commodity production in the smallholder economies. But there was, and recognition of it is key to seeing the historic smallholder development as an achievement in its own right and not simply a by-product of estate development.[2] As Missen (1972: 214) writes, "To see the estates in this role [of teacher] underplays the commercial motivation and awareness of the indigenous cultivator. . . . It seems far more appropriate to view the late nineteenth- and early twentieth-century changes among Outer Island peasants as the continuation of a long-term process rather than as something motivationally new." The view of smallholder rubber development as something altogether new privileges the colonial (and also post-colonial) plantation establishment at the expense of the smallholders.

Historical Context: Trade and the Native Latexes

The once-widespread idea that monetary relations are foreign to traditional, tribal societies has been largely abandoned over the past generation, with the historic linkage of such societies to broader market relations of production and exchange now seen as the rule rather than the exception (Parry and Bloch 1989).

Trade

Bornean tribal communities, for geographic, historical, and political reasons, exemplify the historic depth, breadth, and richness of such market linkages.[3] As Padoch (1982: 107) writes of the Iban and Kenyah, "The involvement of Iban, even far upriver communities, in trade, is therefore of long standing and although often small in actual volume or cost of goods exchanged, trade has been and is considered essential by all Iban. The desire for market products among Bornean groups even far more remotely situated than Sarawak's Iban is pronounced. Some groups of Apo Kayan Kenyah living in a hardly accessible region in East Kalimantan must travel months to reach supplies of desired products. Their trips to and from market sometimes take years." For most of its history, this Bornean trade has involved forest products, the trade in which had great importance both locally and globally. As Cleary and Eaton (1992: 59–60) write, "To conceptualize the important jungle trade as an unsophisticated and anachronistic part of the 'traditional' economy is both misleading and inaccurate. . . . The trade was economically and socially sophisticated, as well as being ecologically balanced."[4] For the tribal participants, this trade was an integral part of their dual household economy; this market-oriented sphere complemented their subsistence-oriented agriculture. The centrality of this trade to tribal society was reflected in its cultural valorization. As Padoch (1982: 106–7) notes, until recently in most parts of the Bornean interior, the most important *adat* fines and ritual prestations could only be made with brassware and ceramic ware, which were obtainable only through long-distance trade. Long-distance trading expeditions themselves were culturally valorized among the Iban and some other Dayak groups. Padoch (ibid.: 113–15), who otherwise critiques the image of the "nomadic Iban," suggests that even in recent times, some Iban have preferred itinerant exploitation of forest products to sedentary cash-cropping. In short, ritual, legal, and cultural structures made a necessity of long-distance trade, which in turn supported the existence of the dual economy.

Failure to note the existence and importance of this trade has led to misunderstandings of the societies involved. In Sumatra, for example, Kahn (1984: 317–18) argues that the trade in forest products was so important to historic Minangkabau society that its disruption, by forest closures under the colonial Dutch government, contributed to the Communist uprising of 1927. He suggests that scholars misinterpreted the effects of the forest closures and the causes of the uprising because they failed to appreciate the importance of this forest-product trade. A similar lack of appreciation has led to misunderstanding of traditional Iban society and economy in Sarawak. Sahlins (1972: 224–26) argues that economic exchange in Iban society was "balanced" rather than "generalized" due to the need to accumulate rice for external trade. Sherman (1990: 287) critiques this thesis based in part on the fact that Sahlins ignored the Iban trade in forest products, which likely eclipsed in importance their trade in rice.

Ignorance of the historic trade in forest products also has contributed to misunderstandings regarding the nature of swidden agriculture. An example is the popular explanation of the well-described seminomadic settlement pattern of the Iban (but see Padoch 1982) in terms of demand for new forest for swidden-making. This explanation overlooks the fact that some of this mobility was likely driven by the dynamics of forest-product gathering. As the epigraph to this chapter attests, the contemporary Kantu' say that their ancestors first explored and settled their present territory in West Kalimantan not in search of fresh swidden territory but in search of forest rubbers for trade.

The Native Latexes

Trade in forest products has a long history in Southeast Asia, with early records of it—between western Indonesia and China—dating from the fifth century (Wolters 1967: 158–59), if not considerably earlier (Dunn 1975; von Heine-Geldern 1945). A major category of forest products throughout this history has been plant "exudates," including gums, hard and soft resins—intraregional trade in which may date back to Neolithic times (Dunn 1975: 120–37)—and latexes. Indonesia is one of the world's largest exporter of these products: at the end of the twentieth century it still exported almost forty-two thousand tons of native gums, resins, and latexes, with a value of almost $25 million (Coppen 1995: 1, 9).[5]

A wide variety of latexes are native to the Indo-Malay region.[6] They were, and are, used traditionally within the local economies for caulking and sealing purposes (for example, of canoes [Jessup and Vayda 1988: 16]); but their greatest importance has lain in their role in trade. The latexes gathered in Borneo are divided within the international trade into three categories.[7] The first is *caoutchouc* (India rubber, or simply rubber). The French term *caoutchouc* (in Spanish *caucho*) was derived from a native Peruvian expression for "weeping wood"; whereas the term *India rubber* stemmed from the discovery in 1770 that the product could be used to "rub" out pencil marks, with *India* referring to its customary sale through London's East Indian merchants (Coates 1987: 7, 20–21; Corominas and Pascual 1980, 1:927; Imbs 1977, 5:130). *Caoutchouc* first referred to any New World forest rubber. Eventually it came to refer chiefly to rubber from *Hevea* in South America, *Ficus elastica* Roxb. in Southeast Asia, and *Willughbeia* spp. in Borneo (Burkill 1966, 2:2300–2304; Purseglove 1968: 146–47). *Caoutchouc* has been known to Europe since the early sixteenth century. One of the first published reference to *caoutchouc* in Europe was in the 1511 "Decades of the New World" (in Latin) of Pietro Martire d'Anghiera, who also documented the first observation of rubber by Spaniards in Tenochtitlan in 1519 (Wolf and Wolf 1936: 23). In the eighteenth century the Frenchman Charles Marie de la Condamine sent samples to Europe and made various articles out of it (ibid.: 26). Regular trade in it—which initially focused on erasers, clothing, footwear, medical syringes, and bottle stoppers—dates from the second half of that century (Coates 1987). With the discovery in 1839 that the elastic properties of natural rubber could be fixed by the application of heat and sulfur (namely, "vulcanization"), what had previously been a minor tropical forest product became the focal point of a global boom. The best source of natural latex proved to be Para rubber (*Hevea brasiliensis*), a tree native to the tropical forest of the right bank of the Amazon, in Brazil, northern Bolivia, and eastern Peru. During the nineteenth-century boom, rubber came to account for nearly 40 percent of the Brazilian economy and brought a level of prosperity to the Amazon that was never seen before or since (Dean 1987: 4).

The second category of forest rubber is *gutta-percha*, which refers largely to latex from trees of the family Sapotaceae, especially the genus *Palaquium* (in particular *P. gutta* [Hook.] Burck), the native habitat of which ranges from India to the Central Pacific, and the genus *Payena*, which ranges from Burma to New Guinea (Burkill 1966, 2:1651, 1708). Its use as an adhesive and as caulking for sailing vessels earned *gutta-percha* a role in the region's ancient trade with China. It was known in Europe by the mid-seventeenth century, but large-scale trade in it dates from the 1840s, when it was discovered that its extreme nonconductivity of electricity suited it for use in insulating marine telegraph cables and its extreme elasticity suited it for golf balls, among other uses (de Beer and McDermott 1989: 40; Eaton 1952: 53–54; Lindblad 1988: 14). A minor trade is still carried on in *gutta-percha*, with Indonesia being the biggest supplier (Coppen 1995: 128).[8]

The final category is *jelutong*, or *gutta-jelutong*, referring largely to latex from trees of the genus *Dyera* (family Apocynaceae), in particular *D. costulata* (Miq.) Hook. f., which are native to Malaysia and Indonesia (Burkill 1966, 1:889–90; Eaton 1952: 63). The market niche into which *jelutong* fits has itself been quite "elastic." Williams (1963: 122–23) writes that during the years 1905–1912 *jelutong* was marketed as a substitute for *Hevea* (that is to say, it was considered to be an inferior India rubber[9]); but during the years 1913–1922 it was marketed as an adulterant for *Palaquium* (in other words, it was considered to be an inferior *gutta-percha*); and from 1923 to the present it has been marketed within yet a third distinctive category of latexes, where it has attained its greatest economic importance. In 1922 it was discovered that *jelutong* could be used as a substitute for Mexican chicle (from *Manilkara achras* [Mill.] Fosberg) in chewing gum, supplies of which fell short of demand during the prohibition era in the United States (Burkill 1966, 1:891; Eaton 1952: 62). A minor trade is still carried on in *jelutong* for the chewing-gum market, with most of it coming from Indonesian Borneo (Coppen 1995: 118).

The change in the market for *jelutong,* from inferior India rubber to inferior *gutta-percha* to chicle substitute, demonstrates the contingent nature of the term *forest product*. Although the botanical sources remain the same, the trade products taken from them may vary considerably. Indeed, the native sources of latex were not necessarily first valued for latex.[10] Many latex-producing trees produce good timber, and so they became known and named for their timber, not their latex (Burkill 1966, 2:1654).[11] Many latex-yielding trees and vines also produce edible fruits and other products (Bock [1881] 1985: 204; Roth 1896, 2:244). Hose and McDougall ([1912] 1966, 1:151) suggest that attraction to the fruit alone caused some Bornean tribesmen to contribute both intentionally and unintentionally to the spread of some of the native rubbers. Burkill (1966, 2:1655) suggests that the aboriginal Jakun of Peninsular Malaysia were familiar with the biogeography of *gutta-percha* trees because, before the *gutta-percha* boom, they had exploited them for their fatty, edible seeds. There was a minor trade in the oil from these seeds long before the market for the latex developed (Burkill 1966, 2:1661; Low [1848] 1968:46–49). Also of great antiquity in the region are the use of various forest rubbers for making handgrips for tools (figure 3.1), for caulking and sealing (for example, of canoes), and for glues, birdlimes, and blowpipe mouthpieces (Burkill 1966, 2:1652; Gianno 1986; Jessup and Vayda 1988: 16; Powell 1976). The recent surge in interest in marketing the wood of *Hevea* (Durst, Killmann, and Brown 2004) shows that this process—whereby different products from the same plant source wax in and out of market favor—continues to the present day.

The Historic System of Latex Gathering

In the nineteenth century, the gathering of the native rubbers deep in the jungles of Borneo, Sumatra, and the Malay Peninsula came under close scrutiny by the colonial authorities.

Figure 3.1. Kantu' using damar, a native resin, to fix a hilt to a brush-sword

Resource Use, Abuse, and Government Policy

An important variable in exploiting the native forest latexes was tap-ping the living tree versus felling it—and, in the former case, tapping with a technique and level of intensity that was sustainable or not. Some variation in techniques is accounted for by variation in botanical characteristics from one latex source to another, but much is not. For example, Bock ([1881] 1985: 152) described the tapping of *gutta-percha* trees in Borneo: "With two sharp strokes of a mandau a deep notch was cut in the bark, from which the juice slowly oozed, forming a milky-looking mucilage, which gradually hardened and became darker in colour as it ran down the tree. The native collectors of gutta-percha make a track through the forest, nicking the trees in two or three places as they go, and collect the hardened sap on their return a few days afterwards." Hornaday (1885: 433) described the felling of *gutta-percha* trees for the same purpose (see also Oxley 1847: 24): "The native found a gutta tree, about ten inches in diameter, and after cutting it down, he ringed it neatly all the way along the stem, at intervals of a yard or less. Under-neath each ring he put a calabash to catch the milk-white sap which slowly exuded." In fact, research decades later showed that felling versus tapping *gutta-percha* trees made some sense. Because these trees are not laticiferous, meaning that the cellular cavities containing the latex are not interconnected, they are simply less efficient to tap versus fell than a tree like *Hevea* (Foxworthy 1922: 162–63).[12]

Colonial observers nonetheless charged native rubber gatherers with exploiting this discretionary element—to tap versus fell—to the disadvantage of the resource, by purportedly favoring less-sustainable methods of exploitation for the sake of short-term gains (Brummeler 1883; Burbidge 1880: 74–76; te Wechel 1911; van Romburgh 1897). The Norwegian naturalist Bock ([1881] 1985: 204), commissioned by the Dutch colonial government to survey southeastern Borneo, writes, "The Dayaks have not yet graduated in the science of forest conservation. Instead of making incisions at regular intervals in the bark of a tree, and extracting a portion of the juice at different periods, by which its further growth would not be prevented, they usually adopt the radical expedient of cutting the whole tree down." Fyfe (1949: 26) came to a similar conclusion regarding exploitation of *gutta-percha* in the Malay Peninsula: "The tree has to be tapped at short intervals along the whole stem and even out on the branches, an operation of some difficulty requiring much effort by the tapper. As a result the gutta collector confined himself to the simplest method of obtaining the latex which is to fell the tree and bleed it at numerous points along the stem and main branches." It was feared that such methods would lead to the extermination of the resource. Burbidge (1880: 74) writes, regarding Borneo, "The rubber-yielding *Willughbeias* are gradually, but none the less surely, being exterminated by the collectors"; and Bock ([1881] 1985: 204) writes, "The consequence is that the material is becoming more and more difficult to procure, and will eventually become scarce, if not extinct, in the island." Such fears were the ostensible basis for government intervention, but the real motives were more political than ecological.

The boom in *jelutong* in the first decade of the twentieth century, for example, triggered progressively tighter control of this resource by colonial authorities (Drijber 1912; Lindblad 1988: 18–19; Potter 1988: 130–34). By 1908 the Dutch colonial government in parts of Kalimantan required a license to tap the trees; in 1910 the government awarded all tapping rights to foreign concessionaires[13]; and in 1913 the government imposed export levies on native tappers. The government justified these measures in terms of the need to avoid overexploitation of the trees and protect the smallholders against middlemen (Lindblad 1988: 19; Potter 1988: 131). But some observers at the time argued that the regulatory measures would not solve the problem and might even exacerbate it (CAPD 1982: 3540; te Wechel 1911); and others insisted that the real motivation for intervention was European profit at the expense of native rights. Van Vollenhoven ([1919] 1932) called it an egregious example of the colonial government's abuse of its rights to "wastelands" (Potter 1988: 134).[14]

Government criticism of felling versus tapping was ironic: the colonial governments that critiqued the overexploitation of forest rubbers were themselves responsible—through their stimulation of trade—for the increased pressure on rubber production, and this pressure favored unsustainable exploitation. *Gutta-percha* trees typically yield one to three pounds of latex at a time by tapping versus ten pounds by felling (Burkill 1966, 2:1664; see also Eaton 1952: 49). In the competitive environment of a colonial-era commodity boom, the motivation to tap a tree for a small yield and leave it standing, in the hope of enjoying more small tappings in another two years, paled against the risk that someone else would fell the tree in the interim for a larger onetime yield. This risk was heightened when native rights to forest-rubber trees were ignored during boom times, when, as the example of *jelutong* illustrates, colonial governments imposed progressively stricter and more-inequitable systems of regulation of the resources. This left the native tappers with increasingly little incentive for sustainable exploitation.

Resource Use, Mobility, and Security

The emergence of a robust European market for forest rubbers, and the exploitation for short-term profit that accompanied it, had important implications for historic patterns of population movement and settlement in Borneo. Intensive exploitation of latex-producing trees, especially if done in a nonsustainable manner with the consequent need to always seek out new stands, promoted a pioneering pattern of latex-related movement. Gathering expeditions that lasted months or even years and sometimes extended beyond Borneo to Sumatra and the Malay Peninsula became common (Burkill 1966, 2:1656; Gomes 1911: 234–35). A number of observers have suggested that gathering native rubbers and other forest products was the genesis of the renowned Iban custom of *bejalai* (expedition) (Lian 1988: 118; Padoch 1982: 25, 109).[15]

Expeditions to gather forest rubbers often led to subsequent migration (Richards 1981: 106). That is, if an expedition led to discovery of a location

that offered large stands of forest rubbers and also met the other requirements of settlement, the group would relocate there. As noted earlier, the
contemporary Kantu' say that their ancestors first explored their present
territory not in search of fresh swidden territory, as the popular image of
swidden cultivators would suggest, but in search of two sources of *caoutchouc*, one they called *jangkang* (*Palaquium* spp. [see Richards 1981: 123]) and
another known as *kubal* (*Willughbeia* spp. [see Howell and Bailey 1900: 81]).[16]
Padoch (1982: 25) gives a similar report of the first settlement of the Kemena
River above Bintulu in the Fourth Division of Sarawak: "These first permanent Iban residents [in the 1860s] had been preceded by Iban 'jungle produce' seekers, tappers, and collectors of damar and other resins, gutta percha, *jelutong*, and other products. These young men brought back reports of
great expanses of available, largely still virgin land to their Second Division
homes." Just as the pattern of movement necessitated by intensive exploitation of forest rubbers favors a pioneering pattern of swidden agriculture, so
does the latter favor—or, perhaps more correctly, permit—a pioneering and
intensive pattern of rubber exploitation.[17] As Psota (1992: 32) said of South
Sumatra, "It was hill rice cultivation that made it possible for the Rejang
to penetrate and settle in remote forest areas, which were at the same time
sources for forest products." A linkage between swiddening and gathering
patterns in Borneo also is suggested by the fact that the group most known
for pioneering swidden cultivation, the Iban, also was known for gathering forest products (Baring-Gould and Bampfylde 1909: 25, 375; Hose and
McDougall [1912] 1966, 1:150; Pringle 1970: 267). This interpretation is supported by the fact that the other groups known for collecting forest products,
the Penan and Punan, were not agriculturalists at all but full-time, mobile
hunter-gatherers (Hoffman 1988; Sellato 1994).

   The long-distance travel necessitated by rubber gathering was associated
with some physical risk, which is reflected in the attendant ritual. Lumholtz
(1920, 1:124–25), for example, described a remarkable 75-centimeter-high
rubber statue from southeast Borneo representing a rhinoceros with a man
on its back, which was offered to the spirits in return for a successful rubber-
gathering expedition. The selection of the rhinoceros (*Didermocerus suma-
trensis*) is apt, since it formerly inhabited the most remote and unfrequented
parts of Borneo (Medway 1977: 144–45)—the same sort of areas that the rubber collectors had to penetrate to find untapped trees. In the ceremony observed by Lumholtz (1920, 1:124–25), a feast was held in honor of the statue
and then the rhinoceros was "killed." This again is an apt symbol: as one of

the largest and potentially most-threatening animals in Borneo, the rhinoceros symbolized the hazards of travel in the uninhabited Bornean interior — although there were other hazards as well.

There was a historical association between gathering forest rubbers and head-hunting. This is reflected in the contemporary Iban/Kantu' language, in which *jangkang* means both *gutta-percha* and a bunch of trophy heads (Richards 1981: 123) — both of which are obtained on expeditions into the forest. Some observers have interpreted this association as evidence of violent conflict over scarce forest products (Lian 1988: 119; Vayda 1961: 354–55). Others have suggested that gathering rubber and other forest products was not per se the cause of warfare, but that it was the attendant travel and migration that led to conflict (for example, Baring-Gould and Bampfylde 1909: 376). Hose and McDougall ([1912] 1966, 1:150, 185) write, "In the course of such excursions [to gather forest products] they [the Iban] not infrequently penetrate into the regions inhabited by other tribes, and many troubles have had their origin in the truculent behaviour of such parties." It is suggestive that the subject of Hose and McDougall's outrage, the Iban, whose reputation for gathering rubber and other forest products has been mentioned, also were renowned for their involvement in head-hunting.[18] Pringle (1970: 21) writes, "Stories about head-hunting may have slandered other pagan groups . . . but the Iban lived up to the reputation" (see Vayda 1976: 48).[19]

In the case just cited by Hose and McDougall, the tribesmen who go on gathering expeditions are the aggressors as opposed to the victims. This may be because adult men go on such expeditions, while the young, the old, and the women remain behind. These age and gender differences favor the tribesmen on an expedition over the inhabitants of any community they chance across. This was not true, however, when the gathering was done by nontribesmen. Bock ([1881] 1985: 118) described gathering by coastal Malays: "When collecting gutta, the Malays take a two or three days' journey into the forest. For fear of being murdered by the Dayaks, they go in parties, from twenty to thirty, for mutual protection, and very often accompanied or joined by friendly Dayaks." This Malay pattern is very different from that described for the Iban and other Dayak. In addition to being much briefer and therefore involving much shorter distances, it is associated with a defensive as opposed to offensive military posture.

Resource Use, Ethnicity, and Sustainability

There were a variety of participants in and patterns of forest-product gathering, varying as the role of the rubbers and rubber collectors fluctuated in the broader political-economic context. The initial gatherers of forest rubber were the forest-dwelling hunter-gatherers and the forest-product specialists of the region (see Guerreiro 1988: 30–31; Hoffman 1988: 103–4; Sellato 1994): the Penan and Punan of Borneo and the aboriginal *orang asli* of the Malay Peninsula. In the peninsula, most of the mid-nineteenth-century collection of *gutta-percha* was carried out by one of these aboriginal groups, the Jakun (Burkill 1966, 2:1655). At that time, the tribal agriculturalists of Borneo, the Dayak, were said to be ignorant of the product. Low ([1848] 1968: 51) wrote, "Gutta percha has been found in Borneo, and . . . the natives . . . know at present nothing of the manner of collecting it, or of its uses." If true, this situation changed quickly as a result of the boom in the *gutta-percha* trade. A quarter century after Low's observations, Dayak tribesmen were even being employed by merchants in the Malay Peninsula for gathering *gutta-percha* (Burkill 1966, 2:1656; Dunn 1975: 109). The Peninsular Malays themselves were not, and did not become, major forest-product gatherers (Andaya and Andaya 1982: 10).

The Dayak offered something to the native rubber trade that was lacking in the Malay Peninsula: the potential for an intensive, pioneering system of extraction made possible by their political economy. The peninsula had no equivalent—neither in its small population of hunter-gatherers nor in its large, peasantized, sedentary, wet-rice-cultivating Malay population—to the populous, often aggressive, semimobile, swidden-based tribal peoples of Borneo. This suggestion is supported by the fact that within Borneo, colonial British authorities gave privileged status in collecting to the most mobile and aggressive of all of the Dayak groups, the Iban (Pringle 1970: 267), thus valuing in this context their mobility and aggressiveness, which they otherwise condemned. In the later stages of market booms, however, even the Dayak could not exploit the forest rubbers as intensively as the colonial markets demanded. At these times more specialized coastal Malayic (see chapter 2, note 4) peoples, or Dayak who became full-time specialists, did most of the gathering, not the common tribesmen (Potter 1988: 131–33; see also Hudson 1967: 66). The tribesmen were not willing to wholly relinquish their swidden cultivation of food crops to concentrate on rubber gathering. Some Dayak tribesmen managed to participate in the forest-product trade while main-

Table 3.1. Different Modes of Forest-Product Gathering

COLLECTOR	INTENSITY	MARKET CONDITION	IMPACT ON RESOURCE
Tribal hunter-gatherer	Low	Normal	Low
Tribal swidden agriculturalist	Medium	Normal/boom	Medium
Malay peasant/specialist	High	Boom	High
Corporate interests	High	Boom	High

taining their involvement in swidden agriculture, by developing partnerships with the Penan and Punan hunter-gatherers.

Sustainability of forest-rubber exploitation varied with these different modes of production (table 3.1). It was probably most sustainable when carried out by any of the native hunter-gatherers (see Dunn 1975: 109) as just one among many activities during normal market times. It might have become less sustainable with the participation of tribal swidden agriculturalists. And it clearly became unsustainable with the participation of full-time specialists, who employed felling or slaughter-tapping—referring to the practice of tapping the trees so intensively as to jeopardize their health—during boom times.[20] As Potter (1997: 289) writes: "Differences could sometimes be distinguished [tapping versus felling] between the behaviour of indigenous groups collecting from their own forests, and that of others, either working with advances from outside employers or ranging independently, seeking sources of dry season income." Potter (1997: 290) adds that this is why the colonial government in Pahang in the Malay Peninsula prohibited gathering of *gutta-percha* by "foreign Malays and Dayaks," but not by local Malays and Sakais.

The Transition from Gathering Indigenous Rubber to Cultivating Exotic Rubber

The development of this system of gathering native rubbers in nineteenth-century Borneo set the stage for the adoption of *Hevea*.

"Domestication" of the Native Rubbers

There are some obvious parallels between the historic system of gathering forest rubbers and the modern system of cultivating *Hevea*.[21] As Dunn (1975: 86) writes, referring to the Malay Peninsula (see also Rambo 1982: 282): "For centuries the ancestors of the modern Temuan presumably collected gums, oils, and resins from forest trees, using for at least some of these resources bark slicing techniques not unlike those employed in modern rubber tapping. *Hevea* rubber, requiring similar techniques and simple technology, has therefore simply replaced traditional gum and resin collecting in the Temuan economy."

The linkage between the cultivation of *Hevea* and the earlier gathering of wild rubbers is in effect one of "domestication": a trade based on gathering wild rubber became a trade based on cultivating rubber, albeit not of the same species. Some such process of domestication in fact took place with a number of forest products. One example is the damar-yielding *Shorea javanica*, which was domesticated late in the nineteenth century and is today planted and managed in sophisticated agro-forests in South Sumatra (de Foresta and Michon 1994; Michon et al. 2000; Torquebiau 1984). Another example is the tallow-yielding illipe-nut tree (*Shorea* spp.), which has been planted in some parts of Borneo for at least 150 years (Blicher-Mathiesen 1994; Sather 1990: 27–28; Padoch 1982: 111–12). A third example is rattan, which grows naturally in the forests of Borneo and has been gathered and traded for centuries. During the second half of the nineteenth century and first half of the twentieth century, rattan began to be planted in parts of Kalimantan (Godoy and Feaw 1989; Jessup and Peluso 1985: 514n6; Tsing 1984: 247). Today it is widely cultivated in East and South Kalimantan in swidden fallows (Fried 2000; Lindblad 1988: 59–60; Peluso 1983b; Weinstock 1983). Pelzer suggests that native recognition of the similarities between Para rubber and the native rubbers was responsible for the dissemination of rubber. He writes (1978b: 282), "The idea [of planting rubber] was brought into these districts [namely, West Borneo and South Sumatra] by Indonesians who had spent some time in Malaya, and also by Chinese traders who traditionally purchased forest products, such as gutta-percha, jelutong, rattan, and damar, and could see the technical possibility of fitting rubber into the agricultural systems of the swidden cultivators." Wolf and Wolf (1936: 152) similarly observe, "Save for its [indigenous rubber's] presence originally in India and Burma and Malaya and Sumatra, it is unlikely that [Para rubber] planting attention would have been turned to this area."

Determinants: Technological, Economic, Ecological, Tenurial

The historic exploitation of indigenous latex-producing trees and vines resembled the subsequently adopted system of Para rubber cultivation in some respects and differed from it in others. The similarities favored this adoption but it is the differences, counterintuitively, that made it happen.[22]

Similarities and Differences

Most obviously, the technology used to obtain the latex of most *jelutong* and some *gutta-percha* was much like that used to exploit Para rubber: cutting or "tapping" the bark, often by V-shaped incisions (Burkill 1962, 1:892).[23] The tool used for tapping the indigenous latex trees was and has continued to be the *parang* (brush-sword). This system of exploitation actually resembled the traditional system for exploiting *Hevea* rubber in its Amazon homeland, where a hatchet was used to tap the latex. In fact, the brush-sword was also used in early exploitation of *Hevea* rubber in Southeast Asia. Only after many years of government-supported experimentation, based on the belief that the use of a sword was harmful to the trees, was the modern "herringbone"-style of cut (see chapter 6, figure 6.3), using a modified farrier's knife, developed (see chapter 4).

Another similarity in the exploitation of both the native and the introduced rubbers involves their lack of conflict with the labor calendar of swidden cultivation and their ability to absorb some of the swiddens' risks. The labor requirements of both native and exotic rubbers are relatively low (Cramb 1988: 112); and there are few constraints in either case on the timing of labor inputs, which minimizes conflicts with swidden activities. As Potter (1997) notes of *gutta-percha*, it was a dry season product, so it did not clash too seriously with normal agricultural pursuits. Even more important, both the native rubbers and *Hevea* can be exploited at short notice in response to fluctuations in either market prices or subsistence crop harvests, with minimal capital investment or risk taking. Well into the twentieth century the Iban of Sarawak still gathered forest rubbers to make up for rice crop failures in the swiddens (Freeman [1955] 1970: 264), which have always been one of the premiere subsistence challenges for Dayak groups.[24] All of these similarities facilitated the adoption of *Hevea*, but this would not have occurred with the speed and magnitude it did if there were not also significant differences.

The most obvious difference between the native and the introduced rubber lies in their respective productive capacities. First, *Hevea* matures and yields latex much sooner than most of the indigenous sources of latex: whereas even indifferently tended *Hevea* will yield in ten years, the sources of *jelutong* (for example) take between thirty and thirty-five years (for *Dyera lowii*) and sixty years (for *Dyera costulata*) to yield (Coppen 1995; Williams 1963: 124). Second, there is an unusually favorable concentration of marketable latex in the exudate from *Hevea:* the balance between latex and resins is eighty/twenty in *Hevea,* but it is the reverse, just twenty/eighty, in the *Dyera* spp. sources of *jelutong* (Burkill 1966, 1:891; Williams 1963: 123). Assuming that production costs are approximately equal, the economic return of *Hevea* would be four times as great as with *jelutong* (Burkill 1966, 1:896). Third, the botanical characteristics of *Hevea* permit its exudate to be taken with an unusually high frequency: *Hevea* actually benefits from being tapped every two days, which yields maximum latex flows (Barlow 1978: 146). Whereas some indigenous latex sources could be exploited with this degree of intensity, as in the case of *Dyera,* which Williams (1963: 116) maintains can be tapped every two to three days for four to five months or more each year,[25] many could not. For example, the rule of thumb for tapping wild *gutta-percha* trees was just once every two years (Foxworthy 1922: 163; Fyfe 1949: 27). Fourth and finally, relative returns to labor with *Hevea* are further heightened by the fact that the tree can be planted by smallholders to densities of at least 500 producing trees per hectare, which compares with much lower densities— and thus much greater costs in travel time during tapping—for the native rubber trees: thus, naturally occurring *Dyera costulata* and *Dyera lowii* reach maximum densities of, respectively, just 0.2 per hectare and 4.9 per hectare (Williams 1963: 114, 115). In a direct comparison in West Kalimantan, Lawrence, Leighton, and Peart (1995: 81, 82, 86) recorded densities of 1,391 *Hevea* trees per hectare in smallholder gardens versus just 181 producing native rubber trees (of all types) per hectare (and for *gutta-percha* in particular, just 3 producing trees per hectare) in the natural forest.[26]

Other differences between *Hevea* and the native forest latexes involve complementarity with swidden cultivation, in particular the central act of the swidden cycle—clearing the forest. Whereas the native rubbers are at risk whenever the natural forest is cleared, *Hevea* seedlings are planted in newly cleared swiddens. As the habitat of the native rubbers is destroyed, therefore, the "habitat" of *Hevea* is created. This habitat is not natural forest, but it does mimic a forest succession (Geertz [1963] 1971: 113; Gouyon, de Foresta, and Levang 1993). The creation of this habitat also was promoted by wider changes in patterns of agriculture and settlement over the past century. Swidden agriculture and settlement patterns in Borneo have both become more sedentary, as a result of demographic and political constraints, which favor *Hevea*. Whereas the supply of forest rubber close to a given settlement is potentially exhaustible, especially if the trees are felled or slaughter-tapped, the productivity of a *Hevea* grove is potentially open-ended, since successive generations of trees will naturally grow on their own from fallen seeds. The sustainability of *Hevea* cultivation permits sedentary settlement, therefore, the unsustainability of forest-rubber exploitation does not;[27] and although sedentariness is inimical to the continued exploitation of natural forest rubbers, it is essential to the exploitation of *Hevea*. Thus, patterns of settlement both affect and are affected by patterns of resource exploitation: possession of *Hevea* gardens both favors and is favored by a more sedentary pattern of settlement.[28]

This past century has seen not only the increasing sedentarization but also the intensification of swidden cultivation, which again favors *Hevea* over the forest rubbers. Swidden cultivation in Borneo has become increasingly concentrated in secondary forest and swampland, which—with the added requirement of weeding and, in swampland, transplanting—requires higher and more frequent labor inputs (Dove 1985c: 377–81; see also Padoch 1982). This labor schedule is better complemented by the timing of economic inputs and returns in the exploitation of *Hevea* than the native forest rubbers. This is because gathering in the forest necessitated the absence of the tribesmen from the village for weeks and months at a time, whereas *Hevea* can be tapped while the tribesmen remain in the village and continue to work in the swiddens.

Tenurial Differences and Cultivation

A final, critical difference between *Hevea* and the native rubbers involves tenure. Under traditional Kantu' *adat* law, for example, the first person to tap a forest rubber tree had the exclusive right to further tapping (see Lian 1988: 118, on the Kenyah). This right lapsed if the person moved out of the area or ceased tapping long enough for the tapping scars to heal. This tenurial principle was not suited to boom markets and state intervention, however, as the progressive loss of local rights during the boom in *jelutong* showed. Even in recent years, individually claimed forest-rubber trees have been cut down with impunity by outsiders, as is evident from this 1989 news-paper report of the destruction of *jelutong* and other trees (*Down to Earth* 1990c: 10): "A logging company identified only as PT SBK with a concession in Kotawaringin Timur district, Central Kalimantan is suspected of cut-ting down thousands of tengkawang [*Shorea* spp.], pantung [local term for *jelutong, Dyera* spp.] and maja [unidentified] trees which had provided local people with a source of income." The nativeness and naturalness of such trees is inimical to outside recognition of proprietary claims, which gener-ally was and is reserved for *planted* trees. If the tree is an exotic, so much the better, since it could not be anything but planted.

   The exotic *Hevea* is thus the ideal vehicle for establishing proprietary rights, not only to the tree planted but to the land on which it is planted. As Gouyon, de Foresta, and Levang (1993: 192–93) write of southeast Sumatra (see also Joshi et al. 2003: 137), "Most farmers in the area lack official land titles; yet rubber contributes to family wealth by bearing witness to land oc-cupancy. An area covered with rubber is usually regarded by local land right as belonging to the planter, and as such can be inherited or sold. Planted land can also be claimed as an individual asset in case of conflict over land property with the government or estate companies." Indeed, the tenurial ad-vantages of *Hevea* are such that for many years local peoples have commonly planted it on a prophylactic basis when government land-clearing programs are in the offing (Angelsen 1995: 1724–25).[29] As Gouyon, de Foresta, and Levang (1993: 192–93) continue, "In some areas, smallholders are planting rubber as fast as they can to occupy an uncultivated area before it is seized by such external bodies." This in turn has led to a predictable counterresponse from government and parastatal managers, as is evident in this report from a Dayak NGO on the encroachment of timber concessions on Dayak lands in Kalimantan (IDRD 1994: 24, 26):

> Di Kecamatan Sungai Laur: Bahkan perusahaan mematok dan membuat plank yang mergerikan seperti; "Ini Tanah Negara," "Jangan Berladang di Areal HTI," "Boleh Berladang Tapi Tidak Boleh Ditanam Karet. (In Sub-district Sungai Luar: The concession even set up frightening boundary poles and signs reading: "This is State Land," "Do not make swiddens in the territory of the timber concession," "It is permitted to make swiddens but it is not permitted to plant rubber.")

Di Kecamatan Sandai: LTW [HTI] mematok dan memasang plank yang isinya melecehkan seperti; "Hutan Milik Negara," "Dilarang Berladang di Areal HTI," "Boleh Berladang Tapi Jangan Ditanam Karet" dan lain-lain. (In Sub-district Sandai: The timber concession set up boundary poles and an insulting sign reading "State Forest," "It is forbidden to make swiddens in the territory of the timber concession," "It is permitted to make swiddens but do not plant rubber," and so on.)

The Dayak *never* plant native rubbers in this way to try to strengthen land claims. This is not a function of botanical constraints: a colonial observer noted that the Bornean source of *caoutchouc* (*Willughbeia* spp.) "may be easily and rapidly increased by vegetative as well as seminal modes of propagation" (Burbidge 1880: 74); and there are records of estate plantings of both *gutta-percha* (Foxworthy 1922; Fyfe 1949: 26) and *jelutong* (van Wijk 1941, cited in CAPD 1982: 1344). Indeed, extensive studies and cultivation experiments were carried out with all of the major indigenous sources of latex. Cramer (1956: 226) writes that the trees experimented with in colonial Indonesia included *Castilloa, Ficus, Funtumia, Manihot* spp., and even lianas like *Willughbeia firma* Bl. Some success was had with *Ficus,* and the colonial Dutch agriculture and forest departments remained strong advocates of *Ficus* up until the second decade of the twentieth century, notably in Java.[30] Even greater success was had with the *Palaquium* sources of *gutta-percha:* plantations of *Palaquium* were established in Java as early as the 1890s, and the last one was still in operation in the 1970s (Coppen 1995: 128). Tenurial implications were irrelevant to the colonial government experiments with domesticating the native rubbers, but not so for native actors like the Dayak.

As a result, and by comparison, Dayak efforts to cultivate their native rubbers were minimal. The Dayak did some planting; the Kantu', for example, say that their ancestors planted some of the native rubber trees, in particular *Palaquium* spp., the major source of *gutta-percha.*[31] But these minor efforts contrast markedly with the enormous effort they eventually devoted to *Hevea.* Although there are multiple reasons for this, including differences in productivity, one of the most important involves the implications for tenure in the eyes of the state. In Borneo, an exotic *Hevea* tree is undeniable evidence of planting and thus tenure, but the same cannot be said of any of the native rubbers: any claim that one was planted can be disputed with the claim that it was naturally grown. Thus, the aforementioned Dayak NGO reported that the manager of a timber concession denied local

Dayak claims for compensation for economic trees he had felled with this explanation (IDRD 1994: 26–27): "Tengkawang, durian, damar, karet, rambutan dan buah-buahan lain tidak ada ganti-ruginya karena tanaman tersebut bukan ditanam kalian melainkan dibawa oleh kotoran kera dan babi." (There is no compensation for illipe nut, durian, damar, rubber, rambutan, and other fruit trees because they were not planted by you, rather they were propagated in the feces of monkeys and pigs.) Fried (2000: 228, 233n19) reports the analogous thesis, ubiquitous among foresters working on timber concessions in East Kalimantan, that all rattan found in their area—which is famous for the historic Bentian system for rattan domestication and cultivation—derives from *tahi burung* (bird feces). This hostility toward the assertion of rights to native trees is one of the key reasons why these tribesmen domesticated not the native forest rubbers but an exotic rubber, *Hevea*, instead.

Consequences: Ritual, Political

The shift from forest rubbers to *Hevea* represented the replacement not just of one tree with another, but of one mode of production with another. Some of the wide-ranging consequences are reflected in the changes in ritual that occurred as a result. For example, whereas Dayak bird augury traditionally was performed both when gathering native rubbers and working *Hevea*, there was a difference: as the earlier-described "rubber rhinoceros" indicated, nineteenth-century ritual in forest-rubber production focused on the hazards of traveling to gather the rubber (Gomes 1911: 234–35); but twentieth-century ritual in *Hevea* production has focused on the hazards of trading the product (Sandin 1980: 107, 112, 113, 115, 122).[32] I observed the Kantu', for example, make spirit-offerings at the start of trading voyages downriver to Pontianak to sell their sheets of rubber (figure 3.2). This reflects the fact that market prices for rubber are volatile and represent the greatest source of uncertainty in rubber cultivation. The focus in the forest-rubber ritual is on the physical dangers and risks of the tribal world, whereas the focus in the *Hevea* ritual is on the economic dangers of the outside world. This shift from "physical" to "fiscal" hazards (see the reference to "the price of rubber" in the poem in the next paragraph) reflects the consequences of a transition from a mode of production based on collection to one based on cultivation.

Since its introduction, *Hevea* has been associated with the cessation of

Figure 3.2. Kantu' making ritual offerings at the start of a rubber-selling trip downriver

tribal warfare. A civil servant in Sarawak wrote that the 1911–1912 rubber boom "banished all thoughts of tribal warfare and head-hunting" (Ward 1966: 145), a change summed up by a colonial poet as follows (*Sarawak Gazette* 1925):[33]

> The tellers' fathers, strong and deep in lung,
> Gave forth great battle cries and fierce
> Mutterings and murmurings to the great Sun God.
> Now all is changed great peace and quiet
> The sharp-edged sword becomes the tapper's knife.
> The carved shield that now becomes a swing
> Wherein is wrapped in clothes the babe whose future lies
> In the price of rubber tapped in a ring.[34]

The shift from mobile gathering of forest rubbers to sedentary tapping of *Hevea* entailed a shift from a more-aggressive, military posture to a more-vulnerable, defensive one. The permanence of rubber gardens impedes the tactical mobility of the tribe, and the solitariness of the rubber tapper makes

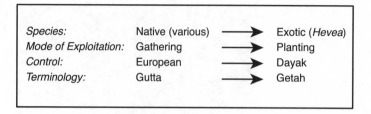

Species:	Native (various)	⟶	Exotic (*Hevea*)
Mode of Exploitation:	Gathering	⟶	Planting
Control:	European	⟶	Dayak
Terminology:	Gutta	⟶	Getah

Figure 3.3. The transition from native forest rubbers to *Hevea*

defense near-impossible. Moreover, although men did most of the historic gathering of forest rubbers, women today do most of the tapping of *Hevea*. Down to the present day, rubber tapping is *the* activity that suffers most (in other words, that is abandoned) when rumors of marauding *penyamun* (headhunters) sweep through the interior of Borneo. Contemporary, solitary tappers of *Hevea* are vulnerable to roving bandits and rebels and even the rumor of them, just as local communities were formerly vulnerable to roving gatherers of forest rubber. This reflects a transition from a political-economic formation in which tribal warfare was the major source of conflict to one in which conflict comes from other sources, including the state itself (Tsing 1993).

These developments are reflected in language. The Kantu' and other Bornean tribesmen use the term *getah* for *Hevea*, not the Malay/Indonesian/Javanese term *karet* (Horne 1974: 259; Richards 1981: 105; Wilkinson 1959, 1:363). *Getah* is the Malay/Indonesian term for "tree sap" (Wilkinson 1959, 1:363–64). This was the source of the Anglo/Dutch trade term *gutta-percha* (*percha* [strip] refers to the sheets of processed latex [Wilkinson 1959, 2:885]).[35] The smallholders' adoption of the colonial cognate term reflects the changing roles both between native rubbers and *Hevea* and between European planters and native smallholders (figure 3.3). It signifies that what the native rubbers were for the Europeans, *Hevea* became for the tribesmen. A fundamental transformation of the political economy of rubber production in Southeast Asia took place, based on critical differences between the native rubbers and *Hevea*. Although tribal collectors could not control exploitation of native forest rubbers, tribal tappers could control exploitation of *Hevea*. The term that colonial planters used to disparage smallholder *Hevea* production, and which is still used by the contemporary estate sector, *karet hutan* (jungle rubber) (Gouyon, de Foresta, and Levang 1993: 182; Lindblad 1988: 66), is also revealing from this perspective. It is doubly

ironic: it unwittingly points to the historic basis for the smallholders' successful adoption of *Hevea* (namely, the gathering of native forest rubbers);
and it disparagingly invokes the commodity that the colonial establishment
successfully controlled (forest rubber), in reference to the commodity that it
failed to control (*Hevea*).[36]

Exception to Conventional Wisdom

The adoption of *Hevea* in Borneo signified not the adoption of trade
but rather the adaptation of a long-standing trade—in forest products—to
a changing political-economic context. This adaptation was driven by a contest between a state and its commercial elite on the one hand, and on the
other hand tribesmen living at the state's periphery. The benefits conferred
upon the Dayak by the adaptation were in part conceptual, therefore, involving the remodeling of the resource landscape in a manner more favorable to their own rights, categories, and interests. Adoption of *Hevea* shifted
the Dayak's activities along the perceived nature–culture continuum, further
from nature (where wild rubbers were gathered) and closer to culture (where
domesticated rubbers are cultivated) which gave tribal communities greater
leverage vis-à-vis the wider society.

Black (1985: 291) characterizes colonial Dutch development of the
forest-product trade in Borneo as follows: "On the one hand, the Dutch
were releasing them [the interior Dayak tribesmen] from some of their old
insecurities, but, on the other, the Dutch were opening up their country to
new traders in jungle produce, and pressing them to become involved with
them. The enticement of working regularly for the new trader organizations,
and their seductively reliable credit, was not easy to resist. A colonial role was
being worked out even for them." My analysis of Dayak involvement with
first forest-rubber gathering and then cultivation of *Hevea* shows the inade-
quacy of such a vision of the tribesmen as the recipients of outside interventions, with no agency of their own. The outcome of the historic competition
over the native rubbers and *Hevea* shows that the intensification of relations
between local communities and the global economic system is complex,
takes many possible shapes, and has many possible outcomes. The latter half
of the nineteenth and first half of the twentieth centuries saw not just more
involvement in the world economy by the tribal communities in Borneo,
but involvement of a different order. In response to the broader political-
economic structures exerting increasing control over commodity produc-

tion, the tribesmen developed new production systems of their own, like *Hevea* cultivation, which maximized the strengths of the local system—for example, a subsistence agricultural base—and exploited some of the weaknesses of the global system—for example, greater recognition of proprietary rights to planted trees. There was much more to this process, therefore, than the "working out of a colonial role" for the native producers.

Kantu' adapt their system to include production beneficial to their dual economy — make CONSCIOUS decisions to cultivate Hevea and indigenous species for their own benefit, including ability to remain competitive in a market in which they'd always been engaged

. How does this change previous ideas about "forced" participation, globalization?

- Does this assertion of agency +/or indigenous community challenge, enhance previous arguments against essentialization? "primitive"/pure indigenous systems?

- why is this the first time we are hearing about this body of literature that challenges colonialism myths/understandings about levels of coercive colonial structures?

PART III

Coping with the Contradictions of Capitalism in the Early Twentieth Century

My analysis of Bornean commodity production moves in this section of the book into the late nineteenth and early twentieth centuries, focusing on two critically important moments: first, the transfer of rubber seeds from the Amazon to Southeast Asia in 1876, and second, the impact of the worldwide Depression in the 1930s. These two periods encompass the initial challenge to develop a distinct rubber industry in Southeast Asia and then, in a remarkably short space of time, to deal with problems of overproduction and falling prices. These challenges raised pivotal questions at the time concerning technology: How much of the South American production technology should be transferred to Southeast Asia? And how much technology should the estates and smallholders in Southeast Asia share with one another? There was a sorting out of places within the rubber industry during these years. What would be the role of South America versus Southeast Asia?—That question was answered remarkably quickly in the favor of the latter. What would be the role of the estates versus smallholders?—That question was answered by the construction of an opposition between the two sectors. And what, in the case of smallholders, would be the role of market versus subsistence activities?—That challenge was answered by the establishment of a dual household economy based on a balance between the two types of activities.

Chapter 4 deals with the construction of rubber knowledge in Southeast Asia, and it compares not only smallholders and estates in Southeast Asia but also the South American and Southeast Asian industries. The process of constructing knowledge about how to cultivate rubber in Southeast Asia commenced with the sundering of the rubber plant not only from its original biological environment in South America, which contained the troublesome—but not determinant—leaf blight, but also from its social environment there, which was based on inefficient exploitation of wild trees and fearful exploitation of the tappers. The fact that this system of exploitation was not transferred to Southeast Asia along with *Hevea* itself shows that, contra staple theory (see chapter 1), it was possible to separate the botanical resource from its associated mode of production, thereby freeing Southeast Asian smallholders and estates alike to experiment and innovate with production technology, tenurial regimes, and other matters. As a result, the histories of rubber production in Southeast Asia and South America are very different, as are the histories of smallholders versus estates within Southeast Asia. In the latter case, whereas the Southeast Asian smallholder and estate systems of production are popularly represented as the distinct products of, respectively, a native and primitive developmental process on the one hand and on the other hand a purposeful and rational scientific process, this is not accurate. The smallholder system was not indigenous, the estate system was not strictly scientific, and the two were not entirely separate. The smallholders did a great deal of innovation in rubber production, some of which was technological but much of which involved the social, economic, and cultural dimensions of production. They also borrowed from and otherwise copied certain aspects of the estates, so that their final product was clearly a hybrid production system. The estates similarly copied smallholder practices, but because the identity of the estate sector was based on complete separation from and superiority to the smallholder sector, this debt could not be acknowledged. For the estate establishment, all rubber history is politicized. They replace a history full of accident and contingency with a heroic and teleological unfolding of the industry's development. This partisan vision can be seen in the historic roles assigned to Ridley and Wickham, respectively deemed the father of the modern system of tapping and the agent of the Promethean "theft" of rubber from the Amazon. Alternate histories could have portrayed the same men as, respectively, a madman and a lucky braggart.

Chapter 5 is a study of two remarkable and interconnected events that took place in the 1930s in Borneo: one was the public retelling of a dream that spread among the tribal societies of the interior, warning them that the introduced *Hevea* rubber tree was hostile to the spirit of their swidden rice;

and the other was the International Rubber Regulation Agreement (IRRA), which attempted to protect the market share of the estates by restricting smallholder production through export duties and other measures. The tribal dream was the product of the threatened loss of importance of the subsistence-food-crop sector as a result of the increasing attraction of rubber cultivation. The IRRA was a product of the same development; it represented a response to the challenge posed by smallholders to the estates' dominant position in the rubber industry. This response was complicated, however, by the fact that the challenge stemmed from the greater efficiency of smallholder production, something that was completely inconsistent with colonial estate ideology and thus had to be obfuscated. This chapter attempts to retrieve the indigenous critique of market production represented by the dream and at the same time problematize the exogenous critique of smallholder production represented by the IRRA. A comparative analysis of these two related phenomena makes the tribal dream look less fantastic and the international regulation look less rational than they otherwise appear. The plantation sector, especially under the market pressures of the Depression, was completely befuddled by the more-efficient production of the smallholders. The international estate community constructed what was essentially a cultural theory of native versus European mentality to invent wholly imaginary problems with smallholder production. At the same time that the tribesmen were astutely perceiving and articulating a challenge to smallholder production through the medium of the rubber dream, the estates were spinning fantastic myths about smallholders to justify the IRRA. The teleological argument of world-system theory and much developmentalist thinking—that market penetration will come at the expense of subsistence economies—is not borne out in this case.

CHAPTER 4

The Construction of Rubber Knowledge in Southeast Asia

> There is really nothing experimental about "fine Pará." It is, and was (probably generations before the advent of the Spaniard into North America), made more durable—of more climate resisting quality—than any factory-made, by certain of the Indian forest tribes (such as the Guyangomo and the Piaroa).
> —*Henry A. Wickham, 1908*

Introduction

The transplanting of *Hevea* from South America to Southeast Asia was a lengthy and contentious process full of surprises. Of most importance, what was transplanted was a plant and not a turnkey system of knowledge and production. Much of the production system in Southeast Asia was created anew, with little reference to South America, and the process by which this came about tells us much about smallholders, estates, and the real and imagined differences between them.

Ellen and Harris (2000: 7) note that the "epistemic origins" of much knowledge, whether folk or scientific, are hidden, and this anonymity has contributed to the emergence of a perceived divide between scientific practice on the one hand and on the other hand indigenous knowledge. When the origins of knowledge can be revealed, the validity of this divide—as between smallholders and estates—becomes questionable. Whereas smallholder rubber cultivation in Southeast Asia is represented by the plantation establishment as a primitive native invention and poor imitation of estate agriculture, in reality it is based on an exotic plant, which is exploited using some of the results of experimentation in colonial botanical gardens along with multiple, original and highly effective smallholder innovations. Similarly, the estate system of cultivation, which has been self-represented as the product of a self-contained, strictly controlled, linear progression of colonial plantation science, is more diverse and chaotic in origin than this suggests. The estate

[handwritten marginalia: Can origins of knowledge even be discovered?]

sector incorporates many more conflicts and mistakes, much more clinging to falsehoods, and much more copying from smallholders than admitted. Such histories are not atypical for what appear at first glance to be localized, self-contained systems of resource use (for example, Frossard 1998; Gupta 1998; Scott 1998: 331). As Agrawal (1995: 422) writes, "In the face of evidence that suggests contact, variation, transformation, exchange, communication, and learning over the last several centuries, it is difficult to adhere to a view of indigenous and western forms of knowledge being untouched by each other."

The Historical Construction of Rubber Knowledge: Smallholders and Estates

The cultivation of *Hevea* by estates and smallholders alike commenced with the sourcing of its seeds in the Amazon in the late nineteenth century.

Southeast Asian Colonial Estates

In the 1870s, a number of attempts were made to transplant rubber out of the Amazon Basin, the most successful of which was made in 1876 by an Englishman named Henry A. Wickham. He collected seventy thousand *Hevea* seeds and brought them to the Royal Botanic Gardens in Kew, England; where twenty-seven hundred were successfully germinated, twenty-five hundred of which were then shipped to England's colonies in Asia and became in large part the foundation of the region's rubber industry.

Wickham became famous—in some quarters infamous—for this one deed. Less well known is the fact that he spent much of the rest of his life trying to ensure that what was transferred to Asia was not just the genetic resource, *Hevea*, but also the Amazonian system of knowledge for exploiting this resource, about which Wickham claimed to be an expert and wrote a 1908 book entitled *On the Plantation, Cultivation, and Curing of Pará Indian Rubber.* Wickham lists a number of points in his book that he deems critical to the success of *Hevea* in Asia. First, he points out that *Hevea* is a forest tree and thus it should be cultivated "on lines of forestry" in a forest-type environment, not, for example, in a garden (Wickham 1908: 3–4, 33). He was critical, however, of attempts to simply plant *Hevea* as a "self-elimination forest product" in standing natural forests (ibid.: 57–58, 63), as the Netherlands Indies Forest Service did with both *Hevea* and *Ficus* up until 1912 (Cramer 1956: 267).[1] Wickham objected to this practice on the grounds that

Hevea took at least three times as long to mature under forest shade as out in the open; so he recommended managing *Hevea* in plantations instead, which is more or less how all *Hevea* came to be managed. His specifications for the plantations included wide spacing, which came to prevail on estates but not smallholdings, and also a no-till, no-burn policy, which was partially followed in different ways by both estates and smallholders (Wickham 1908: 12–23, 65, passim). Wickham was not opposed to allowing some natural undergrowth on plantations, a practice that was completely rejected by the Southeast Asian estates but not smallholders: "Lateral shade to extent required (at first) for formation of a straight trunk is readily got by allowing intermediate *second growth* to come up betwixt the Hevea" (ibid.: 64). Wickham (56–57, 61) claimed that *Hevea* plantations should not be established on swampy lands, an admonition that was widely ignored during the early years of the industry in Southeast Asia and then subsequently embraced when it was found that Wickham was right. He (ibid.: 29, 38–39) also recommended that the latex product be preserved by an "antiseptic smoke cure," advice that was eventually followed by most estates but only by some smallholders (for example, I have observed smokehouses among Banjarese in South Kalimantan [figures 4.1, 4.2] but none among the Kantu' of West Kalimantan). Wickham's chief failure involved his advice for tapping *Hevea:* he insisted that *Hevea* should only be tapped by means of a chisel and mallet, following the native Amazonian system (ibid.: 24–28). But in Southeast Asia this method was thought to be harmful to the trees (Barlow 1978: 21–22; Purseglove 1968: 161–64); and so after many years of experimentation, Henry Nicholas Ridley, then director of Singapore Botanic Gardens, developed the clearly superior V-shaped or "herringbone"-style of cut (see figure 6.3), using a modified farrier's knife and based on the daily reopening of the same cut,[2] which is still in use today (Purseglove 1956, 1957). Although Wickham (1908: 37–38) insisted that this "excision instead of incision," as he put it, would lead to root failure and possible pest infestation, Ridley's system prevailed on its merits and was universally adopted, eventually causing his fame in rubber circles to surpass that of Wickham's (Purseglove 1957).[3]

In large measure, therefore, rubber was transferred from the Amazon to Southeast Asia without the Amazonian system for exploiting it. This was partly due to a *failure* of colonial governance and science. As Wolf and Wolf (1936: 166) write, "Had the British Government's botanists at the Eastern gardens and experimental stations and their planter constituents been well versed in Amazon lore, had Wickham's report to the Government of India

Figure 4.1. Banjarese smoke-house for curing rubber

been broadcast as a Bible instead of bureaucratically being filed away to gather dust, things would have started off on a Brazilian basis." But since none of this took place, the colonial states of Southeast Asia did a great deal of reinvention. As Wolf and Wolf (ibid.) continue: "Needed was the very plantation system that came into being in the East, and it came into being because men, knowing nothing whatever about the Hevea, blundered and experimented and tested through failure after failure until they hit on the methods of planting, of tapping, of coagulating, that gave the sort of results we know today."

Southeast Asian Smallholders

The seedlings sent out from Kew Gardens to Singapore, as elsewhere, were planted, and when they matured and in turn yielded seed and seedlings, these were widely distributed. The first seedlings from the Singapore trees arrived in Sarawak in 1882 (Eaton 1952: 53; Tremeer 1964: 52).

Figure 4.2. Cured and uncured Banjarese rubber slabs

By 1908, the Sarawak government was distributing rubber seedlings to the public (Cramb 1988: 111; Tremeer 1964: 52). On the Dutch side of the border, rubber was introduced to West Kalimantan at about the same time, in 1909 (Uljee 1925: 74). Rubber was first planted in this province by coastal Chinese and Malay farmers (Ward and Ward 1974: 36; Robequain [1946] 1955: 353). Rubber was introduced to Southeast Kalimantan in 1906 (Luytjes 1925, cited in Brookfield et al. 1990: 497). Smallholders started planting rubber almost as soon as it entered their territories. This adoptions was remarkable because, as Penot (2007: 580) writes, "[They] were neither forced to adopt rubber, nor were they under pressure to intensify their land use," and they were not simply following the estates' lead, either.

Contrary to widespread belief (for example, Cramer 1956: 292; Keong 1976: 182), the smallholders of Borneo and elsewhere in the region did not simply copy what was being done on the estates. Most obviously, smallholder cultivation commenced too early to have been greatly influenced by the estates. As Pelzer (1978b: 282–83) writes, "It is frequently claimed that the swidden cultivator and smallholder simply followed the model set by the rubber plantation, and it is assumed that this model was a suitable one. Actually, the first smallholders began planting rubber before the first plantation had reached the production stage." And Sundaram (1986: 64) writes, "Significant peasant participation in rubber cultivation began from 1909, four years after rubber first became a plantation crop on a large scale in Malaya." When seedlings were initially distributed in Sarawak in 1908, the first rubber estate on the east coast of Sumatra was still less than a decade old, and in Java planters were still trying to decide whether to commit themselves to the introduced *Hevea* or the native *Ficus* (Keong 1976: 35–36). Timing aside, smallholder cultivation developed in a radically different direction from the estates' cultivation, influenced both by the smallholders' long experience exploiting native Southeast Asian forest rubbers (see chapter 3) and by the politics and economics of cultivating the exotic *Hevea*.

The smallholders' first key innovation was the development of a linkage between rubber cultivation on the one hand, and on the other hand their swidden cultivation system. Indeed, Cramer (1956: 292–94) suggests that this was the main factor in the rapid spread of *Hevea* in Indonesia after 1915 (see chapters 3, 6). This linkage is based on both temporal and spatial complementarity. A single household can have multiple rubber gardens scattered across its swidden territory. As a result, no matter what corner of the territory the household chooses to make its swidden(s) during a given year, it will have a rubber garden sufficiently close by to be able to tap it without wasting too much time on traveling to and fro (see chapter 6).

A second important aspect of the cultivation system devised by the smallholders was its agro-ecology. Managers in the plantation sector, especially in the British colonies (ibid.: 286), spaced their trees widely and clean weeded their estates—Wickham's ideas on the benefits of undergrowth notwithstanding—in the belief that this would maximize production and minimize the threat from pests and disease, especially root disease. In contrast, the smallholders planted their rubber two or three times as densely (Bauer 1948: 56; Cramer 1956: 305), and they permitted natural secondary growth to come up among the rubber trees during periods of nontapping; and even when tapping they only lightly cut back this growth (figure 4.3). In fact, this undergrowth promotes favorable ecological conditions: it slows down decomposition and establishes a thicker humus layer; it yields dense shade; and it provides ancillary environmental services, including conservation of biodiversity, soil, and biomass, and performance of hydrological functions (Joshi et al. 2003: 143; Ooi 1959: 146; Penot 2007: 579). Of most direct relevance, the undergrowth raises the air temperature and humidity within the rubber grove, which favors latex production and quick recovery of tapping

Figure 4.3. Cutting back
undergrowth around a rubber
tree in a Kantu' rubber garden

scars and also inhibits pests and disease, which actually find the clean and open character of the estates more to their liking (Bauer 1948: 58; Penot 2007: 579; Sundaram 1986: 70).[4] The smallholder practice of allowing natural secondary growth among the rubber trees has a final advantage as well: this growth will include naturally seeded second-generation rubber trees, which can eventually replace those that cease to be productive because of age (see chapter 7).

A third distinctive aspect of the production system devised by the smallholders is its socioeconomic structure, which encompassed a number of important innovations, all of which helped to develop the dual household economy of market-oriented rubber and subsistence-oriented swidden food-crop cultivation. One was the participation of women in rubber production in Kalimantan and most other parts of Indonesia—although the situation in parts of Peninsular Malaysia was different (Kato 1991)—even though this flew in the face of colonial governmental sentiment on the matter.[5] Another innovation was the part-time character of rubber production: most smallholders adopted rubber as just one element in a portfolio of economic activities. As discussed in chapter 1, rubber production typically differed from the other components of the portfolio in being more monetized and focused on the market needs and short-term reproduction of the household, in contrast to the system of food-crop production that tended to be less monetized and focused more on the subsistence needs and long-term reproduction of the community. A related innovation involved the relationship to market fluctuations: given rubber's partial role in the household economy, smallholders could produce more, if they chose, when market prices fell (namely, an "inverse production curve" [Boeke 1953: 125–26]), or they could produce less, or they could not produce anything at all and just live off of their subsistence food-cropping. Yet another innovation consisted of the creation of a new and distinctive set of tenurial rules for rubber gardens, which enhanced the smallholders' abilities to defend valuable rubber groves against the threat of appropriation by extra-local actors, including the state (see chapter 3).⁶

The most important smallholder innovation of all may have been the development of a mechanism for rationalizing the combination of market-oriented cash-cropping and subsistence-oriented food production. The reconciliation of the two systems is exemplified by the dream of the rice-eating rubber tree that swept through the interior of Borneo in the 1930s and catalyzed an effort by Dayak smallholders to balance their involvement in the two types of production (see chapter 5).

The innovative character of the pioneering smallholders has persisted to this day, as contemporary observers continue to document experimentation in smallholdings (Penot 2004). For example, Penot (2007: 585) writes that smallholders in Sumatra and Kalimantan are gradually adopting from estates, on their own initiative, practices of weeding to quicken maturity, planting in rows to reduce tapping labor, and the use of herbicides to combat *Imperata cylindrica* (L.) Beauv. (the ubiquitous, if misunderstood, sword grass [Dove 2008]) during immaturity. Of more importance, because it represents not copying but original development and is more ecologically benign than the aforementioned estate practices, is the observation in South Sumatra by Joshi et al. (2003: 139) of techniques like *sisipan* (filling in) with new seedlings in established rubber gardens: "Recent observations in the smallholder jungle rubber system in the Jambi region in Indonesia indicate that many farmers practice a technique of rubber tree rejuvenation in order to fill in gaps or replace unproductive trees with productive rubber seedlings in rubber gardens." The advantages of *sisipan* are that it avoids burning, mimics

Table 4.1. Comparative Development of Hevea Rubber Production in
Southeast Asia and South America

VARIABLE	SOUTHEAST ASIA	SOUTH AMERICA
Source of rubber	Planted	Naturally grown
Smallholders' rights to rubber	Planters/tappers hold rights	Tappers hold no rights
Structure of production	Smallholders (and parastatal estates)	Patron/estate system
Focus of state/elite control	State focuses on control of taxes and markets	Elite focuses on control of labor (and trees)
Focus of government research and development	Technological research focuses on estates	No technological research
Impact of rubber production system on workers/smallholders	Empowers smallholders but not workers/coolies	Disempowers workers/peasants

natural dynamics, entails minimal capital investment, occasions no break in income, and is farmer initiated (ibid.: 145; see also Wibawa, Hendratno, and van Noordwijk 2005).[7]

Southeast Asia versus South America

The historic patterns of development of both smallholders and estates diverged greatly from those then prevailing in the homeland of *Hevea* in South America, which demonstrates the historical contingency of what took place in Southeast Asia (table 4.1). Para rubber grows wild in its native forests in the Amazon at maximum densities of one to two trees per hectare. The nineteenth-century native tappers, or *seringueiros*, cleared winding paths several kilometers in length through the forest to one hundred to two hundred trees, which they tapped every one to three days in season (Barlow 1978: 17; Romanoff 1992: 124). The tappers worked under traders or patrons, whose authority was based variously on land rights, coercion, or credit and debt, especially for food (Murphy and Steward 1956; Romanoff 1992; Weinstein 1983: chap. 1). The lot of the *seringueiros* in this system was sufficiently bad to have stimulated indignant comment by outside observers almost as soon as the system developed in the mid-nineteenth century (ibid.: chap. 1). This impact of this system on the welfare of the tappers was dramatically different from the impact of *Hevea* on the Bornean tribesmen, therefore (Hvalkof 2000; Padoch 1988b: 131). The ill lot of the seringueiros persisted late in the twentieth century, as was reflected in international attention to their plight, efforts to empower them, and the assassination in 1988 of a leader of these efforts, Francisco Mendes Filho (Cowell 1990: 187–97; Keck 1995; see also Mendes 1992). The far better lot of the smallholder rubber tappers of Southeast Asia was never associated with this sort of overt political conflict (although the lot of coolies on estates in the region, especially in the colonial era, certainly was).

A number of different factors contributed to this distinction between Southeast Asia and South America. A close comparison of agro-forestry sites in West Kalimantan and Peten, Guatemala, for example, demonstrates that patterns of exploitation of rubber and other forest products vary according to differences in ecological factors, such as tree density, fruiting phenology, and sustainability, as well as socioeconomic and political factors, such as tenurial patterns and incentives for conservation, physical and social infrastructure, product demand, and political pressures for alternate uses (Salafsky, Dugelby, and Terborgh 1993). In my view, the tenurial patterns are the most important determinant of the differences between Southeast Asia and South America: Para rubber *had* to be planted in Southeast Asia but not in South America.[8]

The nonplanting of *Hevea* in South America was enormously important because in South America as in Southeast Asia "Cultivated crops, not wild rubber trees, served as proof of possession" (Weinstein 1983: 35). As Weinstein (ibid.: 31) writes, "The entire system of production would have undergone basic changes if the aviadores [rubber dealers] and seringalistas [patrons] had invested in the cultivation of rubber instead of relying on the natural source," but this investment was not made. As a result, the role of Para rubber in South America remained analogous to that of the native forest rubbers in Southeast Asia; and what happened to the native rubbers in Southeast Asia—with local producers losing out to political elites when the resource became economically important—is akin to what happened to Para rubber in South America.

Some analysts have argued that rubber could not be planted in South America because of a native disease, South American leaf blight (*Microcyclus ulei* [P. Henn.] v. Arx.), which has been called "the major limiting factor to rubber production in the New World" (Purseglove 1968: 165; see also Dean 1987: 163). However, the historical evidence suggests that other factors limited cultivation before disease had an opportunity to do so (Barham and Coomes 1994). Market-oriented tapping of South American trees dates from the 1840s, and the first private plantations in Southeast Asia date from the turn of the century, yet the first large-scale attempt to establish rubber on plantations in South America was not made until 1928, by the Ford Motor Company (Purseglove 1968: 147–48, 150–51). The fact that this first effort succumbed to leaf blight does not explain why it took over three-quarters of a century to make it, by which time the Amazon rubber boom had completely collapsed as Southeast Asian rubber came onto the market. Nor does it explain why no such efforts of cultivation were made in the latter half of the nineteenth century, when a number of different trees were being exploited for rubber, including two members of the genus *Hevea* that are naturally resistant to the leaf blight (namely, *Hevea benthamiana* Muell.-Arg. and *Hevea nitida* Mart. ex Muell.-Arg.).[9] *Hevea brasiliensis* was not established as the premier source for rubber until the turn of the century (ibid.: 147). As Weinstein (1983: 32) writes, "These 'ecological' factors cannot be cited as actually having discouraged hevea planting, since it was only after the decline that they were widely acknowledged by the scientific community. . . . Their 'discovery' would have come much earlier if a concerted attempt had been made during the rubber era."

Other obstacles to cultivation of *Hevea*, including the development of a more-productive and sustainable system of tapping, were successfully overcome in Southeast Asia. The contrasting failure to overcome the problem of leaf blight in South America suggests that different incentives were at work. It suggests that the attractions of exploiting natural rubber through the *seringueiros* were, for the elites involved in the industry, so great as to inhibit movement toward cultivation of rubber. The political-economic basis of this attraction is attested to by the observation by some rubber historians that any effort to reproduce this laboring class on plantations would not have been easy. Melby (1942: 465, 467–68) argues that the difficulty in procuring a "large supply of fairly efficient and cheap hands" was in fact the chief obstacle to plantation development in the Amazon, surpassing in seriousness even rubber blight on the Ford plantation.[10] It seems no accident, therefore, that the first South American interest in cultivating Para rubber coincided with the explosion of competition from cultivated Para in Southeast Asia

(Weinstein 1983: 219–30) and that contemporary interest in cultivation co-incides with efforts to empower the *seringueiros* (Cowell 1990).[11]

Knowledge, Agency, and the Colonial Project

The debate about the role played by leaf blight in limiting the ca-pacity for human initiative in the South American rubber industry is of interest, in part, because the polar opposite argument—lionizing heroic, individual, human agency—has characterized so much of the discussion of the development of the industry in Southeast Asia.

Critical Realignments and Knowledge Production

The history of the construction of knowledge of rubber cultivation in Southeast Asia was profoundly affected by two critical "realignments" involved in the transplanting of *Hevea:* first, separation of rubber from not just its biological but also its cultural environment; and second, experimen-tation with the system of rubber production. Regarding the separation of rubber from its cultural context, it has long been known that removing a plant from its native habitat frees the plant from the pests and diseases with which it evolved, and this advantage is often cited to explain why so many tropical crops were most fully developed outside their natural ranges (for example, not just rubber but, cocoa, quinine, coffee, cloves, nutmeg, sugar, bananas, limes, and vanilla [Purseglove 1957: 128]). Following this line of explanation, the fact that *Hevea* was cultivated in Southeast Asia and not in South America is attributed to the absence of leaf blight in the former region. But the benefits of removing a plant from its social, economic, po-litical, and conceptual environment may equal if not exceed those of re-moving a plant from its biological environment, especially with regard to tenurial regimes.[12] The possibility of tenurial innovation was raised as soon as Para rubber was transplanted out of its native habitat: within this native habitat, Para rubber *could* be planted, but it did not have to be, nor was it often (Schultes 1956: 140–41). Outside of its native habitat, in contrast, as in Southeast Asia, Para rubber *had* to be planted. Para rubber was a wild rubber tree in South America; it became a cultivated crop in Southeast Asia, where it is now the most widely planted tree (FAO 2001). By planting or not—and thus by raising or not issues of nature versus culture and public domain ver-sus private—the potential for control by state elites versus smallholders is very different (see chapter 3).

As for the second "realignment," involving experimentation, the evolution of the rubber industry in Southeast Asia was irrevocably affected by the fact that production was not directed from the start by an established, unquestionably superior system of knowledge. As noted earlier, *Hevea* was transferred to Southeast Asia largely without reference to the South American experience (Wolf and Wolf 1936), which led to a prolonged period of experimentation (Brockway 1979: 158–60; Dean 1987: 7). Indeed, the introduction of *Hevea* itself was preceded by considerable experimentation with other species. Even once the choice of planting stock had narrowed down to *Hevea*, the introduction still had a very experimental character. Ridley initially had so little success in persuading Malaysian planters to plant *Hevea* that his continued promotion of it earned him the sobriquet of "Mad Ridley." According to Ridley himself, even the Governor of Malaya "admonished him to waste less time on an uneconomic product such as rubber" (Purseglove 1957: 135).[13] This situation changed only when outbreaks of disease and market reversals led planters to become disillusioned with coffee and tea and more willing to experiment with rubber (Davidson 1927: 677–79; Keong 1976: 35–36; Purseglove 1957: 135). As cultivated rubber spread out into the smallholder population in Southeast Asia, a separate tradition of experimentation was begun and carried on. The biggest experiment of all in the transplanting of rubber to Southeast Asia was in fact an unexpected one, to determine whether the estate or the smallholder would be more competitive—and the answer was the latter.

The experimental character of rubber's transplanting, the sundering of the material resource in Southeast Asia from the body of knowledge previously associated with it in South America, is reflected in the angst this engendered in Wickham, the initial agent of the transplanting. His writings are laced with explicit criticisms of the "experimenting" being done with *Hevea* in Southeast Asia. Indeed, he writes that the transfer of *Hevea* to Asia "can hardly be called an experiment." Wickham (1908: 59) supports his opposition to experimentation with the claim that South American natives had already carried out the needful experimenting and already perfected *Hevea*, which is an unexpected invocation in this context of indigenous knowledge: "There is really nothing experimental about 'fine Pará.' It is, and was (probably generations before the advent of the Spaniard into North America), made more durable—of more climate resisting quality—than any factory-made, by certain of the Indian forest tribes (such as the Guyangomo and the Piaroa)." Wickham's antipathy toward experimentation was based on the fact that experimentation was inimical to the South American heritage, including its cultural as well as biological aspects, to which his status was tied. This is reflected in the fact that whereas Purseglove (1956: 17) credits Wickham among others for the introduction of *Hevea* to Asia, he states that "its exploitation and establishment as a plantation crop was due almost entirely to Ridley [of the Singapore Botanic Gardens]." The separation between the material resource and its technological development that is implicit in Purseglove's judgment was inimical to Wickham's authority, and Wickham appears to have anticipated and lobbied against it. Thus, Wickham (1908: 58–59) writes, "Much time, doubtless, has been lost in 'experimenting,' and it would seem a pity that experience and recommendations, as set forth in my India Office Reports, was [*sic*] not made effective and available for the practical man—the man on the spot."

Promethean Theft, Colonial Project, or Serendipity?

The debate about experimentation with rubber is part of a much larger debate that was taking place, and continues to take place, about the role of agency in the colonial project. The idea of transplanting *Hevea* to Asia and cultivating it there had been discussed in print for more than three-quarters of a century before Wickham's collecting expedition. Wolf and Wolf (1936: 154) write, "It was an old dream, this idea of transplanting and cultivating the American rubber tree, a dream as old as Europeans' knowledge that caoutchouc was yielded by plants native to the eastern hemisphere. In writing we encounter it for the first time in the March 23rd, 1791, issue of *The Bee* or *Literary Weekly Intelligencer* of Edinburgh." And a quarter century before Wickham's expedition, the Scottish explorer Richard Spruce carried out extensive studies of *Hevea* from 1851 to 1855, although he did not gather seeds (Loadman 2005: 81). Wickham (1908: 45), however, claimed credit not just for gathering the seeds but for the very idea of cultivating *Hevea:* "I was at that time as one before my time—as one crying in the wilderness. Dead weight of inertia, not to say opposition, prevailed. The idea of cultivating a 'jungle forest tree' was looked upon as not less than visionary." Wickham ignores the fact that all transfers of plant genetic material at that time were modeled after the successful transfer of the quinine-producing cinchona tree (*Cinchona calisaya* Wedd.) from South America to India by Sir Clements Markham of the India Office. He also ignores the fact that the initiative for his own seed gathering came from this same office and individual: Markham asked Joseph Hooker, director of Kew Gardens, to ask Wickham to gather rubber seed. This initiative was in any case preceded by other efforts along similar lines, including at least one prior collection that was coordinated by Markham and Hooker and two different collecting trips by another Englishman, Robert Cross, under Markham's direction (Davidson 1927: 675–76; Purseglove 1957: 134). Markham actually credits Cross with first collecting seeds of *Hevea* (Davidson 1927: 674–75), which were subsequently sent to Ceylon and reportedly "throve well." In the 1870s, Britain made four separate attempts to ship rubber plants from the Amazon basin to Kew Gardens, involving three different species (*Hevea, Castilloa,* and *Ceara*). Seedlings of all three species were successfully established at Kew and then dispatched—with *Hevea* dominating numerically—to botanical gardens scattered all over Britain's Asian colonies. Of most interest, not only was Wickham not the sole agent that he later represented himself to be, but his characterization of his gathering of rubber seeds as a daring theft was completely imaginary. As Schultes (1987: 91) writes, "The story, endlessly repeated in the popular literature and accepted as absolute truth in Brazil, is wholly without foundation" (see chapter 8). It is likely, for example, that Wickham gathered the seeds with the knowledge of the Brazilian authorities (Dean 1987: 20–21). There was no need for secrecy and theft, because there was then little conception of what could be done with *Hevea* seeds. At the time that Wickham and others were making their collections of rubber seeds, there was no knowledge of how to cultivate *Hevea,* and many mistakes were made in this regard. For example, some of the cuttings grown from Wickham's seeds were sent to Calcutta and then consigned to Sikkim, where they died of cold—reflecting, writes Keong (1976: 4), "a complete lack of understanding of the climatic requirements of *Hevea.* Plans for other destinations—such as a plan to establish a seed depot in Tenasserim in British Burma—foundered on such nonbiological factors as the depreciating Indian rupee (ibid.). At the time, Wickham's seed gathering amounted to nothing more than one of hundreds of investigations into tropical forest products of interest. In the nineteenth century *Hevea brasiliensis* was far from the sole source of latex: it was just one—albeit a prominent one—of dozens of different tropical forest trees and vines that were being exploited for this purpose. One scientist even informed the governor of the British Straits Settlements that *Hevea* would never be anything more than a "botanical curiosity" (Dean 1987: 13). A number of these latex-producing plants were native to Asia itself, including *Ficus elastica,* which was seen by the Dutch in Java as a leading competitor to *Hevea* up until the first decade of the twentieth century.[14]

These facts notwithstanding, historic accounts of the development of the Southeast Asian rubber industry, from within the plantation establishment itself, emphasized its epochal, historic nature. For example, Allen and Donnithorne ([1957] 1962: 106–7) report a 1910 observation within the plantation industry to the effect that the chances that existed in cultivated rubber "exist only once in a hundred years and very likely . . . once in a thousand years." This millenarian tone was established by the accounts of Wickham himself, with his exaggeration of the challenges, risks, and dangers of his seed-gathering expedition. In an explicit counter to this heroic imagery, the rubber historian Dean (1987: 7) has critiqued the idea of a "sudden, dramatic transfer" of rubber to Asia. In an effort to replace the "myth" of Henry Wickham as "hero and rogue" and "bestower and thief" of rubber seeds, with a more prosaic image, he writes, "Alas, it was not so much an adventure as it was a complex bureaucratic project, some fifty years in the execution" (ibid.). Dean's critique is welcome as far as it goes, but it doesn't go far enough. His revisionist view, while purporting to diminish the authority of the state, still overprivileges its authority. Whereas at one level Dean takes power away from the colonial regime by saying that this great project of rubber transplanting was not instantaneous, at another level he returns power to this regime by representing it as a project at all. To characterize the complex, contested, and multifaceted rubber history as the "project" of one of the countries involved is to impose an ex post facto teleology that privileges the role of the colonial plantation establishment and not, most obviously, the local Southeast Asian smallholders. It is true that Wickham's transfer of rubber seeds was part of a wider global movement of genetic material, which was being driven in part by colonial visions and ambitions; but it was far too uncoordinated and happenstance to merit the term *project*.

The problem with this teleology is illustrated by the case of the father of the modern system of tapping, Henry Nicholas Ridley. As noted earlier, Ridley's pioneering work on rubber cultivation initially earned him the derisive epithet of "Mad Ridley." It is significant that what eventually proved to be a hugely successful industry was nonetheless first seen as a "mad" enterprise. This epithet suggests that the transfer of rubber was not a project at all, but a chancy, conflict-ridden historical development, which flew in the face of much accepted wisdom. Dean's critique of the Promethean myth of Wickham arguably applies to Ridley as well, therefore: his fathering of rubber tapping, far from being a seamless, heroic action, was initially ridiculed. Over time, however, the image of Ridley as the father of rubber tapping completely crowded out the image of Ridley the madman. The former privileges the estate establishment and the colonial regimes that encompassed it far more than the latter. Indeed, Ridley's agency in resisting the shortsighted opposition of the government of Malaya was arguably greater than that of Wickham in purloining the rubber seeds from an indifferent Amazonian society. Still, Ridley's real achievement did not come to define either the man or the era in anything like the same way that Wickham's fanciful one did. Ridley's actual triumph over the British colonial government did not "articulate" (in Hall's 1996 sense) with colonial society's views of the world in the same way as did Wickham's imaginary triumph over the native government of Brazil (see chapter 8). What the colonial world wanted was not a successful bureaucrat and researcher but a "conjuror," in Tsing's (2000) sense.

Linkage and Division

The histories of construction of rubber knowledge by estates and by smallholders in Southeast Asia are distinct but also very much intertwined. Knowledge, technology, and other resources have flowed back and forth between the two sectors. Most obviously, the smallholders received the botanical resource of *Hevea* itself, whether intentionally given to or surreptitiously taken from the colonial estate sector. In addition, they received one especially notable product of the state-sponsored research and development by the estate sector, namely the system of tapping. The system of tapping devised by Ridley—involving a spiral, V-shaped cutting of the bark with a modified farrier's knife—was universally adopted among smallholders in Southeast Asia. Another successful if inadvertent transfer of technology involved the use of mechanical rollers to press water out of the coagulated rubber slabs. The International Rubber Regulation Agreement of the 1930s altered the tax structure to favor rubber with lower water content, in an effort to discriminate against the high-water-content rubber of the smallholders. Instead, much to the regulators' surprise, cast-iron "rubber mangles" spread in a few years into even the remote interior of Borneo (figure 4.4).

Smallholders also engaged in their own on-farm experimentation with *Hevea*, just as they have historically done with all of their cultigens, and some of the results of this found their way back to the estates[15]—although this flow was much slower and more complicated, which reflects the politicized nature of rubber knowledge. Knowledge flows from estates to smallholders uphold the reigning ideology, and so they are understood and facilitated; but knowl-

Figure 4.4. Kantu' using a rubber mangle to press water
from the rubber slabs

edge flows in the opposite direction pose a problem, because they undermine
this ideology; they are difficult to even conceive of. One of the most important examples of this reverse flow involved the question as to whether or not
to clean weed the ground among the growing rubber plants. As discussed
earlier, from the very beginning, smallholders in Indonesia and Malaysia
have generally allowed naturally occurring undergrowth to grow up among
the rubber trees. The estate sector, in stark contrast, assiduously practiced
clean weeding in rubber plantations for the first several decades of the industry. The estate sector was aware that the smallholders were not following
their lead in this regard, and this led to decades of invective from the estate
sector regarding the imagined damage that the smallholders were doing to
the productivity and health of their own rubber and even, through the feared
spread of disease, to the estates' rubber as well. After roughly one-half century of insistence upon clean weeding, however, the estate sector recognized
that this practice was a mistake and that some sort of ground cover was desirable. The admission by the estate sector that it was in the wrong on this point
did not amount, however, to an admission that the smallholders were in the
right.

The influential Rubber Research Institute of Malaya officially signaled the change of heart on weeding policy in two editions of Haines's manual on undergrowth: "In his foreword to the first edition of this Manual, in 1934, the then Director of this Institute quoted the words 'The natural bias in favour of clean weeding is slowly breaking down and the present economic conditions have done much to discourage the practice.' Six years have elapsed since then and few will now dispute the undesirability of clean weeding, and the desirability of maintaining a ground cover in rubber plantations, on most Malayan soils" (Haines [1934] 1940: i).[16] This policy change was attributed solely to innovation in the estate sector; there was no mention of smallholders or smallholder practices: "Our present knowledge of the possibilities and methods of management of indigenous cover plants owes much to the enthusiasm and the shrewd observations of the pioneers of the system and of its present day users, to whom the thanks of the industry and of this Institute are due" (ibid.: ii) The pioneers lauded in these remarks are planters, not peasants; they are managers of estates, not smallholders. This nonrecognition of the smallholder wisdom in this regard was neither incidental nor accidental. It represented a major accomplishment by the rubber industry, and it required the investment over time of major institutional resources.

The estate sector's construction of an image of itself as the sole producer of rubber knowledge was the end-product of a major bureaucratic project, which was supported by a complex of bureaucratic resources and mechanisms. The most obvious of these is linguistic: the use in official circles of phrases such as "jungle rubber" to disparage the smallholders' failure to clean weed, or the phrase "slaughter-tapping" in criticism of their supposed overly intense tapping of trees (which was an attempt to explain away the smallholders' bewilderingly high productivity), serve to privilege the estates at the expense of the smallholders. A similar effect has been achieved by the government institutions that gather data on parastatal estates and smallholders in government-supported schemes but that ignore the existence of the smallholders.[17] On the contemporary website of the Indonesia's Central Bureau of Statistics, for example, national rubber production is represented as coming solely from large estates (*perkebunan besar*); smallholdings are not even mentioned (www.bps.go.id, accessed July 2010). In the high modern state, to not be counted is to be discounted. Also extremely important is the exclusive focus of research and development resources on estates.[18] This accentuates and perpetuates the perceived primitiveness of the smallholdings (Gouyon, de Foresta, and Levang 1993: 199; see also Barlow and Jayasuriya 1984).[19] On the other hand, the smallholders' own strengths have not been the object of research, which is another way of diminishing them. The failure to study the smallholder management of undergrowth in the rubber gardens has already been mentioned. One of the signal strengths and defining characteristics of smallholder cultivation, namely the combination of cash-cropping with food-cropping, has also been studiously ignored (see Schneider 1995: 67). This is reflected in the fact that failure to provide enough acreage for food-cropping has been a persistent weakness in government block-planting schemes for smallholders for the past thirty years.

The mental block that rendered the estate sector incapable of seeing the wisdom of smallholder practices of managing undergrowth is still present today, as reflected in the government block-planting schemes for smallholders. As noted in chapter 1, the block-planting schemes are alien in almost all respects to the basic characteristics of the smallholders; they implicitly deny the legitimacy of the smallholding pattern of cultivation. The form taken by these projects is a graphic representation of the estate's privileged epistemological stance. The dominant type of block-planting schemes, the nucleus estate, consists of smallholdings clustered around a central parastatal estate (see chapter 1, figure 1.2). An explicit logic underlies this spatial pattern: it promotes the surrounding smallholders' delivery of produce to the central estate and the central estate's delivery of knowledge and management to the smallholders. As Barlow (1991: 100) writes, "[One] type of group-farming scheme from the late 1970s was the nucleus estate or Perusahaan Inti Rakyat (PIR), which was an institution already tested in other international and especially African contexts. The Indonesian government subsidized land and capital for both PTP [Perusahaan Terbatas Perkebunan (parastatal estates)] and private estate companies, on condition that while establishing their own interests in the nucleus or *inti*, they would also develop a surrounding plasma of supervised smallholdings. The underlying concept was to use the 'repository of expertise' in estate organizations to establish farms for the landless poor, both locals and transmigrants." In short, the principle underlying the design of such projects is for the estates to share their expertise with the smallholders, not the reverse (see ibid.). The highly contingent and political nature of such projects is dramatized by the existence of simple and effective alternatives.

Occasional experimental projects have demonstrated that it is in fact relatively easy—in technological if not political terms—to address smallholder conditions and needs in Indonesia (see Angelsen 1995: 1726; CPIS

1993). This is exemplified by one early project that targeted smallholders on their own smallholdings, the North Sumatra Smallholder Development Project, which was carried out on a pilot basis in the mid-1970s. It was not tied to a government estate, management was quite decentralized, and there was great scope for farmer decision making. For all of these reasons, it was very successful. The central government nonetheless terminated it after the pilot stage, with the admonition, "The government-owned estate groups . . . should be used for future smallholder development" (Dillon 1985: 121). The case of Malaysia is also illustrative. Malaysia raised the average yields of its rubber smallholders by 126 percent between 1965 and 1980 by means of a simple low-cost program of technological assistance, which greatly altered the dynamics of its estate-smallholder relationship (Barlow 1990: 28–30, 30n; Barlow and Tomich 1991: 50; Nonini 1992: 122–26; Rudner 1976). In Indonesia, in contrast, no such assistance was provided, yields rose just 17 percent during the same time period, and this dynamic remained little changed. Indonesian rubber smallholders were left with the most primitive technology among the major rubber-producing nations, employing genetic material and techniques of cultivation and production largely unchanged since the initial decades of rubber's introduction to Southeast Asia (Barlow and Muharminto 1982: 92–93; Barlow and Tomich 1991: 31, 35; Booth 1988: 211–12).

In summary, the estate sector has treated the smallholder sector not as an economic alternative but as an irrational "other"—as something too illegitimate to be even considered a competitor. The aforementioned website of the Central Bureau of Statistics actually states, in a note on definitions, that smallholdings (*kebun rakyat*) are noncorporate, household, even unauthorized enterprises (*tanpa izin*). This view of the differences between smallholder and estate systems of rubber production and knowledge is not sociologically neutral. It is an example of what Foucault (1982: 208) calls "dividing practices," referring to the many ways by which societies objectify the other and privilege the self (for example, by distinguishing between mad and sane, sick and healthy, criminals and law-abiding citizens). By conjuring this type of division between estates and smallholders, actual linkages between them are obscured; and by emphasizing the need to make the smallholdings more like estates (for example, in nucleus-estate projects), the legitimacy of the smallholders' own mode of production is denied; and by depicting the relationship of the estates to the smallholders in almost a pedagogical light, the fact that the relationship is really one of economic and political competition is obfuscated.

Depression-Era Responses to Smallholder Rubber Development by Tribesmen and Governments

Rice that people were drying in the sun kept disappearing. Then one day the people found this rice in a hollow rubber tree that they had felled to use for firewood.
—*Kantu' recollection of dream from the 1930s*

Introduction

In this chapter I move from the initial development of the rubber knowledge and technology in Southeast Asia to its first major market crises. Geertz ([1963] 1971: 123) has written of this period: "As the bulk of the Javanese peasants moved toward agricultural involution, a small minority of the Outer Island peasants moved toward agricultural specialization, frank individualism, social conflict, and cultural rationalization. The second course was the more perilous, and to some minds it may seem both less defensible morally and less attractive aesthetically. But at least it did not foredoom the future." This chapter is an analysis of how some agricultural development choices foredoom the future, how some don't, and how the consciousness of this choice is culturally mediated.

Background

My focus here is on two events during the Depression years of the 1930s: a government agreement and a tribal dream. The International Rubber Regulation Agreement (IRRA) was ostensibly designed to stabilize world rubber prices by limiting production through taxation, sales quotas, and prohibition of planting. In practice, as noted in earlier chapters, the agreement was used to try to perpetuate the early domination of the industry by estates against an increasingly competitive smallholder sector, through the imposition of planting restrictions and onerous taxes on smallholder rubber. The ideological underpinning of the IRRA was a complex of unsubstantiated beliefs about the economic and ecological shortcomings of the smallholdings. The gist of the tribal dream, as summarized in the epigraph to this chapter, was that rubber was hostile to swidden rice. The public telling of the dream spread throughout the interior of Borneo. News of it caused great consternation among the Dayak of the interior, so much so that in some cases they felled their rubber trees upon hearing of it. Sutlive (1978: 129) cites independent records of the dream from the Third Division in Sarawawk, and Pringle (1970: 203n) cites records of it from the First and Second as well as Third Divisions. Geddes (1954: 97) maintains that in some parts of Sarawak the effects of the dream lingered into the post–World War II era: "Throughout the Kayan district today, most people are still restrained from planting rubber by this same threat of spiritual harm to their padi, a threat which now has the support of tradition in the legend of the cutting down of the trees." Both the dream, in a direct sense, and the IRRA, indirectly, represent efforts to come to terms with the unique dynamics of a dual peasant economy, which encompasses both subsistence- and market-oriented activities. For the Dayak, the challenge was to maintain the balance between the two parts of their economy; for the colonial estate sector, the challenge was to compete against the efficiency and resiliency of that dual economy.

Taussig, in his pioneering work (1980) on the way that the challenge of capitalism to the traditional moral economy is articulated within indigenous cosmologies in Colombia and Bolivia, shows that devil belief, which scholars might have dismissed as either unimportant or anachronistic, is in fact a gesture of resistance to a new mode of production. Taussig (ibid.: xi) asks, "What is the relationship between the image of the devil and capitalist development?" Here I will ask, "What is the relationship between the dream of the rice-eating rubber and export-crop development in Borneo?" Taussig (ibid.: 96) calls devil belief an "image illuminating a culture's self-consciousness of the threat posed to its integrity." I suggest that the dream of the rice-eating rubber illuminates Bornean tribesmen's consciousness of the threat posed to them by overcommitment to global commodity markets. In an effort that extends back to the materialist/functionalist interpretation of ritual by Harris (1966) among others, anthropologists have sought to link the study of political economy with the study of symbols (see Roseberry 1991). These efforts have been criticized, in part, because of their reductionism, their explanation of one thing in terms of something else. Taussig (1980: 17) suggests that political-economic analysis of native cosmology should be based on readings that are as literal and nonreductionist as possible: "Instead of reducing the devil-beliefs to the desire for material gain, anxiety, 'limited good,' and so on, why not see them in their own right with all their vividness and detail as the response of people to what they see as an evil and destructive way of ordering economic life?" Rappaport (1979: 174), whose earlier work was more vulnerable to this charge of reductionism, later in his career similarly writes, "It may be suggested that in their eagerness to plumb ritual's dark symbolic or functional depths, to find in ritual more than meets the eye, anthropologists have, perhaps increasingly, tended to overlook ritual's surface, that which does meet the eye." In keeping with these admonitions, the premise here will be that the Dayak dream of the rice-eating rubber actually is about rubber that "eats"—or at least displaces—rice.[1]

Local Bornean history, which is more about rice, and global history, which is more about rubber, can be linked (see Roseberry 1991: 132). Although local culture is, in part, a product of interaction with the global political-economic system, it also is more than this (see Marcus and Fischer 1986: 39, 78). There is more history here, in short, than that which "arrives, like a ship, from outside the society in question" (Ortner 1984: 143). On the other hand, international regulatory regimes are not unaffected by this local history. The global history of commodity regulation in the 1930s is intertwined in a number of different ways with the local tribal history of commodity production. As Tsing (1993: 74–75) writes, with reference to Southern Borneo, "It is important to remember here that the rational development rhetoric of the state is not a representation of truth obscured by hillbilly ignorance; it has its own bizarre, tenuous association with local events."

In the Depression-era clash between tribal smallholders and international rubber regulators, the former did not have a monopoly on mythmaking. As Obeyesekere (1992: 10) writes in his critique of analyses of colonial-era clashes between Pacific peoples and Europeans, "One of my basic assumptions is that mythmaking, which scholars assume to be primarily an activity of non-Western societies, is equally prolific in European thought." I will both attempt to "naturalize" a native view that normally is seen as bizarre and "denaturalize" an official view that normally is not seen as bizarre. By problematizing not just Dayak actions in the 1930s (namely, the rice-eating rubber dream) but also the actions of the global economic system (namely, the International Rubber Regulation Agreement), the former is shown to be more tied to reality and the latter less objective than had been thought to be the case (see Bloch 1989: 167).

Dreams in Borneo

Many of the tribal peoples of Southeast Asia traditionally regarded the relationship between dreams and everyday life differently than is the case in most modern Western societies (Dentan 1982; Domhoff 1985; Roseman 1991; Tedlock 1992: 5).[2] Gomes (1911: 161) writes as follows of the attitude toward dreams among the Dayak: "The Dayaks place implicit confidence in dreams. Their theory is that during sleep the soul can hear, see, and understand, and so what is dreamt is really what the soul sees." The Dayak traditionally regarded dreams as omens of the future (Tsing 1984: 225–26). As such, dreams could affect the decision whether to undertake a journey or not, what type of work to do on a given day, and even where to locate a field.

Dreams that are deemed to be particularly meaningful are told to other members of one's own household or longhouse, and occasionally they are disseminated to other longhouses as well. During my fieldwork among the Kantu', it was not unusual to awake to find that someone had an inauspicious dream during the night, leading to a longhouse-wide discussion, proscription of all work that day in the swiddens, and staging of a prophylactic ceremony that evening to protect the longhouse's inhabitants from harm (figure 5.1). The motivating factor in sharing a dream with kinsmen in the longhouse is the dreamer's desire for assistance in interpreting and responding to the dream (Richards 1972: 80). In these cases, it makes a difference who the dreamer is: since the elders of the society are thought to be more skillful in interpreting messages from the spirit world, their dreams are the ones most likely to be retold and analyzed. However, in a case of wider dissemination, like that of the dream of the rice-eating rubber, it is the significance of the dream for the wider society that motivates its retelling and spread. In such cases, the original dream agent is less relevant. And indeed, I never heard any information on or even speculation regarding the identity of the person or persons from whom the rice-eating rubber dream first came.

The wide dissemination of the dream of the rice-eating rubber marks it as a "collective representation," in Durkheim's sense.[3] The circumstances of its original production, who first dreamt it, are less significant than the circumstances of its proliferation, the fact that many Dayak in many different areas were receptive to its message.

Figure 5.1. Prophylactic Kantu' ceremony held after an inauspicious dream

The International Rubber Regulation Agreement

At the time that the dream of the rice-eating rubber occurred, tribal rubber was also much in the thoughts of colonial policy makers; and if tribal anxiety over rubber was manifested in the dream, then government anxiety was manifested in the International Rubber Regulation Agreement (IRRA). The forces driving the IRRA are aptly summarized by Barlow and Jayasuriya (1986: 641):

> The usual response of what have most often been colonial governments to these smallholding developments is one of unfolding surprise, sometimes accompanied by measures to "protect" the farmers concerned from what is regarded as a much too wholesale switch from traditional to commercial agriculture. As the output of the tree crop increases, however, its revenue potential is appreciated, and some form of tax is commonly imposed. Where estate interests are also cultivating the same crop, the official response may involve positive hostility. Thus attempts may be made, generally through land regulation, either to suppress smallholder cultivation or push it to remote peripheries beyond the interest of estate bodies. Where smallholder output of the crop poses some threat to estates, as often occurred in the 1930s, discriminatory attempts are made to reduce it. In no case is any substantial positive assistance given to promote small-

holder cultivation of the new crop, except as a flow-on of measures to help the estate subsector.

The Political-Economic Context

Efforts to restrict smallholder production date back at least to the Dutch effort early in the seventeenth century to erase native spice production on islands not under their control in eastern Indonesia. In more recent times, the nineteenth-century booms in natural forest rubbers led to government allocation of exclusive rights to European concessionaires and prohibition of further exploitation by local communities (see chapter 3). Similar attempts were made in the twentieth century to wrest exploitation of the Para rubber tree away from smallholders. The first, called the Stevenson Restriction Scheme, attempted to maintain high prices for estate rubber on the international market by restricting the amount of rubber that could be sold by producers, in particular smallholders (Drabble 1973; Ghee 1974).[4] The scheme was limited to the British colonies—the Dutch did not join it, and so it did not apply to Dutch Borneo—and it was in effect from 1922 to 1928.[5] The second and more important effort to regulate smallholder cultivation of rubber was the International Rubber Regulation Agreement, in which the Dutch did join, and thus it did apply to Dutch Borneo.[6]

The IRRA was a response to dramatic increases in the supply of rubber and decreases in its price. The drop in price—1932 prices were just 16 percent of 1929 prices—was a result of both a Depression-driven drop in demand and the increase in supply. This increase was due to the planting of high-yielding clones in the estate sector and the expansion of acreage under nonclonal rubber in the smallholder sector (Ricklefs 2008: 222; Tucker 2007: 126). Enacted by the Netherlands, Great Britain, France, India, and Siam in 1934 and lasting until 1944, the IRRA was in theory designed to stabilize world rubber prices by limiting production through taxation, imposition of sales quotas, prohibition of planting, and even in some cases the felling of planted trees and the uprooting of naturally grown trees (Bauer 1948; Ghee 1974; Thee 1977). In practice, however, the IRRA imposed the burden of price stabilization, through limitations on production, largely on the smallholders.

As Bauer's authoritative work (1948) makes clear, the IRRA, like the Stevenson Restriction Scheme before it, was essentially an attempt to protect the European estates' initially dominant role in the rubber industry from an extremely competitive smallholder sector. As Barlow and Jayasuriya (1986: 647–49) write, "Both the Stevenson and the International Rubber Regulation Schemes devised to counter low prices by supply restriction were highly discriminatory against smallholding interests through a mechanism of low quotas, and certainly reflected political pressures in favour of the estates" (Nonini 1992: 85–88, 96–98). Both regulatory schemes were confounded by the smallholders' response, however. As Robequain ([1946] 1955: 354) wrote regarding the failure of the Stevenson Restriction Scheme to check the expansion of rubber cultivation: "The big producers had counted without the natives. As prices had risen, so rubber trees had multiplied in the *ladangs* [swiddens] in Sumatra and Borneo, more quickly than on European plantations, and without the formation of companies or the issue of shares and advertisements." The problem for the regulators was that smallholders could establish rubber for less than 10 percent of the estate's costs, by integrating the rubber into their swidden cycles and using few if any capital inputs (Bauer 1948: 68; Barlow 1990: 32). Furthermore, because the smallholders did not have to depend on rubber for their daily subsistence, they were willing to tap rubber for prices that were as little as one-fifth of those that the estates insisted on as a reasonable return (Bauer 1948: 206; Barlow and Jayasuriya 1986: 640).[7] These economic realities of smallholder production were ultimately too much for the IRRA. Despite the fact that special export taxes on smallholders alone were increased to the point where the ratio of tax to net return ranged from twenty- to as much as sixty-to-one (Bauer 1948: 38–39, 142, 142n), smallholders continued to increase both the quantity and quality of their production.

The unanticipated response of the smallholders is just one of the many counterfactual dimensions to the IRRA. Contradiction was inherent to its very design: some of its key premises were based on the perceived shortcomings and developmental needs of smallholder rubber production, and yet in practice the major impact of the agreement was to not support but suppress this production.[8] The contradictions in the IRRA do not appear to have been entirely contrived. Most colonial officials appear to have sincerely believed that the IRRA was designed to support the entire industry and not just the estates at the expense of smallholders (Nonini 1992: 87). This is reflected in the fact that colonial planters and officials seemed genuinely surprised—recall Barlow and Jayasuriya's earlier-cited remark about the "unfolding surprise" of colonial governments—by the fact that the smallholders proved to be innocent of promoting disease and degradation and that they did not curtail their production under the IRRA. The sincerity of the estate sector's mistaken beliefs regarding the smallholders is further reflected in contradictory statements made with no hint of cognitive dissonance. For example, writing about smallholder production at the time, the preeminent tropical geographer Robequain ([1946] 1955: 361–62) states in successive paragraphs both that native agriculture had to be "protected" against the "rude blows" of the external world and that the native producers were less damaged than others by the depression of the 1930s. He writes, "In 1935 the economic depression was seen to have less serious effects on the people of the country than on Europeans, 10,000 of whom were unemployed in Indonesia. . . . The elasticity of native economy was admirable" (ibid.: 362). The weight of colonial estate dogma is reflected in Robequain's ambivalent, backhanded, and contradictory comments on smallholder production (ibid.: 355): "Rubber raised in an extremely acute form one of the most serious problems connected with colonisation, namely competition between Europeans and peasant producers, one armed with his capital, proud of his organisation and technique, and helped by his knowledge of the market; the other having the advantage of a low standard of living and securing unexpected profits from casual and slovenly cultivation." These puzzling statements, views, and practices were supported by the development of an estate ideology surrounding smallholder cultivation.

The Ideological Context

The colonial estate sector viewed—just as its modern-day counterpart still views—the smallholder sector as a minor, troubled part of the industry. Throughout the duration of the IRRA and down to the present day, rubber has been associated in the minds of government officials with estates, not smallholdings. In the early post–World War II years, Bauer (1948: 212) writes, "Officials, research workers and others closely connected with the industry still regarded the smallholder as a minor and rather inefficient factor in rubber production." This impression was reinforced by a variety of bureaucratic mechanisms that rendered the smallholders unimportant or invisible (as noted in chapter 4), based on all of the ways in which smallholders differed from estate cultivation.

There were and are marked visible differences between the estate and smallholder sectors. Smallholder cultivation is characterized by planting densities over twice as high as those on estates, the absence of clean weeding, and spontaneous coverage of the rubber groves by secondary growth during extended periods of nontapping. These visible differences were thought to be associated with serious management failings involving disease, degradation, and inefficiency. Colonial planters and officials believed that the small-holdings were subject to "rampant root disease," which was proving to be a serious problem on European estates at the time, and it was thought that the source of this disease was the smallholdings.[9] This specter of diseased smallholdings was used to help justify the IRRA (Ghee 1974: 109–10). When smallholdings were finally surveyed in Malaya in 1931–33, however, almost no evidence of root disease was found (Bauer 1948: 58). Only eight out of nine thousand trees examined were found to have succumbed to the disease. Root disease proved, ironically, to be a product of the peculiar microecology not of smallholdings but of estates, not in spite of but because of their cleaner and more open character (ibid., chap. 4).

Colonial officials and planters believed that smallholdings were subject not only to disease but also to degradation of the rubber trees. It was an article of faith in the estate sector that a majority of smallholdings were degraded. This belief was invoked repeatedly during the years of rubber regulation in an attempt to explain the troubling fact that smallholder yields exceeded estate yields both on per-acre and overall bases. Colonial observers attributed the smallholders' high yields to their purported "slaughter-tapping" of trees, meaning the cutting of the bark of the rubber trees at a rate exceeding that of natural bark production (ibid.: 37, 68).[10] Again, when the Malayan smallholder survey was carried out, the rate of bark usage was found to be well in line with the rate of bark production (ibid.: 36). Not a single tree examined had been degraded by overtapping, which was attributable to the intermittent character of smallholder tapping (Ooi 1959: 146–47), rational tapping techniques, and a favorable microclimate. The dense vegetative cover in the smallholdings produces higher air temperature and humidity than in the estates, and this in turn promotes quicker bark renewal after tapping (Bauer 1948: 58). The belief and the reality were nicely juxtaposed in an exchange at the time in the *Sarawak Gazette*. A European observer who had spent a year inspecting the rubber in Sarawak writes, "Practically all of the Asiatic-grown trees have been ruined by bad tapping" (*Sarawak Gazette* 1938a: 64). But the next number of the *Gazette* included a diametrically opposed comment from another reader: "Nor is this high yield [among small-holders] due to severe knife-work, as this [previous] author would have us believe. On the contrary, experts consider the bark reserved on this type of rubber as good, and the tapping conservative" (*Sarawak Gazette* 1938b: 96).

Colonial planters and officials also maintained that the smallholders were not "efficient producers," a critique that was central to the regulatory environment of the day. The guarantee of a "reasonable return to the average efficient producer" was the purported and oft-repeated purpose of the IRRA (Bauer 1948: 200). However, when the Rubber Manufacturers Association — representing the principal international buyers of rubber and thus already inclined to be skeptical of the real motives behind the scheme to "stabilize" rubber prices — requested a definition of an "efficient producer" from the International Rubber Regulation Committee, the latter could not provide one (ibid.: 195).[11] The closest the committee ever came was to state, "Efficient producers are those who produce efficiently" (ibid.: 196n). There was less obfuscation of this sort during the earlier Stevenson Restriction Scheme, which was explicitly justified as a defense against a pro-smallholder philosophy of "the survival of the fittest." Drabble (1973: 167) writes, "The R.G.A. [Rubber Growers Association] group stressed the need for unanimity among producers, the importance of the industry as an Imperial asset and the unwisdom of a policy of 'survival of the fittest.'" By the time of the IRRA the following decade, however, rubber industry ideology had sufficiently matured so that the estates identified their smallholder opponent not as the winner of Darwinian competition but as just the opposite.[12] Ironically, the principal beneficiaries of the IRRA were in fact the *least* efficient producers, the heavily capitalized estates with their high overheads (Bauer 1948: 215);[13] and the true efficient producers, the smallholders, were severely penalized by it. In a remarkable demonstration of their efficiency, the smallholders continued to plant and tap rubber and improve their production techniques (see also Barlow 1991: 93), in spite of low incentives (namely, prices) from the market and severe disincentives (namely, taxes) from the government.

The colonial community accounted for the "inexplicable" aspects of smallholder behavior in terms of the theory of "economic dualism," exemplified by the writings of the onetime "Professor of Eastern Economics" at the University of Leiden, Julius Herman Boeke (1953), which held that the smallholders' economy and indeed mentality was fundamentally different from that of the European planters. In keeping with this thesis, it was thought that export cropping should be left to the European planters and that the natives should concentrate on their traditional food crops. In colonial Malaya, in particular, government policy explicitly discouraged native cultivation of rubber and other export crops and encouraged their cultivation of rice. This dichotomization of rubber and rice aptly expresses the disharmony and potential conflict that Europeans saw between export crop production and native society: it was thought that if the natives did not destroy the export crop through poor cultivation or overexploitation, then the export crop would destroy native society by undermining its subsistence basis.

The errors in the colonial estate sector's views of efficiency and dualism were self-serving. Scott (1998: 139) asks, "How do we explain the decided colonial preference for plantation agriculture over smallholder production? The grounds for the choice can certainly not have been efficiency. For almost any crop one can name, with the possible exception of sugar cane, smallholders have been able historically to out-compete larger units of production." The preference for plantations over smallholdings, Scott (ibid.) suggests, has to do with what sort of efficiency is being measured: "The paradox is largely resolved, I believe, if we consider the 'efficiencies' of the plantation as a unit of taxation (both taxes on profits and various export levies), of labor discipline and surveillance, and of political control." In short, the colonial governments favored estates because they were far and away more efficient, in terms of colonial governance, than smallholdings.

The Rubber Dream

Like the economic–dualism theorists, the native societies of Borneo also saw rubber and rice as separate and distinct, but in this case the relationship between the two was conceived as, ideally, one of complementarity rather than opposition.

Complementarity of Rice and Rubber

The literal meaning of the dream of the rice-eating rubber is that rubber can eat rice, meaning that overinvolvement in rubber production can lead to a diminishment in rice cultivation—if sufficient care is not taken. Some versions of the rubber dream make it clear that the rice is "eaten" when no one is looking, and it is only when people mount guard that they catch the predatory rubber tree in the act. The rice is "eaten" when it is being dried in the sun in preparation for husking, which is in fact a period of vulnerability for the grain: drying rice is exposed to predators (for example, domestic fowl, birds, rats), and constant protection is essential. The dream can be interpreted, therefore, as calling attention to the potential vulnerability of the rice base at a time of increasing involvement in commodity production, and to the need for vigilance in protecting this base against any ill consequences of such involvement.

The emphasis in the dream is not on the extermination of rubber but on the protection of rice, not on rejecting new cash crops but on protecting the traditional subsistence crops. The danger does not lie in producing for the market but in producing *only* for the market.[14] Those tribesmen who responded to the dream by felling their rubber trees were guilty of an overly literal interpretation of the dream, of focusing on the threat from the rubber trees as opposed to the rubber sector. The most common response to the dream, in any case, was not to fell the rubber trees but to balance development of the rubber sector against the continued importance of the subsistence rice sector; and this response was far more important in the long run than any felling of rubber that took place. The felling that did take place is important more for what it says about the seriousness with which the dream was greeted.

The interpretation of the rubber dream as a warning against overcommitment to rubber at the expense of rice is supported by the contrasting ecological logic of the dream and the reality. In the dream, rice is found in or among the rubber; no rubber is found among the rice. In practice, according to the customary ecology of Dayak agriculture, it is the other way around: rice is never found among rubber, but rubber often is found among rice. Rubber is usually planted in rice swiddens after the planting and before the harvesting of the rice, with the result that a rubber garden eventually grows up on the erstwhile swidden site. In contrast, rice would never be planted among standing rubber trees: the trees would block too much sunlight for the rice to grow. After the passage of several decades, when the rubber trees have passed their productive peak, the rubber garden may be cleared and burned for a rice swidden again, bringing the cycle full circle.

In this real-life cycle, rubber might be said to eat the rice, in the sense that it succeeds the rice on the land, but then even more clearly rice eats the rubber, when the no-longer productive rubber is felled and burned for a new rice swidden. This relationship becomes asymmetrical—rubber eats but is not eaten by the rice—only if the swidden cycle is abandoned for complete dependence on rubber cultivation. This is what was warned against in the dream. The dream was a mythologically condensed expression of an undesirable trajectory in agricultural development. At the time of the dream, neither the desirable nor undesirable trajectories had yet been experienced; they still lay in the future. The dream was not a comment about past trajectories, therefore, but about possible future ones. The dream did not reflect the existence of a cycle in which the rubber does not eat the rice; rather, it helped to bring about such a cycle.[15]

The Timing of the Rubber Dream

Smallholder rubber development reached a critical juncture in the 1930s, the time of the rice-eating rubber dream, due to a number of different factors. The global Depression and crisis in capitalist markets presented the lower orders of global trade with opportunities for development that they would not otherwise have had (Frank 1967), as well as challenges that they would not otherwise have faced. These opportunities and challenges coincided with the maturation of the smallholder industry: rubber planting stock was not widely available in Borneo until the first decade of this century, and it was not widely planted in the tribal interior until the second decade nor tapped, accordingly, until the third decade. Not until the fourth decade, the 1930s therefore, was rubber sufficiently well established to raise the specter of rubber-rice competition. Not until then did the question have to be asked whether rubber would fit into the existing shifting cultivation cycle in a complementary fashion or, conversely, establish its own competing cycle of land use. The significance of the decade of the 1930s in the evolution of smallholder rubber production is reflected in a comparison of production statistics for the 1920s—the first decade in which significant smallholder production took place—and the 1930s (table 5.1). Smallholder rubber production for all of Indonesia, with the exception of Java, increased by more than 900 percent between 1920 and 1930, compared with less than 300 percent between 1930 and 1940, after which it took almost one-half century for another 300 percent increase.[16]

The 1930s was also a critical time because of the plunge in rubber prices triggered by the global Depression.[17] Some rubber cultivators reacted to these falling prices by tapping less or not at all, shifting the labor previously devoted to rubber either to some other income-earning activity or to subsistence rice cultivation;[18] whereas others reacted by tapping more, in an inverse production curve (see chapter 6), in an attempt to maintain the same level of income from rubber.[19] The falling rubber prices provoked other responses as well. Sutlive (1992: 85–86) describes how Iban in Sarawak, who had planted rubber at the encouragement of the English rajah there, interpreted the fall of prices during the 1930s as a breaking of faith on the rajah's part. They became angry, refused to pay their taxes, and joined in rebellions against the rajah.

The pressure to tap more rubber to maintain given levels of income was exacerbated by the onerous exactions of the IRRA, which taxed and constrained smallholder production in the ways cited earlier. It was no coinci-

Table 5.1. The Growth of Smallholder Rubber Production in the
East Indies / Indonesia

YEAR	ANNUAL PRODUCTION*	PERCENTAGE INCREASE
1920	10,000 metric tons	
1930	90,496 metric tons	909 percent vs. 1920
1940	264,464 metric tons	292 percent vs. 1930
1987	795,200 metric tons	301 percent vs. 1940

These figures exclude Java, where the smallholder pattern of cultivation was quite different from that on the outer islands.

dence that the IRRA and the rubber dream occurred at the same time. Both addressed the same development: a competitive and threatening production environment. The estates were threatened by loss of market share to the smallholders; and the smallholders were threatened on the one hand by the punitive regulations that the estate lobby put in place against them and on the other hand by the attractions of rubber cultivation.

The association of the rubber dream with a particular stage in the political-economic evolution of tribal Bornean society is reflected in an indigenous assessment of the dream recorded four decades after the fact, from a Kantu' elder in West Kalimantan:[20] "This story of [the rice-eating rubber] dream was spread by those who opened the first rubber gardens at Sejiram [the name of a Catholic missionary settlement on the Kapuas River], so that they could develop their own gardens more rapidly than otherwise." The elder's comment is certainly accurate in implying that the Depression years were marked by intense competition in rubber production; but it is wide of the mark in identifying the Catholic Church as the culprit, for which there is no historical evidence. On the contrary, historians suggest that the various Christian missions generally encouraged the Ibanic peoples of western Borneo to plant rubber (Pringle 1970: 203). And indeed, the Kantu' themselves say that they obtained some of their first rubber seeds from this same Catholic mission at Sejiram. Iban across the border in Malaysian Sarawak attribute the story of the rubber dream to Malays, and impute similar motives to them, but here too there is no historical evidence to back up this charge.[21] It is at first glance surprising that neither the Iban nor the Kantu' blamed the colonial states for spreading the story of the rubber dream, given what the tribesmen recall about the role of the state in restricting smallholder rubber cultivation at that time.[22] The Kantu' still call the Depression years *jaman kupon* (the coupon era), referring to the coupons issued by the colonial government that dictated how much rubber smallholders could cultivate and market. This case demonstrates that any interpretation of tribal politics in terms of simple tribal-state opposition is too simplistic, and that for Dayak the "wider society" is not a monolithic whole but comprises diverse parties, some of whom are perceived to be more immediately threatening than others. This also reflects the fact that a Dayak group like the Kantu' is to some extent obliged to articulate its political situation in the local terms available to it (Scott 1984).[23] It does not mean that they do not grasp the political realities of their situation, only that their critiques are necessarily couched in the means available to them (Scott 1985). However inaccurate the Kantu' elder's critique was, the fact that he could make it at all reflects the extent to which a critical self-consciousness has arisen since the 1930s, one that recognizes the role of competition and misinformation in modern market dynamics. Although the Catholic Church may not have been trying to convince tribal smallholders not to become independent commodity producers, a host of other parties were trying to do exactly that.

Change and Continuity

Although these Dayak avoided the historic threat that rubber posed to their basic way of life in the 1930s, they did not avoid all rubber-related change. Rubber cultivation has contributed to greater socioeconomic differentiation;[24] it has played a key role in the development of individual household rights to land, involving the progressive shift of the balance of control from the longhouse to the household (Dove 1985b);[25] and, perhaps of greatest importance, it has reduced household interdependence. The traditional mechanism for coping with environmental constraints on swidden agriculture was the reciprocal exchange of labor among households; and the traditional mechanism for coping with uncertainty in agricultural yields was the interhousehold exchange of rice for labor. But rubber, the cultivation of which requires no reciprocal exchanges of labor or anything else (see chapter 7), became increasingly important as the twentieth century progressed as a means of covering harvest shortfalls; and the ability to rely on rubber has lessened the need to rely on others. These changes are reflected in the difference between the rubber dream and the Kantu' elder's critique of the dream: in the 1930s the Dayak were preoccupied with the contest between subsistence agriculture and commodity production; forty years later they were more concerned with the contest between smallholders and state elites. This reflects the political, economic, and cultural changes that the tribal societies of Borneo have undergone in the past three-quarters of a century.

Rubber cultivation underwent tremendous expansion in Borneo during the remainder of the twentieth century, in part because it was not a system of cultivation to which an exclusive commitment was made; it was not a system of rubber cultivation that "eats" the rice cultivation. That threat did not come to pass — at least not until near the end of the twentieth century in most of Borneo — and this is perhaps presaged in the dream. The dream has, after all, a happy ending: in it, the missing rice is found. And in real life, the rice base was safeguarded, as was also the case in most parts of the Indonesian archipelago during the surge of commodity production early in the twentieth century. Today, however, there are an increasing number of cases where this no longer holds. Potter and Badcock (2004: 346) report on a Minang village that cultivates only rubber and no rice; Peluso (2009) reports on similar conditions among the Salako Dayak of West Kalimantan; Cramb (1988, 2007) reports on Iban villages in Sarawak that grow only pepper; and Heersink (1994: 69) reports on a shift in eastern Indonesia from a dual economy of subsistence swidden agriculture and cultivation of coconuts for market to monocropping of coconuts, which she calls "a time-bomb for the local society in several respects."[26]

The Genesis of the Rubber Dream

There is a dichotomy in explanations of the rubber dream between those who attribute it to an external agency and those who attribute it to the internal dynamics of Dayak society.

Conspiracy Theory: The State against the People?

The rubber dream has drawn passing comment from a number of Bornean ethnographers, most of whom — focusing on the felling of rubber that followed the dream — conclude that the dream was not in the best interests of the smallholders. Sutlive (1978: 128–29), for example, says that the story of the rice-eating rubber and the subsequent responses to it reflect the conflict between the values of traditional rice farming and modern rubber tapping and the benefits of choosing the latter over the former. He writes, "Those men who refused to destroy their trees — to accede to tradition —

reaped large profits during rubber booms."[27] This is true, but it is only part of the picture. If the men whose behavior Sutlive endorses had completely rejected traditional values and rice cultivation, they would have profited greatly from the periodic rubber booms, but they would have been hard put to survive the inevitable busts without a subsistence base to fall back upon.

The ethnographers who take a negative view of the dream's impact on smallholders look for its origin in an external, malign agency. This interpretation is influenced by the obvious historical "irony" that at the same time that the colonial governments in Borneo were taking steps to restrict smallholder plantings, a story was circulating that panicked some smallholders—in a well-publicized minority of cases—to take steps to restrict plantings. Several observers note this coincidence in timing and outcome and suggest that the rubber dream may have been disseminated as part of a government "disinformation" campaign (Geddes 1954; Uchibori 1984). Even if this suggestion is true—and there is no evidence to suggest that it is—it is beside the point: the dream would not have achieved the currency that it did, regardless of its source, if it had not accurately reflected the feelings of the smallholders.

The interests of smallholders and government, respectively, in restricting smallholder rubber cultivation were the reverse of those imagined by these ethnographers. History has shown that the real threat to the estate sector was not total commitment to rubber by smallholders but partial commitment. The smallholders' ability to resist wider political and economic forces is based on their retention of a subsistence agricultural base. A healthy fear that rubber would eat the rice—a fear that commodity production would usurp subsistence production—far from supporting estate production, was the basis of the smallholder threat to this production. The threat to the estate sector lay in the fact that the Dayak would *not let* rubber eat their rice. Conversely, the threat to the smallholders lay not in any short-term loss of either rubber profits or rubber trees, which can be regrown in fewer than ten years, but in any weakening of the dual nature of the economy that protected them from market turbulence (to which the estate sector itself was vulnerable).

The failure to correctly interpret smallholder interests is based on a tendency to see the quandary of the rubber dream as the need to choose between rubber versus rice. It is true that the danger warned against in the dream is the abandonment of rice for rubber; but the ideal that it supports is not the abandonment of rubber for rice. The historical success of Dayak smallholders stems from embracing neither rubber nor rice alone, but both together. Anthropologists have sometimes been slow to see that monetary/

nonmonetary divisions are possible not only between but within societies (Bloch and Parry 1989: 7, 29; Shipton 1989).[28]

Different Transactional Orders: Society against the Individual

The rubber dream is the product of the threatened convergence of two distinct transactional orders (Bloch and Parry 1989: 23–24), which are as much indigenous as they are foreign. These are the subsistence-oriented system of rice cultivation and the market-oriented system of rubber cultivation. The rice system focuses more on the long-term reproduction of the social and cosmological order, while the rubber system focuses more on the short-term economic interests of the individual (ibid.: 23–24, 25, 26). The reciprocal exchange of labor and grain is central to the rice system but absent from the rubber system. The group-focused rice system addresses needs internal to the community, whereas the individual-focused rubber system addresses the need for articulation with external political-economic structures. The rice system is heavily ritualized; the rubber system is strictly secular, as reflected in the application of omen taking—an elaborate system that governs relations between the Dayak and the spirit world—to all of the stages of rice cultivation but none of the stages of rubber cultivation. This pattern of differentiation of the two transactional orders is not uncommon, with mining versus subsistence agriculture (Clark 1993; Nash 1994; Taussig 1980) and cattle versus market agriculture (Evans-Pritchard 1940; Ferguson 1990; Gudeman 1986) being two other examples.

The differences between the rice and rubber systems make the rubber dream possible in the first place. The central image of the dream, the consumption of rice by rubber, is a powerful statement of opposition. The dream did not just reflect this opposition, however; it enhanced it and thereby helped to counter the threatened convergence of the two sectors. By showing that rubber and rice are opposed, the dream showed that the two are fundamentally distinct. The dream symbolically dichotomized rice and rubber, probably for the first time in Bornean tribal history. The dream helped to further define two distinct indigenous sectors—one monetary and market-oriented, and the other nonmonetary and subsistence-oriented.[29] The dream was one episode, in short, in an ongoing, historical process of differentiation between the two transactional orders, rice and rubber.[30] Kopytoff (1986: 89) writes that it is this mediation between the forces of singularization, as in the ritualized rice sector of the Dayak, and commoditization, as in the market-oriented rubber sector, that explains "the striking viability, historically, of

parochial economic systems in the midst of worldwide networks of trade."
This was probably not the first time that subsistence and market sectors
were distinguished in this fashion in Borneo—given that the Dayak were
engaged in trade in native latexes and other forest products for centuries if
not millennia before they obtained Para rubber, but it may have been one of
the sharpest distinctions up to that point in their history. Another obvious
example, involving the Banjarese, was the seventeenth-century death-bed
injunction against cultivating pepper (see chapter 2).

The rubber dream helped to differentiate the two transactional orders by
portraying their threatened convergence. The threat of this convergence, of
the transformation of rice into rubber, is the central message of the dream.
The message is not that rubber is something to be feared by itself; rather,
the message is that rubber is something to be feared when it is eating rice.
It is significant that rubber does not destroy the rice in the dream but rather
"consumes" it. This consumption represents transformation by one of the
most universally understood means, alimentary processes (Bloch and Parry
1989: 25).[31] The dream, indeed, is about transformation.

Most transformations between the short-term transactional order of the
individual and the long-term transactional order of the community move
from the former to the latter (Bloch and Parry 1989: 25):[32] this directionality is usually culturally valorized. Transformations that move in the opposite direction are usually not and cause anxiety (ibid.: 27–28).[33] There is a
directional and moral hierarchy here. An example is the Kantu' belief that
the Catholic mission at Sejiram is inhabited by a *naga* (dragon), which is fed
human dead and excretes gold coins.[34] This type of image is widespread and
dates from the beginning of the modern money economy. Bloch and Parry
(ibid.: 18), citing Little's (1978) observation that at the end of the thirteenth
or beginning of the fourteenth century the pictorial theme of men and apes
defecating coins started to appear in the margins of scholarly manuscripts,
conclude that as the importance of the money economy grew, so too did "the
attention devoted to money, trade and avarice as a moral peril." The rubber
dream, with its transformation from the sacred rice system to the secular
rubber system, clearly falls into this category of moral peril as well. All transformations in this wrong direction are associated with excess consumption.
In the case of the Catholic dragon, the excess consumption is inferred from
the perceived material wealth of the Church's missions in the hinterlands of
Borneo; in the case of rubber, it is inferred from the wealth to be had during
rubber booms.

In most Bornean societies, excess wealth and conspicuous consumption was traditionally seen as a violation of indigenous norms governing redistribution or reciprocity; indeed, they were seen as being made possible only by such violation.[35] Rubber, as has been discussed, involves little if any reciprocity, either in inputs—there is no exchange of either land or labor in rubber cultivation—or outputs; unlike rice, rubber sheets are not given, loaned, or exchanged among households to cover economic shortfalls. The rubber dream, which shows the reciprocal rice order succumbing to the nonreciprocal rubber order, thus shows the threatened end of reciprocity. It shows the last exchange: like the "devil contract" made by sugar plantation workers in Colombia, it is "the exchange that ends all exchange" (Taussig 1980: 118).[36]

Historical Singularity: The Past against the Future

As with the dream in the 1930s, alarming stories—these days typically regarding head-hunting or human sacrifice—still today periodically sweep across the island. Drake (1989: 271) calls such phenomena "diving rumors," because they characteristically appear, disappear, then reappear, and so on (see also Barnes 1993). This does not characterize the rubber dream, however, which occurred only once and has not recurred since. This suggests that the rubber dream was a product not of recurring aspects of Bornean society but of a unique historical circumstance: namely, the increased involvement in commodity production represented by the cultivation of Para rubber, and the increased pressure against this involvement on the part of self-interested national and international political-economic structures.[37] External pressures against Dayak rubber production reached their peak during the International Rubber Regulation Agreement, which brought the attention of five nations to bear on the activities of all tribesmen living in the hinterlands of Southeast Asia who owned rubber trees. This may have been the most intense level of state attention that these interior populations had received up to that time (see Robequain [1946] 1955: 361). The dream was provoked by a true fork in the road in the history of these communities,[38] but not by the end of the road or "the end of history." The dream was not the "last gasp" of a dying way of life. There was no millenarian character to it: the tree felling aside, it lacked most of the other features associated with millenarian movements, such as a prophet.[39]

Interrogation of involvement in rubber cultivation through the medium of the rubber dream was a historically decisive act for institutional, not agricultural, reasons. A number of anthropologists, focusing overly much on the scattered fellings of rubber that followed the dream, have concluded that this felling had a "fatal" impact on the subsequent economic fortunes of the tribal populations involved (Freeman [1955] 1970: 286; Uchibori 1984: 231), but this overlooks the fact that rubber can be planted and brought to exploitation in fewer than ten years. The error here stems from focusing on the shorter-term effects of undercommitting to rubber, as opposed to the longer-term effects of overcommitting. A complete shift from an economy based on rice, or a mixture of rice and rubber, to one based on rubber alone— as happened among some smallholders in the Malay Peninsula and Suma- tra (Geertz [1963] 1971: 122–23; Pelzer 1945: 24–25)—might have proved difficult to reverse, as Cramb (2007) has said with regard to the abandon- ment of swidden cultivation by full-time pepper farmers in Sarawak. Thus, Kathirithamby-Wells (2011) argues that there was a historical possibility of developing smallholder rubber cultivation in Malaysia in an environmentally sound fashion, which was not seized and thus was forever "lost."[40]

Denaturalizing Western Beliefs

For some time anthropologists have been trying to shift the ana- lytical emphasis from developing external critiques of other societies to un- earthing or "retrieving" these societies' own self-critiques. As Marcus and Fischer (1986: 132, 133) write, "[I]t is no longer the critique of the detached intellectual: rather it is the critique by the subject unearthed through ethno- graphic engagement. . . . The cultural critic becomes in effect a reader of cultural criticisms, discovered ethnographically rather than an independent intellectual originator of critical insight." The rubber dream represents an indigenous critique of involvement in commodity production, the "read- ing" of which has been the subject of this chapter.[41] This reading shows how one of the exotic plants and systems of cultivation introduced by Euro- peans was absorbed into, and critiqued within, Dayak mythic structures.[42] I have not limited myself to the indigenous critique, however. As Taussig (1980: 10) writes, "It would be a mistake to emphasize the exotic quality of the reactions of these peasants if, by virtue of such an emphasis, we overlook the similar beliefs and ethical condemnations that characterized much eco- nomic thought in the history of Western culture." This is all the more im- portant, given that Western economic thought tends to present itself as not just another moral order, but as a nonmoral and therefore privileged order (Ferguson 2006: 80). The aim of this chapter, accordingly, has been both to naturalize the native beliefs represented by the rubber dream and to denaturalize and critique the beliefs regarding smallholder cultivation represented in the IRRA. Each was a product of confrontation with the other, during a time when a global economic crisis was heightening their diverging self-interests. As Hobsbawm (1994: 213) writes, the Depression changed the apparent remoteness of the world economy: "For the first time the interests of dependent and metropolitan economies clashed visibly." The Dayak dream of rice-eating rubber was a product of confrontation with capitalist reality, and the IRRA myth of diseased and degraded smallholdings was a product of confrontation with smallholder reality (compare to Fabian 1983).

Central to the ideology of the IRRA was the belief that the smallholder rubber stands were diseased and posed a threat to the plantations. The truth of the matter is that the ecology of smallholder cultivation, with its more densely planted and partially overgrown stands, minimized disease, while the ecology of estate cultivation, with its sparsely planted and clean-weeded stands, exacerbated it. This difference in the ecology of rubber cultivation was associated with a difference in its economy: namely, the intermittent nature of tapping and integration into the swidden cycle in the smallholdings, versus the unremitting exploitation and heavy capitalization in the estates. It was this difference in economics that posed the real threat to the estates. Smallholder disease did not threaten the estates, but smallholder economics did. The perception on the estates of a threat from disease on smallholdings was incorrect, and perversely so, since it reversed the facts of the matter; but the perception of some type of threat was not incorrect. Therefore, it may be most useful to see the perception of smallholder disease as symbolic of estate perception of a threat on the smallholdings that was beyond their understanding. Thus, this perception of diseased smallholdings was, in effect, a perception of smallholdings that attack estates. We might, indeed, say that it was a perception of "estate-eating smallholdings."

The history of competition between estates and smallholdings suggests that the plantation establishment was quite right to see the smallholdings as threatening, attacking, or "eating" the estates. The smallholdings did, over time, in fact "eat" most of the estate's market share, accounting today for more than 80 percent of production in Indonesia (Government of Indonesia 2004: 1, table 1). This official myth of the diseased and threatening smallholdings was thus quite as structurally correct as the smallholder myth of the rice-eating rubber. Both were equally correct—and equally partisan—expressions of real economic tensions. Both can be seen as cultural statements, or warnings, about matters of import. Their sources of authority are very different, however. Whereas the Dayak were invoking the authority of their spirits, regarding the offense to the rice spirits, the IRRA was invoking the authority of capitalist ideology and the efficiency of production. As a result, the tribal myth has been represented *as* a myth, whereas the official myth has been represented as economic policy, which is a difference with vast implications for the structure of power.

myth as myth for tribe
myth as policy for state
POWER DIFFERENTIALS
to expose this is dangerous.

PART IV

The Indigenous Resolution of the Subsistence/Market Tension

In this section of the book, I move forward in time to the latter half of the twentieth century, again focusing on smallholder rubber cultivation. By this time, the events attending the transfer of *Hevea* from South America to Southeast Asia had become history, the major initial adaptations of Para rubber to the new social and biological environment had been made, and mature, well-functioning smallholder systems of production were in evidence. The aim of this section is to examine more closely the details of these systems, in particular their dualistic nature. The aim is to ask how the dual household economy works. What are its benefits and how are they reaped? What are its costs and how are they borne? In particular, how do the differences and even oppositions between the two sectors of the household economy complement as opposed to undermine one another? And finally, how does the articulation of this local household economy to the wider global economy help us to better understand both?

Chapter 6 examines the ecological, economic, and social dimensions of the combination of cash-crop and subsistence-food-crop production, focusing on rubber and swidden rice and taking the Kantu' as a case study. The dual economy does not simply consist of two proximate but separate production systems. It is the fit between them that makes the dual economy work. Rubber complements swidden cultivation in some obvious, temporal ways: it is easily fitted into the calendars of work versus idle time, hunger versus abundance, ritual versus secular observance, rain versus dry, and the inter-annual movement around a swidden territory. Less obvious is the fact that systems of swidden agriculture create surpluses of labor and land in a way that is perhaps unique among systems of agriculture; and rubber, which itself is unique among cash crops in its flexibility in being exploited or left idle, is ideally suited to make productive use of these surpluses. As a result, rubber helps swidden cultivators overcome fundamental techno-environmental factors that constrain production, producing a beneficial positive feedback cycle between rubber and swiddens. This complementarity between the two production systems is built upon both similarities and differences. The most important similarity is the partial and episodic character of resource use in both rubber and swidden production. At any given time, most land in the swidden cycle is idled after a brief period of cropping in order to restore its biomass and fertility. In the case of rubber, trees are ideally rested after periods of tapping in order to restore the volume of latex production or, in the case of longer periods, to restore the bark. The differences between rubber and swiddens are equally important: there are a variety of ways in which strength in one complements weakness in the other. The secular character of rubber production offers some respite from the restrictions attendant upon the heavily ritualized swidden cycle. Of great importance, rubber complements swiddens by enabling smallholders to make much more authoritative proprietary claims to land than they can make based on their swidden cultivation alone. Rubber and swiddens complement but are not alternative to one another. Through most of the twentieth century, at least, Bornean smallholders could not dispense with one by doing more of the other; and, indeed, each was made more productive by the presence of the other.

Chapter 7 focuses on the Kantu' belief that when they plant rubber in their swiddens or swidden fallows, the land thenceforth becomes *tanah mati* (dead land), in contrast to the remaining "living land" contained in the swidden agricultural cycle. Rubber is seen as killing the land because it is not part of the traditional exchange system involving both society and environment. This exchange system is based on three principles: resource bounty bears a cost, bounty should be distributed not held, and the creation and destruction of resource wealth are linked. Rubber is exempt from all three principles: its bounty does not carry a cost, its bounty is accumulated instead of being distributed, and it is not part of a cycle of creation and destruction. Rubber is not part of the systems of either social or ecological exchanges. The fact that rubber is different, the fact that it does not fit into the local resource cosmology, is central to its role in the tribal economy. Most analysts have misunderstood this question of fit. The key to the success of the cash-crop half of the dual economy is not to mimic the subsistence production sector but to differ from it in critical ways. These differences help to preserve the subsistence sector in its own right. Like the belief in the rice-eating rubber, thus, the belief in the land-killing rubber helps to establish the subsistence/market distinction. Rubber's lack of fit with the local subsistence system is also a prerequisite to its fit with the extra-local market system. What fits in the wider world will not fit, by definition, locally. The fact that smallholder rubber thrives at the extra-local level is related to the fact that it "kills" at the local level. Rubber's lack of local fit also inhibits access to the local subsistence sector for extraction-minded outsiders. This analysis reveals some of the challenges of discussing sustainable natural-resource management cross-culturally.

CHAPTER 6

The Dual Economy of Cultivating Rubber and Rice

Agi' bisi' padi. (There is still rice.)
— *Kantu' explanation for why a household is not tapping rubber*

Introduction

A number of studies have noted the historic association of small-holder rubber cultivation with swidden cultivation of food crops (Chin 1982; Colfer, Gill, and Agus 1988; Cramb 1988, 1993; Dove 1983; Padoch 1980; Pelzer 1978b; and Thomas 1965). Valuable data on rubber cultivation by swidden agriculturalists also is presented in broader analyses of tribal agriculture and economics (Chin 1985; Drake 1982; Freeman [1955] 1970; Geddes 1954; and Hudson 1967). Beyond noting the association between smallholder and swidden cultivation, however, with the exception of some studies of swidden-based agro-forestry (for example, de Jong 1997), there has been little in-depth analysis of the relationship between the two systems and, thus, little understanding of why this combination historically proved to be so successful. This failure is notable, given the great deal of research that has been done on swidden communities in Southeast Asia. Scholars have largely defined and studied these communities in terms of their swidden activities alone, overlooking the fact that a determining characteristic of these communities is the combination of subsistence-oriented swidden agriculture with export-oriented cash-crop cultivation. One ill consequence of this failure is that it has supported the formulation of policy for cash-crop production and swidden cultivation in isolation from one another (Cramb 1993: 213–14).

The Kantu', for whom communication was historically easier across the border to Sarawak than to the distant Kalimantan coast, obtained their first rubber seedlings from Iban tribesmen in the Saribas River drainage

Table 6.1. Rubber Production at the Kantu' Longhouse Tikul Batu

PER DAY:			PER YEAR:	
Per person:	Per 100 trees:	Per garden:	Per hectare:	Per household:
1.0–1.5 kg	1.5–3.5 kg	2.0–7.0 kg	150–350 kg	150–350 kg

All figures are given in kilograms of dried sheet rubber (viz., rubber that has been run through a cast-iron rubber mangle to remove water).

of Sarawak, as well as from the Catholic mission at Sejiram on the Kapuas River, in the late 1920s. Drake (1982: 169–70) reports that the Mualang, of the Belitang River system to the west of the Kantu' territory, started planting rubber trees in the early 1930s. A majority of Kantu' households had planted some rubber by World War II, although households with mature rubber were still in the minority. During the second half of the twentieth century, however, rubber became their primary source of cash or tradable commodities, used to obtain the basic trade goods of salt, tobacco, clothing, and kerosene (see also Hudson 1967: 305). At the time of my initial fieldwork among the Kantu', the fourteen households in the longhouse of Tikul Batu owned a total of sixty-six separate rubber *kebun* (gardens) (figure 6.1), for an average of almost five gardens per household. The gardens averaged a little less than a hectare in size and contained two hundred to four hundred trees, for a total of over four hectares and one thousand to two thousand trees per household. At that time, 61 percent of the gardens contained mature trees. Production characteristics are given in table 6.1.[1]

Rubber and Swidden Agriculture

The rubber gardens of Borneo's swidden agriculturalists have been called "managed swidden fallows" (Cramb 1988: 112; Padoch 1988a: 23). Smallholder rubber is not simply cultivated by people who also happen to be swidden agriculturalists, it is integrated into the swidden cultivation cycle (Barlow and Jayasuriya 1984: 87; Barlow and Muharminto 1982: 90). Most observers have characterized this integration as an easy one (Muzzall 1925, cited in Booth 1988: 205; Cramb 1988: 112). Rubber is in many respects a challenging crop, however, as attested to by Tomich (1991: 256):

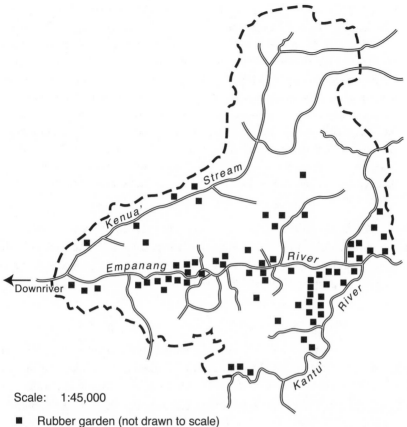

Scale: 1:45,000

■ Rubber garden (not drawn to scale)

– – Border of Tikul Batu's territory

Figure 6.1. The rubber gardens of the Kantu' longhouse Tikul Batu.
This figure includes some rubber gardens that lie within the territory of
Tikul Batu but belong to other longhouses, and it does not include a number
of gardens that belong to Tikul Batu households but lie within the territories
of other longhouses.

Indeed, if there were ever a commodity in which significant market failures were likely to occur, it is smallholder rubber. The gestation period of six to ten years is among the longest for commercial tree crops and the productive life can extend to thirty years. This compounds the effects of risk and uncertainty on planting decisions, which are perfectly rational worries for a smallholder household attempting to meet its needs from a meager income. Furthermore, rubber smallholders must make investment decisions in an environment that includes high investment costs relative to cash income; capital market imperfections; limited access to information about markets and technology; output price variation around a declining trend; breakdown of traditional land tenure practices in the absence of formal tenure institutions; and uncertainty about future rubber export policies.

Given all of these challenges, the success of the smallholder system of cultivation—which indeed is able to make virtues of some of these vices—is all the more notable. It is based on the use of land and labor resources that are in surplus within the swidden system.[2]

Rubber and Swidden Labor

An important characteristic of swidden agriculture is the seasonal nature of its labor demands.[3] Labor is in great demand during some stages of the swidden cycle, in less demand in other stages, and not in demand at all during the time between stages. In the Kantu' case, the greatest demands for labor occur during planting, weeding, and harvesting (Dove 1984: 111; see also Drake 1982: 141) (figure 6.2). These three stages together account for approximately four months of work. During the remaining eight months of the year, swidden labor is in surplus, since if swidden cultivators have sufficient labor to meet the demand during the three intensive stages, they will by definition have more than sufficient labor to meet demands during the remaining less-intensive stages. The number of potential surplus calendar days per year varies by swidden type, ranging from 163 days for swiddens made in secondary forest to 211 days for swiddens made in primary forest (Dove 1984: 111). Since labor and not land is the primary factor of production in swidden societies, the productive use of this surplus labor is a major economic challenge. Further complicating this picture is the fact that the labor surplus varies from year to year as the household moves through its domestic cycle (Dove 1984).[4] The most active participants in rubber tapping are schoolchildren needing tuition money, mothers whose mobility is limited by

Figure 6.2. Kantu' woman harvesting dry rice in a swidden

infant children, and elderly men and women who are less fit for the more-strenuous work in the swiddens.

Rubber cultivation is well suited to making use of this idled swidden labor because it is uniquely adapted to intermittent exploitation. Periodic idling of rubber trees actually benefits them and results in higher peak latex flows when tapping is resumed. Barlow (1978: 146) suggested that tapping should ideally be limited to no more than 15–19 days per month to achieve maximum latex flows. The only cost entailed in intermittent exploitation, and then only after relatively long periods of idling, is a reduced flow of latex during the first few days after resuming tapping (Chin 1982: 32; Colfer, Gill, and Agus 1988: 203). The Kantu' say that the flow of latex reattains its maximum on just the third day after tapping is resumed. This gives the Kantu' great flexibility to start and stop tapping as labor is freed from or required in their swiddens (figure 6.3).[5] As Geddes (1954: 98) observed in Sarawak, one of rubber's advantages as a cash crop is that "it is not a crop which needs constant attention, so that an owner may go about any other urgent business while still keeping an account at the rubber bank to be drawn upon whenever he finds time to do so."

Figure 6.3. Kantu' man
tapping rubber

The integration of the rubber and swidden cycles is facilitated by a variety of cultural factors. For example, when work is halted in the swiddens due to ritual proscriptions—following ritual sacrifices, curing ceremonies, or ill omens—tapping usually is permitted in the rubber groves (see also Freeman 1960: 87n).[6] What Kato (1991: 151) said of Malays historically is true for the Dayak today: rubber gardens are considered to be "ritually neutral zones." The number of days of swidden work proscribed by ritual is considerable. In one twelve-month period, I calculated that just two sources of ritual proscriptions—the phases of the moon and curing ceremonies— accounted for a total of 51 proscribed days on which no one in the longhouse could work in the swiddens (Dove 1985c: 28–29). Another cultural attraction of rubber production is that it is much less governed by the social norms of equity and exchange that govern swidden rice production, thereby affording rubber tappers much more freedom to attend to meeting their own economic needs. On the other hand, the lack of ritual and group labor also makes rub-

rituals associated w/ labor time consuming but give purpose would prepose

ber relatively less enjoyable work (Kato 1991: 153), which makes its leavening with intermittent periods of swidden labor attractive.

Rubber trees cannot be tapped during or immediately following a rain. Rain in the morning or even on the previous evening can fill the latex collection cups, bring about premature coagulation of the latex, and also, according to the Kantu', overstimulate the flow of latex to the point of harming the tree. When tapping of rubber is not possible because of rain, however, work can still be done in the swiddens. This is an important advantage in Kalimantan, where at one interior site in West Kalimantan I recorded an average of 16.2 days per month on which more than 1 millimeter of rain fell, and a total annual rainfall of 4,290 millimeters (Dove 1985c: 43). In Peninsular Malaysia, which is considerably drier than Kalimantan, Barlow (1978: 137) estimated that rain interferes with tapping on 30–40 days per year.

If labor is needed in both the swidden and the rubber garden on a given day, the household workforce can be divided—as noted in the epigraph to chapter 1—or the day can be divided in two. Rubber is tapped by preference early in the morning, when, because of lower air temperature, higher humidity, and correspondingly lower evapo-transpiration, the hydrostatic pressure in the latex vessels and the speed of the latex flow are greatest (Dijkman 1961: 72; Purseglove 1968: 162). The Kantu' say that a rubber garden that yields six kilograms of latex when tapping begins at dawn, will yield just four kilograms if tapping is not begun until late morning or midday.[7] Households with severe rice shortages, which need to tap rubber at the same time as they are working in their swiddens, may thus tap in the morning and work in their swiddens in the afternoon. While this schedule is possible, it is onerous (Drake 1982: 299). The need for labor on the same day in both rubber grove and swidden is, in any case, the exception rather than the rule.

The Kantu' are able to time most of their tapping during those months of the year when there is little or no work in the swiddens, as illustrated in figure 6.4 (compare Geddes 1954: 95, 98). As Hudson (1967: 308) similarly writes of the Ma'anyan in southern Kalimantan: "Tapping operations are begun or terminated as the rhythm of the *dangau* [household] family's activities may dictate." The Kantu' especially try to avoid tapping during the three most-intensive swidden stages: planting, weeding, and harvesting. I calculated that the average Kantu' household did just 4 percent of its yearly tapping during these three stages, while doing the other 96 percent during the remaining eight months of the year. This inverse association of rubber

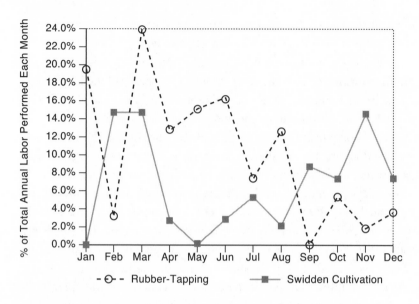

Figure 6.4. Calendar of Kantu' rubber tapping and swidden cultivation

tapping and intensive swidden labor is statistically significant (table 6.2). The tapping calendar is determined not only by when the Kantu' can tap but also when they need to tap. The most intensive tapping occurs during January, the time of year closest to the next rice harvest and farthest from the last one. This is the traditional *musim rapar* (famine season) of the Kantu', when the proceeds of rubber tapping are most likely to be needed for the purchase of rice for daily subsistence.

The use of surplus swidden labor in rubber cultivation is facilitated by a special characteristic of this labor: it is exceptionally productive, which is ultimately based on an energy subsidy from the tropical forest. The swidden system, by means of brush-sword, adze, and fire, releases and then exploits the energy stored up by the tropical forest (Hecht, Anderson, and May 1988; McGrath 1987; Rambo 1980). This energy subsidy contributes to the highest returns on labor in any known system of tropical food-crop agriculture. I calculated that the returns on labor in Kantu' swidden agriculture averaged 7.9 kilograms of unmilled rice per person per day, which compares with just 4.2 kilograms in the irrigated rice fields of Java, which are famous for their purported productivity (Dove 1985a: 4–8). This labor productivity permits the swidden system to guarantee basic household subsistence during most years using only a portion of the available labor. It permits the household to

Table 6.2. Timing of Intensive Swidden Labor and Rubber Tapping

		DAYS OF INTENSIVE SWIDDEN STAGES:	
		NO	YES
Days on which rubber	No	79.5 days	120.5 days
tapping is carried out:	Yes	158.0 days	7.0 days

n = 365 days in the year; chi squared, $X^2 = 124.6$; level of uncertainty, $P < .001$

devote surplus labor to rubber cultivation and to accept low returns on this labor during periods of low rubber prices, or to cease tapping entirely, while still preserving the rubber gardens for future use.

Rubber and Swidden Land

Swidden labor requirements are not only staggered unevenly across the annual calendar, they also are unevenly spread out across the spatial landscape. Households need to apply their swidden labor resources in widely dispersed locations, which change from one year to the next. At the time of this study, each Kantu' household owned approximately two dozen plots of land, two or three of which were cultivated in any given year, while the remainder recuperated under a fallow forest cover. The dynamics of land use and inheritance ensure that each household's two dozen plots are scattered all over the ten-square-kilometer longhouse territory. The distances and travel times that result from this scattering are so great that during at least one-half of each year, most households do not live in the central longhouse but rather in farmhouses built in or near that year's swiddens. It would be difficult during this seasonal dispersal for the Kantu' to tap rubber in any central location.

The Kantu' avoid this difficulty by dispersing their rubber gardens—each household owned an average of five at the time of this study—around the longhouse territory (see figure 6.1) and exploiting them in a rotation that matches that of the swiddens. Selection of which garden to tap in a given year is determined by proximity to that year's swiddens. As the Kantu' say: "Asa nadai bumai din, kami nadai motong din" (If we do not make a swidden there, we do not tap rubber there) (compare Hudson 1967: 308). Freeman

([1955] 1970: 163n) maintained that the Iban of the Baleh River system in Sarawak followed a different system, planting their rubber close to the longhouse and exploiting it by dividing the household labor force between the longhouse and the rubber gardens on the one hand and on the other hand the distant swiddens. Among the Kantu', this determinate role of the swiddens vis-à-vis the rubber gardens may be reversed under conditions of economic duress. If a household reaps an exceptionally poor swidden harvest, it may base its decision on which plot of forest to open for the next year's swidden on proximity to its most-productive rubber garden, to assure itself of a source of income to buy rice until the next harvest. The nonexploitation of gardens not located near any swidden in a given year is beneficial: the Kantu' maintain that long-term idling of a garden gives tapping scars a chance to heal and ultimately enhances the garden's longevity and productivity. This is in line with Barlow's (1978: 137) estimate that it takes the bark of a rubber tree six to nine years to completely renew itself after a period of tapping. This is another reason given by the Kantu' for having multiple rubber gardens, most of which are idled in any given year.

The periodic, long-term idling of rubber gardens is possible because of the absence of important alternative uses for the land, the absence of significant opportunity costs. Much of the land that was traditionally planted by the Kantu' and other Bornean smallholders in rubber had little or no value within the swidden system (Geddes 1954: 99; Cramb 2007; Dijkman 1961: 253). Rubber is planted by preference along the banks of major streams and rivers (see figure 6.1) because access to water is essential for processing and transporting the rubber (Barlow 1978: 165) (figures 6.5, 6.6). The threat of periodic flooding makes this location highly problematic for swiddens (Dove 1985c: 44–46) but less so for rubber, which can tolerate temporary inundation by flowing water (Ghani, Huat, and Wessel 1986: 155). Geddes (1954: 97) reported a case in the 1930s when some Dayak in Sarawak tried to evade a government proscription on planting rubber on rice land by planting it on land prone to riverine flooding, meaning land that would not normally be thought of as potential rice land. Still, the Kantu' believe that rubber is generally healthier above the floodplain than in it, due to the greater prevalence of *sampok* (termites [*Coptotermes* sp.]) — which can do great damage to rubber trees — in the floodplain.

A second location that is problematic for swiddens but not rubber gardens is *kerangas* (heath forest). The low level of nutrients and absorption capacity of the soils in this forest type is inimical to the cultivation of swidden

Figure 6.5. Kantu' stirring coagulant into the raw latex

Figure 6.6. Kantu' washing rubber slabs in the river

rice (Brunig 1974: 138–39) but not, the Kantu' say, rubber, so long as no standing water is present. On the other hand, rubber does not grow well in some of the locations that are most productive for swidden crops, notably the marshy areas where the Kantu' practice their highly productive swamp-rice cultivation (Dove 1985c) but where the constant moisture stress is too much for rubber.

Finally, even when rubber is planted on land that also could be used for swiddens, the overall impact on swidden cultivation usually is limited by the minimal amounts of land involved (Geddes 1954: 98–99). At the time of this study, just 8.5 percent (4.4 hectares) of the average Kantu' household's landholdings of 52 hectares was planted in rubber, 8.8 percent (4.6 hectares) was under active swidden cultivation, and 82.7 percent (43 hectares) was under swidden fallow. Hudson (1967: 310–11) similarly calculates that even if the planting rates that obtained at the time of his study among the Ma'an-yan were maintained for fifty years, rubber would cover only 2.5–4.4 per-cent of their territory, concluding "Therefore . . . fears that rubber trees will soon usurp all productive swidden land seem unfounded." These appear to be typical figures for smallholder rubber acreage, as reflected in Angelsen's (1995: 1722) calculation, for a smallholder village in Riau Province of Suma-tra, that rubber covered just 4.3 percent of its territory.

There is one last consideration in the allocation of land to rubber that may surpass all others in importance: establishment of tenure (see chap-ter 3). Under the *adat* (customary law) of the Kantu' and many other of Indo-nesia's ethnic minorities, rubber-planting establishes greater rights to land than does clearing the forest for a swidden (Barlow and Muharminto 1982: 92–93; Cramb 1988: 122–23; Drake 1982: 102). One of the reasons, and some-times the sole reason, that the Kantu' plant rubber is to take advantage of this fact, to strengthen their claim to a particular piece of land, especially when this claim is being contested (compare Angelsen 1995: 1724–25; Gouyon, de Foresta, and Levang 1993: 192–93). This tactic is used in contests over land not only with fellow tribesmen but also with the government. Under colo-nial as well as post-colonial regimes, land without evidence of cultivation has routinely been claimed as state property. Successive Indonesian gov-ernments have consistently, all evidence to the contrary, perceived fallowed swidden land as lacking such evidence. In contrast, rubber and other peren-nial commodities—especially if planted, and most especially if nonnative in origin—are more likely to be acknowledged as evidence of cultivation. This fact has not been lost on Indonesia's swidden cultivators, many of whom in recent years have planted rubber or other tree crops in swidden fallows in large part to forestall appropriation by the government as "uncultivated land."

Rubber and the Household Economy

The intensity of rubber production among smallholders like the Kantu' is relatively low, which is explained by the role that it plays in the dual household economy.

Intensity of Cultivation and the Household Economy

Rubber's role in a smallholder economy like that of the Kantu' was traditionally to provide whatever subsistence agriculture does not provide (Ward and Ward 1974: 38). Resources available for use in the market-oriented sector of the household economy are not necessarily available for use in the subsistence-oriented sector, and the reverse also is true. Thus, rubber was never viewed as an "alternative" to swidden rice; the latter could not be dropped by doing more of the former—although the reverse was not impossible. There is a definite asymmetry in this regard, which reflects a traditionally strong cultural emphasis among many smallholders on the subsistence sector. Even during rubber booms, when returns on rubber might rise to ten times that of rice, rice cultivation remained the first priority—at least through most of the twentieth century (Cramb 1988: 115; Cramb 2007; Freeman [1955] 1970: 269–70). There is evidence, however, as noted in chapter 5, that this incommensurability between rubber and rice has started to break down in some parts of Borneo in recent years.[8]

Smallholders often differentiate between motives for tapping rubber "in season" versus "out of season." The tapping season is commonly defined as either the slack period in the swidden cycle or as the famine period just before the harvest—and in fact the two periods often coincide. Indeed, the Kantu' told me that they only tap rubber when they are *lapar* (hungry). When the rubber is tapped "out of season," it is usually to fill some discrete need for cash or market goods (compare Geddes 1954: 95; Hudson 1967: 307).

Rubber most often is tapped to obtain either cash or rice. In the first instance, the goal is to obtain basic trade goods and pay children's school fees and expenses (see Best 1988: 78; Chin 1982: 33; King 1988: 237). Among smallholders like the Kantu', dwelling in the interior of Indonesia's outer islands, other opportunities to obtain currency or tradable commodities were traditionally somewhat limited. Local wage-labor opportunities are restricted by the agricultural calendar and by the availability of households with sufficient surplus rice to pay wages. The advantage of owning a rubber garden is that a household can, in effect, pay itself a wage whenever desired. As Geddes (1954: 95) writes, "The rubber gardens are in the nature of a bank to be drawn upon when money is needed."[9] Tapping rubber to obtain rice is of course a function of harvest failure (Freeman [1955] 1970: 267, 271; see also Drake 1982: 145, 293, 298; Ward and Ward 1974: 38). A great deal of rubber is used to purchase *beras ili'* (downriver rice) from traders to cover swidden harvest shortfalls (Freeman [1955] 1970: 271; Geddes 1954: 95; Hudson 1967: 307; Thomas 1965: 102). The prominence of this use is reflected in the common Kantu' statement "Agi' bisi' padi" (There is still rice), the epigraph for this chapter, to explain why a household is *not* tapping rubber.

The episodic character of the need for cash or rice explains one of the most distinctive features of rubber cultivation among the Kantu' and other smallholders: its low level of intensity. The production figures given in table 6.1 are far below the potential output of the Kantu' rubber groves. Not all mature gardens are tapped—in an average year only 60 percent of mature gardens are tapped—and those that are tapped are tapped irregularly. If all mature gardens were tapped, average production per household per year would rise by two-thirds; and if all mature gardens were tapped at a uniform intensity of 160 days per year, production would rise an additional 57 percent—for a total increase of 162 percent.[10]

Intensity of Cultivation and Market Conditions

The intensity of tapping is affected not only by household variables but also by market variables. Market demand, and thus price, is not a constant, and the way that market and household dynamics interact is of key interest. Market conditions for rubber are characteristically volatile, with rubber prices historically following a forty-eight-month trading cycle (Ghani, Huat, and Wessel 1986: 153). When market prices drop, smallholders have historically demonstrated considerable freedom of response (Cramb 1993: 217; Geertz [1963] 1971: 122). They may continue to tap at the same rate, and live with less income; they may increase tapping in inverse proportion to the fall of market prices, along an inverse production curve; or they may let their rubber stand untapped and benefiting from the respite, until the next upswing in the international market (Robequain [1946] 1955: 355, 362). Some analysts, such as Drake (1982: 144) and Thomas (1965: 103), report a direct relationship between production and price level, meaning the higher the price, the more the tapping. Geddes also says that there is a direct relationship but maintains that, due to the nature of rubber cultivation, increases in prices do not prompt "commensurate" increases in tapping. He writes (1954: 96), "Since the money is generally sought for specific ends, the amount of rubber tapping tends to be governed more by the nature of these particular cash demands than by the value of rubber itself." This sort of logic often produces not a direct but an inverse relationship between price and production, which Booth (1988: 210–11) sees as a general characteristic of the smallholder sector in Indonesia. This means that during a time of declining market prices, when estate production is decreasing—following a direct curve—smallholders tap more; and during a time of rising market prices, when estate production is increasing, smallholders tap less.

One of the most prominent early descriptions of this inverse production curve came from the colonial Dutch economist Boeke (1953: 40), mentioned in chapter 5: "Anyone expecting western reactions will meet with frequent surprises. . . . When rubber prices fall the owner of a grove may decide to tap more intensively, where high prices may mean that he leaves a larger or smaller portion of his tappable trees untapped." The period when Boeke among others first observed such behavior, on a scale sufficient to draw attention, was during the Depression years of the 1930s. As discussed in chapter 5, this was a time of challenge to estates and smallholders alike. Falling prices led to falling production in the estate sector, as expected; but what was not expected was the increase in production that occurred in the smallholder sector during the same period, in spite of not only lower prices but higher export taxes (Boeke 1953: 125–26; Geertz [1963] 1971: 122; Lindblad 1988: 71, 117). Writing at the time, and with specific reference to the IRRA, the Dutch economists de Wilde, Neytzell, and Moll (1936: 28–29) described this response as follows: "With regard to native rubber remarkable reactions have been witnessed. These reactions vary in different regions. Wherever the population has other sources of income besides rubber, the system [the IRRA] works to satisfaction and a rise in duty will cause a drop in production. In areas, however, where rubber is the principal means of livelihood, a rise in the duty, dictated by an excess over the export quota, will, at a given price level, cause a drop of the amount in money which the individual cultivator receives for his output and will, therefore, induce him to produce a bigger quantity of rubber in order to restore some sort of equilibrium in his earnings. The effect is that, in such a region, the system leads to the opposite effect." Penot (2007: 594) suggests that the inverse production curve is now less common in Indonesia, however, and that "Farmers are now acutely sensitive to price signals."

The inverse production curve drew the attention of colonial observers in part because it was so alien to the estate mode of production. Estate production of rubber is "inelastic" with regard to market demand, because of the long lag time (namely, at least seven to eight years) between the planting of rubber trees and their readiness for tapping. This lag time is much less relevant in the case of smallholders, however. Since smallholders like the Kantu' typically have almost as many trees out of production as in production at any given time, and since they typically tap at only two-thirds the normal frequency, increasing production in response to changing prices is usually a simple matter of tapping more trees more often.

Kahn (1982: 11) attributes the inverse production curve to labor immobility: "Specifically, increased production in the face of falling prices is likely to take place only when labor is relatively immobile. When labor mobility exists, falling prices can be expected to produce a drop in both enterprise and aggregate production as peasants switch to branches of production in which the 'return to labor' is more favorable." However, Kahn's explanation applies only to smallholders who depend largely on a given commodity production for their livelihood, who would completely abandon it for some other economic endeavor if their labor was mobile, and who would have no choice but to intensify production if their labor was immobile. Mobility of labor does not explain as well the behavior of smallholders with dual economies whose allocation of labor between the two sectors is not based solely on market considerations. The Kantu' participation in swidden cultivation historically met subsistence needs and freed land and labor for use in rubber cultivation, which permitted them to produce not as much rubber as possible, nor as much as the market or state demanded, but rather as much rubber as they needed or wanted themselves.

This dual economy, this combination of market-oriented rubber production and subsistence-oriented swidden production, has enabled smallholders like the Kantu' to participate actively in the global market economy while avoiding many of its risks.[11] As Hudson (1967: 311) writes from southeastern Borneo, "Most villagers feel that the rubber market is a chancy thing. World demand varies and prices fluctuate. No one of them wants to be totally dependent on factors over which they have no control." This is a sensible view. As Booth (1988: 231) writes, "Faced with uncertain world markets, and discriminatory treatment from government, the most obvious 'survival strategy' for smallholders has been to diversify their holdings so that they are not dependent on any one crop." Indeed, Sulistyawati (2011) believes that it is the fact that swidden cultivation relieves them from complete dependence on volatile commodity markets that guarantees swidden's future among the Kantu'.

The dual economy thus partly removes the household from a direct dependence on the market, which is crucial to what Gudeman and Rivera (1990: 52) call the household's "project of survival": "The house is not susceptible to economic cycles, for it represents a distancing from the economic intentions of others." This distancing, this independence, this contrary behavior is of interest to economists and policy makers because, although it seems to be good for smallholders, it is thought to be less good for the wider economic system. The Dutch economic historian de Vries (1976) presents the orthodox position when he argues that the transition to a demand-driven capitalist economy is dependent in part on the eradication of consumption-driven production, the disposition to work no more than required, the backward-sloping supply curve of labor.

Overall Impact on the Household Economy

Exploitation of rubber at a low and variable level of intensity, with considerable independence from the state of the markets, has an overall, beneficial influence on the household economy: households with rubber tend to be better off than those without. This is true not just because of the added benefits of rubber but because even swidden cultivation itself is more productive when pursued in rubber-owning households. Figure 6.7 shows that the more rubber gardens a household owns, the greater the likelihood that its swiddens—alone, without drawing on the production of the rubber groves—will fulfill its subsistence requirements for rice. Geddes (1954: 96) also found this to be true in Sarawak in the 1950s: villages and households with rubber tended to be better off in rice than those without rubber. The basis for this association is easily understood. When rubber-owning households experience swidden harvest failures, they can tide themselves over to the next swidden cycle by tapping rubber whenever their labor is not needed in the preparation of the new swiddens. Non-rubber-owning households do not have this luxury: their need to look for wage-labor opportunities and other

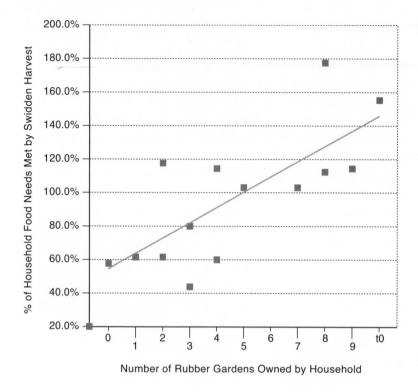

Figure 6.7. Kantu' rubber garden ownership and swidden success.
A regression analysis of the independent variable—number of rubber
gardens—and the dependent variable—harvest sufficiency—yields the
following results: r^2 = .562084, the standard error of coefficient = .023512,
and the X coefficient = .092277.

means of meeting their harvest shortfall may disrupt their labor inputs into
their new swiddens, which will in turn jeopardize the next swidden harvests
and so on, in a process of negative feedback. In addition, if a rubber-owning
household taps rubber during the slack periods in its swiddens, it can use
the proceeds of the tapping to hire wage labor during the intensive periods
in their swiddens (namely, planting, weeding, and harvesting). This enables
them to partially overcoming the major techno-environmental constraint on
swidden production and thereby make larger swiddens than otherwise possible (Dove 1984), which will lead to larger harvests, the proceeds of which
can be invested back into the swidden cycle in a positive feedback process
that is beneficial for the household economy.

The principles that make combined rubber and swidden production so beneficial for the farm household also apply to the other major export tree crops (for example, coconuts, coffee). This is reflected in co-variation, among Indonesia's provinces, between the amount of land area under swidden agriculture and the amount under tree crops. When Indonesia's twenty-four provinces (as of 1991) were ranked (using data from Barlow and Tomich 1991: 32, table 3) according to percentage of agricultural land devoted to swiddens and then ranked according to the percentage of agricultural land under tree crops, a comparison of the two rankings yielded a Spearman's rank-order correlation coefficient of 0.61,[12] demonstrating a positive association significant beyond the .01 level.

Other Trajectories

The path of development taken by smallholder rubber producers in Kalimantan is a historically contingent one. This is illustrated by the rather different path followed in Negeri Sembilan in Peninsular Malaysia, based on differences in gender relations and politics. Among Dayak groups like the Kantu', there is considerable gender equality in property relations. There is no differentiation between men and women in owning or inheriting farmland. Intracommunity post-marital residence tends to be virilocal (with the husband's family), while intercommunity post-marital residence tends to be uxorilocal (with the wife's family), as a result of which women have traditionally played a role that was equal to if not greater than that of men in knowledge of and control over household and community landholdings. In Negeri Sembilan, in contrast, a matrilineal pattern of property historically prevailed. According to traditional *adat perpatih*, proprietary rights to houses, house compounds and irrigated rice fields were held by women not men.

When *Hevea* rubber was introduced into Negeri Sembilan early in the twentieth century, it was treated as falling outside of *adat perpatih*, as belonging to a separate and different moral economy, as not infrequently happens with introduced cash crops (see chapter 7). This made it possible for men to exert greater proprietary control over rubber gardens than they had traditionally exerted over other sorts of landed property (Kato 1991: 146; 1994: 151). As a result, as rubber became more important in Negeri Sembilan, men increasingly focused on it and women increasingly focused on irrigated rice cultivation, which over time accentuated a gender-based division of labor (Kato 1991: 144, 145; 1994: 147–48, 157; Hobsbawm 1994: 212–13).[13]

This was not a strictly parochial process, unaffected by wider political-economic forces. The colonial British regime in Malaya saw rubber as a modern, market-based introduction that should be exempt from traditional *adat perpatih* (Kato 1994: 156); and the rise of more orthodox Islamic teachings in Malaysia during the twentieth century also contributed to the development of a stronger position for men in property inheritance and ownership.

Whereas the gender and religious politics of Negeri Sembilan were important factors in the adoption and spread of rubber, the equivalent factors among the Kantu' and other Dayak smallholders were largely market related. Whereas the former involved gender-based differences between rubber and irrigated rice, the latter involved differences in the transactional orders of secular market rubber and sacred household rice. Whereas the former led to male dominance of rubber tapping, the latter led to a slight dominance of tapping by women.

CHAPTER 7

Living Rubber, Dead Land, and Persisting Systems

Indigenous Representations of Sustainability

Tanah ditanam ngau getah nyadi tanah mati. (Land planted in rubber becomes dead land.)
— *Kantu' explanation of change in status of land planted with rubber*

Rubber That "Kills" the Land

Kantu' traditionally said that when they plant rubber (*Hevea brasiliensis*) in their swiddens or swidden fallows, the land thenceforth becomes *tanah mati* (dead land), in implicit contrast to the remaining "living land" contained in the swidden agricultural cycle, a linguistic usage that is widespread in Borneo (for example, see Cramb 2007).[1] Rubber appears to be the first and so far the only cultigen to have this impact. No swidden crop, nor any aspect of the swidden cycle, is ever said to kill the land, not even when opening primary forest. The meaning of "dead land" is based on three indigenous processes of social and ecological exchange: (1) bounty carries a cost; (2) bounty (or wealth) should be distributed, not accumulated; and (3) the creation and destruction of bounty are linked. None of these principles apply to the system of rubber production, which carries no such costs, in which distribution is not necessary, and in which there is no cyclic linkage between resource creation and destruction.

The understanding of sustainable environmental relations across cultures is challenging. International environmental policy is often marked by overly facile exercises of crosscultural translation. For example, Goldman (2005: 177) writes, "In the mid-1990s, when the Wildlife Conservation Society (WCS) and IUCN [International Union for the Conservation of Nature] described the state of the environment in Laos, they unambiguously stated that *no* conservation practices existed. Indeed, one report (IUCN

1993) stated that the word did not exist in the Lao language." The inference from the purported absence of a word for "conservation," that no resource conservation is being practiced, is based on an extremely limited and Western-biased notion of this practice. Even some anthropologists have suggested that management practices that conserve resources but do not do so consciously do not qualify for the label of "conservation" (Stearman 1994). Conversely, anthropologists and conservationists have also been accused of projecting Western intentions onto inadequately understood native practices. Thus, Richards (1992) critiques the Western notion of "saving" the rain forest in light of the perspective of the Mende of West Africa, who see the forest as the patron, and themselves as clients, not the reverse. Many other anthropologists have noted the shortcomings of Western environmental concepts in analyzing non-Western environmental relations (for example, Ellen 1999; Keller 2008; Lye 2004, 2005; West 2005, 2006).

The challenges involved can be illustrated by the story that the Kantu' and related groups tell of their mythical culture-giver and rice deity Pulang Gana. According to this story, the ancestors of the Kantu' cleared forest for swiddens every day, but overnight Pulang Gana made the forest grow back. This continued until the Kantu' finally agreed to make offerings in their swiddens to Pulang Gana. Only then did cleared forest stay cleared. The untimely regrowth of forest in this story is, thus, a curse—in part because of the way it erased human labor. This represents an attention to labor that is often missing from Western conservation discourse (Williams 1980: 78). The story of Pulang Gana also highlights the centrality in Dayak beliefs of cycles of living and dead land, of creation and destruction. Whereas Western environmentalists often still idealize a static harmony with the environment, Dayak beliefs emphasize the reality of dynamic, fluctuating relations between society and environment. In this sense, Dayak beliefs are consistent with the post-equilibrium scientific paradigm: disturbance is not seen as something outside history, rather disturbance *is* history (Worster 1995: 74).

In the same way the regrowing forest in the story of Pulang Gana confounds Western assumptions of conservation versus degradation, and balance versus perturbation, so too does the land that is killed by rubber. In an effort to explain this concept, I will join other anthropologists in trying to retrieve indigenous concepts for understanding complex processes like environmental degradation and conservation. The concept of "dead land" raises the issue of what Obeyesekere (1992: 175) called, in his critique of the ethnographic belief that Western explorers were viewed by the indigenous peoples of the Pacific as "gods," "this problem of literalizing tropes." I will show that whereas it is correct to translate land planted in rubber (*tanah mati*) as "dead land," the meaning of this "deadness" must be interpreted within a "context of utterance" (ibid.) that encompasses not just agricultural economy and ecology but also society and cosmology, the history of land-use change, and relations with global market systems. The Kantu' characterize rubber lands as "dead" as part of a pervasive discourse of exchange involving both society and environment. Rubber is not part of this system and, accordingly, it kills exchange and thus the land. This contradiction at the very heart of the logic of the Kantu' system of land and resource use cannot be divorced from their relationship with the wider political economy. As Wolf (1982: 390) writes, "There is thus an economic and political side to the formation of idea-systems, and idea-systems, once produced, become weapons in the clash of social interests. Sets of ideas and particular group interests, however, do not exist in mechanical one-to-one relationships. If a mode of production gives rise to idea-systems, these are multiple and often contradictory." The contradiction in the Kantu' case reflects the fact that their economy is based on mediation between two separate and conflicting production systems, the subsistence-oriented rice swiddens and the market-oriented rubber gardens (compare Robbins 1995: 220).

Social and Ecological Exchange

In order to understand how the land becomes dead under rubber, it is first necessary to understand how the land otherwise is alive. The life of the land, among the Kantu' and many of the other societies that adopted rubber at the beginning of the twentieth century, comprises pervasive relations of exchange in which not only land but also people participate. The most fundamental principle underpinning these relations is that of reciprocity, which has implications for the cost of resource abundance and views of distribution versus accumulation, and permanence versus impermanence (compare Lye 2004).

Bounty Bears a Cost

The operation of the principle of reciprocity can be seen first in the Kantu' belief that wealth or bounty bears a cost (Dove and Kammen 1997). This is aptly illustrated by tribal beliefs concerning the mast (synchronized) fruiting of the trees in Borneo's rain forest. Every three to five years, the

Figure 7.1. Kantu'
sacrifice of pig to
spirits

rain forest's dipterocarps (a family of trees that dominate Borneo's lowland
rain forest) bear a heavy crop of fruit.[2] Borneo's tribesmen welcome mast
fruitings as an opportunity to increase personal consumption of and trade
in the forest fruits. But they also believe that the increased consumption of
fruit in the mast year entails a cost: the Kantu' say that the spirits of the forest demand "sigi' kolak mata mensia" (one basket of human eyes) during a
mast-fruiting year, meaning that the spirits demand human dead in sufficient numbers to fill a basket with their eyes.[3] A corollary to this principle
that bounty bears a cost is the reverse principle that cost yields a bounty: the
most important statement that most animist tribesmen of Borneo can make
to their spirit pantheon involves the sacrifice of one or more domestic pigs
(figure 7.1). Such a sacrifice entails a significant economic cost to the tribesmen, but it is one they justify by saying that any household that makes this
sacrifice is certain to reap better harvests as a result, or at least better harvests than those households that do *not* make the sacrifice (Dove 1988: 151).[4]

The converse of the spirits rewarding the Dayak in exchange for a sacrifice is their withholding the reward because, in effect, such a sacrifice has not
been made. The Kantu' say that their relations with the spirits are governed

by a number of proscriptions as well as prescriptions, and prominent among the former are sexual proscriptions against adultery, illegitimate birth, and incestuous unions. The Kantu' say that when they honor these sexual proscriptions, the spirits will assist them in enjoying the fruits of the land and forest, and when they don't they won't.[5] Thus, the Kantu' say that because of repeated violation of these sexual proscriptions, mast fruitings are less frequent today than formerly, and when they do occur they are still less abundant than formerly. The only way to avoid this withdrawal of the spirits' favor, in the event of a sexual offence, is to make a compensatory sacrifice to the spirits. Formerly, the lives of the offending couple, namely those who committed the sexual delict, were sacrificed to the spirits.[6] In contemporary times, domestic pigs are sacrificed instead. For a serious sexual offense, seven pigs should be sacrificed: one each at the oldest *rian* (durian tree, *Durio zibethinus* Murr.), *engkabang* (illipe-nut tree, *Shorea* spp.), *tapang* (a bee tree, often *Koompassia excelsa* [Becc.] Taub.),[7] and *buah* (any other forest fruit) in the territory; and one each in the *rumah* (longhouse), on the *tanah* (ground), and at the *sungai* (river). The cultural centrality of this reciprocal relationship of sacrifice and favor between humans and spirits is reflected in a story that the Kantu' tell about their historic foes, the Iban. To the Kantu', the Iban are a true "other," marked off by such purported habits as eating head lice and so on. In keeping with this otherness, the Kantu' say that the Iban summon the spirits with the promise of a sacrificed chicken, but then they set the chicken free instead of killing it. This purported (and apocryphal) practice of reneging on the principle of reciprocity with the spirits fills the Kantu' with horror, and they say it will guarantee the perpetrators a *panda' umur* (short life).

A related dimension of the principle of reciprocity in Kantu' society is that too much bounty, as discussed in chapter 5, can be a bad thing. That is, there is a point at which the accumulation of material wealth violates indigenous norms for redistribution and reciprocity and, indeed, is made possible only by such violation.[8] Thus, the majority of swidden rice surpluses are typically distributed each year, from households enjoying surpluses to those households experiencing shortfalls. As a result, any long-term accumulation of rice stores by a given household is suspect, since it implies that requests for rice to tide others over harvest shortfalls have been denied. Rice stored for more than a few years goes bad and becomes unfit to eat, which makes its accumulation all the more immoral. Thus, to say that a household has such large and long-standing rice stores that the rice has gone bad is the ultimate Kantu' expression of both farming success and social failure. The assumed immoral origins of such accumulation are reflected in explanations of the perceived material wealth of the Catholic Church in Borneo. As noted in chapter 5, the Kantu' say that the loft of the Catholic mission nearest to their territory is inhabited by a *naga* (dragon) that excretes gold coins when it is fed human dead. The implication, therefore, is that only such a gross violation of the moral order as feeding one's dead to a dragon could produce the kind of accumulated wealth that they associate with the Catholic Church.[9]

Creation and Destruction of Bounty

Overaccumulation of bounty can be avoided by its distribution or destruction. As the story of the Catholic dragon suggests, there is a linkage between the destruction and creation of resource wealth. This linkage, and the principle of cycling and recycling that underlies it, is central to the cosmology of many Dayak groups and, indeed, to the cosmologies of indigenous peoples throughout Southeast Asia.[10] An example is a myth held by the Ngaju, a people of south-central Borneo, concerning the Tree of Life, a central symbol of their cosmology: "When the Tree of Life bears its fruit . . . it does not simply stand in solitary height, for then its time has come. The birds fly to it. They peck at the fruit of the Tree, they destroy it, and from the destruction and self-destruction arises the whole cosmos" (Schärer 1963: 128).

The image of cosmic fruiting in this myth resembles the phenomenon of mast fruiting discussed earlier. The stochastic character of production underlying both mast fruiting and Ngaju cosmology has an ecological basis. Mast fruiting in Borneo is triggered by dry air masses, caused on the western side of the island by "a chance fluctuation in the subtropical monsoonal circulation system" and on the eastern side by the El Niño-Southern Oscillation (ENSO) phenomenon (Ashton, Givinish, and Appanah 1988: 61). The evolutionary purpose of the mast fruiting is to overload seed predators during the mast years and thereby enhance the prospects for seed survival, while denying predators food during the intervening years and thereby suppressing their population growth. Mast fruiting represents an adaptation to the generally impoverished environment of the tropical forest, and the more extreme the impoverishment, the more extreme the mast (in other words, the less frequent but the greater in magnitude [van Schaik, Terborgh, and Wright 1993: 358]). There is increasing evidence that stochastic, even catastrophic, patterns of perturbation characterize forest history and, indeed, the natural history of Earth's environment in general. This has led to a new generation of Bornean studies focusing on such topics as the ENSO cycle and other climatic perturbations, as well as drought and fire (Goldammer 1990; Harwell 2000; King 1996; Knapen 1997; Leighton and Wirawan 1986; Mayer 1996; Salafsky 1994).

According to traditional Dayak beliefs, creation and destruction are linked in a cycle, and anything that interrupts or resists this cycle is seen as a violation of the cosmological order. This is reflected in the traditional Kantu' *pantang* (proscription) against the use of Borneo's foremost timber, from the ironwood tree (*Eusideroxylon zwageri*), in house construction.[11] The Kantu' rationale for this proscription was that the durability of this wood and anything constructed from it surpassed and thereby "trumped" the life span of the people using it.[12] The problem with such long-lived construction is that it represents a bounty taken from nature with no fixed time for returning it to nature. Such construction breaks the cycle of destruction and creation, the cycling between nature and culture.[13] Many scholars have observed that it can be culturally meaningful when trees outlive human beings, but few have discerned that this also can be problematic. Thus, Bechmann (1990: 276) suggests that such trees are venerated for their "memories" of what they have "witnessed"; and Davies (1988: 34) similarly calls such trees "historical markers." Davies (ibid.: 41) continues by suggesting that long-lived trees have "fed the flames of creative thought . . . because they stand over and against human generations in a way which demands acknowledgment."

A type of acknowledgment unimagined by Davies is reported for the Merina of central Madagascar, namely a proscription—analogous to that of the Kantu' regarding the use of ironwood—against planting trees whose life span surpasses that of humans. Bloch (1989: 179–80) interprets this in light of the tension in Merina society between the transitory life of the individual and the eternal life of the descent group. The former opposes the latter because it terminates with death. This opposition is mediated, and the problem of death is dealt with, by a prescription that all individual property must be distributed before death. Such distribution is complicated, however, if the dying individual has planted and still owns long-lived trees. The problem with planting long-lived trees, therefore, is that they interfere with this cyclic relationship between the individual and the descent group. As Bloch (ibid.: 179) says, such planting "would therefore compete with descent in an absolute way. It would render something of the individual permanent."[14] Bloch's explanation is evocative of the principles elucidated in this chapter concerning the need to distribute versus accumulate wealth and the need to destroy in order to create. Long-lived trees present a challenge to the moral order and the moral cycle not because something has been destroyed forever but, counterintuitively, because something has been *created* forever.[15] Permanent life presents as much of a problem to this moral ecology as does permanent death.[16]

The principles of this cosmological order are recognizable in the everyday processes of rapid decay and then reuse of organic matter that characterize the tropical forest,[17] as well as in the forest-farming system that prevailed throughout much of the interior of Borneo and the rest of Indonesia's outer islands up to the end of the twentieth century: swidden agriculture. The cyclic linkage of creation and destruction is obviously central to this system: the sudden destruction of the forest by fire creates the swidden (figure 7.2); whereas the gradual destruction of the swidden, through both natural and anthropogenic processes of afforestation, re-creates the forest (figure 7.3). An emphasis on distribution versus accumulation also is central to the labor regime of the swidden system. The existence of environmental constraints on the timing of planting, weeding, and harvesting, discussed in chapter 6, obliges swidden operators to exchange labor with one another to cope with these labor bottlenecks; and the inherent unpredictability of the environmental conditions that determine the swidden harvest obliges each successful swidden operator to distribute grain to the less successful as an investment against the time when he or she also will be less lucky (Dove 1988: 162). As noted earlier, accumulation versus distribution of grain stores, which violates this principle of exchange, is socially sanctioned. Finally, the principle that bounty bears a cost also applies to the swidden system. The Kantu' believe that if they perform the requisite rituals and offer sufficient sacrifices to the spirits, this will be reflected in bountiful swidden harvests.

According to a traditional folk classification in Indonesia, there are two types of societies: *kebudayaan batu* (cultures of stone) versus *kebudayaan kayu* (cultures of wood). The former are sedentary, centralized, permanent, state based, and state valorized—and build with stone; whereas the latter are mobile, scattered, impermanent, and marginal to the state and state values—and build with wood. Societies like the Kantu' clearly fall into the latter category, which is used by government representatives as a term of deprecation to refer to them and their ilk. However, the Dayak themselves have their own concepts of permanence and their own worries about threats to it. For example, the Simpang Dayak of southwest Borneo sum up as fol-

Figure 7.2. Kantu'
swidden burn (in
background, afforest-
ing former swidden
in foreground)

lows the changes that have been wrought on their landscape in recent years
by state elites intent on resource extraction:[18] "Batu sudah berobah, gunung sudah berinsit. Gunung tidak bermacan, telok tidak bernaga." ([Even]
the stones have changed, [even] the mountains have fallen. The mountains
have no tigers, the river holes have no dragons.) These changes in stones
and mountains are the product of a disenchantment of the landscape, which
transcends, as the use of these metaphors implies, normal instances of resource extraction and destruction. Stones and mountains are not supposed
to change; and when they do, it signifies something that violates the normal
cosmological order of creation and destruction. Whereas the state representatives pejoratively label people like the Dayak as failing to attain social fixity,
therefore, the Dayak themselves accuse state elites of erasing fixity, of turning their world into a place that lacks fixity in the most fundamental sense.

Figure 7.3. Natural afforestation on former Kantu' swidden (in foreground, current swidden in background)

Lack of Exchange in Rubber Cultivation

The principles of exchange that apply to the system of swidden cultivation do not, for the most part, apply to the system of rubber cultivation.

Bounty without Cost or Distribution

The Kantu' do not believe that the bounty produced by rubber cultivation bears a cost in the way that the bounty produced by swidden cultivation does. When rubber was first introduced to the Dayak early in the twentieth century, it was feared that the rubber trees would eat the spirit of the swidden rice (see chapter 5), which clearly says something about the perceived costs of rubber cultivation. In addition, there is some ritual associated with the marketing of rubber (see chapter 3), which imply some sort of human-spirit exchange. In general, however, the beliefs that pervade the system of swidden agriculture, regarding the ritualized exchange of bounty between spirits and humans, is absent from the system of rubber cultivation. The fact that rubber lies outside this belief system is reflected in the fact that rubber is not included among the trees mentioned earlier at which pigs are sacrificed upon the occasion of a major sexual delict.

Figure 7.4. Kantu' exchange-labor planting party

Not only is there no exchange between humans and spirits in rubber production, there is no exchange among humans. Thus, little or no interhousehold reciprocity or exchange is involved in providing the inputs to rubber
cultivation, the foremost of which is labor, or consuming the outputs, namely
sheets of rubber, in sharp contrast to the inputs and outputs of swidden cultivation (figure 7.4).[19] Unlike the case in swidden cultivation, there are no
ecological imperatives for such exchange: the seasonal variables and labor
bottlenecks that necessitate such exchange in swidden production are absent
from rubber production. There also is greater commoditization in rubber
cultivation of inputs such as labor, and greater separation of the laborer from
the product of his or her labor than is the case in swidden rice cultivation.
Thus, while sharecropping was traditionally unknown in swidden cultivation, it became a common practice early in the history of rubber cultivation,
notably in the form of the *bagi dua* (split in two) system, wherein laborers
who have no rubber trees of their own tap the trees of others in exchange for
one-half of the yield. The use of an adopted Malay expression, *bagi dua,* for
sharecropping, instead of a native Kantu' expression, reflects the distinct and
market-oriented transactional order of rubber cultivation.

Bounty without Creation and Destruction

Just as there is little or no social exchange in rubber cultivation, so there is little or no ecological exchange: there is no automatic cycling back and forth between rubber and forest. Unlike most of the economic plants planted by the tribal peoples of Borneo in their swidden sites, rubber does *not* succumb to the secondary afforestation that naturally occurs on these sites; rather, it becomes part of the succession, within which it thrives. In its native habitat in South America, rubber is a denizen of mature forests, not younger successions (Dean 1987: 60). Rubber trees are long-lived: individual rubber trees can have a productive life of thirty to forty years. This does not mean that the life of the rubber garden is limited to even thirty to forty years, however, because naturally grown seedlings typically replace the planted trees with a second generation of trees. Further iterations of this natural process make the productive life of rubber groves potentially open-ended. In practice, however, the productivity of older rubber groves tends to decline. Gouyon, de Foresta, and Levang (1993: 194) note that the impact of shade on seedling growth will result in a drop in tree density in the third and higher generations, such that the spacing of the rubber trees gradually moves from the artificial spacing of five hundred per hectare in rubber groves toward the two to three per hectare that naturally obtain in the Amazon, which eventually makes the rubber grove unprofitable to tap. And indeed, it is not uncommon for Dayak to clear older rubber groves for new swiddens. Such reentry into the swidden cycle does not alter the status of the land as *tanah mati* (dead land), however.[20]

The nonparticipation of rubber land in these exchanges, whether ecological or social, is reflected in its unique tenurial status, as discussed in chapters 3 and 6. For example, after a Kantu' *bilek* (household) undergoes partition, its swidden forest land will continue to be held in common (*kuntsi*) by the resulting households, at least until the children of those carrying out the partition mature and begin to make their own swiddens (Dove 1985b); but any rubber gardens will immediately be divided. Similarly, if a household moves out of a longhouse, its forest lands must be returned to the longhouse to be held and used in common, but not its rubber gardens; the departed household can continue to exercise exclusive proprietary rights to these gardens.

The phrase "dead land" (*tanah mati*) uses not the Kantu'/Iban term for death, *parai*, but the Malay term, *mati* (Richards 1981: 210, 254–55; Wilkinson 1959, 2:749–50). The use of a Malay versus Ibanic term reflects the distinction between the more locally oriented transactional order of swidden production, where a vernacular language is spoken, and the transactional order of the rubber that is more outward oriented toward markets and the wider society, which was traditionally Malay speaking. Whereas the Malay term *mati* does have the literal meaning of "death," it also has a figurative meaning of "fixed," which dominates its uses in Iban (Richards 1981: 210; Wilkinson 1959, 2:749–50). Accordingly, the term *tanah mati* (dead land) can be interpreted as a statement about how planting rubber fixes the land within the context of a wider, swidden landscape that is by implication not fixed.[21] Counterintuitively, this fixing of the land does not mean its death biologically. Land planted in rubber is dead forever because the rubber is, at least potentially, alive forever; just as the accumulation of wealth from rubber trees is unending because of the lack of social exchange in its cultivation. The continuum against which rubber cultivation is being measured is not, therefore, life versus death, but rather the cycle between life and death, creation and destruction, field and forest, which was described earlier. Unending life without death jeopardizes this cycle, just as does unending accumulation without distribution. The former severs the ecological cycle of creation and destruction, the morality of exchange between nature and culture; whereas the latter severs the economic cycle of interdependence and reciprocity, the morality of exchange between people.

The Rubber-Swidden Fit and the Threat of Subsidy

The relationships between systems of cash-cropping and systems of swidden cultivation have not been well interpreted, even by respected scholars. For example, Wolf (1982: 330) and Pelzer (1945: 24–25) argue that cash crops like tobacco, coffee, and pepper fit well into native swidden systems during the colonial era but suggest that rubber competed with and disrupted these systems.[22] Thus, Pelzer (ibid.) writes, "A shifting cultivator, may, over a period of years, convert his old ladangs into rubber gardens, for example, until he is assured of a sufficient income from his permanent tree crop to buy his food from the outside and no longer requires a ladang for the production of food. . . . Although this modification of the old economy [by planting perennials in swiddens] has led to permanent gardens of rubber, coconut, and benzoin trees and thus to a partial abandonment of shifting cultivation, where pepper and coffee supplement the traditional crops of the shifting cultivator no fundamental change takes place, because these gardens are not permanent." Based on Pelzer's research, Wolf (1982: 330) writes regarding Deli, Sumatra, "In this area, the Dutch had long grown tobacco on plantations, which developed in symbiosis with the slash-and-burn agriculture of local Malay and Batak villagers. The plantation took over the labor of burning off the covering vegetation. It then raised the first crop, tobacco. When productivity decreased in the second year, the plantation opened a new field, allowing the villagers to take over the tobacco plots in order to raise food. When rubber was introduced in 1906, this symbiotic relationship came to an end. Rubber trees were a perennial crop and could not be alternated with annuals. Instead, rubber cultivation, carried on by imported Javanese and Chinese laborers, now engulfed the subsistence plots of the native population." Wolf's and Pelzer's thesis of symbiosis is partially correct, in narrow agronomic terms, as can be seen in the case of black pepper (*Piper nigrum*). Pepper cultivation, unlike rubber cultivation, has a highly deleterious impact on the land, as discussed in chapter 2. The exactions of pepper cultivation are reflected in the short productive life of pepper gardens: the average Kantu' pepper garden can be cultivated for a maximum of seven to eight years, after which it must be abandoned. Pelzer and Wolf are partly right in thinking that this pattern of land use in some sense resembles and thus fits with swidden cultivation. The same fundamental ecological principle underlies both systems of cultivation: cultivation exhausts available nutrients, which obliges a cessation in cultivation until such time as the nutrient base is restored.[23] The similarity between pepper cultivation and swidden cultivation in this respect is reflected in the fact that the Kantu' do not say that land used for pepper is "dead" but only that it is "barren."

The ecological principles underlying rubber cultivation are quite different. In rubber cultivation, the decline in productivity of older gardens is much more gradual and it is not driven by a decline in the stock of available nutrients; rather, it is driven by the natural progression of older-generation gardens toward a lower density of rubber. Rubber cultivation resembles swidden cultivation and pepper cultivation in that the act of cultivation eventually undermines the conditions necessary for its continuation or reproduction, but the principles by which this takes place differ: whereas in the case of tobacco, pepper, and most swidden crops, the process is driven by a fast shift to a younger, impoverished succession, in the case of rubber the process is driven by a slow shift to an older, richer succession. There is a clear opposition between the two processes: whereas the former depends on interrupting natural processes of vegetative succession, the latter promotes them; whereas land subject to the latter process becomes fixed or dead, land subject to the former process remains unfixed or alive. In terms of this opposition, rubber can indeed be seen as conflicting with swidden cultivation, as Pelzer (1945: 25) and Wolf (1982: 330) suggest. But the significance of this conflict needs to be interpreted in light of the extraordinarily successful history of joint swidden and rubber cultivation.

Despite the seemingly poor fit between rubber and swidden cultivation, despite their ecological opposition, the spread of their combined practice has been very successful, as measured by the number of people and amounts of land involved and their contribution to the international rubber trade. This success is explained by the fact that the combination of rubber and swidden cultivation has been politically as well as economically empowering, as discussed in earlier chapters. This empowerment is a function not just of the relationship of the rubber system to the swidden system, but of the viability of this relationship in the wider context of colonial and post-colonial political-economic relations. In this wider context, the fit or complementarity between a system of cash-cropping and a system of subsistence agriculture is not necessarily beneficial. On the contrary, it bears a risk: it may be seized by superordinate political and economic authorities as an opportunity to "piggyback" a centralized regime of extractive agriculture on a local regime of subsistence agriculture, as happened with tobacco and swidden cultivation in Deli, Sumatra.

The colonial tobacco planters and swidden cultivators of Deli did not contribute equally to their so-called symbiosis. Wolf (ibid.) implies that the swidden cultivators benefited because "The plantation took over the labor of burning off the covering vegetation"; but burning is actually the briefest stage by far of the swidden cycle, taking, in successful cases, as little as an hour or two to complete. The slashing and felling of the forest that precede the burn, in contrast, are onerous tasks; and by integrating their tobacco into the Deli swidden cycle, the planters could avoid expending this labor themselves. This arrangement was ironic, in that colonial planters were in effect drawing a subsidy from a traditional system of agriculture that was otherwise fiercely criticized and suppressed by the colonial establishment. This irony reached a peak in the famous *taungya* system of colonial British Burma, in which state teak cultivation piggybacked on indigenous swidden cultivation. Bryant (1994) has exposed the dual and paradoxical function of *taungya* in Burma, noting that it was intended to extract an economic surplus from the swidden peoples in the form of assistance with the planting of teak at the same time as it was intended to eliminate swidden cultivation by putting all potential swidden lands under state teak plantations.[24]

In the end, the Burmese swidden cultivators did not succumb to the *taungya* system (ibid.: 249–50), but the potentially debilitating effects of such subsidies of state enterprise are well documented in Geertz's 1963 study of the piggybacking of colonial and post-colonial sugarcane cultivation on peasant irrigated rice agriculture in Java. In order to assure parastatal sugar mills of a supply of cane, colonial and post-colonial governments obliged Java's rice farmers to plant sugarcane on their lands, between crops of rice, and then sell the crop to the mill at fixed, often below-market rates. Cultivation of sugarcane fit well, agronomically, into the cultivation of irrigated rice fields. The fit was so good that peasant rice production in effect subsidized state sugar production, which contributed to the historic failure of rice agriculture to develop—its "involution," in Geertz's words.[25] Where outsiders seek such subsidies, a system of cash-cropping that offers—by means of its goodness of fit—the requisite easy avenue into local systems of resource use is not empowering; and one that does not offer this fit, like rubber, *is* empowering.[26] In this sense, the lack of fit between rubber and swidden cultivation, and the "death" of the land under rubber, indicate social and ecological relations that are sustainable as opposed to unsustainable from the local perspective. Conversely, the so-called fit of pepper and swidden cultivation indicates locally *un*sustainable social and ecological relations. As Schneider (1995: 31–32) writes of seventeenth-century West Sumatra, "In theory, pepper production fitted well into swidden cultivation. A newly cleared field could be planted first with *ladang* rice which was then followed by pepper as a perennial crop. . . . In practice, however, production demands on pepper planters by the British were such that subsistence agriculture was severely affected and the previous self-sufficiency in rice could hardly be maintained."

There is an analogy in the contemporary forest industry. The forest-dwelling peoples of Indonesian Borneo have been bedeviled over the past several decades by the explosive growth of logging concessions, called HPH (*hak pengusahaan hutan*). Notwithstanding all the ills that attend logging concessions, Dayak activists say that they are less worried about them than about the more recent HTI (*hutan tanaman industri*), or commercial pulpwood plantations and now oil palm plantations as well. The Dayak say that whereas the logging concessions will eventually go away, after the last tree has been felled, the tree plantations may stay forever.[27] Whereas the logging concessions are essentially part of a forest cycle of opening and closure, the tree plantations are fixed, like the rubber gardens. This analogy is reflected in the fact that many of the tenurial conflicts that arise in the development of pulpwood plantations involve locally owned rubber gardens, whereas most conflicts in the development of logging concessions have involved locally owned and managed swidden lands. The pulpwood plantations and the rubber gardens are in greatest conflict because both are tenure-making projects.

The ability to establish or strengthen land claims is one of the most important dimensions of the fit between rubber and the extra-local political-economic system. As discussed in earlier chapters, the fact that rubber plantings win this tenurial recognition from the state has become an important motivation among smallholders for planting rubber. It is probably inevitable that a production system that wins this much recognition from the overarching state system and that fits well into the logic of this wider system would *not* fit well into the logic of a local subsistence system like the swidden system of the Dayak. That is, it is probably inevitable that what thrives in the wider political-economic system would be "dead" in the local system. Opposition to the local system was probably a prerequisite, by definition, for success in the extra-local system.

Exchange between People and Trees

Underlying many of the Dayak beliefs regarding social and environmental exchange are ideas about relationships between people and trees.

People-Tree Metaphors

Many societies around the world have used metaphoric linkages between people and trees, or more generally between people and plants, as a mechanism to conceive of and structure social relations.[28] A traditional Javanese example of this is the folk saying "A king is to his people as the tiger is to the forest" (Moertono 1981: 22).[29] A still-current example of the metaphoric linkage of people and plants in Indonesia is called *ilmu padi,* which literally means "rice knowledge" but which Echols and Shadily (1992: 220) translate as "the ability to be well educated but humble." A common example of this body of norms and knowledge is the aphorism "Makin berisi, makin berunduk" (The fuller it is, the more it bends over) (Schmidgall-Tellings and Stevens 1981: 121). This statement refers literally to the agronomic fact that the fuller a rice panicle is, the more it bends over. Metaphorically, it refers to the norm within Javanese and to a lesser extent all Indonesian culture that the more one has to say, the quieter one is.

One of the most important metaphoric linkages of people and trees involves a comparison of age.[30] The dimension of age is implicit in most discussions of trees and other perennials in Indonesia: they are colloquially called *tanaman umur panjang* (long-lived plants) in the Indonesian language. The Kantu' say of land planted in rubber, "tanah mati s'umur idup" (the land is dead for as long as [one] lives).[31] In this context, the meaning of *s'umur idup* is actually, and counterintuitively, "for *longer* than [one] lives"; that is, it means forever.[32] The significance of this life span lies in its comparison with the human life span, as was illustrated in the earlier-mentioned proscription by the Merina of Madagascar regarding planting long-lived trees (Bloch 1989) and by the Kantu' regarding the use of long-lived timber, both of which have negative connotations and are enjoined.[33] With respect to land rights, however, the fact that a tree exceeds the human life span may be constructively utilized: this is why durian trees (*Durio zibethinus* Murr.) are planted in West Kalimantan as tenurial markers.[34]

Comparison of age between people and trees is often part of a wider belief in their shared interest and welfare. For example, the *Hikayat Banjar* discussed in chapter 2 tells of a battle in which the king's standard fell to earth and was reerected with a branch of the *jingah* tree[35] (Ras 1968: 175–76, 432, 438). This pole took root and grew; and then, whenever it lost a branch in still weather, this foretold the imminent death of a member of the royal family.[36] An identification of person and tree also was found traditionally among some of the Dayak groups of southwest Borneo, as described by Frazer (1951: 790):[37] "Amongst the Dayaks of Landak and Tajan, districts of Dutch Borneo, it is customary to plant a fruit-tree for a baby, and henceforth in the popular belief the fate of the child is bound up with that of the tree. If the tree shoots up rapidly, it will go well with the child; but if the tree is dwarfed or shriveled, nothing but misfortune can be expected for its human counterpart." One of the closest identifications of all between person and tree was achieved in the traditional treatment of the dead among some Bornean tribes: there are several nineteenth-century accounts of Dayak burying their dead in apertures in living trees, which then grew around the bodies (Maxwell 1992: 8–9).[38] The lifelines of people and trees may also converge at the cosmic level. The conception of the cosmos as a tree of life is common throughout Indonesia,[39] indeed throughout the world. The Ngaju

Tree of Life was mentioned earlier, along with the belief that its cyclic creation and destruction represents the creation and destruction of the cosmos.

The tree-mediated relationship between humans and spirits, between culture and nature, is addressed explicitly in the symbolism of Dayak head-hunting, as Davison and Sutlive (1991: 191, 203) write: "Trophy heads are like the fruit of the forest: they are gathered, and their seed is planted to provide the Iban with sustenance. . . . In symbolic terms, to take heads is to gather the fruits of the forest: Iban warriors must go headhunting, to bring back the fruit of the mythical *ranyai* palm and thereby supply their community with the means for their continued existence, namely rice seed and children." In head-hunting, therefore, human death is linked to the life of both crops and people; and just as spirits are seen as taking the eyes of humans in exchange for giving them fruit, so is head-hunting seen as taking human heads *as* fruit. The images of fruiting, fruit gathering, and consumption thus form a key linkage between people and trees, between human-culture and spirit-nature.

Theories about People-Tree Metaphors

Davies (1988: 32) notes, but does not analyze, the centrality of tree symbolism in Western thought: "We . . . wish to see how natural phenomena assist thought. In scaling the tree of knowledge without getting too far out on any limb, in exploring the many branches of thought, and in attempting to get at the root of the matter, we pursue a branching task." There have been efforts to denaturalize such ubiquitous, metaphorical uses of the tree, as in Bouquet's (1995) analysis of Dubois's family tree of *Pithecanthropus erectus,* Haeckel's phylogenetic diagram of human evolution, the Tree of Jesse showing Christ's earthly ancestry, and River's genealogical tree for anthropological inquiry. Bouquet (ibid.: 44) suggests that unthinking commitment to treelike conceptual structures is reflected in the fact that evolutionary theory contested the biblical creation story but borrowed the same genealogical motif to represent its own version: "This replication of the genealogical motif seemed to me a very clear example of how scientific discourse is rooted in what I will call local cultural discourse."[40] She cites Bourdieu's ([1972] 1977: 38) critique of anthropology's preference for official or logical, as opposed to practical, genealogical trees;[41] and she also cites Deleuze and Guattari's ([1980] 1987) discussion of tree-based versus rhizome-based models of reality (Bouquet 1995: 42, 51). Deleuze and Guattari's ([1980] 1987: 18) discussion is sufficiently interesting to merit citation at some length. They write:

It is odd how the tree has dominated Western reality and all of Western thought, from botany to biology and anatomy, but also gnosiology, theology, ontology, all of philosophy. . . . The West has a special relation to the forest, and deforestation; the fields carved from the forest are populated with seed plants, produced by cultivation based on species lineages of arborescent type; animal raising, carried out on fallow fields, selects lineages forming an entire animal arborescence. The East presents a different figure: a relation to the steppe and the garden (or in some cases, the desert and the oasis), rather than forest and field; cultivation of tubers by fragmentation of the individual; a casting aside or bracketing of animal raising, which is confined to closed spaces or pushed out onto the steppes of the nomads. The West: agriculture based on a chosen lineage containing a large number of variable individuals. The East: horticulture based on a small number of individuals derived from a wide range of "clones." Does not the East, Oceania in particular, offer something like a rhizomatic model opposed in every respect to the Western model of the tree?

Deleuze and Guattari are correct in suggesting that there are important symbolic differences between systems of cultivation based on vegetative propagation and systems based on reproduction from seed. The historic transition from the former to the latter during the evolution of agriculture in Southeast Asia is marked to this day, centuries if not millennia later, in the mythology of many Bornean groups (Dove 1999). Deleuze and Guattari are wrong, however, and themselves fall victim to Orientalism, in characterizing the rhizome versus seed/tree distinction as one of East versus West. There are trees in Eastern history, as shown by the earlier discussion of the Tree of Life, as well as seeds, such as the rice spirits of Borneo, just as there are rhizomes in the West.

A more illuminating approach to this topic might consist of comparing the use of tree analogies or metaphors in East and West. Fox (1988) does this in an analysis of descent "trees" on the island of Roti in eastern Indonesia.[42] He notes that the cross-cultural meaning of the image of the tree is far from given. He writes, "Trees present protean forms. They can grow up but they can also grow outward. Some, like the waringin, can grow up and then set down new roots. Hence, tracing relations using the image of a tree can take many forms" (ibid.: 16). He illustrates this point by noting that whereas descent is conceptually represented by a tree on Roti, as in the West, the directional orientation of the two images is not the same. Thus, he writes of Roti, "Here we have the conception of an ancestral tree, which is the opposite of that of the West: instead of being read from the top down, as a form of descent, it is read from the bottom up as a kind of ascent—from trunk to tip" (ibid.: 9). For another example, consider the comparison of tree and sap. It has been argued here that because rubber's socioecology opposes but complements the swidden cultivation cycle, the Dayak conceptually move it outside this cycle and say that the land under it has died. In contrast, the Western plantation complex, in colonial as well as post-colonial times, has often focused not on the wider socioecological context of rubber production, nor even on the tree, but on particular interpretations of the sap/latex itself, which receives no attention whatsoever in Dayak cosmology. In the colonial plantations (not smallholdings) of Indochina, Woodside (1976: 210, cited in Murray 1992: 60) says that the rubber tree's sap was called "white gold" by the planters, whose workers countered by calling it "white blood." Ehrenburg (1976: 49–50) writes, "The coolies and the trees understand one another. They bleed in the same way." Shifting to the Western Hemisphere, Schultes (1987: 93–94), following the lead of a 1940s Brazilian novelist, calls the sap the "blood of the gods." The intimate, informed link between rubber tree and human being that is suggested by these powerful anthropomorphic images is deceptive. The Dayak believe in a special identity between people and trees, for example, but they do not anthropomorphize the rubber.[43] Whereas the Dayak image of the dead land under rubber addresses the principal social and ecological parameters of rubber cultivation, as does the image of white blood, albeit to a lesser extent, the images of white gold and god's blood address neither.

External Representations and Sustainable Environmental Relations

External observers have a poor record of understanding the rubber-swidden dynamic. As the manager of a nucleus-estate project in West Kalimantan said, regarding how he wants the Dayak participants to relate to their rubber trees: "Dapat diibaratkan seorang ibu yang mengandung dan melahirkan bayi, akan memelihara serta mengasuhnya dengan kasih sayang, jangan sampai bayi anak tersebut sakit atau luka." (It can be compared to a mother who is pregnant and then gives birth to a baby, who will take care of and rear it with love and affection, so that the aforementioned baby does not get sick or hurt.)[44] This vision diverges in almost all respects from the indigenous Dayak concept of rubber that kills the land and eats the rice spirits. First, whereas the estate manager focuses on the relationship of human to plant, the Dayak focus on the relationship between plants, the relationship of one system of production to another. Second, whereas the estate manager wants a relationship of succoring, the Dayak see a relationship of conflict. Third, whereas the estate manager focuses on the household, the Dayak focus beyond it; the manager invokes a domestic image, the Dayak do not. Fourth, whereas the manager assumes that the Dayak are in a superordinate relationship to the rubber—as mother to child—the Dayak do not assume this, which is reflected in the fact that they actually make offerings to many trees, albeit not to rubber trees.

International social scientists and ecologists view smallholder rubber with possibly even more adoring eyes than the aforementioned estate manager, as attested to by the citations in chapter 4. From the perspective of Western environmentalists, smallholder rubber cultivation is so admirable that it is touted as not a complement to but a replacement for swidden agriculture—which would destroy the dual economy, however—and its wood became one of the first "eco-labeled" tropical timbers (Durst, Killmann, and Brown 2004; Gordon 1993).[45] But there is nothing in these environmentalists' views, however positive, that addresses the Kantu' concept of dead rubber versus live swidden lands. There is certainly nothing that would help to explain why the crop that Western environmentalists consider far more unsustainable and unnatural, namely pepper, is seen in a sense as more "natural" within the Kantu' agricultural logic than rubber. This shows us again how challenging the crosscultural analysis of conservation is; it shows us how concepts of nature and culture can be affected by the intersecting opposition of local and global; and it shows us how non-Western ways of grappling with the contradictions of production and conservation, like "dead land," may challenge in sophistication impoverished Western concepts like "sustainable development."

This chapter offers two final insights into the elusive ideal of sustainable resource management. First, there are no strictly local solutions to sustainability. The swidden-rubber system described here is Janus-faced: it is oriented toward both local and extra-local needs, constraints, and opportunities. In an interconnected world, sustainable systems will not just partake of such interconnections, they will focus on them; they will focus on balancing the costs and benefits of these connections in a way that is sustainable for the local community. This balance necessarily involves the political as well as the economic arena: Dayak successes with rubber came at the expense of, and in spite of the opposition to, a state-supported plantation sector. Second, there

solutions must evolve

are no static solutions to sustainability: in a world of change, sustainability is, in part, necessarily *about* change; it is about incorporating change into what already exists, so as to protect existing advantages and diminish existing disadvantages. Joshi et al. (2003: 154) write of smallholder rubber in Sumatra, "Although we use the term 'permanent' to describe the system, the history of rubber is too short to actually evaluate the permanence of the system." This misses the point. The history of smallholder rubber actually is long enough to show both that it is not permanent and that permanence is not, in any case, the goal.

The swidden-rubber system of the Kantu' is not "traditional," if by this term we mean to signify something from an "unchanging past." It is, at least in part, as new to Borneo as the *Hevea* rubber on which it is based. The change implied in the term *tanah mati* (dead land) reflects the changes in Dayak society that accompanied the introduction of *Hevea*.[46] This is not to suggest that Dayak society was "traditional" before the introduction of rubber. On the contrary, as discussed in earlier chapters, Dayak society experienced analogous transformations during the prior boom in native forest latexes in the mid-nineteenth century; and for many centuries before that native Bornean society experienced changes related to the cultivation of pepper. There was always, thus, a history, not an "unchanging past."

PART V

The Conundrum of Resource
Wealth versus Political Power

In this section of the book, I bring my analysis of commodity production and trade in Borneo into the near present and present,
focusing in chapter 8 on contemporary views from smallholders in South
Kalimantan and in chapter 9 on contemporary views from parastatal estate
managers from throughout Indonesia, and drawing on data from the past
several decades. Chapter 8 revolves around the analysis of a folk parable concerning the perils of resource riches in the hands of a politically weak person, which sums up the theme of asymmetrical wealth and power that runs
through the entire book. Chapter 9 shows how this asymmetry is sustained
by the institutionalized, discursive undermining of the character of smallholders by the plantation establishment. I examine the self-description of
smallholders in chapter 8 as "little men," meaning politically weak men;
and in chapter 9 I look at the derogatory representations of the character of
smallholders by estate managers. This differential emphasis of questions of
power versus character is telling and reflects the realities both of power and
power's need to disguise itself. Both chapters raise issues of wider theoretical and policy relevance beyond the shores of Borneo.

Chapter 8 begins with the Banjarese parable of "the little man" who
finds "the big stone," a diamond, and reaps misfortune as a result. The
tragedy of the poor man who comes into possession of riches coveted by
those more powerful has been a theme in world literature, exemplified by
stories from Dekker's *Max Havelaar* and Steinbeck's *The Pearl*. The misfortune in such cases stems from the incongruous and unstable combination of resource wealth and political poverty. This incongruence, with all of

its ill consequences, aptly characterizes the circumstances of places like the interior of Borneo, where great wealth of natural resources is coupled with politically disenfranchised human communities. The resulting imbalance explains some of the key dynamics in the history of forests and forest peoples in Borneo, in particular the degradation of the former and the immiseration of the latter. This interpretation of underdevelopment and resource degradation in terms of lack of political power directly contradicts prevailing development theories and policies, which instead attribute these problems to lack of resources. Prevailing development ideas are exemplified by rain forest marketing, the premise of which is that forest peoples degrade their environment because they are poor, which can be remedied by bringing new forest products to market. It is argued here that the contemporary search for new nontimber forest products (NTFPs) to bring to market has in effect been a search for nonvaluable forest products (NVFPs) of so little interest to the wider society that they can be left to marginal forest peoples. The forest peoples' real problem, lack of political power, has been obscured by the dominant development discourse. This focuses—using seemingly apolitical language—on problems of addition not subtraction, helping not hurting, and economic as opposed to political solutions, and thereby ties a discursive knot. Rain forest marketing illustrates the fact that corrective actions tend to be in line with hegemonic power. The persistent but groundless myth of Wickham's so-called theft of Brazil's rubber illustrates how power needs to view itself and be viewed by others.

Chapter 9 presents a sustained comparison between the planters' views of the natives and the natives' views of themselves. Information on the planters' views is based on participant observation that the author carried out while a member of a research team working for Indonesia's national Lembaga Pendidikan Perkebunan (Plantation Training Institute) in Yogyakarta, Central Java. The team's analyses of the problems encountered on plantations scattered all over Indonesia revealed a striking consistency in the plantation managers' rhetoric regarding workers, peasants, and tribesmen, irrespective of place, ethnic group, crop, and other variables. The existence of the Plantation Training Institute, among other related institutions, contributes—in ways discussed by Anderson (1983)—to a uniformity of outlook among the managers. A diversity of outlook among plantation workers and proximate peasant and tribal communities reflects the absence of any such homogenizing institutions in their case. The plantation managers regard these natives as "strange," "obtuse," "lazy," and "thieving"; they construct an image of the natives as, in short, the "other." My studies suggest that this construction of the "other" obfuscates the real challenge on these plantations, which is a contest between planters and peasants for control of the mobilization of labor and responsibility for its reproduction. The planters' discourse represents a political-economic conflict as a problem of cultural discontinuity between them and the natives and as a psychological problem of native mentality. A variety of hierarchical baffles keep this reality of the political-economic basis for native unhappiness from infiltrating the planters' understanding of the problem. The planter-native contest is not just a struggle over resources, thus, although it is certainly that, it is also a struggle over meaning.

CHAPTER 8

Material Wealth and Political Powerlessness

A Parable from South Kalimantan

Siapa yang mendapat batu besar, dia pasti susah nanti. (Whoever
finds a big [gem] stone, he will inevitably suffer [as a result].)
—*Saying among Banjar diamond miners in southeastern Borneo*

The Big Stone and the Little Man

This chapter begins with a parable that I heard when working with
Banjarese villagers in the foothills above Martapura in southeastern Kalimantan. One of the sources of nonagricultural income for these villagers is
small-scale, part-time, alluvial mining of gold and especially diamonds. The
parable that I heard regarding the paradoxical outcomes of good fortune
helped to crystallize for me many of the ideas that I have presented in this
volume. As Andrew P. Vayda (2009: 18) writes, "Far from taking the form of
strict statements of invariant sequences, the generalizations deployed by us
may refer to sequences seen as recurrent but not necessarily invariant and
may be encapsulated for us not in formal propositions but rather in plati-
tudes, proverbs, and homely phrases or sayings."

The Parable

All Banjarese can tell of the misfortunes that befell men who found
truly large, valuable diamonds. The problem with such stones is that they
cannot readily be sold: their value is out of proportion to the marketing
channels normally used by these part-time miners, who gather diamonds in
the same way that they gather other nontimber forest products like rattan
and aloes-wood.[1] Big gemstones become sources of dissonance within the
local and regional political-economic structure, because they become points

in this structure where power is not commensurate with wealth. Big gemstones represent "big wealth" held—though never for long—by *orang kecil*
(little men). News of such finds quickly comes to the attention of *orang besar*
(big men) in the district capital Martapura, the provincial capital Banjarmasin, and even the nation's capital Jakarta.[2]

A problem is then posed: how can the finder of the stone be relieved of
it without giving him more wealth than is deemed appropriate for a poor villager in a remote corner of the country? How can the "center" extract such
wealth from the "periphery" while still maintaining the appearance of a just
society, as demanded by the national ideology of Pancasila?[3] The answer
typically is to carry out this extraction in the name of the nation. For example, it may be announced that the stone will be deposited in a "national
museum," with the finder being paid an honorarium or even a lifelong pen-
sion. In some cases the stone actually may go to a national institution, but
in many such cases it goes directly to state elites, who refer to the "national
museum" as a way of invoking powerful national images to justify their behavior and as a gloss for their hierarchical resource extraction. In either case,
the essential injustice of the extraction is perceived by all of the parties involved.[4] This is reflected in the folk wisdom about big stones and little men:
far from improving the position of the finder in the political-economic structure, it worsens it; far from endearing the finder to the political structure,
it usually estranges him from it. The finder suffers (he is *susah*) because of
the ill luck that brought him fortune that would never have come to him
by virtue of his place in society and that, when it does come to him by mischance, thereby reveals—as it brings into play—the political-economic inequity of society. Knowledge of this threat engenders secrecy about resource
wealth, as the early twentieth-century explorer Beccari ([1904] 1986: 122)
writes, "During my stay in Borneo I did not hear of any big diamond being
found in the Sarawak river, but it is not in the Malay character to talk much
about any such stroke of fortune; and if any were found it is not improbable
that they were quietly smuggled out of the country. Perhaps the fear of attracting other prospectors, or making the Government augment the license
tax may also contribute to this." This is an ancient theme in the region, as
Reid (1993: 208) writes of the early colonial period: "The political context
made it dangerous for a small man to show his wealth unless he had sufficient
dependents to defend and legitimate it."

Foucault (1984: 266) has noted that the "normalizing power" of the
modern state means that "it does not have to draw the line that separates

the enemy of the sovereign from his obedient subjects." But this is precisely what happens in Borneo, when the mischance that brings the big stone and the little man together instantly and dramatically redefines which side of this line he is on. Another example of the way this line gets redefined occurred during the former rule of Ferdinand Marcos in the Philippines. In 1971 a poor Filipino locksmith by the name of Rogelio Roxas discovered a tunnel full of gold and diamonds that was presumed to be long-lost Japanese war booty (Associated Press 1996). Under Philippine law, one-half of the find belonged to Roxas. Instead, Roxas was arrested, tortured, and imprisoned by the Marcos regime. When he was released, the tunnel was empty—and he has since died. In 1996, separate courts in Switzerland and the United States respectively ordered Imelda Marcos to pay Roxas's family $460 million and $22 billion (*Honolulu Advertiser* 1996, 1997).

Diamonds

There is an age-old association of diamonds with traditional rule in the region,[5] which is itself partly explained by the big stone/little man pattern of extraction. Diamonds symbolize the ruler because he or she is located at the extreme end of this pattern of extraction: the ruler can take priceless gemstones from all others in the society, but no one else can take them from him or her. The value of such gemstones is based, therefore, on the fact that they are objects of desire and contest; and their value is most clearly expressed when this contest ceases—namely, when the supreme ruler holds them. The gemstones' value, like that of any commodity, is expressed in their devolution, in their passage from one owner to another; yet their ultimate value is attained when devolution is no longer possible, when they are held by the paramount ruler. In the flow of resources, thus, the point where the most valuable gemstones cease to flow is the point of greatest power; and the character of the flow up to that point is revealing of the structure of power in society.[6]

In general, of course, very valuable stones move *up* the hierarchy of power: thus, the *Hikayat Banjar* (see my chapter 2) tells of the historic Sambas kingdom in southwest Borneo sending a large diamond, called "Si Misim," as tribute to their overlords in the Banjar kingdom, which in turn sent the stone on to their overlords in the court of Mataram on Java (Ras 1968: 481, 483, 485).[7] Contested, sideways movement also is possible, as attested to by this comment of the mid-nineteenth century observer, Spenser St. John ([1862] 1974, 2:47), in a passage presciently titled in his contents page (ibid., 2:16), the "Discomfort of Possessing a Large Diamond": "I may even see the great diamond now in the possession of a Malau chief, whom [sic] would even give it me if I would help him to destroy a Malay noble who attacked his house in order to get possession of this famous stone: the Malay was driven off, not however before he had lodged a ball in the jaw of the Malau chief." One of the most detailed gemstone "biographies" is given by Raffles, pertaining to one of the largest diamonds to have come out of Borneo at the time of his writing early in the nineteenth century, the "Mátan Diamond" (named after the seat of an old sultanate in West Kalimantan, where it was originally found), which weighed 367 carats. Raffles ([1817] 1978, 1:239) recounts the movements of the Mátan Diamond up to his own day as follows: "This cele-brated diamond was discovered by a Dayak, and claimed as a droit of royalty by the Sultan of the country, Gurú-Láya [Raffles subsequently refers to this stone as an "appanage of royalty"]; but was handed over to the Pangéran of Lándak, whose brother having got possession of it, gave it as a bribe to the Sultan of Súkadána, in order that he might be placed on the throne of Lán-dak." The history of the Mátan Diamond and that of the others mentioned thus afford a window into the history of power in the society. The way that such gemstones move through society, in a seemingly inexorable response to the dynamics of hierarchy and power, is not unique to Indonesia; this wider currency is reflected in the tales told around the world of gemstones so linked to human trauma and tragedy that they are thought to be "cursed."[8]

The texts just cited focus almost entirely on the dynastic portion of this history; the other part, involving the nameless Dayak or Malay who initially discovered the gem stones, is passed over quickly or ignored entirely; but it is remembered in folk accounts.[9] An example comes from the oral history of the Dayak living in the Meratus Mountains of southeastern Borneo. As recounted by Tsing (1993: 277–78), the Meratus tribesmen sent diamonds and gold to Banjarmasin, the seat of the coastal sultanate of Banjar, "to ob-tain a king," and in return they were sent the Ratu Intan (diamond queen), who "instituted the dewa rituals performed today, bringing adat, ceremony, and well-being to the local area." Compared with the earlier-cited dynastic accounts, this account recognizes greater agency on the part of the Dayak; it shows the periphery not simply having its wealth appropriated by the cen-ter but proactively using it to negotiate with the center. This account makes it explicit that there was supposed to be a quid pro quo for the flow of dia-monds and other resources to the center: namely, they were supposed to get both a ruler and rule in return. Whereas the perspective from the center fo-

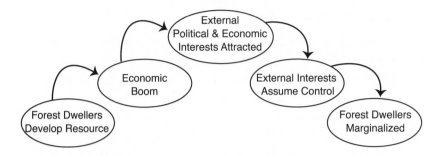

Figure 8.1. Pattern of tropical forest resource development

cuses only on royal right, therefore, this perspective from the periphery adds the issue of royal obligation. The folk belief that the transfer of wealth to the rulers should be reciprocated is, of course, intrinsic to the expressed irony in the folk comment that commoners who get involved in such transfers—as little men with big stones—typically do not benefit but rather suffer as a result: injury is negative reciprocity.[10] This is the central and counterintuitive lesson of the parable of the big stone and the little man: tropical-forest resource flows can engender not positive but negative reciprocity.

A Characteristic Pattern of Resource Appropriation

The story of the big stone and the little man is obviously analogous to the other folk image that gives this book its title, "the banana tree at the gate." Both are about a rich resource that is too attractive to outside actors for the owner to hang on to; and both are about the multiplying misfortunes that attend the inevitable loss of the resource. The big stone or diamond is analogous to the historic wealth of pepper and the contemporary wealth of rubber, both of which smallholders have had trouble hanging on to. The dynamics involved similarly apply to virtually every other natural resource that has been exploited in Borneo in the modern era, including the native rubbers in the nineteenth century, and in the twentieth century edible birds' nests (from cave-dwelling swifts, *Aerodramus maximus* and *Aerodramus fuciphagus*), rattan (from the stripped stems of climbing palms, commonly species of the genus *Calamus*), and gaharu wood or aloes-wood (from *Gonystylus* spp. and especially *Aquilaria* spp. [especially *A. malaccensis*]), among others (figure 8.1). But there is also a universal element to this story that transcends Borneo, which is reflected in accounts found in the world's literature.

Examples from Literature

Long before recognition of this pattern of resource appropriation began to grow in the natural resource field, it was a recurrent theme in literature. Writers in many different societies and at many different periods of history have drawn their readers' attention to something analogous to the tragedy of the big stone and the little man. In a discussion of this particular variant of human tragedy, Pollan (2001: 92–93, 93–94), notes that Alexandre Dumas, *père*, wrote *The Black Tulip* as a fictional account of the misfortunes that befall the man who breeds the first black tulip, to which he adds a "possibly true" story about a poor shoemaker who discovers a black tulip, which the union of florists in Haarlem buy and then unexpectedly throw to the ground and stomp to a pulp. They then tell the stupefied shoemaker that they have the only other black tulip in the world, and they mock him, saying: "'If you had asked ten thousand florins for your bulb and a couple of horses on top of it, we would have paid without a word. And remember this, Good fortune won't smile on you a second time in your entire life, because you are a blockhead.' The shoemaker, devastated, staggers to his bed in the attic and dies."[11] More well-known literary examples come from Eduard Douwes Dekker ([1859] 1982), whose pen-name was Multatuli, and John Steinbeck ([1945] 1974).

Max Havelaar

In the novel *Max Havelaar*, Dekker's famous critique of nineteenth-century government in Indonesia, written in response to the excesses of the *cultuurstel* (mentioned in chapter 1), the recurrent symbol of oppression is the "official theft" by the native aristocracy of the villagers' water buffalos (Multatuli [1859] 1982: 275). Buffalos were the villagers' chief material asset and were essential to the intensive irrigated rice cultivation that enabled them to both eat and pay their onerous land taxes. Villagers whose buffalos are stolen thus have lost not just their chief possession but also their means of fulfilling their obligations to the state, starting them on a downward spiral to both economic and political ruin.

The main protagonist in *Max Havelaar* is Saijah, a boy of twelve living in the regency of Lebak in West Java (ibid.: 255–80). Saijah's daily charge is to work the family's land with their buffalo, an animal whose *ontong* (good fortune) was indicated by the unusual whorls in its coat (Prawiroatmodjo 1981, 2:36, 423). This fortune is demonstrated one day in the fields, when a tiger tries to attack Saijah and the buffalo gores it to death. The buffalo is deeply clawed in the encounter, but Saijah's mother—thankful that her son was not clawed instead—nurses it back to health. But then, in one of the "official thefts" of which Dekker writes, the buffalo is taken from the family by the local district chief and slaughtered for his table. In consequence of this outrage against the very basis of their household, Saijah's mother dies of a broken heart, and Saijah's father, unable to plow his land and pay his taxes, tries to flee the district but is caught, flogged, and imprisoned—where he shortly thereafter dies. As a result of another official buffalo theft, Saijah's sweetheart is raped and then murdered by Dutch soldiers, and Saijah himself is subsequently murdered as well (Multatuli [1859] 1982: 274–76).

Dekker says that this is not a story just about one boy and his buffalo. He insists, "There were *many* . . . Saijahs, and that *what is fiction in particular is truth in general*" (ibid.: 278). His novel and the contemporary film version of it were banned in Indonesia during the Suharto era, which was popularly attributed to the fact that this account of the colonial period shows more collusion between native Javanese rulers and the Dutch than the post-colonial and Java-centric government wanted to acknowledge. But this is perhaps too narrow an interpretation. It seems more likely that contemporary sensitivity over Dekker's work is due to the fact that his account illustrates a persistent structure of power that cannot be blamed on the Dutch and that indeed to some extent still prevails—witness the pattern of the big stone and the little man—in post-colonial Indonesia.

The Pearl

One of the most famous explorations in English literature of the image of the great treasure and the little man is Steinbeck's 1947 novel *The Pearl*, which is set in Latin America. Steinbeck tells of a great pearl—the "Pearl of the world"—found by a poor pearl diver, Kino, and of the conspiracy by society to defraud him of it. Instead of bringing him wealth and happiness, the pearl brings Kino and his family violence and tragedy, so that at the end of the story he hurls it back into the ocean from whence it came. Robbed of his right to benefit from the pearl, Kino destroys it.[12]

At one point in this novel, Steinbeck's protagonist recalls a sermon that the local priest delivered after the pearl divers tried, and failed, to bypass the local pearl-buying syndicate: "The Father made it clear that each man and woman is like a soldier sent by God to guard some part of the castle of the

Universe. And some are in the ramparts and some far deep in the darkness of the walls. But each one must remain faithful to his post and must not go running about, else the castle is in danger from the assaults of Hell" (ibid.: 59–60). In the Bornean story of the big stone and the little man, the place of "the castle of the universe" is taken by "the national museum in Jakarta." The rationale of placing the big stone in a national museum in Jakarta invokes a millennium-old tradition of centralized stateship, which is sustained by resources flowing to it from the periphery. Indonesian society, like Steinbeck's castle, is internally differentiated, and any attempt to alter or transcend these differences is problematic. The little man in Borneo who finds himself in possession of the big stone is like the dweller deep in the darkness of the castle walls who might aspire to stand on its ramparts. Either one is a violation of the natural and—as the Father points out—moral order. This is what the story of the big stone and the little man is: a violation of the established order, a violation of the status quo. Both this story and Steinbeck's are similarly concerned with how such violations are dealt with by society and what this tells us about the society in question.

Both stories, Steinbeck's most explicitly, are also concerned with how the little man responds to the way he is dealt with by society. Kino's destruction of the great pearl at the end of the story illustrates how people can respond when deprived of that which is theirs by right but the enjoyment of which is unjustly denied them. Examples of this were noted in chapter 2 when, in response to mounting colonial pressure to produce, some cultivators of pepper and cloves (for example) not merely refused to continue cultivation but destroyed all of their plantings. Another historic example of this involves Indonesia's sandalwood tree (*Santalum album* L.). Because of the interest of native rajahs and subsequently the colonial Dutch regime in controlling and profiting from this trade, it is said to have "caused the common Timorese more pain than pleasure" (Ormeling 1957: 177). As a result, "Wherever possible the population tried to get rid of the troublesome sandalwood tree by clandestine felling, or by other means" (ibid.: 177–78).[13]

Wider Applicability

The parable of the big stone and the little man is applicable to a great deal of rural resource development. Whenever politically marginalized peoples develop a resource, the more successful the development becomes, the more likely it is that extra-local political and economic forces will

become involved, and the less likely it is that the local population will retain control and continue to benefit from this development.[14] This principle
still largely applies in the post-Suharto era in Indonesia, with the difference
being that in some cases provincial- and district-level elites have supplanted
those of Jakarta. The application of this principle beyond Borneo is attested
to by Gudeman and Rivera's (1990: 155) description of a similar cycle of local
development and extra-local appropriation in Colombia:

> From the perspective of the dominant economy, the house is located "off
> the margin." It occupies, and sometime has to fight for, spaces left empty by
> the larger system. As soon as these rural spaces become profitable, however, the
> capital-backed organizations enter, buying land and controlling resources, and
> the local people are pushed again beyond the frontier of profit. . . . For the last
> 150 years and more, campesinos have been expanding the spatial frontiers of the
> Colombian economy only to find that after they cut down the forest, planted it
> in domestic crops, and built homesteads, the land is taken over by large owners
> by political and economic means. The house economy, thus, remains in a state
> of perpetual marginality relative to the corporate system.

There are several corollaries to the principle of the big stone and the
little man. The first is that the greater the extent to which control over resources is shifted from local to extra-local forces under these circumstances,
the greater the likelihood that the resources will be degraded (see also Brookfield et al. 1990: 499).[15] A second corollary is that whenever the value or importance of a particular resource diminishes, local communities will likely
be able to reassert some control and resume some benefit—and the process
of degradation may begin to be reversed.[16] The obverse is also true, which is
the third and final corollary principle: whenever extra-local forces encourage resource development by local peoples and permit it to remain in local
hands, this development is by definition likely to be of less interest to the
wider world, and for this same reason it is likely to be less beneficial for the
local peoples themselves.

When the twentieth century's purportedly biggest gold discovery was
made in East Kalimantan in 1997, by Bre-X Minerals Ltd., the primary
battle over rights to the claim was fought between the children of then-
President Suharto—the possibility of a rightful claim being made by local
communities was not even discussed. But when the claim was proven to be
fraudulent two years later, small North American investors got stuck holding
most of the worthless stock. The association between little men and worth-

less resources was aptly expressed in the title of a *New York Times* (1997) article on the subject, "Small Investors and Big Money Taken by Tale of Jungle Gold" (see also Tsing 2000, 2005). In short, the claim proved to be so worthless that it was passed off to "little men."

Contrary Development Theory

The big stone and little man pattern of local resource development followed by extra-local appropriation is widespread but scarcely recognized. Marginal tropical forest communities are commonly seen as challenged not with the loss of the resources that they already have but with not having the resources that they need. This obfuscation of reality can be seen clearly in the rain forest marketing of such goods as breakfast cereals.

Rain Forest Marketing

The belief that underdevelopment and environmental degradation are linked on the one hand, and on the other hand that economic development and conservation also are linked, led to the rise of integrated conservation and development projects (ICDPs) in the 1980s. Problems with these projects led to a backlash from conservationists, which is the subject of an ongoing debate. An important type of ICDP was based on the idea of rain forest marketing, which was initially popularized by some northern nongovernmental organizations (NGOs), including Cultural Survival[17] and its marketing arm Cultural Survival Enterprises, Inc. (Clay 1991, 1992a, 1992b). The goal of rain forest marketing was to help forest peoples replace unsustainable agricultural uses of the forest with sustainable gathering and marketing of nontimber forest products. The physical manifestation of this solution came to be seen on the shelf of any grocery or health food store in the northern industrialized countries in the form of cereals such as Rainforest Crisp and Rainforest Flakes, cookies like Cashew Crunch, drinks like Rainforest Tea, cosmetics like the Body Shop's Rainforest Bath Beads,[18] as well as Rainforest Crunch ice cream,[19] and Rainforest Crunch candy. Even a Rain Forest Dog Food became available. These were important forerunners of today's much vaster green consumerism movement.

The premise of rain forest marketing is that if the return to market-oriented exploitation of the forest can be raised high enough, purportedly destructive nonmarket, subsistence-oriented exploitation will cease. The corollary premise, therefore, is that the problem of tropical deforestation is a problem of economic miscalculation: the forest is being cleared because its marketable riches have been overlooked and/or underexploited. Thus, a container of Rainforest Crunch ice cream states "Rainforest Crunch helps to show that the rainforests are more profitable when their nuts, fruits & medicinal plants are cultivated for traditional harvest than when their trees are cut and burned for short-term gain." And a box of Rainforest Crisp breakfast cereal[20] states that its marketing venture helps to raise the economic returns to forest residents from forest nuts by 2,000 percent, and that the "increased revenues from the nut harvest make the trees too valuable to cut down." The implication, therefore, is that when the incomes of local forest dwellers are too low, the forest is *not* too valuable to cut down. Deforestation thus is linked to local poverty, which in turn is linked to exploitation of the wrong products of the tropical forest in the wrong way. The key is presumed to be finding the right products and the right way. The underlying premise of rain forest marketing, in short, is that global market mechanisms are inefficient or faulty—they overlook exotic products and marginal peoples—but they are basically benign, when they can be made to work properly through outside experts' efforts at discovery and integration.

According to the thesis of rain forest marketing, local forest communities are primarily responsible for degradation of tropical forests and lands;[21] and the proposed solution to this is to intensify their exploitation of non-timber forest products (NTFPs). Thus, proponents of rain forest marketing argue that sustained Brazil nut production can provide three to five times as much income from a given area of land as forest clearance and cattle raising (Clay 1992b: 34). One box of Rainforest Flakes states: "Rainforest Products [the name of the firm involved] and other related companies are working together with Cultural Survival to demonstrate that forest residents can make more money per year from the sale of nuts and fruits than they can by logging and ranching." The clear implication is that it is the forest residents who are doing the logging and ranching and so the challenge is to make sustainable forest uses more profitable for them than nonsustainable uses. But the real question is not how profitable logging and ranching are compared with the sale of nuts and fruits, but rather *who* is doing the logging and ranching and *who* would be doing the selling of nuts and fruits? In most cases, the two groups are very different;[22] and whereas the latter are likely to be local forest residents, the former are not. Local communities are usually not the perpetrators but rather the victims of large-scale resource degradation. What is needed is not to make forest protection more profitable for local forest dwellers, therefore, but to make forest destruction less profitable for outsiders—and it seems unlikely that breakfast cereal can play a role in this. We cannot, for example, imagine reading on the back of a cereal box, "Purchase of this rain forest product will enable timber kings and cattle barons to make more money per year from the sustained production of forest nuts and fruits than from laying waste the forest." What is needed to mitigate deforestation, therefore, is not better identification and valuation of forest resources, but rather better identification of and discrimination between the beneficiaries of deforestation and its victims.

A recent synthesis of work on the topic concludes that market involvement produces mixed effects on resource conservation and the well-being of local peoples, which are hard to assess in any case because rigorous studies are lacking (Godoy et al. 2005). But the premise that tropical forest conservation will be promoted by not less but more engagement in the global economy is contradicted by the history of tropical forest resource development (Corry 1993a, 1993b; Lohmann 1991). In addition, the premise that there are resources in the tropical forests that are underexploited by the forest peoples is directly contradicted by the historic depth of exploitation of such resources for global markets, with its characteristic recurring pattern of the big stone and the little man. This history should lead us to ask: If these forest products are as valuable as rain forest marketers suggest, why have local communities not exploited them before? And why are extra-local elites likely to allow such exploitation instead of appropriating the products for themselves? One danger of rain forest marketing is that it will attract the unwanted attention of outsiders to the few forest resources still left in the hands of local communities, with the result that these resources will be lost as well.[23] There also are underlying biogeographical contradictions in rain forest marketing schemes that have received little attention. Romanoff (1992: 132) points out that the same factors that make exploitation of forest products practical in some parts of the world, through such means as extractive reserves, also foster hierarchical political-economic systems that mitigate against broad-based sharing in the benefits of this exploitation.

An even greater danger for forest communities is that the focus of rain forest marketing on developing new commodities like Rainforest Crunch will deflect the attention of sympathetic outsiders from the fact that these communities already have valuable resources that they are not allowed to fully exploit for their own benefit. The structure of many commodity markets is biased in favor of national and international elites and against the local community who produce or first developed them. Indeed, World Bank analysts have suggested that the quickest and most productive way to improve the economic welfare of Indonesia's marginal communities, like those in Borneo's forests, would be through deregulation and rationalization of these markets. Buying a box of Rainforest Crunch will not help these marginal communities, but forcing a government to terminate ruinous commodity monopolies might.

The smallholder cultivation of *Hevea* rubber is a good example of a valuable commodity that forest communities have long possessed and whose further development would benefit from supportive as opposed to punitive intervention from the wider society. The developmental history of rubber suggests that there is less need to find new forms of resource use for local communities, than to find political mechanisms to combat the self-interested domination of existing forms of resource use by national elites. Some rain forest marketing efforts now recognize this political calculus and are attempting to build it into their programs, empowering local producers through the formation of cooperatives, for example. The lesson of the big stone and the little man for conservationists is that they would, in practice, better attain their ends by protecting the people in the tropical forest than protecting the forest itself.

"Neglected" Forest Products

A premise of rain forest marketing is that tropical forest resources have been neglected. Work over the past two decades on nontimber forest products has focused on showing that the prevailing calculus of the wealth of tropical forests has been in error. Peters, Gentry, and Mendelsohn's (1989) widely cited study concludes that the market value of sustainable exploitation of nontimber forest products (NTFPs) in the Amazon exceeds that of exploiting the timber or converting the land to other uses. But if Peters, Gentry, and Mendelsohn are correct in their calculations, this raises the question: Why was the prevailing calculus of where value lay in the tropical forest so ill-informed? Surprisingly little systematic effort has been made to answer this question, beyond assuming that the subject is understudied. De Beer and McDermott (1989) carried out a pioneering baseline survey of NTFPs in Southeast Asia with the support of the International Union for the Conservation of Nature.[24] They call NTFPs a "neglected resource," the role of which in the national and local economies of Southeast Asian countries has been "overlooked," which they explicitly blame on lack of study: "That policy-makers tend to forget the role of non-timber forest products is not surprising given the lack of readily available information on the subject" (ibid.: 13, 125). As to why this subject is understudied, the only explanations offered have been economic ones. Thus, Homma (1992: 25) writes, "Given the nature of Amazonian forests, with their generally low densities of individual species, large distances to market, difficult living conditions, and lack of information about the market potential, the best stocks of forest resources are sometimes not even recognized." Peters, Gentry, and Mendelsohn (1989: 656) attribute differential knowledge of forest resources to differences in market structures: "We believe that the problem lies not in the actual value of these resources, but in the failure of public policy to recognize it. Tropical timber is sold in international markets and generates substantial amounts of foreign exchange; it is a highly visible export commodity controlled by the government and supported by large federal expenditures. Nonwood resources, on the other hand, are collected and sold in local markets by an incalculable number of subsistence farmers, forest collectors, middlemen, and shop owners. These decentralized trade networks are extremely hard to monitor and easy to ignore in national accounting schemes."

There is a political dimension to this neglect and understudy, however. When forest products are important to national governments, they are studied; and the reverse also is true.[25] For example, the colonial Dutch government's major economic interest in *gutta-percha* and *jelutong*, products that are today of minimal economic importance, was clearly reflected in the Netherlands East Indies' colonial forestry literature, a compendium of which lists sixty-four and thirty-two references, respectively, on these two products alone (CAPD 1982). The association between state interest and research attention is reflected in de Beer and McDermott's (1989: 17) own observation that research interest in rattan had increased significantly in recent years, a development that closely paralleled the explosion of the global market in the 1970s and 1980s and the attendant increase in the value of Indonesian rattan and involvement in its exploitation by state elites. What de Beer and McDermott (ibid.) see as an imbalance in scholarly inattention to forest products is actually an imbalance in governmental and institutional interest. NTFPs were ignored during much of the twentieth century and deemed "minor" because central governments were focusing their extractive interest on timber.

Nonvaluable Forest Products (NVFPs)

Much of the effort to reveal the hidden value in tropical forest re-sources, in order to combat deforestation and degradation, is focused on the wrong actors and resources. One contributor to the field wrote, "Recent studies on indigenous peoples and the impact of their traditional life-styles on tropical forests appear to indicate that crafts development represents a constructive alternative to destructive land-use practices" (Kerr 1991: 33). A similar conclusion was reached in a United Nations (UNESCO/FAO) study of the potential efficacy of developing forest-based handicrafts and other resources to contribute to forestry development and protection in Kalimantan (reported in Ohlsson 1990). The authors of the United Nations study concluded that in addition to handicrafts, the income of forest peoples can be supplemented by "agriculture or other activities, such as butterfly farms, crocodile farms, fish farms, and medicinal plant collection" (ibid.: 69). Notably absent from this list are the tropical forest resources of greatest importance to global society: valuable hardwoods, trees for pulp, gems and other minerals, the world's greatest botanical gene pool, rubber, and other smallholder export crops such as coffee, tobacco, and coconuts. The omis-sion of these resources from the list in the United Nation's study implicitly endorses the claim of extra-local interests to these resources and weakens the claims of the forest communities themselves.

The concept of nontimber forest products itself is highly politicized. Whereas the term NTFP appears to be a politically neutral botanical refer-ence to a slice of tropical forest resources, it has hidden premises, and its power comes precisely from the fact that they are hidden. There are two key premises here: the first is that NTFPs are resources that local people may be allowed to exploit; the second and associated premise is that NTFPs are resources that no one *but* local people would want to exploit. That is, NTFPs are not just nontimber forest products, they are in fact nonvaluable forest products, or NVFPs. The rhetorical constraints of the concept of NTFPs/ NVFPs are reflected in the fact that these terms are never applied in the context of any large-scale development of tropical forest resources. For ex-ample, there is no reason to not think of mineral resources as NTFPs, but it is difficult to imagine the world's biggest gold-and-copper mine, the Free-port mine in the rain forests of West Papua, being called a "nontimber forest product project." By "unpacking" the reasons that lie behind this semantic difficulty, further insights into the subjective underpinnings of contemporary understandings of tropical forest resource use can be obtained. Terms like *nontimber forest products* used in discussing tropical forest development and conservation, though appearing to be politically neutral, in fact have far-reaching implications for power and equity.

For a part of the world as rich in resources as Borneo's tropical forests, a list of potential income sources for local communities that cannot transcend butterfly and crocodile farms is a recommendation not for the empowerment of the forest peoples but for their impoverishment (see also Li 2007: 141). The list of potential sources of income in the United Nations' study is a list not of what the broader society values most, but of what it values least. It is a list of what the broader society is likely to *allow* the forest peoples to keep—so long as some twist of fate or the market does not suddenly render one of these products more valuable (like the big stone)—than is deemed appropriate for marginal peoples.[26] The search for additional forest products for lists such as this, the search for "new" sources of income for marginal forest inhabitants, often seems to be a search for opportunities that have no other claimants, a search for the least coveted development alternatives.

The Problem of Wealth and Powerlessness

According to prevailing development policies, poor forest peoples need to be helped to develop. Alatas (1977: 8) sees the image of the developmentally needy native as the contemporary equivalent of the colonial image of the lazy native: "The image of the indolent, dull, backward and treacherous native has changed to that of a dependent native requiring assistance to climb the ladder of progress."

Rich Forests and Poor People

The history of resource exploitation in Borneo is at variance with the rain forest marketing premise that forests are overexploited by forest communities due to inadequate income from forest products. The analysis here suggests that there has been no lack of such sources of income in the past and that the problem has lain in maintaining the forest communities' control of them. This analysis suggests that the nature of the relationship between resource degradation and the underdevelopment of forest peoples often is the reverse of that commonly claimed. Resources are not degraded because forest peoples are impoverished; rather, these peoples are impoverished by the degradation of their resources by extra-local actors. Ironically, this degradation, the instrument of their impoverishment, is blamed on the forest communities themselves. Their proximity to the resource base makes them an easy target for blame for degradation, and their lack of political capital makes it difficult for them to contest this charge. The problem is not that forest communities are poor in resources, therefore, but that they are politically weak; and the problem is not that the forest is environmentally fragile, but that it is politically marginal. The forest peoples of Indonesia are not just physically but also culturally and politically distant from the nation's seats of power. From ancient times in Indonesia, forest residence has been associated with antiestablishment views, held by those using the forest as a place from which to flee, or assail, the central state (Dove 1985a, 2003). This political poverty often coincides geographically with resource wealth (Dove 1996). The resulting problem for the forest peoples is that they inhabit a resource base that is coveted by groups more powerful than they. From the standpoint of conservation, the problem for the forest is that it is inhabited by peoples who are too weak to insist on its sustainable use—hence my earlier observation that it is not the forest but its peoples that conservationists should be trying to protect.[27] For two decades, anthropologists influenced by post-structural theory, like Escobar (1994) and Ferguson (1990), have been studying the discourse of development, including the way that politics are imbricated in expressions of concern for the needy.[28] The conservation-and-development discourse about how best to "conserve" tropical forest resources and "develop" forest dwellers appears to be apolitical. But in fact, it represents forest dwellers as uninformed agents of resource degradation and extra-local elites as informed agents of "improvement" (see Li 2007). This hegemonic interpretation of resource use focuses attention on the microeconomics of subordinate forest communities, thereby diverting attention from the broader political-economic causes of resource degradation and underdevelopment and masking the need for more challenging change in the superordinate structures of power.

This discursive relocation of responsibility is well illustrated by rain forest marketing: the rhetoric of this approach frames the challenge of tropical resource conservation as the question, Will the wider society "help" impoverished tropical populations to improve their economic returns from alternate uses of the forest so as to reduce their destruction of the forest? But the real challenge is not whether the wider society will decide to help or not; rather, it is whether the wider society will be willing to recognize its own role

in creating the problem in the first place. There is considerable irony, therefore, in the offer of "help" by the agents of resource degradation to the victims of this degradation. The colonial novelist Dekker referred to the "cow-
ardice" of "*invoking public charity* for the *victims of chronic piracy*" (Multatuli
[1859] 1982: 319). As Li (2006: 33) writes a century and a half later, with
respect to the World Bank's current village development program in Indonesia, "The benevolence of a program does not excise the element of power."

This poverty-based explanation of forest degradation confers several
distinct benefits on political elites. First, it focuses the public discourse on
the need to develop the economy and culture of the forest communities. This
adds to the benign tone of the discourse and thereby strengthens it (see also
Tsing 1993: 296). Second, the emphasis on poverty precludes recognition
of the actual resource wealth of distant forest communities. It is much less
problematic to assume that forest peoples have no resources than to explain
why the resources that they have are being taken away from them. The emphasis on what the state needs to do *for* such communities effectively precludes attention to what the state has done and is doing *to* them. Li (2006: 34)
has similarly critiqued the World Bank's view of development in Indonesia
as "a matter of addition" instead of "altering existing economic relations."
Ironically, the emphasis on the forest communities' purported lack of resources, and on the need to remedy this, supports their resource disenfranchisement and helps to make this fictional resource scarcity a reality. Third
and last, the poverty thesis affords the central government another excuse for
further extending its bureaucratic authority into the lives of forest communities, which, as Ferguson (1990: xv) argues, may be the actual objective of
much rural development planning. The association of resource degradation
with poverty as opposed to wealth constitutes a "discursive knot" (Rabinow
1986: 253). It is tied by asking, How can we help? and, What do we need to
give *to* tropical forest peoples? This knot can be untied by asking instead,
How are we hurting? and, What have we taken *from* tropical forest peoples?

Wickham's "Theft" of Brazilian Rubber

The modern conservation and development discourse of what resources need to be given *to* tropical forest communities, which obfuscates the
actual history of taking resources *from* them, is illuminated by the famous
case in which the opposite occurred: the nontaking of a resource that was
trumpeted worldwide, referring to Wickham's collection of rubber seeds (see

chapter 4). The story of the gathering of seventy thousand seeds of *Hevea* in the Amazon in 1876 by Henry Wickham, which eventually became the basis of the rubber industry in Southeast Asia, has been widely recounted as the "theft" by England of Brazil's rubber. A typical version comes from the historian Melby (1942: 464):[29] "The Far Eastern rubber industry owes its beginnings to Henry A. Wickam [*sic*], a British planter from Santarem. In 1876 he smuggled several thousand rubber seeds from Brazil and sowed them in Kew Gardens in London." In addition to Melby, many other scholars have repeated this story of Wickham "smuggling" and "hoodwinking" Brazilian officials in an operation of "Bondian intrigue" (Brockway 1979: 157; Kano 2008: 180; Kloppenburg 1988: 156; Wolf 1982: 329). As Schultes (1987: 91) writes, "Tales concerning the 'British seed steal' are [still] rife." Wickham was eventually knighted by Britain for this exploit. Brazilians, on the other hand, to this day revile his name, reproach their government for permitting the theft, and reproach themselves for failing to domesticate rubber in its native land. Contemporary critics of the global economic order cite Wickham's "theft" as an example of the perfidy of the global North. Shiva (1993: 79) says that the North "stole" the rubber heritage of Brazil in particular and the South in general. Wickham's exploits are also widely cited by critics of contemporary collecting of biogenetic materials in southern countries by northern scientists (Brush 2004).

The thesis that rubber's theft served colonial power relations is not entirely consistent with the historical facts, however. The transplanting of rubber empowered an entire class of smallholders in Southeast Asia—although it *dis*empowered an entire class of coolies on rubber estates in Southeast Asia, including in Indonesia (Stoler 1985a)—and by ending the rubber industry in the Amazon it freed a class of laborers there from a notoriously exploitative system (Schultes 1987: 90). The colonial histories of other commodities, like cloves and cinchona, similarly show that it was regional monopolies—not the breaking of them—that tended to produce the most oppressive conditions for the laboring classes.[30] Nor can rubber's transplanting be faulted on equity grounds at national or international levels. Whereas Brazil "lost" rubber, for example, it gained coffee—which was long its foremost export—from French Guyana, and this case actually does appear to be a theft. As Schultes (1984: 9) writes, "[M]any Brazilians are persuaded to believe that rubber seeds were 'stolen' or 'smuggled' out of the country, however, and fail to realize that Brazil's major agricultural industries are based on plants introduced from foreign countries: coffee (originally from Abyssinia), rice (from India), sugar (from Southeast Asia), soybeans (from China), jute (from India), cacao (from Colombia and Ecuador)." Moreover, Kloppenburg (1988: 182) notes that the global history of circulation of biogenetic resources does not simply show a flow from South to North: "Genetic 'dependence' is not exclusively a characteristic of the northern regions. The Africa region [for example] has a dependency index of 87.7 percent [meaning that 87.7 percent of its food crops are non-native to Africa]." Whereas the transplanting of rubber benefited the northern industrialized countries during colonial times, this is obviously not true today when the Southeast Asian rubber-producing countries themselves belong to the southern block.

The correction of the historical record on Wickham has long been public. Wolf and Wolf critiqued it at length in 1936, and in 1944 Ashplant published an article entitled "Wickham Not a Smuggler" in a rubber industry journal. Recent scholarly debunkings of the myth include Keong (1976: 3), Purseglove (1968: 148–50), Schultes (1984, 1987), and Wycherley (1968), as well as Dean's authoritative 1987 monograph. These critiques have had little impact, however. As Dean (1987: 7) writes, "Although the documents lie near at hand, abundant and unfaded, a marvelous version of events prevails. . . . This is the myth of Henry Wickham, the English rogue, thief of rubber seeds." Why has this version prevailed, in spite of the facts, for so long, and for so many disparate audiences? Theft is a prominent theme in cultural myths about the origins of agriculture. Pollan (2001: 84) writes, "Very often in myth, a theft, and its consequence of shame, lies at the root of a human achievement—think of Prometheus's theft of fire from the sun or Eve's tasting of the fruit of knowledge." Theft, the Promethean act, is one of the ultimate acts of agency. Dean (1987: 7), who titles his chapter on the theft "Prometheus in Reverse," suggests that the bounty of agriculture is so great that it must be seen to have been paid for by human sacrifice and suffering.

The myth of Wickham's rubber theft is premised on stasis in the ownership and management of biogenetic resources—but nothing could be further from the truth. The norm throughout human history has been *movement* of economic plants through migration, travel, and trade. It is nonmovement, enforced by the extreme exertions of the power of the state and its corporations—as in the Dutch clove monopoly or today's patent-based agribusinesses—that is the anomaly. Quite often, theft plays a role in this movement: the global history of agriculture is rich with cases of theft (Brush 2004; Harms 2003). In addition to attributing the spread of the potato in France to a theft from the royal gardens of Louis XVI, Pollan (2001: 83–84) similarly derives the development of the tulip industry in Holland from a theft from Carolus Clusius, who introduced tulips to Leiden from Vienna but unwisely refused to part with any. Even such a pillar of probity as Thomas Jefferson was apparently guilty of smuggling Italian rice to the United States (Brush 2004). The Dayak share Jefferson's passion and tactics: the surreptitious removal of interesting-looking plants from one another's fields has long been a custom. As noted in Chapter 1, even the *Hevea* of smallholders in the Indo-Malay region owe their origins, in many cases, to surreptitious removal of seed or seedlings from colonial plantations early in the twentieth century. But these actual cases of plant theft have failed to attain anything like the role in the global imagination of Wickham's nontheft.

The enduring appeal of the myth of Wickham's theft derives from what it says about history, or about what people would like to think is history. In the rubber myth, it is Brazil and the less-developed world that suffer and the colonial powers and the industrialized North that reap the bounty—and of course there is an element of historical truth to this framing. From the standpoint of Brazil in particular and the global South in general, which feel that the colonial and post-colonial industrialized North has misappropriated the biogenetic heritage of the South, Britain did indeed transplant a vital industry from one part of the world to another and benefited hugely as a result. In this sense, there is a some structural truth to the theft. In this light, the mythical dimensions of the rubber story can be seen as a powerful, discursive way of mobilizing resources in current critiques of the North by the South.

The myth of Wickham's theft can be read as a statement about North-South relations and the role of agency and reward therein; it is a "myth model" (Obeyesekere 1992: 10) of North-South relations. The myth of the rubber theft is premised on a particular vision of the world. It assumes a dichotomy between North and South; it assumes that relations between the two can only be ones of violation and not collaboration (compare to Tsing 1999, 2000); it assumes that if the colonial British took something, it could only be by theft. It further assumes that all agency lies with the North: whereas the North can only steal, the South can only be stolen from. These are characteristically "modernist" assumptions regarding agency, power, and the global order, in which power is localized and consciously wielded by central, monolithic authorities in clearly defined oppositional relations with others (see also Dove et al. 2008).

CHAPTER 9

Plantations and
Representations in Indonesia

Kalau sudah punya uang, tidak mau bekerja. (Once the Dayak have money, they do not want to work.)
—*Official from a nucleus estate in West Kalimantan, interviewed at the headquarters of the National Plantation Training Institute in Yogyakarta, Central Java*

Asal sama makan, sama kerja, tidak ada yang tidak mau. Kalau pemerintah adil, tidak ada yang tidak mau. (If [everyone] eats [profits] the same and works the same, there is no one who will not want [to cooperate with the plantation program]. If the government is just, there is no one who will not want [to cooperate].)
—*Temenggung (traditional Dayak leader), interviewed near Sanggau, West Kalimantan*

The Challenge of Plantation Representation

In the early 1980s, what was to become an infamous tea party was held along the banks of the Kapuas River in West Kalimantan. The hostesses were the Javanese and Sumatran wives of the managers of a rubber nucleus estate being developed there, and the guests were the wives of local Dayak tribesmen. When the guests arrived, they gathered up the food that had been prepared and then left, taking the food with them and leaving their shocked hostesses behind. The managers of the plantation attributed this behavior to the purportedly strange and difficult culture of the tribesmen. I suggest that the tea party foundered not on cultural differences between the tribesmen and the plantation officials, however, but on conflicting economic and political interests that were couched as cultural differences. The Dayak behavior at this tea party was an attempt to make a public statement about this conflict. The planters' interpretation of the tea party represented a countereffort not to argue with this statement but to deny that it was a statement at all and, by implication, to deny the existence of any such conflict.

Peasant-Planter Conflict

Conflicts between plantation management and local communities are a salient component of Indonesia's rural ethnoscape. The national bureaucratic elite that manages the plantations largely attributes these conflicts to the cultural, economic, and political backwardness of the local peoples, often ethnic minorities, which is an explanation that privileges planter interests and decisions at the expense of local interests and decisions. This planter discourse is quite uniform across different provinces, ethnic groups, and plantation types and crops. The issues at stake are not merely rhetorical: as Berry (1988: 66) writes, "Struggles over meaning are as much a part of the process of resource allocation as are struggles over surplus or the labor process." In Indonesia's contemporary plantation sector, power does not work merely through the self-serving scheming of elites; it also works through the discourse by means of which the planters perceive and represent the plantation world. The planters' representations do not merely support plantation extraction but, more powerfully, these representations deny legitimacy to local community efforts to resist or temper that extraction. A premise of local cultural, economic, and mental backwardness—which enables plantation managers to misinterpret conflicts over the economic and political rights of local communities as conflicts over their culture—is integral to the institutional culture of Indonesia's parastatal plantations.

Much of the material in this chapter concerns problems on nucleus-estate schemes, which consist of smallholdings clustered around and selling their produce to a nucleus government estate, as described in chapters 1 and 4. Most of these problems stem from conflict between the estates and local communities over the issue of land compensation, arising from the fact that many of these projects have been developed on land consisting of swidden fallows, groves of fruit trees, and rubber gardens developed and of course claimed by local communities. Indeed, the managers of one nucleus estate near Singkawang in West Kalimantan openly acknowledged that most of the land on which they developed this estate was formerly *hutan karet* and *hutan sekonder* (jungle rubber and secondary forest on fallowed swiddens).[1] When such lands are appropriated for nucleus-estate projects, local claimants are hard-pressed to obtain any compensation from the estate. If the claimant joins the estate project as a smallholder, he or she usually must give up this chance of partial compensation, on the ground that participation in the project is sufficient compensation in itself. The problem with this reasoning lies in the government loans that each farmer must assume as a condition of project participation, to cover the cost of government investment in the farmer's share of the project infrastructure. The size of the loan is the same for the local farmer whose lands are appropriated for the project as it is for the transmigrant from Java or Bali who brings nothing to the project. The inequity of this policy predisposes some local farmers against participation in these projects; it lessens the commitment to repay the loans of those who do participate; and it has convinced some local government officials of the need for policy change. Provincial officials in West Kalimantan have stated that the key to making nucleus-estate projects successful is to "membedakan antara pendatang dan orang lokal" (distinguish between the newcomers [namely, from Java and Bali] and the local people), because the latter contribute land to the project whereas the former do not.[2] Even in the absence of this problem, however, many nucleus-estate schemes founder on their own internal economics or ecology. In one case reported from Cimerak in West Java, actual earnings averaged as little as 4 percent of official projections, forcing participants into prostitution to stave off hunger (*Down to Earth* 1990b: 10–11). In another case in Mendjalin sub-district, Pontianak district, West Kalimantan, mortality rates for the high-yielding rubber clones provided by the scheme averaged 70 percent, in spite of which the government still insisted upon full repayment of the loan that was provided to the participants to purchase these clones in the first place[3] (compare to Gouyon, de Foresta, and Levang 1993: 198–200).

Studying Planters' Views of Peasants

The data presented here on plantation managers are drawn primarily from a unique year-long study carried out for the Lembaga Pendidikan Perkebunan (LPP, Plantation Training Institute) in Yogyakarta, Central Java. The study brought together a three-man team of social scientists, including myself—from Gadjah Mada University where I worked as a visiting professor and research advisor for six years—senior officials in the institute, and visiting plantation managers. The visiting managers came from plantations (and some sugar mills) from all over Indonesia but principally from Java, Sumatra, Sulawesi, and Kalimantan. The managers were mostly Javanese or Batak and, in most cases, in particular on the outer islands, did not hail from the local ethnic group.

The Plantation Training Institute study was structured around a visit to the institute each month by a different team of managers from a different plantation, selected on the basis of a marked level of conflict with local workers or communities. These conflicts involved one or more of four distinct categories of people: (1) permanent plantation employees (*karyawan*), (2) smallholder participants in nucleus estates, (3) day laborers (*buruh harian*) hired from nearby villages, and (4) other inhabitants of proximate, often-tribal communities who came into conflict with the plantation over land appropriation or other matters.[4] The visiting plantation managers would present written and oral accounts of these conflicts, upon which the university team and officials from the institute then commented. In addition to participating in this commentary, I took notes during the formal presentations, analyzed the planters' written texts, and gathered data as an institutional participant-observer. Since these monthly seminars were not public, and since most of the visiting managers had studied formally at the institute, my premise was that their reports largely reflected the actual views, policies, and practices of plantation managers. This premise was supported by subsequent field visits by the university team to specific plantations—in my case, to plantations in West Kalimantan and Southeast Sumatra—where this process of reporting and commenting was continued with plantation officials, workers, and local peoples. At the end of the year, the university team presented summaries of our findings to a large assembly of plantation managers at the Plantation Institute.

The expectation of the plantation managers regarding this study was that the university-based social science study team would help them to better understand the behavior of workers and local peoples that they deemed inimical to plantation policies. Instead of problematizing the peasants' reality of the intended subjects of the study, however, we wound up more often than not problematizing the reality of the planters. In my own part of the analysis, I attempted to transcend the particularistic aspects of individual conflicts by isolating what seemed to be common and distinctive features of them all, namely, a discourse that privileged the reality of the planters at the expense of the reality of the peasants. This study of planters joins the few exceptions to the general neglect of this important topic by anthropologists (but see Errington and Gewertz 2004).

Planters' Interpretation and
Representation of Peasant Behavior

Plantation managers consistently invoked the same set of purported failings of workers or local villagers to explain conflicts on the plantations: two have to do with their general "otherness," namely, their *aneh* (strange) and their *bodoh* (obtuse) behavior; and two have to do in particular with perceived weakness in their economic behavior, namely, their *kemalasan* (laziness) and their *pencurian* (thievery).

"Strange" Behavior: The Tea Party

Criticisms of local culture and personality punctuated the oral and written reports of the plantation managers who were interviewed in the Plantation Institute study, especially those working on the outer islands. For example, managers from a sugar mill in South Sulawesi referred to Bugis workers as having "low IQs" and being *serik* (jealous), *emosionil* (quick to anger), and *keras watak* (hardheaded).[5] Managers from a rubber nucleus-estate project in West Kalimantan referred to Dayak tribesmen as *masyarakat terbelakang* (backward people) and criticized them as follows:[6] "kurang disiplin karena cara hidup yang bebas dan berpindah-pindah sehingga merasa kurang terikat oleh peraturan-peraturan/norma-norma hidup dalam lingkungan masyarakat yang sudah menetap" (undisciplined because of a way of life that is free and nomadic so that they feel less bound by the rules and norms of a society that has settled down)."[7] The plantation managers also reported numerous cases of "strange" and disturbing peasant behavior.

The tea party described at the beginning of this chapter was represented as one of the most disturbing cases encountered. The managers of the plantation attributed this *perilaku aneh* (strange behavior) of the Dayak women to the problematic culture of the tribesmen; and they cited this tea party as an example of how—even with the best of intentions, when inviting them to tea—it was impossible to get along with them. The plantation managers who reported the tea party incident said that it was not the loss of the food that bothered them; of that, they said, "Tidak apa-apa" (It does not matter). They said what upset them was that this behavior had "frightened" their wives. These planters regarded the incident as but one more example of the strangeness of Dayak culture and of the planters' consequently understandable difficulty in dealing with them.

In actuality, the plantation managers' interpretation of the tea party ignored the two central facts of the incident. First, the Dayak clearly *intended* their behavior at the tea party to be if not strange and frightening, at least offensive. When the Dayak of this region attend feasts in other households or villages, all food and drink are customarily consumed on the spot: the guests take nothing home for later consumption (Dove 1988: 165n24). Ironically, it is the ethnic group of many of the plantation managers, the Javanese, whose custom it is to take food home from rituals like the *slametan* (Geertz 1960: 13); but the reaction of the plantation hostesses—some of whom were Javanese—indicates that they did not expect the tea to follow Javanese norms in this respect. The second salient fact of the tea party is that the Dayak forcibly took *food* from the planters. Other reports indicated that these Dayak did not believe that they had received proper compensation for hereditary lands appropriated by this plantation. The Dayak appropriation of plantation food must be viewed as a counterpoint to the plantation's own appropriation of the source of Dayak food, their land. By saying that the loss of the food was unimportant and that the real problem was the bizarre culture of the Dayak, the planters' rhetoric diverted attention away from the economic dimensions of the conflict in favor of spurious cultural dimensions.[8] The planters' interpretation of the tea party also may be disingenuous. There is a tradition going back to colonial times, with which these planters would have been acquainted, of feeding plantation workers before negotiations in an attempt to improve the planters' negotiating position (Stoler 1985a: 147). The behavior of the Dayak women can be seen as an effective method of countering this ploy: by forcibly appropriating the food, they contested the planters' construction of the situation as one of planter generosity and worker indebtedness.

In addition to stories of behavior that they found strange, plantation managers told stories of peasant behavior of which they approved. Typical is the following description of a Dayak village head and participant in a rubber nucleus-estate project, as he appeared for a meeting with project officials: "Perilaku Tero menimbulkan ciri-ciri tersendiri yang tanpa disadari sedang adaptasi sistim nilai baru dengan cara-cara sebagai berikut. Menjelang rapat yang kami adakan, ia telah dua kali berganti pakaian. Achirnya ia berpakaian safari dan membawa surat (seperti orang kantor). Biasanya ia hanya pakai kaos oblong." (Tero's behavior revealed that he was unconsciously adapting to the new system of values, in the following manner. As the time for our meeting approached, he twice changed his clothes. Finally, he wore a safari suit and carried a letter file [just like an office worker]. Usually he wore only a T-shirt.)[9] By dressing not like the tribal farmer that he was but like the government civil servant that he was not, Tero self-consciously paid public obeisance to the plantation officials' belief in their own social superiority. The officials saw Tero as honoring not their system of values, however, but as honoring some more universal and modern "new system of values." The officials also stated that Tero was adapting "unconsciously" to this new system, but the report that Tero changed clothes twice before the meeting suggests a very conscious recognition of the difference in clothing norms between Dayak farmers and Javanese officials and a deliberate attempt to manipulate these norms for political and economic advantage.

"Obtuse" Behavior: Uncomprehending Workers versus Misunderstanding Planters

Another current of planter criticism of workers and local peoples locates the source of their "otherness" in various sorts of mental deficiencies, which are blamed for their incorrect behavior. The focus on mental shortcomings is reflected in the fact that the Plantation Training Institute had a staff psychologist to study problems with workers, as opposed to a sociologist, an anthropologist, or even an agricultural economist. Criticism of the workers' mental capacities is common: "Suku Dayak tidak mau bekerja pada bidang kegiatan yang memerlukan pikiran. Yang memerlukan latihan pun tidak mau. Hanya mau bekerja dengan menggunakan tenaga, misalnya tebas/tebang. Dayak mengerjakan sesuatu yang perlu mikir, tidak mau. Tidak bisa." (The Dayak do not want to work at anything that requires thinking. Not even anything that requires training. They only want to use their labor, for example in slashing and felling [the forest]. [As for] the Dayak doing anything that requires thinking, they are not interested. They cannot.)[10] Some plantation managers maintain not that their workers refuse to understand, but that they cannot understand. Plantation managers interviewed routinely attributed any reluctance to embrace plantation priorities on the part of either laborers or locals to thinking that was *negatip* (negative) or in which there was *kesenjangan* (asymmetry).[11] One manager from a rubber nucleus-estate in West Kalimantan suggested that the Dayak objected to his appropriation of their land because *mereka kurang mengerti* (they did not comprehend) the agrarian laws that purportedly permit this (but that in fact do not).[12] Another plantation manager (quoted in Sinar Harapan 1984) used a similar explanation to dismiss complaints about inadequate housing and the difference in lifestyle between laborers and managers on a nucleus (oil palm) estate project in Sumatra:[13] "Heboh mengenai perumahan peserta PIR lokal . . . sebenarnya tidak perlu terjadi kalau masyarakat mengerti tentang jiwa PIR lokal. . . . Barangkali hal itu lahir karena masyarakat kurang mengerti bagaimana posisi perkebunan negara waktu itu." (The fuss about housing for local participants in the nucleus estate . . . in fact did not need to occur if the people had comprehended the spirit of the project. . . . Probably that [envy] arose because the people did not comprehend what the role of the national plantation was at that time.) In short, in the eyes of the plantation officials, one of their main problems is that they are misunderstood by their workers.

Plantation managers believe that the solution to this lack of comprehension is mental change on the part of the workers or smallholders. As the managers of a rubber nucleus-estate project in South Kalimantan write, "Permasalahan yang utama adalah bagaimana mengubah sikap mental dan pola berpikir agar mereka mau bersikap dan berpikir sebagai petani pengusaha dalam usaha tani." (The main problem is how to change the [farmers'] mental character and pattern of thinking so that they have the attitude and thinking of entrepreneurial farmers in their farming activities.)[14] In a particularly egregious case, after officials of a nucleus-estate project in Sumatra's Riau Province reneged on promises to include local farmers in the project despite having appropriated their land, destroyed one thousand hectares of their rubber, and shot one farmer during an ensuing protest, the head of a government investigating commission concluded that if the local people were still *bodoh* (obtuse), then they should be taught the "right skills" (*Merdeka*, 12 January 1990, cited in *Down to Earth* 1990a: 3).[15] A typical proposal for changing the farmers' incorrect attitudes and pattern of thinking, made by a provincial official in West Kalimantan, included "pembinaan mental-spiritual, latihan dan pendidikan, kursus-kursus serta P4" (mental-spiritual indoctrination, training and education, and courses and indoctrination in the state ideology). The sweep of this proposal reflects not just official bewilderment over how to deal with the problem, but the fact that the problem itself—the crippled mentality of the workers and smallholders—is a conceit of the plantation imagination. These proposals are also characterized by the rhetoric of "helping" that was discussed in chapter 8: the "uncomprehending worker" is one that can and should be helped to overcome the source of his or her incomprehension. The rhetoric of helping is stretched to encompass the use of force with difficult workers, when this is necessitated by their purported immaturity. For example, a plantation manager in West Kalimantan told the

Plantation Training Institute study team that whenever his Dayak laborers cause him any trouble, he reports them to the local military garrison, which sends a patrol to intimidate them. As he ingenuously put it, "Saya tahu kelemahan suku Dayak: mereka takut baju hijau" (I know the weakness of the Dayak tribes: they are afraid of the green shirts [namely, the military]).

Many workers and smallholders share the planters' perception that the basic problem in their relationship is one of misunderstanding, although they attribute this to the planters, whereas the planters attribute it to the workers. It is noteworthy that the workers, like the planters, attribute the problem to a mistake of communication or interpretation as opposed to a conflict of interest. This is reflected in a comment made to me by Dayak activists in Pontianak in 1993, regarding the widespread and extremely disturbing felling of groves of fruit and rubber trees belonging to local tribesmen in the course of land-clearing operations for government plantation projects.[16] The Dayak activists believed that these clearances were due to the fact that their fruit and rubber groves cannot easily be distinguished from natural forest in the government's aerial surveys, especially given the Dayak practice of allowing undergrowth and secondary forest to fill in the spaces in these groves. As a result, the activists suggested, government surveyors often misclassified their groves of economic trees as unmanaged, public, and therefore available forest. These Dayak were correct that the government misperceives and misclassifies their landed resources; but they were incorrect in seeing this as an anomaly as opposed to an inevitable product of the government system of knowledge production.

"Laziness": Full-Time Workers but Part-Time Employees

Plantation managers claim that the tribesmen and peasants involved in their projects are not only culturally and mentally but also economically deficient. Thus, the managers of a rubber nucleus-estate project in South Kalimantan described the local Banjarese and Dayak to my study team as "kurang tekun dan kurang ulet" (not diligent and not persevering),[17] while one official of a rubber nucleus-estate project in West Kalimantan similarly berated the Dayak involved in their project as hopeless: "Ada prestasi rendah, karena hanya trampil dalam kegiatan tebas-tebang, karena tidak bisa menggunakan cangkul dan sebagainya. Menurut persepsi kita, mereka suka bermalas-malasan, tidak ada kemauan kerja." ([They] have low [work] output, because they are only skilled in slashing and felling [the forest], because they do not know how to use hoes and so on. According to our perceptions, they like to loaf around, and have no desire to work.) As the Plantation Training Institute staff psychologist said during one of our meetings (18 June 1984): "Banyak pendapat yang menyatakan bahwa penduduk lokal malas-malas. Hal ini tidak sama dengan pendapat Pak Michael Dove, yang menyatakan bahwa penduduk setempat baik." (Many are of the opinion that the local people [the Dayak of West Kalimantan] are lazy. This differs from the finding of Mr. Michael Dove, that the local people are good.) The plantation managers attribute this perceived low intensity of labor to the tribesmen's lack of needs, something that has concerned planters since colonial times. As Boeke (1953: 40) writes, "The most characteristic phenomena in the eastern society . . . find their simple explanation in the eastern premise of the limitedness of needs. . . . If three acres are enough to supply the needs of the household a cultivator will not till six." As another official from the aforementioned nucleus-estate project in West Kalimantan put it, in the epigraph to this chapter, "[Dayak] bekerja hanya untuk mendapatkan uang. Kalau sudah punya uang, tidak mau bekerja." (Dayak only work to get money. Once they have money, they do not want to work.)[18] Speaking of Bugis plantation workers in South Sulawesi, the manager of a sugar mill told the team, "Mereka bekerja di pabrik hanya untuk mencari uang tunai guna membayar pajak." (They work in the sugar mill only to obtain cash to pay their taxes.)[19] This same manager further told the study team that the Bugis continue to cultivate their own fields while working on the plantation. As a result, "Kesulitan: bagi karyawan, bekerja di pabrik bukan merupakan ketergantungan." (Problem: for the workers, working in the sugar mill is not something they must depend on.) The absence of this dependence is a "problem" for the plantation managers because an unvarying labor supply is one of the ingredients in successful plantation agriculture (for example, Murray 1992: 52–53). Yet avoidance of precisely this dependence is a principal desired outcome of many peasant and tribal household labor strategies in Indonesia.

Diversification of the household economy in time and space is a time-honored dimension of resource management in smallholder households throughout the world (see chapter 6). This diversification often involves not merely exploiting different resources but participating in completely different modes of production. As Coomes and Barham (1997: 183) write of forest dwellers in the Amazon: "With changing conditions, whether from price-cost shifts, ecological shocks, external policies or access to new resources,

Figure 9.1. New oil palm plantation in West Kalimantan

forest peoples have moved readily among the peasant, hired labour and petty capitalist classes . . . and in some cases effectively participated in more than one class at the same time." Thus, the Dayak and other ethnic minorities in Indonesia often work off-farm on plantations as part of a portfolio of activities designed to achieve a desired balance between needs and resources, and risks and rewards. This portfolio may include not only wage labor on plantations, but also swidden cultivation of food crops, cultivation of cash crops, and gathering of nontimber forest products for international markets. The place of wage labor in the overall portfolio, as just one activity of many, is not as determinant as planters would like it to be, because when a need for cash has been met, the workers may cease their wage labor and turn their attention to other parts of their portfolio, thus unexpectedly reducing the planters' labor force.

Over time it is possible for the conditions underlying the portfolio to change, however, elevating the role of wage labor to a more determinant position. This is illustrated by the case of one oil palm nucleus-estate project near Sanggau in West Kalimantan (figure 9.1): the conversion of tribal forests to state plantations and rising population/land ratios, among other factors, convinced many of the Islamicized Dayak living around this project that their best prospects for the future lay in full-time plantation work (see Dove 1986b: 7–8; compare to Stoler 1985a: 185–86).[20] As a result, these tribesmen said that they felt *susah* (aggrieved) when the planters placed a thirty-five-year-old age cap on candidates for *karyawan* (full-time employees), leaving many of them with no option but to work as *buruh harian* (day laborers).[21] The uncertainty and low wages of this daily labor makes it impossible, the tribesmen said, to "memikir tentang masa depan" (think about the future). In this case, where a deteriorating local subsistence base makes it easier for the plantation to find willing laborers, the tribesmen's desire to make a long-term commitment to the plantation is less welcome than in circumstances of labor scarcity. The underlying issue, therefore, is control of the mobilization of labor and responsibility for the reproduction of labor, which are recurring issues associated with the plantation mode of production. As Mintz (1959: 46) writes, "The plantation normally seeks to reduce its dependence on labor, while thriving in situations where labor is regularly or seasonally oversupplied."

Independence, Dependence, and Off-Estate Sales

The extent of autonomy granted to smallholders in the system of nucleus estates, however limited, still concerns a number of plantation officials. A manager from an oil palm nucleus estate near Sanggau in West Kalimantan maintained that the central mills that serve such smallholders must have some land of their own under palms, "supaya jangan tergantung kepada rakyat" (so that [the mill] will not be dependent upon the people). According to this manager, therefore, if the government-owned mill has to depend entirely upon the production of smallholders—who can in theory withhold their crops if they are dissatisfied with the price offered by the mill—then the mill's profits can be jeopardized. The plantation managers' pervasive concern for control also is reflected in the view that they take of peasant and tribal political institutions. They view any strong indigenous institution with suspicion, as posing an implicit threat to the exercise of total control by the plantation. Thus, in detailing the difficulties that they faced with Dayak and Buginese, plantation officials noted as problematic the fact that the former are "taat pada agama" (devoted to religion) and their "kehidupan kelompok kuat" (group life is strong), while the latter's "sifat sukuan masih kuat" (tribal nature is still strong). Indigenous institutions of land control are seen as particularly threatening to the plantation. In the words of an official on a plantation in West Kalimantan: "Perasaan mereka tentang memiliki tanah ulayat sangat kuat, sehingga terhadap undang-undang Agraria yang berlaku kurang mengerti, dan hal ini kepada pekerjaan mengalami hambatan karena banyak areal-areal yang telah digarap oleh kebun dipersengketan." (Their feeling that they own the communal land is very strong, as a result of which they do not understand the relevant Agrarian laws, due to which the [plantation] work is encountering difficulties because many areas that have already been planted by the plantation are being contested.)

Government planners in the provinces see one of the greatest problems with the rubber nucleus-estate projects as sales of produce by participating smallholders to outside buyers.[22] Planners object to these outside sales on the grounds that they jeopardize repayment of the loans that each of the smallholders assumed when joining the project to cover the cost of infrastructural investment. When the smallholders sell rubber to the estate, they receive only 70 percent of the price, the remaining 30 percent being taken by the project to pay off their loans. When they sell rubber to outsider buyers, however, they receive 100 percent of the sales price; and in some cases the outside buyers will also pay higher prices than the estate, which estate managers attribute to the fact that the estate has to deduct "infrastructural costs" from the price paid to its smallholders. In addition, outsiders buyers will usually buy anytime a smallholder wants to sell, whereas the nucleus estate only buys at certain times and on certain days. Government planners note that the outside buyers often pay in trade goods, which makes it that much more difficult for the smallholders to amass the currency needed to repay their loans. Government planners say that the problem of outside sales is especially hard to control when the nucleus-estate smallholdings are mixed in amongst traditional smallholdings, the product of which can legitimately be sold anywhere the smallholder wants. As noted in chapter 1, the response of many officials to this problem is to try to eliminate any such traditional smallholdings, called *daerah kantong* (enclaves), either near or within nucleus-estate projects.[23]

Estate managers regard outside sales as *pencurian* (thievery), and the most generous explanation that they can give for them is that they reflect a *masalah mental* (mental problem).[24] On the other hand, smallholder views of such sales are affected by their perception of the wider legitimacy of the estate projects, clouded as this is by such issues as uncompensated or poorly compensated appropriation of local lands and the failure to lessen the credit obligations of local participants to take into account their contribution of land to the project. Far from acknowledging these extenuating factors, however, government planners in West Kalimantan suggested that the problem with repayment of nucleus-estate loans had nothing to do with local issues at all but was due to the involvement in the projects of troublemaking transmigrants, including people who were involved in the attempted Communist coup of 1965.[25] Participants in the Cimerak nucleus-estate project in West Java who complained about the inequity of the terms of repayment of their loans were similarly accused by government officials of involvement in the outlawed Communist Party (*Down to Earth* 1990b: 11). The massacre of suspected Communists and others in the wake of the purported 1965 coup ranks as one of the twentieth century's worst episodes of communal violence. The implicit specter of such violence made an accusation of complicity on the Communist side the most potent threat in the political arsenal of the former "New Order" regime of Suharto.

What is achieved by these representations of plantation workers and smallholders, peasants, and tribesmen, as "thieving," "lazy," "obtuse," and "strange"? "Strangeness" and "obtuseness" have to do with "otherness" in general, whereas "laziness" and "foolishness" have to do with economic otherness in particular. Purported laziness and foolishness clearly have something to do with issues of control of labor and the products of labor, as do peasant strangeness and obtuseness, albeit less directly. Control of labor and the products of labor is a real problem in the real world for planters. Their characteristic representations of workers and smallholders as strange/ obtuse/lazy/foolish helps them cope with this problem, to the extent that they are able to represent it as a different, more tractable sort of problem. That is, it is in the planters' favor to represent resistance to the plantation's management policies as merely resistance to its cultural values (Stoler 1985a, 1985b).

The Construction of Planters' Knowledge of Workers and Smallholders

Plantation managers' views of plantation workers and smallholders as "strange," "obtuse," "lazy," and "thieving" are part of a wider, self-serving plantation discourse about the native "other."

Planters' Views of Workers and Smallholders

Leach (1982) writes that people discriminate themselves from "other" people according to food, sex, and attire. Borsboom (1988: 429) adds to this list reason versus emotion and communal versus private ownership. The examples just presented from the planters' anti-smallholder and anti-worker discourse—involving criticism of their cultures, emotions, intellect, labor, settlement patterns, temporal horizons, clothing, and eating customs—cover most of these points of discrimination. Indonesian plantation managers, therefore, characterize plantation workers and smallholders, local peasants and tribesmen, as the quintessential "other." Managers characterize workers in "polar" terms (Rosaldo 1978: 242), which emphasize the differences as opposed to similarities between them and thereby privilege the managers' interests over those of the workers.

In every case of conflict examined in the Plantation Institute study, problems that I attributed to differences between planter and peasant in economic self-interest were attributed by plantation managers to differences in culture, mentality, industry, and morality. There was no variation in this regard: plantation managers all over the Indonesian Archipelago, despite great local variation in ethnicity, economics, ecology, history, and politics, leveled the same criticisms, using the same words and phrases. There is a culture of plantation managers, a shared world view, that is a product of the centralized training at the Plantation Training Institute and of the subsequent mobility of plantation staff as they rotate between centers of plantation administration on Java and Sumatra and field postings in Kalimantan and elsewhere in the country.[26]

The way that planters represent workers and peasants today is remarkably like the way that planters represented them in the colonial era, even down to the use of the same pejorative terms and phrases. As Alatas (1977: 62) writes, "The theme of the lazy Javanese . . . functioned as a major constituent of the colonial ideology" in support of coercive agricultural policies. Similarly, Stoler shows that colonial planters in Sumatra varyingly blamed peasant resistance on social causes—the "child-like," irrational, and rapacious character of the coolie (1985a: 48, 51)—or political ones, depending upon whether their priority lay in respectively discouraging or encouraging interference by the colonial government in planter-coolie relations; but in neither case did they blame resistance on the embattled economic self-interests of the coolies. In the same vein, Elson (1979) notes reluctance on the part of colonial officials to link intentional burning of sugarcane fields to the deleterious impact of sugarcane cultivation on the economy of the Javanese peasantry. The continuity with the colonial plantation establishment is not surprising, since at independence Indonesia received the "wiring" of the plantation system more or less directly from the Dutch (Anderson 1983:

145): "Like the complex electrical-system in any large mansion when the owner has fled, the state awaits the new owner's hand at the switch to be very much its old brilliant self again." On the other hand, the Dutch themselves did not move into an empty mansion. As the initial chapters in this volume show, involvement in commodity production by native states in the archipelago predates the colonial era by nearly a millennium.

Workers' and Smallholders' Views of Planters

The views of plantation officials by workers, peasants, and tribesmen do not mirror the officials' views of them. In none of the cases examined do workers and local villagers impugn the culture, intelligence, or emotions of the officials. For example, disgruntled Dayak said of an oil palm nucleus-estate project in which they were involved near Sanggau in West Kalimantan, "Kami takut penipuan" (We are afraid of deception [on the part of the managers]) and "Kami takut Batak jadi Rajah" (We are afraid that the Batak [managers] will become lords).[27] They did not say, however, that they were afraid of the managers doing something "stupid," "irrational," or otherwise reflective of an unfathomably different cultural tradition. Villagers and workers assume that the managers share the same general interests and values as they do themselves. The peasants and tribesmen worry that the managers will maximize their interests to the detriment of their own, but they do not worry that the managers will maximize some alien and incomprehensible interest. The workers and villagers view the managers as potential adversaries, therefore, but not as alien "others."

Smallholders' and workers' views of planters also differ from planters' views in being less consistent: they do not characterize plantation officials in the same way in different parts of Indonesia, much less with identical terms or figures of speech. Rather, their characterizations vary according to their own ethnic group and the character of individual plantations and, especially, plantation managers. Stoler (1985a: 197) similarly notes that in North Sumatra, "Specific estate managers are singled out as individuals for being especially demanding, aloof, or compassionate, without any generic attributes commonly and consistently applied to them." While planters clearly think of workers as a "class," therefore, in the sense that they see most workers as sharing certain problematic characteristics, the reverse is not true.[28] This does not necessarily mean that the workers fail to recognize that much of the behavior of plantation managers is in fact determined by their membership in a wider managerial class, only that they use an idiom that is culturally and politically more appropriate. Scott (1984: 209) argues that it is both convenient and strategic for oppressed groups to focus on the "local and personal" causes of distress: it is convenient "to blame those who are most immediately and directly responsible for . . . reverses," and it is strategic "because it focuses on precisely those human agents which are plausibly within their sphere of social action."

The idiom of resistance used by plantation workers and smallholders is drawn from the value systems of the local peasant and tribal communities. As noted in the epigraph to this chapter, a Dayak *Temenggung* (traditional leader) levied this judgment regarding disputes over an oil palm nucleus-estate project near Sanggau in West Kalimantan: "Asal sama makan, sama kerja, tidak ada yang tidak mau. Kalau pemerintah adil, tidak ada yang tidak mau." (If [everyone] eats [profits] the same and works the same, there is no one who will not want [to cooperate with the plantation program]. If the government is just, there is no one who will not want [to cooperate].)[29] This comment reflects the fiercely egalitarian values of most of the Dayak groups in this part of Kalimantan (see Dove 1986b: 14, 17). Even the Islamicized Dayak groups vouchsafe similar values, as is reflected is the following commentary on the problem of increasing population/land pressure created by this same nucleus-estate project: "Cara disini, setiap suku punya tempat sendiri; tidak bisa lebih, tidak bisa kurang." (The way of things here, is that each group has its own niche, no more and no less.)[30] It is deviation from such local values that causes concern, as reflected in the aforementioned comment by other tribesmen in this area, that they feared the Batak managers were trying to become their *rajah* (lords). The tribesmen did not, for example, say they were afraid that the Batak managers would become *kaya* (rich). Acquiring wealth is an acceptable if not always socially esteemed goal in this tribal culture, but acquiring lordlike power over the lives of others is not.

Adas (1981: 228) writes that this sort of resistance was characteristic of the pre-colonial era, when "Peasants responded as members of a particular community and especially as the clients of particular landlords, local officials, or royal appanage holders." Adas (ibid.: 240–46) suggests that colonial-era penetration of the countryside by the mechanisms of state bureaucracies lessened the efficacy of peasant resistance and prompted its evolution toward more open confrontation, at the same time as the particularistic concerns of the peasantries evolved toward more generic, class-based forms. A similar transformation is currently under way among the groups reported on here: the views of planters by workers and smallholders are becoming more consistent and ideological, as a result of the development of more institutionalized resistance to plantation policies, which in turn is linked to the politicization of ethnic identity and the rise and involvement of local, national, and international nongovernmental organizations (see Davidson 2008).

Maintenance of Planters' Beliefs

The managers' belief that resistance to their policies is based on mental and cultural backwardness is not cynical in tone; it appears to be entirely sincere. This sincerity is made possible by a system of plantation administration that implicitly minimizes and misconstrues peasant and worker feedback.[31] Plantation officials demonstrate great aversion to critical feedback, especially when delivered directly to the person responsible.[32] Among all of the examples of untoward peasant behavior reported by plantation officials during the Plantation Institute study, the one that disturbed them most was a demonstration by disgruntled Dayak tribesmen in front of the manager of an oil palm nucleus-estate project near Sanggau in West Kalimantan, which was termed *ancaman-ancaman mental* (psychologically threatening). The prevention of further demonstrations became a primary goal of the plantation management, which proposed the following solution to the problem: "Pemecalah masalah: mencegah adanya demonstrasi penduduk yang ingin menyalurkan kehendaknya langsung kepada PTP dan Bupati/Kepala Daerah atau langsung kepada Petugas PTP dengan kekerasan seperti pernah terjadi bulan Pebruari 1984." (The solution to the problem: prevent the holding of demonstrations by people who want to make known their desires directly to the plantation and the regent/district head or directly and with force to plantation officials as happened in February 1984.)[33] Direct communication to higher officials, thus, was intolerable. The implication is that any plantation worker or smallholder or villager with a complaint should, at most, make it to his or her immediate superior; the latter may then pass it on to his immediate superior and so on, until and if the upper levels of plantation management and government are reached.[34] This idealized hierarchical structure shields upper-level officials from contact with the workers and smallholders who bear the consequences of their management decisions and, thereby, it shields their views of workers, smallholders, and villagers from confrontation with a contrary reality. This tradition and emphasis reaches back to the colonial era. Schrieke ([1955] 1966: 145) writes as follows of what he calls the "effort to maintain a degree of outward quiet": "Complaints were smothered. Anybody who ignored one of the steps of the hierarchy was punished 'according to the *adat*' and was in danger of being summoned to appear before the district court for making false charges. This even happened to persons who had been bold enough to send a petition to the governor general." These norms were deeply embedded in culture. A traditional Javanese proverb (Moertono 1981: 19) governing communication between ranks was "Dupak budjang, semu mantri, esem bupati" (A kick for a slave, an insinuation for a lower official, a smile for a high dignitary).

If the way for planters to support their view of the world is to resist feedback from the workers and smallholders, then it follows that the way for workers and smallholders to support their own views and contest those of the planters is to insist on feedback to the planters. The obverse of the planters' antipathy toward feedback, thus, is a folk predilection for it. There is, indeed, a folk tradition of protest to higher authorities in Southeast Asia, which can be effective precisely because it is so little in keeping with the public culture of Southeast Asia. Thus, Adas (1981: 229) writes of pre-colonial Java: "In Java, disgruntled villagers—at times led by their headmen or, in other instances, in opposition to them—organized processions to the residence of the most powerful lord in the region, which in the vicinity of the capital meant the royal palace" (compare to Moertono 1981: 76). Adas (1981: 229) goes on to write that he doubts whether specific protests were all that effective in traditional state systems in Southeast Asia, but he adds that the mere possibility of such protest from below must have been unnerving to those above. The suggestion that the medium of demonstrations by common folk has an impact in and of itself, regardless of the specific circumstances and message, is reflected in the aforementioned plantation "solution" to the "mental threat" of demonstrations, which focused on preventing demonstrations regardless of their content. Thus, the basic principle of access to and communication with planters is itself contested.

The plantations explicitly support information-gathering activities, but they are structured in ways that will not subvert the plantation's norms of knowledge production. Meetings between workers or smallholders and planters, for example, are structured as occasions of information presentation, *by* planters to the workers and smallholders, and not information gathering, *to* planters from workers and smallholders. The possibility in such meetings for critical public feedback from common folk to planter—like

Table 9.1. Attitudinal Scale in Planter's Survey of Peasants

worst	(1) *Belum pasti senang* (Not yet satisfied for sure)
|	(2) *Lumayan* (Relatively satisfied)
best	(3) *Senang* (Satisfied)

the "terroristic demonstrations" described earlier—is minimized at all costs. Thus, when meetings are held between either estate workers or local villagers and visiting officials or researchers such as myself in the Plantation Training Institute study, the local plantation managers invariably attend, and their presence—especially given the Indonesian reticence for direct confrontation—suppresses most possibilities for candid feedback from the attendees (see Dove 1986b: 23–26).[35] These possibilities are further minimized by simply excluding from such meetings anyone known to disagree with plantation policies. When I met with plantation managers and smallholders on a rubber nucleus estate near Sambas in West Kalimantan in 1993, the senior manager informed me that he had only invited to the meeting *petani yang baik* (good farmers), which he defined as farmers who did not sell any of their rubber to buyers outside the estate. Although such outside sales were one of the primary concerns of the plantation management, the manager's approach to the problem consisted of giving less, not more, "voice" to its proponents.

When formal research is carried out on workers or smallholders by the plantation establishment, it is structured to ensure that nothing untoward is discovered. For example, the earlier-mentioned Dayak demonstration of "mental terror" prompted the management of the nucleus-estate project in question to carry out a survey of local tribesmen's attitudes toward plantation policies. The tribesmen were asked to rank their attitudes on a three-part scale (table 9.1), the lowest and thus least satisfactory ranking of which was "Not yet satisfied for sure." Thus, even on a plantation on which demonstrations and "terrorism" on the part of the local tribesmen were being reported, the structure of the study did not allow for the possibility that dissatisfaction with plantation policies ran deeper than "Not yet satisfied for sure." The possibility that anyone was "unsatisfied" was literally off the cognitive scale. The point is not, of course, that the planters in question simply needed to add one or two further steps to their measurement scale; rather, the way this scale was structured reflects the institutional limitations on their ability to accept candid feedback. Aversion to acknowledging dissatisfaction with plantation projects is ubiquitous: thus, a local government official told critics that a much-troubled coconut nucleus-estate project in West Java could not be canceled and disagreed that the project had "failed," saying instead that it had "not yet achieved ideal results" (*Kompas*, 25 August 1990, cited in *Down to Earth* 1990b: 11).[36] There is a rich historical tradition of such obfuscation of agricultural realities in Indonesia, which was ridiculed in Multatuli's ([1859] 1982: 214) *Max Havelaar*: *"Export* [of rice] from a Residency meant prosperity; *import* into it means want. Now, when those [import/export] returns are examined and compared, it will be seen that rice is so abundant everywhere *that all Residencies combined export more rice* than *all the Residencies combined import. . . .* The conclusion of all this is therefore the absurd thesis *that there is more rice in Java than there is."*

In the rare case when the extent of worker or smallholder unhappiness is so great and so focused as to render the official representation of their misunderstanding untenable, the two great *deus ex machina* of Indonesian rural affairs may be invoked: namely, Chinese usuriousness and political extremism. Regarding the former, for example, one plantation official explained the unsatisfactory development of smallholder programs as follows: "Banyak petani di sektor perkebunan yang belum mampu mencari harga yang baik. Ada yang mensinyalir bahwa petani mau saja ditipu, apalagi kalau yang menipu dari golongan Cina." (Many farmers in the plantation sector are not yet capable of obtaining good prices [for their crops]. There are indications that the farmers just want to be deceived, especially if the one who deceives is Chinese.) As for political extremism: when the planters involved in the tea party incident described it to another planter, whose long career in Kalimantan qualified him in their eyes as an "expert" on Dayak culture, this planter suggested, as I did, that the behavior of the Dayak women at the tea party violated Dayak cultural norms. Whereas I explain this anomalous behavior in terms of Dayak unhappiness with plantation policies, however, this planter suggested that the Dayak women involved in the incident must have been put up to it by some *pihak ketiga* (third party), with the intention of frightening the planters' families and disrupting the operation of the plantation. The term *third party* is used in Indonesia to refer to shadowy and often in fact imaginary political extremists (see Stoler 1985a: 63 on similar colonial suspicions of "outside instigators"). Similarly, in an armed clash with smallholder coffee growers in Sumatra, which grew out of a conflict over land appropriation, the government claimed, "It is probable that the rioters were from left-wing or right-wing extremists or a combination of both" (FEER 1985: 25). As noted earlier, the threat of being labeled—and treated—as a member of the political fringe was one of the most important classificatory tools used by the former Suharto regime to keep dissidents in line.

The Challenge of Ethnographic Representation

The planters' representation of the worker/smallholder "other" has material consequences. As Scott (1985: 204) writes of the dialogue between rich and poor in his Malaysian study village, "What we observe, in brief, is not some trivial difference of opinion over the facts, but rather the confrontation of two social constructions of the facts, each designed to promote the interests of a different class."

The Planters' Audience

The immediate source of the conflict between workers and smallholders on the one hand, and on the other hand the planters, is political and economic in nature. The plantation managers want the workers and smallholders to be completely dependent on the plantation, to facilitate the mobilization of labor on the plantation's own terms; but they do not want the plantation to be completely responsible for reproducing the conditions of the workers' and smallholders' existence, for example, housing and social security, in addition to reasonable hours and wages (see also Stoler 1985a). The smallholders and workers want the reverse: they want the plantations to make a greater commitment to them and assume more responsibility for their welfare; but they still do not want to become completely dependent upon the plantations. This difference in views is reflected in the rhetoric of the two sides. The plantation managers complain that the workers are not always ready and willing to work in the plantations, and the workers complain that the work is not always available to them when they want it. The managers worry that the alternate sources of income available to proximate villagers give them too much independence, and the villagers worry that if they lose these sources—swiddens and smallholdings (Dove 1986b: 8–9, 11–13)—they will have too little independence. Stoler (1985a) describes how North Sumatran plantations maximized reduction of their responsibility but minimized reduction in their control by relocating their workforce to pseudoagricultural communities on the plantations' peripheries. She regards this "part-proletarian, part-peasant positioning of workers as an ingenious cost-cutting device on the part of capital" (ibid.: 6), but she acknowledges that in other cases it might represent a bid for self-sufficiency on the part of the peasants. Both forces are likely at work.

The goal of the plantation managers' discursive depiction of the conflict between planters and workers/smallholders is a battle for the moral high ground. As Stoler (1985b: 647) writes of the rhetoric of Dutch colonial planters, "This written rhetoric was not a reflection of a secure colonial base but a site of negotiation over the nature of it. . . . How the planters talked and wrote about dangers and the way they classified violence determined the jurisdiction of various problems." The rhetoric of contemporary plantation managers suggests that resistance to plantation plans and policies by workers and smallholders is due to their irrationality. The workers and smallholders, in contrast, suggest that their resistance stems from the managers' desire for too much power. The workers' and smallholders' rhetoric suggests that there is a difference in self-interest between themselves and the managers, whereas the managers' rhetoric rejects the possibility of any such difference. Any construal of the conflict as one based on competing self-interests is inimical to the managers' privileged position.

The audience for the plantation managers' rhetoric is neither tribesmen nor peasants, neither workers nor smallholders; rather, it is the managers' peers and supporters in the wider structures of the state.[37] The managers, as officers in state or parastatal enterprises, have needed, especially during the Suharto era, to publicly demonstrate commitment to state ideology (*Pancasila*) regarding the welfare of the common citizen; and their rhetoric preserves an image of this commitment by focusing attention on alleged worker and smallholder shortcomings, thereby deflecting attention from plantation policies that are inimical to the welfare of these same workers and smallholders. Of most importance, their rhetoric deflects attention from opposition to plantation governance: according to long historical traditions in the region, the commoners' resistance to rule can be interpreted as a sign of the ruler's loss of the right to rule (Anderson 1990). Once public perception of this loss takes hold, power can evaporate literally overnight, as was demonstrated by the precipitous fall from power of former President Suharto in the spring of 1998. This is why popular resistance is seen as so disturbing in government circles, not just in the plantation sector but throughout government. This is why managers of government plantations deem it so important to publicly represent such resistance as something else.

Defining the Boundaries of the Shared Moral Community

From one perspective the conflict between plantation managers and workers or smallholders is about whether both parties belong to a joint moral community — with the workers and smallholders arguing for this membership and the planters arguing against it. If planters, workers, and smallholders all belonged to the same moral community, then the planters must assume more responsibility for the latter than would otherwise be the case. Accordingly, much of the worker and smallholder rhetoric is devoted to invoking joint values, as exemplified in the earlier-cited statement by a tribal elder, "If everyone profits the same and works the same, there is no one who will not want to cooperate with the plantation program." Similarly but conversely, the planter rhetoric is devoted to invoking differences in values: all of the planter rhetoric discussed earlier, regarding the "strange," "obtuse," "lazy," and "foolish" workers and smallholders, emphasizes not the proximity but the distance between them. Whereas the peasants' rhetoric argues for their inclusion in the same moral community as the planters, the planters' rhetoric argues for the peasants' exclusion. Inclusion would empower the peasants, whereas exclusion further empowers the planters.

The planters' rejection of the idea of a joint moral community with the workers and smallholders helps to further explain the incident of the tea party. This solitary effort to encompass the local Dayak community in some sort of social relationship with the plantation community was belied by everything else that the plantation was doing, all of which was interpreted by the Dayak as exclusionary. This discontinuity was perceived by the Dayak as not just ironic but insulting. Their explicit response to this implicit insult was to resolve this discontinuity by wrecking the tea party. Just as the planters were violating the norms of an inclusive community in their treatment of Dayak land and labor, so the Dayak violated the norms of the planters' social outreach, in order to reveal its theatricality.

Some scholars would argue that the Dayak response to the tea party is characteristic of the way that tribal societies confront overarching authorities. As Sider (1986: 30, 33) writes:

> Peasants serve their overlords "according to custom" (Hilton 1975: 21); tribespeople serve precisely because their customs are different. In both cases, custom can become an arena of confrontation, but the structure of these confrontations will be profoundly different. . . . Peasants, being excluded from and included in elite culture, can use their own folk culture to express confron-

tational claims upon their dominators, which tribespeople cannot do. Tribespeople can rise up, they can withdraw, they can develop their own cultural and
social transformations of the domination that confronts them and more—but
they ordinarily cannot make influential or effective culturally rooted appeals to
their colonizers—such as is done by peasants in the context of a "moral economy," or "just price" uprisings.

Following Sider, we might interpret the Dayak behavior at the tea party as
"withdrawal" instead of engagement, as rejecting the cultural structure of
this encounter instead of attempting to manipulate or employ it themselves
to challenge the planters.

The validity of this interpretation can be examined by comparing the
account of the tea party with one of the accounts cited by Sider (ibid.: 71) to
illustrate the "peasant" pattern of behavior:[38] "I repeat the story of an incident that occurred in the early twentieth century—a story told across three
generations, which took place in a village outport in Placentia Bay around
the turn of the century: 'I heard me father say one man came up to the
door [of the rich merchant's house] and asked for a drink [of water] and he
pointed to the water in the harbour and said, "plenty of water there."'" In
this story, community values of sharing and reciprocity are being manipulated by both the man seeking water, who seems to have gone to the merchant's house not for water but to make a social statement, and by the merchant, who intentionally misinterprets the man's request. In fact, it seems
as if something very similar happened in the tea party. The social values
underlying the tea party were manipulated both by the planters, who were
not otherwise conducting their relations with the Dayak according to these
values, as well as by the Dayak, whose open subversion of the tea party was
intended to focus attention on this discontinuity. As noted earlier, the plantation managers correctly perceived that the behavior of the Dayak women
was extraordinary, but they failed to perceive that it was extraordinary to
the Dayak as well as themselves and, hence, that it was intended to convey
a message. The actors in Sider's story could not have denied knowledge of
and complicity in this manipulation; whereas the planters, but not Dayak,
in the tea party story could and did deny this. Instead of seeing the tea party
debacle as the product of different value systems, therefore, it may be more
accurate to see it as an example of the way this difference is constructed.

Granted that the "otherness" of tribal peoples is marked, should this be
attributed to the fact that tribesmen have "different customs," as Sider sug-

gests, or to the fact that the similarity of their customs to those of the wider society is denied while dissimilarities are emphasized? It may be more productive to treat tribal otherness not just as a given but as something that is constructed and not just by tribesmen. The planters' rhetoric is all about the otherness of tribesmen as well as peasants, workers, and smallholders, which systematically distinguishes them from the planters. Indeed, this is the purpose of the planters' rhetoric: it is an attempt to place all of these peoples beyond the bounds of the planters' moral community.

how we use otherness

Responses to This Study

When I described the purpose of the Plantation Training Institute study to a gathering of Dayak in West Kalimantan, who were losing their lands to a state plantation, and asked them how they wanted the plantation managers to address their concerns, their response was an explosion of laughter (Dove 1986b).[39] The idea that the way to resolve conflict between government and tribesmen was to ask the tribesmen what they wanted was perceived as hilariously ingenuous. Clearly, these Dayak had not been asked before to participate in this fashion in the public representation of their problems. The invitation to do so left not just the tribesmen but the government officials accompanying me completely nonplused. Both sides were used to beginning and ending with the government's representation of both the problem and the solution. This was reflected in the subsequent non sequitur of a conclusion by the manager of the government plantation in question, who said that what these tribesmen needed was "penyuluhan yang betul-betul" (extension that is really extension). *Penyuluhan* (extension) is the standard Indonesian gloss for imparting government information and instructions to the rural population, and thus it is the quintessential government representation of the community-state relationship. *Penyuluhan* also can have connotations of coercion (Hansen 1973: 5–6), as the response of the aforementioned plantation manager suggests.

Just as marked as the Dayak's reaction to my invitation to participate in their representation was the planters' reaction to my effort to exclude them. When I presented the major points from this analysis to a meeting of plantation managers in Central Java, the public response was polite; but the real response took place the previous day, when the meeting organizers saw the text of my talk for the first time. The response involved a hasty reshuffling of the meeting program, moving my presentation from a prominent position at the beginning to a less-prominent position in the middle and closure of all but the opening ceremony to the press. The meeting organizers had expected a synthesis of and response to the plantation managers' views of the problematic workers and smallholders, not a critique of these views nor an attempt to generalize about problematic planter behavior. The planters had expected a study of the folk "other," not a study of themselves. By presenting the latter, I challenged the fundamental principles that (1) plantation managers solve problems, and they are not the source of problems; and (2) plantation managers are the sponsors not the subjects of objective study.

In short, the response to this study from the local community reflected the fact that they are normally excluded from participating in their representation; and the response from the plantation managers reflected the fact that they are not normally represented by others. My ability to move back and forth between the roles of analyst of workers and smallholders and analyst of planters was revelatory, as was the planters' response to this movement. For the past decade or so, anthropologists have been suggesting that one productive way to rethink the traditional ethnographic role is to create multiple roles for the ethnographer among which he or she moves. It is suggested that this movement itself can reveal aspects of the field situation that would not be revealed if the ethnographer remained within one role. As Pierce (1995: 96) writes, of what she calls "outlaw ethnography": "The outlaw position is multiple and discontinuous identity whose movement between positions proves to be a critical advantage in uncovering the 'regimes of power' in the workplace. Further, I suggest that it is through the responses I elicit in my movement between positions . . . that I unveil the complex operations of gender and power in the field." My fieldwork with the planters involved the same sort of movement, from carrying on a dialogue with the planters about the "problems with workers and smallholders" to beginning a dialogue with these same workers and smallholders about "the problems with planters." The extremity of the planters' reaction to this movement, not so much because of what I said about the planters but because I said anything at all about them, helped to clarify the power implications of studying versus being studied.

PART VI

Conclusion

What are the implications of this study of Bornean smallholders for our understanding of globalization and in particular for the thesis (Appadurai 1996) that it has enlarged the scope of the imagination? This is the subject of this final section of the book and its concluding chapter. The imaginative, interpretive dimensions of trade in the ancient, much less contemporary Indo-Malay region have received scant attention. Van Leur ([1955] 1967: 54–56) carried out pioneering work in this direction, beginning with the highly unorthodox position that work like that of Malinowski on the "magic" of the kula ring trade in the Trobriand Islands is relevant to the study of the history of Indonesian trade and society.

I will argue that globalization has indeed produced an imagination "at large," in Appadurai's sense, but that this process began millennia ago in the case of Southeast Asia. The Southeast Asian case of commodity production and trade not only moves globalization back in time, it belies the teleological thesis that globalization has unwound at all times and in all places in the same way and with the same logic. The analysis here suggests a new perspective on the relationship of local smallholders to the global economy, one that permits the possibility of a more balanced mutual causation. Returning to the image of "the banana tree at the gate," it is suggested that future work in this field should focus less on the economics of the banana—the natural resources—and more on the political empowerment of the gatekeeper—the local holder of resource rights.

who owns / controls resources?

CHAPTER 10

Smallholders and Globalization

I show that the work of the imagination . . . is neither purely emancipatory nor entirely disciplined but is a space of contestation in which individuals and groups seek to annex the global into their own practices of the modern. . . . In dreams, finally, individuals even in the most simple societies have found the space to refigure their social lives, live out proscribed emotional states and sensations, and see things that have then spilled over into their sense of ordinary life.
—*Arjun Appadurai,* Modernity at Large

There is no "magical period" in the past of mankind, over and done with. . . . The category "trade," too, shares to a large extent its imprint. . . . The standard point of view on the history of trade . . . "from barter to world trade," gives no thought to such things.
—J. C. van Leur, *Indonesian Trade and Society*

Introduction

This book began with a vignette of a day in the life of a tribal family in the interior of Borneo, a scene that seems quintessentially "local." But a large part of the aim of this study has been to question this understanding of the local and thus the nonlocal as well—the global. One of the principal conclusions to this analysis of smallholder agriculturalists is that we cannot understand local smallholders unless we understand their relationship to extra-local political and economic systems. A corollary conclusion is that we cannot really understand the wider, global systems either, if we do not understand these local actors.

For much of the past generation, our understanding of global systems was dominated by neo-Marxist approaches, which sought to explain local societies in terms of the hegemonic operation of global capitalism. This represented a salutary reaction against a strong tradition in anthropology and human ecology that had ignored such wider processes and treated local communities as self-contained units of study (see Netting's 1990 critique). But the pendulum swung too far, and the new insights were attained at the cost of robbing local society of their history and agency. As Kahn (1982: 3) writes early on about smallholder commodity producers in West Sumatra, "There is a need for forms of economic and political analysis not easily derivable from Marxist theories of the capitalist mode of production, or from theories of the 'articulation' of modes of production in which the modes subordinated to capital are deduced directly from the functional prerequisites of capitalism conceived as an abstract, global structure." As a result, explanations of the local in terms of the global became discredited. Scholars like Taussig (1980) argue that such approaches deny us a reading of the local in its own terms, at the same time as they fail to problematize, and thereby privilege, extra-local actors.

The reaction against the biases of neo-Marxist approaches helped to spur the development of global studies, which purport to examine the interaction of local and global in a more balanced way. This field of study was also driven by developments in economics, politics, religion, culture, and the environment toward the end of the twentieth century, which increasingly convinced scholars, including many anthropologists, of the need to study at a global scale. The escalating concern with global climate change is of course only adding to this trend. Globalization has become one of the hottest subjects in academia, and global studies has become a privileged optic for looking at the world. There is a natural tendency to think that the scholarly enthusiasm and the phenomenon itself have coevolved, and as a result globalization is typically studied as a matter of the here and now. Leading texts, like Edelman and Haugerud (2005), focus on the present. But global trade networks are age-old; they have knit parts of the world together for millennia. The analysis in this book demonstrates the way in which Borneo and the rest of Southeast Asia have long been, in effect, "globalized." The aim here has been to historicize the local and thereby to restore a missing dimension to the history of the global. It has also been to take a more balanced reading of local and global, one that sees the strengths of the local as well as the vulnerabilities of the global, not just the reverse.[1]

Imagination and Globalization

Arjun Appadurai (1996), as noted in the epigraph to this chapter, argues that contemporary global media and migration have pushed projects of imagination beyond the local, such that modernity is now "at large." His work has helped to make imagination into an important topic for scholars of globalization. Tsing (2000: 133), for example, has shown the role that imagination plays in contemporary views of the resource frontier in places like Kalimantan. But in other works she also hints at the historical depth to this imagination in her work on the rich and much older tradition of stories of diamond queens, refugees from Javanese kingdoms, and shipwrecked Chinese traders (Tsing 1993). The history of trade in this region is imbued with such imaginative constructions, beginning with the trade of fantastically named products like "dragon's blood" and "dragon's brain perfume" to the Chinese, leading up to the Dutch besottment with spices, and extending into the modern history of rubber production. The conceptual groundwork for the transfer of *Hevea* from the Amazon to Southeast Asia was laid down by the ability of people like Clements Markham to imagine engineering the global circulation of biogenetic resources.[2] Imagination is also responsible, of course, for depicting the transplantation of rubber as a heroic North-South theft instead of the far more mundane act that it was at the time. Imagination subsequently played a potent role in the lurid vision of diseased and degraded rubber smallholdings that was invoked to justify the Stevenson Restriction Scheme and the International Rubber Regulation Agreement. So there is much reason to believe that modernity has long been "at large" here.

Imagination has arguably been from the very start an integral part of the ancient global commodity trade. This is in part a function of the distances involved and the many intermediaries participating, as a result of which there was often a complete break between the knowledge systems of the producers and the knowledge systems of the consumers. For most of the history of this trade, the end users had no real idea where the products came from. As Freedman (2008: 91) writes of the trade in the Middle Ages, "Where spices were *thought* to originate tells us more about medieval ideas concerning how the world was organized than knowledge of where they actually came from" [emphasis in original].[3] Similarly, Donkin (1999: xiv) writes that the Chinese term *dragon's brain perfume* for camphor reflects its pungent aroma and also "centuries of uncertainty over its provenance and mode of origin." The corollary point is that the producers usually did not know where their products were going and had no idea to what use they would be put. As Freedman (2008: 108) continues, "The producers and most of the middlemen had no idea of the end user, while the European consumers thought that these treasures came from a magical far-off realm, perhaps the land of the monstrous races, or the domain of Prester John, or an imagined India."[4]

One of the great paradoxes of this global commodity trade, which has persisted into modern times, is that the producers often do not use the products themselves. Whereas this is less perplexing in the case of Para rubber, it is more surprising that most of the Southeast Asian producers of pepper, which dominated global trade for several centuries, did not use pepper themselves.[5] As Crawfurd (1868: 191) writes, "There is, however, one exception to this [the universal consumption of pepper], and it is a singular one: it is that of the producers themselves, and this observation applies equally to the clove and nutmeg. These commodities are hardly used at all by their growers, and are all produced by them for strangers." The use of the product by the consumer but not producer raises questions about the fundamental character of the trade. The spice trade, for example, was long interpreted in light of the supposed material function played by spices in preserving and making palatable the food of the European consumers. Freedman (2008: 225), however, has definitively skewered this thesis, demonstrating that the desire for spices was not material or hygienic in origin but social: "Spices were simultaneously valuable commodities, social signifiers of discriminating taste, pleasurable substances, and yet vessels of higher, even sacred meaning." Given Freedman's work, it seems clear that the distances and discontinuities in knowledge associated with this ancient commodity trade were not obstacles to it; rather they were what constituted the trade, what made it possible, desirable. Freedman (2008: 99–100) writes that for centuries Europeans thought that spices came from the lands of so-called "monstrous races," which represented a "conjunction of the alluring with the frightening." He continues, "There is a long-standing association of precious substances with dangerous creatures, an aspect of the same pairing of the alluring and the perilous exotic found in accounts of the earthly paradise surrounded by deserts or monstrous races, the same relation between images of India as wealthy yet replete with frightening animals, humanoids, and bizarre customs" (ibid.: 134). In short, what was distant, unknown, and frightening drove this commodity trade. If it was proximate, known, and familiar—like some of Europe's own home-grown spices (Freedman 2008)—it was not as valuable or desirable. This holds for both ends of the trade: the Dayak who once sent dragon's brain perfume to China received back bronze gongs and ceramic jars, which were as exotic and thus valued in their society as camphor was in China.

The fact that lack of knowledge was intrinsic to this trade does not mean that ignorance and knowledge were not constructed and contested. The earliest traders of aromatics in the Middle East are thought to have invented some of the fabulous stories surrounding them, in order to elevate their prices and deter others from seeking them (Freedman 2008: 135); the early traders of the Malay Archipelago surreptitiously substituted their own pepper for that from India in the China trade; and Banjar and other coastal trading states exaggerated to Europeans the dangers of dealing with the interior tribal collectors of forest products. Given the misinformation campaigns on which the trade rested, it is little wonder that the initial European voyages of discovery were explicitly charged with getting the facts. As Freedman (ibid.: 191) writes, "Europe was entranced by the flavor, scent, and aura of spices, obsessed with finding out where they came from, and eager to figure out how to profit from direct contact with those who grew them. Ignorance was as much a spur to commercial adventure as was knowledge."[6] It is no surprise that the study of natural history became a cornerstone of the colonial project, producing over time in the region people like Georg Everard Rumpf (Rumphius), Thomas S. Raffles, Alfred Russel Wallace, and I. H. Burkill. The colonial European powers sought to change their roles in this game of global misinformation, but not to end the game itself. The Portuguese, for example, tried to prevent the late-coming English and Dutch from competing for the rich pepper trade of Jambi in Sumatra by keeping secret the route from the coast to Jambi's capital 120 kilometers upriver. One of their stratagems involved printing maps that placed Palembang, Jambi's neighbor, in Java (Andaya 1993b: 46–47). The Dutch, when confronted with a Moluccan native who traveled to Europe and asked too many questions about the economics of the spice trade, never allowed him to return to his country (Meilink-Roelofsz 1962: 157–58).

Colonial and post-colonial projects of knowledge production notwithstanding, the scope for the imagination in thinking about natural resource wealth and commodity production in the region has not lessened.[7] As Freedman (2008: 137) writes, the pre-modern stories of the wondrous aromatic and spice lands were replaced by modern stories of El Dorado. An example is the earlier-discussed Bre-X gold mine of East Kalimantan (Tsing 2000). In this case, national and international elites imagined something that was simply not there. Tsing (ibid.) also describes how these same elites reimagine what *is* there in the alluvial gold fields of East Kalimantan, how they conceptually reconstruct a natural resource landscape to suit their purposes. An analogous example from the export-crop sector, discussed in this book, is the estate and nucleus estate, both of which reimagine and reconstruct the natural resource landscape in a partisan way. This is based on the imaginative depiction of the character of the lazy native, the isolated native, the pre-monetary native; on wholly fictitious perceptions of diseased, degraded, inefficient, and unproductive smallholdings; and on imagined heroic acts of theft, creation, and control. The reimagination of the landscape that makes parastatal plantations possible is far from being a subject of mere historical interest. It is equally relevant today, given the fantastic proliferation of oil palm estates across Borneo, covering nearly three million hectares by 2004 (Potter 2008: 70; see also Acciaioli 2008; Cooke 2002; Sandker, Suwarno, and Campbell 2007; Sheil et al. 2009).[8]

The ongoing development of environmentalism, and in particular environmentalism as an optic with which people in the global North look at the global South, also offers new scope for the imagination.[9] Global environmentalists display an increasing ability to assess local landscapes in terms of abstract systems of value, such as provision of ecosystem services, biodiversity, and habitat conservation, promotion of ecotourism and education, and most recently carbon sequestration. Perhaps the most important future policy mechanism impacting tropical forests and peoples will be the so-called Reduced Emissions from Deforestation and Degradation (REDD) projects, which are wholly an exercise of the imagination, based as they are on the slippery concept of "avoided deforestation" (Chhatre and Agrawal 2009; Griffiths and Martone 2009; Schwartzman and Moutinho 2008; Survival International 2009). As a result of all of these multiplying and overlapping ways of valuing local tropical forest landscapes, more and more natural resources are potential "big stones (chapter 8)."[10] These represent ever more numerous possibilities for the disenfranchisement and disempowerment of the local "little people."

The Teleology of Globalization

The history presented here of participation in global trade by Bornean peoples is not the one we have been accustomed to hearing. I debunk the age-old colonial narrative of Promethean acts of invasion, plunder, and loss; and I question the accepted wisdom of stereotypical transformation of native societies in confrontations with global capitalism. Murphy and Steward (1956: 353) present the orthodox view in their well-known study of rubber tappers in South America and fur trappers in North America: *"When the people of an unstratified native society barter wild products found in extensive distribution and obtained through individual effort, the structure of the native culture will be destroyed, and the final culmination will be a culture type characterized by individual families having delimited rights to marketable resources and linked to the larger nations through trading centers"* [emphasis in original].

World systems scholars (for example, Wallerstein 1974, 1980) offered a theoretical framework for this teleology, based on the perceived determinism of the capitalist world system. But most scholars have subsequently argued that incorporation—or changes in the type and intensity of incorporation—of local societies into the global economic system does not initiate a sequence of predetermined change. Kahn (1982: 9) has argued this for the Minangkabau in Central Sumatra. Errington and Gewertz (2004) present the case of a sugar mill in Papua New Guinea, which they say represents an exception to hegemonic studies of globalization. And in a powerful study, Ferguson (2006) argues that much of Africa actually represents a countertrend to globalization. He calls Africa an "inconvenient" case for theories of globalization because "most of the dominant theories of globalization have been theories about worldwide *convergence* of one sort or another" [emphasis in original], but it is a *divergence* that is taking place in Africa (ibid.: 27). He writes, "Perhaps this is why so much of the critical literature on globalization seems oddly out of place in Africa. Most Africans can hardly feel that they are being dominated by being forced to take on the goods and forms of a homogenizing global culture when those goods and forms are, in fact, largely unavailable to them" (ibid.: 21).

The Bornean and Southeast Asian case is quite different. Whereas Ferguson is arguing that Africa is not yet global, or even is becoming less global, Borneo was global before we started talking about globalization; but clearly both cases reveal problems with the current globalization discourse. Whereas this study of smallholder history belies any kind of global determinism, it unequivocally shows the local impact of global forces. Global processes constrain the local—there is indeed a "political economy" factor—but this does not thereby erase the self-determination of local populations. A middle ground must be sought between these two perspectives, as Tsing (2005) does in her work complicating the simplistic idea of a globalization-driven clash of cultures.

The corollary to the critique of a single path in globalization is the critique of a single driving logic to globalization. As Moore (2005: 8) writes in his study of Zimbabwe:

> Despite their considerable insights, such [post-structural] analyses of colonial power and postcolonial governmentality have tended to emphasize an underlying "grammar of modern power," a coherent "regime of intelligibility," or a unified "political rationality." At times, a Weberian specter of bureaucratic rationality haunts these formations. Assertions of a unitary "logic" purge

heterogeneous practices, struggles, and alternatives from analytical recognition. Michael Hardt and Antonio Negri confidently proclaimed that globalization has produced a "single logic of rule," which they term sovereignty. Such blanket pronouncements elide attention to the microtechniques through which power relations work in historically and geographically specific contexts.

Similarly, my study shows no single logic driving global commodity production throughout Southeast Asia's history. The political economy of the earlier trade oriented toward India and China was very different from the succeeding Europe-focused trade; and that of the Portuguese was different yet again from that of the Dutch and English, and there were also differences between early and late Dutch rule. The extractive logics of the nineteenth- and twentieth-century rubber industries in the Amazon and in Southeast Asia were dramatically different, although they were clearly producing for the same global capitalist markets. And much of this book has been dedicated to showing the fundamental differences over the past century in estate commodity production, smallholder commodity production, and smallholder subsistence production.

Because there has been no single driving logic in these stories of globalization, there has been no single axis of either alliance or opposition. Turning again to Moore (ibid.: 7), he writes, "I stress shifting alignments and contingent constellations of power rather than a single ruling rationality."[11] Scholars like Moore suggest that a vision of "the local" and "the global" locked in opposition is too simplistic. Much of the present study, it is true, focused on a unitary opposition between the Indonesian estate and smallholder, but there have been many other axes of differentiation in the history of this complex trade. For example, there were complicated historical relations between coastal sultanates, their Malay subjects, their Dayak vassals, and the Dutch. There was the late nineteenth-century schism in the global rubber industry occasioned by the transplanting of rubber from South America and Southeast Asia, leading to the emergence of opposing hemispheric industries, in open competition with one another. Within this schism, there were differences in interests between two of the principals involved, Henry Wickham, wedded to the South American rubber technology, and Henry Nicholas Ridley of the Singapore Botanic Gardens, committed to experimenting with new methods. During the 1920s and 1930s there was a divergence of economic interest not only between estates and smallholders but also between the rubber-producing nations and the rubber-consuming ones—a divergence that produced odd bedfellows. As Wolf and Wolf (1936: 237) observed at the time, the Southeast Asian smallholder became the greatest ally of the rubber-hungry United States in its battle against the rubber cartel, because both shared an interest in supporting the most efficient producers, the smallholders, and in not protecting the least efficient ones, the estates: "It is, then, the native of the tropics, exploited since the birth of the caoutchouc industry, who looms today as the controlling figure in the market, an act of poetic justice long delayed but now particularly welcome to the American consumer to whom the brown man represents his best guarantee against highway robbery prices in the future."

Revisiting the Smallholder

If globalizing forces are ancient, then so too is the smallholder, and the reverse also holds true, for both are part of the same process. The involvement of the native peoples of Borneo in production of commodities for global trade is indeed old, which makes all the more remarkable the tenacious popular belief that markets—and perhaps even money—are foreign to them (Tsing 1999). The evidence presented here shows the Bornean smallholders to be quintessential global actors, yet an apparently important if paradoxical part of that identity today is its vigorous denial by outsiders.

That denial of millennia of history illustrates how important the imagination has always been to smallholder dynamics, including their own imagination. My analysis historicizes the role of the imagination in the smallholders' engagement with global markets.[12] It suggests that well before the modern era the scale of imagination had already transcended the local, was already "at large." It suggests that before there were global migration and mass media, mechanisms as varied as dreams, court annals, and folk parables were being used to communicate and interpret, contest and co-opt the forces of globalization. Imagination played a direct and immediate role in the way smallholder production evolved. The cases of the deathbed injunctions against planting pepper and the dream of the rice-eating rubber, among others, all attest to the way that multiple, alternative possibilities of production for global markets were imagined and accepted, rejected, or modified. As these cases demonstrate, imagination was here not just the product of globalization; it helped to articulate the difference between the local and the global. These historic examples suggest that Appadurai is right in seeing imagination at large as a product of globalization; but they also suggest that this was a pre-modern phenomenon.

This exercise of imagination has contributed to the smallholders' ability to forge their own path toward involvement with the global economy, one that was not predetermined by any logic of the global economic system. This is reflected in the fact that smallholders have continually surprised on-lookers. The withdrawal of some producers from pepper production in the seventeenth century is one example; another is the response of tappers to the boom in native rubbers in the mid-nineteenth century, which was so enthusiastic that the colonial states had to create cartels to suppress it. Yet other examples are the swift adoption of and innovative experimentation with *Hevea* rubber early in the twentieth century, and production of rubber in inverse relationship to market prices and government duties during the 1930s Depression. Overall, the fact that the smallholder sector did not simply survive but thrived, and indeed dominated the rubber industry during the twentieth century, was completely outside the reckoning of the state and its plantation sector. The basis for the unending surprise of this smallholder sector is its dual economy, which allows smallholders to behave in a way that cannot be predicted by market signals alone. Mirroring the complexity of the overarching world system, the dual economy is not dominated by a single logic. It encompasses the differing but complementary logics of two very different enterprises—one subsistence oriented and one market oriented.

This analysis complicates our understanding of the smallholders' relationship to the global economic system. The orthodox view has long been that this relationship was antagonistic, leaving the smallholders at best in a marginal or anomalous position and at worst hard-pressed and teetering on extinction. But the critiques of the single logic of global capitalism have opened up space for rethinking this view. As Bernal (1994: 794) writes, "Counter to evolutionary expectations regarding the rise of market relations and the decline of subsistence values, market pressures . . . not only have failed to transform subsistence production into commodity production, but are also one of the driving forces behind subsistence farming. . . ." Based on his research on swidden cultivation and commodity production in Southwest Sumatra, Schneider (1995) similarly concludes that new opportunities to produce commodities for global markets actually resulted in an expansion of swidden cultivation in this region that would not otherwise have taken place.[13] Schneider shows how local society uses modern means to stay pre-modern (see also Hirtz 2003), how local society uses global ties to stay local. Given the way that commodity production supports swidden cultivation, as well as the reverse, Schneider further argues that swidden cultivation is not a pocket of resistance to the global system, as it has been commonly regarded, but is one of its integral components. He suggests that just as the global helps the local to be local, so does the local help the global to be global. The same conclusion can be drawn from the analysis here of smallholder production of global commodities like pepper and rubber. Tucker (2007: 149–50) has insightfully suggested that global rubber consumption created rubber smallholders: "American buyers purchased much smallholder rubber from middlemen in Singapore. . . . On behalf of American consumers they thus provided a large portion of the global market that sustained massive small producer rubber expansion. In a real sense, that demand created even the smallholder groves." But it could be said with equal validity that the rubber smallholders created — made possible — the global rubber consumers and consumption, which perhaps requires us to rethink what is meant by the humble term *smallholder*.

Further Study

The origins of smallholder commodity production in Indonesia date to early in the Christian era, but the issues raised by their study are still very much with us. Current developments in Borneo—as in Indonesia's other outer islands—raise anew the question of the viability of estate versus smallholder agriculture. One prominent example is the earlier-mentioned development of huge oil palm plantations, which are displacing smallholders— although Feintrenie, Chong, and Levang (2010) suggest that smallholder development of oil palm is equally possible—and posing all the political, economic, and environmental risks of the estate model that have been discussed here. This development threatens to add to a growing level of political insecurity in Borneo, which has already been amplified by estate development. For example, outbreaks of large-scale ethnic violence in West Kalimantan beginning in the late 1990s between Dayak and immigrant Madurese were concentrated in the vicinities of existing centers of government estate development (Davidson 2008; Dove 2006; IDRD 1994). There has been little effort to study the role played in these conflicts by the estate-driven transformation of the landscape. The tension between local smallholders and parastatal plantation development is likely to be exacerbated by the new interest in tropical forest lands stemming from climate change, which is producing the latest effort by outside actors to reimagine the natural resource landscape of Borneo. There is enormous international interest in reducing emissions of greenhouse gases through REDD programs. Indonesia, because of its abundant forests but also high rate of deforestation, is one of the major global targets for these programs; and rubber, with its carbon-fixing potential, is a plant of interest (Penot 2007: 579). Efforts to implement REDD programs in Indonesia and thereby secure carbon credits are reinvigorating centuries-old debates about the roles of local communities versus central government, and smallholder versus estate patterns of development. After the fall of Suharto, top-down models of resource development are being challenged by local communities, strengthened in Kalimantan as elsewhere in Indonesia by the rising political capital of indigeneity and *adat* (Bedner and van Huis 2008; Davidson and Henley 2007). Finally, not just in Indonesia but around the world, the block-type, single-logic, concession model of development is proliferating with little scrutiny of its political implications (Hardin 2002).

This returns us to the line from the *Hikayat Banjar,* which provides the image and title for the book, "the banana tree at the gate." This image of the rich but vulnerable resource typifies many tropical forest communities around the world. What is the solution to the quandary that it poses? To begin with, we make progress by simply recognizing this quandary for what it is. This is not an image of a community that *needs* a resource that it doesn't have; rather, it is an image of a community that cannot afford to *lose* a resource that it does have. This is not a quandary of the lack of resources, therefore; it is the quandary of a lack of power to hold on to an existing resource—and this completely transforms the problem.

The orthodox response of the wider world toward this situation has been to offer, in effect, another banana tree, but this is based on a complete misreading of the problem. More productive would be an effort to develop the existing resource base. As noted throughout this study, government efforts to develop the smallholder sector have been surprisingly limited in Indonesia. Even a modest investment in Indonesian smallholder agriculture would pay enormous dividends. But this alone will not suffice, because it does not directly address the central issue of "the banana tree at the gate," namely the threat of its appropriation. What is needed, in effect, is a stronger gate. What the smallholders need above all else are the means to hold on to their lands, their natural resources; and this entails political empowerment at the local level and wider development of the institutions of civil society. Anything else is missing the point of two thousand years of local, and global, history.

Notes

Chapter 1. The Study of Smallholder Commodity Producers

1. *Swidden agriculture* is the scholarly term for "shifting cultivation" or "slash-and-burn agriculture." It refers to a diversity of agricultural systems in which fields are cleared and prepared using sword, adze or axe, and fire and are cultivated for a short period and then fallowed for a longer one (Conklin [1957] 1975: 1). The term *swidden*, which refers to the cultivated field and was probably first used by Izikowitz (1951: 7), at the suggestion of Ekwall (1955), is derived from the old English *swithen* and before that the Old Norse word *sviðna*, meaning "to be singed" (*Oxford English Dictionary, CD-ROM version*, 1999).

2. Terminology is important, as Kahn (1982: 11) notes, in his study of commodity production in West Sumatra: "The use of blanket terms like peasant, small producer, household production and the like all lead to a misleading conflation of rather different forms of petty production."

3. See Stoll (2006) on continued academic interest in smallholder agriculture.

4. Cf. Hecht and Cockburn (1989: 173) on political obfuscation of the contribution of Brazil's smallholders to national food production.

5. The figures are 96 and 97 percent, respectively, for West Kalimantan, which ranks fifth among Indonesia's provinces in rubber production (Government of Indonesia 2004: 5/ table 3.3).

6. The fact that rubber and the other export crops — palm oil, sugar, rubber, tea, cocoa, and coffee — are termed "estate crops," despite the fact that many of them are mostly raised on smallholdings, reflects the extent to which estates are privileged over smallholdings in public discourse.

7. For a recent work on commodity production in Southeast Asia, albeit from outside of anthropology, see Nevins and Peluso (2008).

8. Van Leur ([1955] 1967: 5) cites as evidence of early Indonesian trade "westwards" the Indonesian settlement of Madagascar, ship motifs in the stone reliefs of Borobudur, and references in "The Thousand and One Nights."

9. See Ellen (2003) for a production-end account of the spice trade in the Moluccas.

10. The magnitude of Java's trade to the east is given by Van Leur's ([1955] 1967: 209–

10) estimate that in the early seventeenth century Java was sending to the Moluccas 30,000 tons of rice per year by 375 junks.

11. See Kano's (2008: 178–206) detailed analysis of corporate identities in the colonial-era plantation sector in Indonesia.

12. By the time of the OPEC oil embargo in the 1970s, which suddenly made the economics of natural rubber much more attractive, petroleum-based synthetic rubber was meeting two-thirds of global demand (Tucker 2007: 138).

13. The earliest uses of aromatics date from the third millennium B.C. in Egypt and Mesopotamia (Donkin 1999: 5, 16), although the world's largest historic concentration of natural aromatics was in Southeast Asia (ibid.: 11). One of the latter region's signature products was "dragon's brain perfume" or camphor (*Dryobalanops aromatica*), which was traded to China before the sixth century and is the subject of Donkin's exceptional 1999 book-length treatment. Borneo is the center of origin of the genus of *Dryobalanops* (ibid.: 51).

14. Freedman (2008: 76) argues that fragrance more than gastronomy explained the historic allure of spices.

15. This was not the end of pepper cultivation, however, even if it never again attained its earlier importance. By the time of Marsden's ([1811] 1966: 129) study of West Sumatra in the 1770s, for example, pepper was again of sufficient importance for him to write, "Of those productions of Sumatra, which are regarded as articles of commerce, the most important and most abundant is pepper. This is the object of the East India Company's trade thither, and this alone it keeps in its own hands." In addition, the trade to China was not necessarily affected by the boom-and-bust cycles of the European trade (Andaya 1993b: 122).

16. Cf. Airriess (2003) on the importance of upstream–downstream integration in the trade and politics in the premodern Malay world.

17. Andaya (1995: 185–86) suggests that pepper was one of the first crops in the archipelago to undergo the transition from small-scale household cultivation to large-scale production with state involvement.

18. Mintz (1985: 48, 50–51) suggests that the "plantation form" was first developed and perfected in the eastern Mediterranean at the end of the first and beginning of the second millennium A.D., was subsequently developed on the Atlantic islands (the Azores and the Madeira, Canary, and Cape Verde islands), and by the middle of the fifteenth century was then redeveloped in the New World colonies.

19. Barlow and Muharminto (1982: 86) define a rubber smallholder as someone with fewer than twenty-five hectares.

20. Compare Geertz's ([1963] 1971: 14–15) famous contrast between inner and outer Indonesia, but based largely on the distinction between swidden and irrigated rice cultivation.

21. The Chinese also cultivated rubber, the history of which in West Kalimantan has been "erased" (Peluso 2009).

22. The model of a mixed agrarian economy, exploiting multiple types of different resources and ecotypes, has ancient roots in Indonesia (Day 1994; Foley 1987).

23. "Malayic" refers to a hybrid ethnicity comprising elements of Malay and Dayak cultures as well as older elements from beyond Borneo; see chapter 2.

24. Cairns's (2007) compendium, perhaps the most comprehensive work on swidden agriculture within the past quarter century, shows that the linkage of swidden communities to markets is ubiquitous worldwide.

25. Kato (1991) analyzed the relationship between rubber cultivation and irrigated rice cultivation in the Malay Peninsula in the early twentieth century and found only partial dis-

placement of one by the other as their relative market prices fluctuated. Despite the "see-saw" relationship between rice cultivation and rubber prices, *most* rice fields continued to be cultivated because of "peasant conservatism," hedging against market fluctuations, colonial regulations, matrilineal *adat*, lack of ecological competition, differing labor schedules, and a developing gender-based division of labor (ibid.: 144). See Cramb (2007) for an analysis of a more recent case in Sarawak in which the balance seems to have tipped in favor of the cash crop, in this case, pepper.

26. This firewall is integral to the historic ability of upland peoples in Southeast Asia to be linked to, but not completely governed by, lowland states (Scott 2009).

27. Bauer (1948: 64–65) notes the paradoxical fact that beginning in the early 1920s colonial policy in Malaya was to discourage smallholder rubber cultivation to ensure food production, and yet the food deficits that prompted this policy were concentrated not among smallholdings but on the estates.

28. The thesis of economic dualism led to many contradictory policies, an example being Dutch efforts in West Sumatra to restrict commercialization of the peasant economy while at the same time attempting to increase peasant production of coffee (Kahn 1982: 5–6).

29. See Ortiz's ([1947] 1995: 4–5) classic study of sugar and tobacco in Cuba: "Sugar and tobacco are vegetable products of the same country and the same climate, but the biological distinction between them is such that it brings about radical economic differences as regards soil, methods of cultivation, processing, and marketing. And the amazing differences between the two products are reflected in the history of the Cuban nation from its very ethnological formation to its social structure, its political fortunes, and its international relations."

30. Paige (1975: 53, 56) argues that it is in part due to the potential for smallholder competition that rubber estates must rely on political as opposed to economic power to discipline their workforces and take action against smallholders.

31. A much more "satisfactory" plantation crop is oil palm, which helps to account for the astonishing expansion of oil-palm acreage in Indonesia over the past three decades (see chapter 10).

32. As van Leur ([1955] 1967: 240) notes, since the Moluccas produced more cloves (and nutmeg and mace) than the whole world could consume, "[Dutch] policy in the Moluccas was that its servants should not so much exert themselves to obtain a great deal of cloves as above all keep watch and take care that the cloves were not shipped away by the inhabitants or by foreign nations."

33. Of course the Dutch efforts in the seventeenth century to eliminate spice cultivation in eastern Indonesia except on a few closely monitored islands were an earlier and more extreme effort to construct "state space."

34. As Bonneuil (2001: 278) writes: "Read from an epistemic perspective, the repression of indigenous knowledge helped to subordinate the farmers' sphere of knowledge and practices to the realm of experimental design (whose keystone was the isolation and control of individual variables). Farmers' practices were considered invalid until their scientific validity was proven by controlled experiment."

35. The *Oxford English Dictionary* (1999) defines *plasma* as: "The living matter of a cell, protoplasm; sometimes *spec.* the general body of protoplasm as distinct from the nucleus."

36. As Tomich (1991: 252) writes of these nucleus-estate schemes, "Then, as today, large-scale plantations in Indonesia and elsewhere in Southeast Asia provided the main reservoir of organizational experience and technical information on rubber production, as well as a ready supply of expatriate advisors."

37. Tomich (1991: 258) assessed the real priorities of these block-planting schemes as

follows: "Thus, a project setting designed to replicate plantation conditions is seen by some as an opportunity to control smallholder decision making and ensure that it conforms to the requirements of modern technology."

38. For further discussion of panoptic vision in Indonesia, see Dove (2009).

39. Hardin (2002: 23) writes, "Concessionary actors operate to constrain information flow in the interest of protecting their interests, and shoring up their competitive advantages."

40. Penot (2007: 583) writes that by 1990, 80 percent of smallholders in Malaysia and 65 percent in Thailand had been reached by clonal rubber improvement schemes, but by the time of his writing almost three decades later, fewer than 15 percent of rubber smallholders in Indonesia had been reached by such schemes, and only two-thirds of those eventually developed productive plantations. Tomich (1991: 251) observes that "The focus on projects meant that virtually no development assistance was going to the majority of rubber smallholders." For example, Joshi et al. (2003: 138) write that at the time of their study, rubber smallholders in Jambi in South Sumatra were still tapping one-hundred-year-old trees grown from the earliest plantings of rubber in the archipelago.

41. This model of smallholder development proved to be so unsuccessful as to weaken government support for it (Barlow and Tomich 1991: 48).

42. For example, the administrative director of a plantation project in West Kalimantan, who was attempting to develop an estate of high-yielding rubber where traditional rubber stood, dismissed the existing rubber's value with the epithet *hutan karet* (jungle rubber) (interview at the nucleus estate PIR VI Sambas, Monterado, Samalantang sub-district, Singkawang district, West Kalimantan, 29 September 1993).

43. As Tomich (1991: 257) writes, "Despite the importance of the answer and the amount of resources put into smallholder rubber development, a good estimate of how much unassisted rubber planting takes place in Indonesia each year is surprisingly difficult to obtain because virtually no attention is paid to 'spontaneous' planting. Local government office charts indicate precise areas of rubber projects, often down to the last tenth of a hectare. Yet, statistics on unassisted planting are incomplete, if they are kept at all. Thus, most official statistics support the official line."

44. Cf. Alfred Russel Wallace's accounts (1869: 419) of his difficulties in collecting specimens of the bird of paradise, which was being traded in this region even before the first Europeans arrived. This is the one category of fauna that involves Wallace in what he calls "difficulties" in collecting specimens, which stemmed from his efforts to *directly* contact the interior tribesmen who catch the birds (ibid.: 437–38). Such contact would have undermined the long-established authority of the coastal natives, which was based on ensuring that no one but them had such access to the interior peoples. This was a point of contention for centuries between coastal native states and Europeans who wanted to eliminate the middlemen and so maximize their own profits.

45. The term *Dutch disease* was coined in 1977 by *The Economist* to describe the decline of the manufacturing sector in the Netherlands after the discovery of a large natural gas field in 1959.

46. The trope of heroic "transportation" of rubber trees has even found its way into popular thinking, if Sammy Cahn's 1959 lyrics about the solitary ant "moving" a rubber tree plant, cited in the epigraph to this book, are any guide. I am grateful to Barry Muchnick for this reference.

47. There also was a conviction that these projects needed to be big: Tomich (1991: 256) writes of ". . . a large scale project bias in smallholder development strategy. In other words,

to raise yields, planting was necessary; to induce planting, it was believed projects were necessary; and to make significant progress in the enormous task, big projects were necessary."

48. Foucault's (1986) work helps us to appreciate how the condition of modernity can create landscapes characterized by persistent contradictions or incompatibilities, which he termed "heterotopia."

49. Most of these plantation studies are part of the gray policy literature, much of it coming from the Center for Research on Forestry, based in Bogor in West Java, or the International Center for Research on Agroforestry, also with offices in Bogor but with headquarters in Nairobi, Kenya (e.g., Potter and Lee 1998; Kartodihardjo and Supriono 2000). One of the few sources of critical, analytic views of Indonesia's parastatal plantation operations while Suharto was in power was the activist newsletter on Indonesia, *Down to Earth*, published by the International Campaign for Ecological Justice in Indonesia, a project of the Asia-Pacific Peoples' Environment Network (Penang, Malaysia), published in London. Just as social scientists have ignored estates, so have natural scientists in the estate sector ignored smallholder cultivation. As Tomich (1991: 260) writes, "An important, but unfortunate, result of the block planting strategy that restricted supply of high-yielding planting material to project participants is that there is very little evidence on performance of improved rubber varieties under typical smallholder conditions in Indonesia. Furthermore, one outcome of the plantation bias in rubber research is that important questions regarding the application of technology in smallholder settings have not received serious attention."

50. The fact that real-world importance is not always reflected in scholarly attention is demonstrated by this academic focus on historic sugar cultivation. As Li (1999: 25–26) writes, "The labor mobilized for upland coffee at the height of the Cultivation System was two to three times that mobilised for lowland sugar . . . [and] colonial profits, ecological impacts and social dislocations associated with coffee were immense . . . , yet they have received less scholarly attention [than sugar]."

Chapter 2. A Native Court's Warning about Involvement in Commodity Production

1. Compare the bleak native vision of pepper in the *Hikayat Pocut Mohamat* with this colonial paean to the pepper gardens of Sumatra: "A pepper garden cultivated in England would not, in point of external appearance, be considered as an object of extraordinary beauty . . . ; yet, in Sumatra, I never entered one, . . . that I did not find myself affected with a strong sensation of pleasure. Perhaps the simple view of human industry, so scantily presented in that island, might contribute to this pleasure, by awakening those social feelings that nature has inspired us with, and which makes our breasts glow on the perception of whatever indicates the prosperity and happiness of our fellow-creatures." (Marsden [1811] 1966: 139)

2. There are reports of similar cases from around the globe during the colonial era, including the nineteenth-century uprooting of peanuts in Senegal for fear they were attracting the colonial French (O'Brien 1975).

3. There is an older and more fundamental relationship between resource wealth and political instability in the region, as Ricklefs (2008: 80) writes, "Whenever a lucrative trade product was produced in areas not immediately under the control of the king (as was often the case with gold, tin, pepper, and other products) the growth of external markets brought wealth into the hands of local lords who might choose to challenge the authority of the centre. Trade growth was thus often the cause of state disintegration."

4. I use the term *Malayic* rather than *Malay*, in part because the Banjarese distinguish themselves from Malays, listing Malays among the "foreign traders" (Ras 1968: 431; cf. Saleh 1976: 206). Also, Ras (1968: 8) describes the Banjarese language as "the independent continuation of a rather archaic type of Malay, superimposed on a substratum of Dayak dialects, with an admixture of Javanese."

5. Ras (1968: 173) says that one version of the chronicle includes a sketchy continuation of dynastic history up to the beginning of the nineteenth century.

6. Ras (1968: 2) says that the text was recopied several times in the first half of the nineteenth century, but there is no evidence that this involved substantive rewriting; thus, the chronicle can be taken to reflect the views of its sixteenth- and seventeenth-century authors.

7. See also Koster (2005) on Malay historiography and the Dutch.

8. Ras (1968: 98) argues that parallels with other Malay chronicles, like the *Sejarah Melayu* or *Salasilah Kutai*, are due not to borrowing but rather to the fact that they share a common "proto story" of the region that has been developed differently in each chronicle according to its needs.

9. Compare Florida (1995) on writing and reading in the historic Javanese courts.

10. Contemporary government statistics on pepper cultivation in South Kalimantan, for example, indicate that 100 percent of it is produced on smallholdings, none of it coming from estates (http://kalsel.bps.go/id, accessed July 2010); see Creutzberg (1975: 133–34) on the period 1925–1930. De Waard (1964: 24) writes that the same pattern long prevailed in the other major regional producer, Sarawak, East Malaysia (cf. Purseglove et al. 1981: 38–39, 85).

11. The Kantu' say that they have had pepper for "generations" and that they first obtained it from Dayak living across the border in Sarawak, East Malaysia.

12. The Kantu' plant former pepper garden sites in rubber; and Heidhues (1992: 215) writes that degraded former pepper lands on Bangka are planted in not only rubber but also durian (*Durio zibethinus* Murr.), coffee, and cloves.

13. A number of observers have noted a link between pepper cultivation and grassland succession (e.g., Blacklock 1954: 42, 47; Brookfield et al. 1990: 497; Burkill 1966, 2:1779; Potter 1988: 129; Reid 1995: 101–4); and some have suggested that the mark of historic pepper cultivation can still be seen in contemporary grasslands. However, whereas pepper cultivation may precipitate grassland succession, other factors are necessary to perpetuate them, because they are unstable on their own. In addition, succession to grassland—even to the much-maligned *Imperata cylindrica*—does not necessarily reflect environmental degradation (Dove 1986a, 1986c, 2008). *Imperata* grasslands may serve a wide variety of economic and ecological functions, including that of being used for further cultivation, which is laborious but far from impossible.

14. See Osche ([1931] 1980: 588): "A plantation of pepper is very exacting as regards quality of the soil and care to be bestowed."

15. Duke and duCellier (1993: 398) write that pepper can be stored off the vine, and thus withheld from the market, for several years without loss of quality. Instead of empowering small producers, as Duke and duCellier suggest, this characteristic is exploited by international speculators (see de Waard 1964: 24), which adds to the problems faced by the smallholder. As Andaya (1993b: 79) writes, "Pepper can be stored for several years without deteriorating, and by the middle of the seventeenth century, warehouses in Europe were filling up as sellers tried to keep the price high and as consumers turned to ginger as a substitute. By 1652 Europe was said to be glutted with pepper, the surplus sufficient to last for at least three years."

16. The negligible cost of starting or stopping rubber tapping in an existing rubber

garden permits smallholders to respond adroitly to fluctuating market prices (see chapter 6). This capability, coupled with the minimal costs of establishing rubber and the ability to self-exploit household labor, even permits the Kantu' to respond inversely to price fluctuations (viz., to increase production as prices fall or decrease it as prices rise) (see chapters 5, 6).

17. This inherent volatility is reflected in Chau Ju-kua's comment on the fluctuation in the cost of pepper from thirteenth century Central Java (Su-ki-tan): "At the right season and in good years, twenty-five taels of 'trade money' will buy from ten to twenty packages of pepper, each package holding fifty pecks. In years of dearth or times of disturbance, the same sum will buy only half that amount" (Hirth and Rockhill 1911: 83). Schrieke ([1955] 1966: 56) writes of these disturbances: "It happened repeatedly that because of troubles between *negeri* [kingdoms] in the interior there would be no pepper shipped to the market in Jambi." Burkill (1966, 2:1779) attributes fluctuation in nineteenth-century pepper production to variations in political conditions, variations in market prices, and the inherent ecological dynamic that necessitates periodic relocation and replanting of the pepper gardens.

18. Pepper also appears in the writings of the physician Dioscorides and the botanist Theophrastus (Burkill 1966, 2:1776; Flückiger and Hanbury 1879: 576; Watt [1889–1896] 1972, 6:264).

19. Van Leur ([1955] 1967) disputes the idea of actual Indian Hindu colonization as opposed to cultural influence.

20. Wolters (1967: 184) writes that Lévi's (1918: 83) identification of She-yeh with Java is "reasonable."

21. The role of pepper in Java's prominence as a source of valued trade goods is reflected in the fact that China eventually had to prohibit trade with Java because purchases of its pepper were draining China's currency reserves (Hirth and Rockhill 1911: 78, 82).

22. Reid (1993: 12) writes that the Ming trade missions "were probably responsible for the introduction of Indian pepper plants to northern Sumatra [. . .]," but this would give a much later date for this introduction than that given by other authorities.

23. See also Hobhouse (1985: xi): "The starting point for the European expansion out of the Mediterranean and the Atlantic continental shelf had nothing to do with, say, religion or the rise of capitalism—but it had a great deal to do with pepper."

24. See Crawfurd (1868) for a useful discussion of the etymology of early regional names for black pepper.

25. This custom of trans-shipment created confusion concerning the actual origins of trade goods since, as Wheatley (1959: 33) writes, "Authors all too often described commodities as natural products of regions from which they were only re-exports" (cf. Donkin 1999: 133). In some cases, however, the fact of trans-shipment was noted, as in this comment from Chau Ju-kua on woven mats: "The mats called *yé-sin-tién* come from Tan-jung-wu-lo [Banjar]. The foreign traders carry them to San-fo-ts'i [Palembang], Ling-ya-mön [Lingga?] and *Shö-p'o* [Java] for trade" (Hirth and Rockhill 1911: 220).

26. See Tagliacozzo (2005) on the history and environmental implications of China's trade with Borneo and Logan (1848a) on the history of Chinese trading linkages to Borneo.

27. The fact that one of the trade items from Tan-jung-wu-lo reported by Chau Ju-kua is fine woven mats (Wheatley 1959: 64) supports the identification of Tan-jung-wu-lo with Banjar, given the salience of this item in the *Hikayat*'s lists of trade goods. Also supportive of this identification is Chau Ju-kua's comment that "large numbers of horses are raised" in Tan-jung-wu-lo and one of its "native products" is yellow wax (Hirth and Rockhill 1911: 84–85). Beeswax is one of the historic trade items of Banjar, and it is mentioned in the *Hikayat*'s tribute lists. Raising horses for use in deer hunting is reported from Banjarmasin in the

mid-nineteenth century (Low [1848] 1968: 91; see Medway [1977: 15] for references to the large herds of deer that were the object of this activity). The concurrence of hoofed game and horses in Southeast Kalimantan makes sense given the historic presence of extensive grass-lands in the region, which are noted in most of the historic accounts of horses and deer, since these grasslands would sustain these animals and make possible such things as horse-borne hunting in the first place (see Dove 1986a, 1986c for contemporary accounts of these grass-lands). In all such attempts to identify toponyms from the early Chinese sources, however, Wolters's (1967: 169) caution should be borne in mind.

28. Indeed, Borneo was known to the fourteenth-century Javanese as Puradvipa, "Dia-mond Land" (Cleary and Eaton 1992: 40).

29. Banjarese have a reputation to this day as one of the archipelago's foremost trading groups (cf. Peluso 1983a: 99). The dispersion of Banjarese traders around the archipelago was amplified by the capitulation of the Banjar sultanate to the Dutch at the end of the Banjarma-sin War of 1859–1863 (ibid.: 98). See Hudson (1967: chap. 3) for a brief introduction to Banjar history.

30. Forest products continue to be important to the Banjarese and native people even today. In the contemporary highland Banjarese village of Rantau Balai (visited by the author), during the slack agricultural period between weeding and the harvest, most people leave the village to seek tradable products in the forest, including diamonds, gold, damar (a resin), rat-tan, fish, and *kemiri'* (candlenut, *Aleurites moluccana*)—which is much the same list of goods that the Banjar kingdom was sending abroad three and four centuries ago. Compare to Tsing (1993: 55–56) on the forest-product trade of the nearby Meratus Dayak: "Meratus hike or raft down to these [Banjar] markets, where they sell rattan, rubber, peanuts, mung beans, iron-wood, incense woods, wax, and numerous other minor crops and forest products."

31. The historic concern for navigable waterways in the region is reflected in the story told by the villagers of Rantau Balai about a Banjarese rajah from the pre-Dutch era who tried to cut a channel between two loops of the Riam Kanan River and also between two loops of one of its tributaries, the Pa'au River. The two attempts are said to have ultimately failed due to encountering bedrock formations. The villagers of Rantau Balai believe that two long gul-leys stretching inland from the two aforementioned rivers—both of which were shown to the author—mark the sites of these attempts. They refer to them, both located upstream from their village, as either *lobang rajah* (the crater of the rajah) or *bekas rajah* (the remnants of the rajah). The villagers insist that the purpose of these excavations had nothing to do with irri-gation, but was intended to *mempercepat jalan* (quicken the way) (see Hudson [1967: 76] on inter-river linkages built in the Banjar region by the Dutch at the end of the nineteenth cen-tury).

32. Groeneveldt's (1960) list (cited in Hudson 1967: 64) of the trade products sought by China in Southeast Borneo at this time resembles the lists in the *Hikayat:* "rhinoceros horns, peacocks, parrots, gold dust, crane crests, wax, rattan-mats, [chilies], dragon's-blood, nut-megs, deer hides, and so on." Dragon's blood, damar, mats, pepper, coral, pearls, civets, and beeswax—all mentioned in tribute lists in the *Hikayat Banjar*—each merit separate sections in the second part of Chau Ju-kua's *Chu-fan-chï* (Hirth and Rockhill 1911: 197, 199, 220, 222, 226, 229, 234, 238). One other commodity mentioned in the *Hikayat*'s tribute lists, gold, is discussed in Chau Ju-kua's section on P'o-ni (Borneo), where he says that gold vessels are both used and traded, and gold is used in barter (ibid.: 155, 156, 158). Chau Ju-kua identifies the Indonesian Archipelago as the source, or one of the sources, of most of these goods; thus, he identifies kingdoms in Java, Sumatra, or Borneo as the source of the mats, pepper, coral, pearls, civets, and beeswax (ibid.: 77–78, 81, 83–85, 220, 222, 230n1, 234, 239n). Hirth and

Rockhill (ibid.: 198n) themselves identify Borneo and Sumatra as the source of the "ordinary" dragon's blood (*hüékié*) traded to China.

33. *Damar* is a generic term for resin from a variety of trees from the family Diptero-carpaceae, especially of the genus *Shorea*.

34. "Dragon's blood" is the sap of certain rattans, especially of the genus *Daemonorops* Blume ex Schult. f.

35. The Sumatran trading states of Jambi and Palembang were similarly dependent on Java (Andaya 1993b: 66; Schrieke [1955] 1966: 56–57).

36. Cf. Tsing's (1993: 280) report on the vow to not eat rice, by a female Dayak shaman in the Meratus mountains in Southeastern Borneo: "Uma Adang is different. She sees as the distinguishing mark the fact that she does not eat rice. Symbolically and practically, rice is central to Meratus livelihood. Uma Adang positions herself outside the world rice consumption creates, to see beyond it. And, indeed, because she does not eat rice, she also does not plant, weed, harvest, thresh, pound, sun-dry, cook, or serve rice. These are time-consuming, identity-creating activities for almost all Meratus women." For Uma Adang, as for the people of Negara Daha, the disavowal of rice is a statement about an unorthodox relationship both with local society and with translocal forces.

37. There must also have been substantial numbers of artisans in Banjar in earlier times, given that the seventeenth-century *Hikayat*'s lists of forest products sent abroad include not only raw materials like precious stones, beeswax, and rattan but also items manufactured from forest products, such as woven dish-covers, roofing, and especially mats. The fame of Southeast Borneo's fine woven mats is noted in official accounts of Sung-era maritime trade to China (Wheatley 1959: 64) and in the nineteenth-century colonial accounts of Crawfurd ([1856] 1971: 59) and Bock ([1881] 1985).

38. Hudson (1967: 66) similarly writes, "Banjarmasin had begun planting and exporting pepper on a small scale at the beginning of the seventeenth century in response to the needs of Chinese traders who were finding it increasingly difficult to secure pepper at Patani and Bantem [viz., Banten], the ports previously utilized."

39. Cf. Hudson (1967: 65): "It was the introduction of commercial pepper cultivation into the Banjar sultanate in the seventeenth and eighteenth centuries, rather than the conversion to Islam in the sixteenth, that led to the growth of Banjarmasin's importance in the Indonesian trade sphere and the expansion of Banjar-Malay peoples throughout the whole Banjar region of the Southeast Barito basin at the expense of the indigenous Dayak population."

40. "Myrobalans" is the trade name for fruits of a variety of tannin-rich species of the genus *Terminalia*, which are used in the manufacture of tannin for leather, dye for cloth, and ink (Burkill 1966, 2:2173–80).

41. The memory of this period of international fame and exchange is remarkably fresh among contemporary Banjarese. Villagers in the remote upland Banjarese village of Rantau Balai proudly told me that Martapura, one of the historic capitals of Banjar, was once known as "Little Singapore." Since Singapore was not founded until early in the nineteenth century (1819), Martapura could not have been known as "Little Singapore" until much later than the period under discussion here, the seventeenth century. Nevertheless, the contemporary claim that Martapura was once known by this term still can still be read as a contemporary effort to retrieve a more cosmopolitan past (cf. Marsden 2008). I am grateful to Barbara Andaya for this insight. The memory of a time when the region figured more prominently in international affairs is retained in other ways as well. For example, the villagers of Rantau Balai retain a legend of a "Chinese Rajah of Brunei" who attacked and defeated an early, pre-Islamic Banjar ruler, then was attacked and defeated in turn by [the kingdom of] "Majapahit," whereupon he

"fled" (*lari*) to, "fasted' (*betapah*) atop, and "disappeared" (*hilang*) on nearby Mount Payangan. A similar story is recounted in the *Salasilah Kutai*, a Malay chronicle from East Kalimantan, which tells of a Chinese prince who comes to Kutai by ship, loses a cockfight, and flees to and settles in the interior (Ras 1968: 82). Ras (ibid.:120–21) notes that a visiting Chinese prince is a recurring figure in many Malay and Javanese stories. The villagers of Rantau Balai also retain a memory of the ruler of South Kalimantan formerly paying tribute (*bayar upati'*) to the ruler (Rajah Betawi) of Java, just as they say Indonesia as a whole once paid tribute to the Dutch. These comments have something of the flavor of the unique historical consciousness of the Dayak inhabitants of the mountain hinterlands of southeast Kalimantan studied by Tsing (1993: 74). Compare McWilliam (2007) on the history of the fluctuating, complex, creative engagement with external others of the coastal entrepôt of Com in East Timor.

42. Schrieke ([1955] 1966: 53) says that pepper production in Pidie on Sumatra's east coast was "mentioned as early as 1416 in the Chinese records."

43. The *Hikayat* elsewhere describes the "good state" of society as one in which "food *and* clothing were very cheap" (Ras 1968: 335; emphasis added).

44. Cf. the comment in Chau Ju-kua's trade manual on pepper cultivation in Central Java: "The pepper gatherers suffer greatly from the acrid fumes they have to inhale, and are commonly afflicted with headache" (Hirth and Rockhill 1911: 83).

45. The Dutch established monopolies on the pepper trade in Palembang in 1662 and in Jambi in 1679 (Andaya 1993b: 244).

46. Reid (1993: 250) writes, "Banjarmasin's ruler began in the 1660s to force growers to sell to his agents at low prices in order to fulfil his contract with the Dutch United East India Company and still make a profit."

47. Pepper contracts with foreign traders were integral bargaining chips in all local conflicts (Andaya 1993b; Schrieke [1955] 1966: 62–63).

48. *Diupamai* literally translates as "to be taken as examples" (Ras 1968: 612).

49. Another version of the *Hikayat* gives *Saki* and *Sakie* as alternate wordings for *sakai* (Ras 1968: 240n6, 330n37).

50. *Kaparak*, from *parak*, translates literally as "persons who during the audience-meetings have their seats nearest to the king" (Ras 1968: 579).

51. Most of the references to *rakyat* in the *Hikayat* involve audiences before the king or the king's responsibility for his "subjects"; and most of the references to *sakai* involve waging war on, exacting tribute from, or sending instructions to the upland tribal peoples.

52. The contemporary swidden system of the Meratus Dayak of this region is still notable for its highly mobile character (Tsing 1993).

53. Slaves also played a prominent role in the system of pepper cultivation in Jambi (Andaya 1993b: 80, 96), in spite of the fact that the interior agrarian population there was larger than in Banjar, just because the labor demands of pepper—especially as state demands for production accelerated—are so onerous.

54. Hudson (1967: 56) reports that Banjar even raided the Dayak for slaves.

55. Hall (1995) examines the Banjar's use of cultural-historical means to bring the upstream Dayak within their orbit.

56. This also held true in Jambi, as Andaya (1993b: 244) writes "Following the English and Dutch arrival . . . the bonding [between upstream and downstream] created by the exchange of gifts, the acceptance of mutual obligations, and putative kinship ties was frequently undermined by the commercial tensions injected into the marketplace."

57. Peluso (1983a: 28, 30, 32, 61, 70) describes in eastern Borneo a loose and shifting political-economic relationship between upriver Dayak gatherers of forest products, the

downriver Malay Kutai sultanate, and Bugis traders, with the sultanate at first mediating between the Dayak and Bugis, and then the Bugis mediating between the sultanate and the Dayak—a situation further complicated by the arrival of the Dutch.

58. Hudson (1967: 66n25) adds: "This Dayak reluctance to becoming overly dependent on a cash or trading economy at the expense of subsistence agriculture continues to the present day. It is one of the economic and psychological characteristics that sets the majority of the Southeast Barito Dayak off from the contiguous Banjars."

59. Andaya (1995: 175) cites the *Hikayat* recommendation of five to ten clumps in making her point. In fact, the various passages in the *Hikayat* suggest "about four or five clumps per head," "about ten or twenty plants per head," "some ten or twenty plants only," or "a few pepper trees per head" (Ras 1968: 265, 331, 375, 443). Burkill (1966, 2:1778), writing of pepper growing in the sixteenth century and earlier, says, "Pepper was probably grown all through Malaysia at that time in a very haphazard way. Later a more intensive cultivation came in, with special plantations, in the place of a vine or two near the homestead."

60. Van Leur ([1955] 1967: 127) estimates that in 1619 approximately 280,000 pieces of Coromandel cloth went to from India to Indonesia in this trade.

61. "Marhum Panambahan" literally translates as "the deceased one to whom homage is paid" (Wilkinson 1959, II: 742, 876).

62. There are two mentions of "Hollanders" in the *Hikayat* prior to this passage on the bombardment of Banjar: one is in the listing of foreign styles of dress that they should avoid, and a second in the listing of foreign traders who visited the kingdom (Ras 1968: 263, 265).

63. Suntharalingam (1963: 47) estimates that the annual exports of pepper from Banjarmasin averaged just over 1,000 tons at the beginning of the eighteenth century; Raffles ([1817] 1978, 1:215) puts this figure at the beginning of the nineteenth century at "about twelve to fifteen hundred tons"; Lindblad (1988: 31) puts the figure at about 1,000 tons early in the twentieth century; and government statistics put the production of South Kalimantan at 366 tons in 2005 (http://kalsel.bps.go.id, accessed in July 2010). Crawfurd ([1856] 1971: 65) suggests that there was a marked reduction in pepper cultivation during the early nineteenth century in southeastern Borneo, as a result of Dutch policies.

64. Thus, Hudson's (1967: 70) suggestion that the compiler of the *Hikayat* was a member of the Banjar court's "isolationist faction" is, although on the right track, beside the point. The *Hikayat* statements on pepper were not so much an articulation of an isolationist position as an articulation of what the implications were for Banjar society of isolation versus nonisolation.

Chapter 3. The Antecedent to Cultivating Exotic Rubber

1. See de Jong et al. (2003) on current issues in the forest product trade in Indonesia.

2. As Bunker (1984: 1033) writes regarding the Amazon: "Even though market opportunities inspired the local reorganization of modes of extraction in the Amazon, the specific socioeconomic forms which modes of extraction took were influenced more by the socioeconomic and environmental conditions created by prior local modes of production and extraction than by the political and economic characteristics of the capitalist world system."

3. See Morrison and Junker (2002) for a rare effort to put the forager-trader groups of South and Southeast Asia into historical perspective.

4. See also Hecht and Cockburn (1989: 154): "There is an academic pastoral fallacy about collectors, which holds them to be backwoodsmen whose activities are entirely oriented to subsistence. This condescending vision of an Amazon sheltering millions of rural Calibans

is far wide of the mark. Forest collectors have been supplying international markets for almost five hundred years and are also part of lively regional markets."

5. Gathering of native rubbers was stimulated in the 1980s by the efforts of the former Suharto regime to take control of the rattan market, which led many collectors and traders to shift their activities to other products, such as the native rubbers (Safran and Godoy 1993: 296). Nonetheless, the various native gums (e.g., balata, *gutta-percha*, guayule, chicle, and others) still account for only .06 percent of Indonesia's rubber exports by USD value (Government of Indonesia 2004: 35, table 12.2).

6. Latex-producing plants of commercial interest in Indonesia early in the twentieth century included, in addition to the introduced *Hevea,* five other introduced trees and, among native plants, two trees, two climbers, five lianas, and one climbing shrub (Anonymous 1935, cited in CAPD 1982: 3525).

7. See Low ([1848] 1968: 49–52) for a mid-nineteenth-century European sketch of Borneo's latex resources.

8. See Lawrence, Leighton, and Peart (1995: 80): "Prior to the introduction of *H. brasiliensis* around 1950 [in their particular study area in West Kalimantan], forest rubber, or *geta hutan* (*Palaquium* sp. Sapotaceae), was collected from the primary forest and marketed by the Dayaks of Kembera [West Kalimantan]."

9. Coppen (1995: 118) writes: "Before *Hevea* plantations were developed in Southeast Asia, jelutong was produced and exported for the manufacture of inferior rubber items, in which elasticity was not a prime consideration. With the advent of large-scale rubber production, exploitation of jelutong ceased almost completely."

10. Similarly, the limited traditional cultivation of *Hevea* in its native habitat in the Amazon was driven by the importance of the tree for food, not latex (Schultes 1956: 146).

11. The fact that *jelutong* trees yield a timber preferred for use in making coffins (Williams 1963: 123) may explain one of the most enigmatic historic trade names for this rubber, namely "dead Borneo."

12. Foxworthy (1922: 163) argued that the only nonlethal method that ever proved practical for exploiting *gutta-percha* trees, even in plantations, was based on extracting latex from their leaves by means of mechanical grinding.

13. Even the English "rajah" of Sarawak, Charles Brooke, otherwise known for his hostility to European plantation interests, gave Europeans a *jelutong*-processing monopoly in Sarawak (Reece 1988: 28–29).

14. Another observer defended the right of the Kalimantan tribesmen to tap *jelutong* by likening it to the right of the Javanese to cultivate rice land (CAPD 1982: 5519).

15. Up until World War II the principal economic activity engaged in by Iban men on *bejalai* was collecting jungle produce; since then it has been wage labor (Padoch 1982: 109).

16. See Potter (1997) on the spread of *gutta-percha* collecting through the Kapuas River basin during the mid-nineteenth-century boom.

17. Padoch (1982: 109, 115) writes: "'Jungle produce' is found and collected in old forest, and therefore pioneering Iban can obtain these products close to their homes, while those in older settlements must travel to other districts. . . . Longer settlement and increasing agricultural use of land lead to both a drop in farm productivity and exhaustion of nearby forest product sources, and make traveling [viz., relocating] to areas of abundant old forest and/or wage labor opportunities more profitable."

18. It is also suggestive that a contemporary of Hose and McDougall described Iban dressing in war attire for expeditions to gather forest products like camphor (Donkin 1999: 178).

19. Wadley (2007) correctly points out, however, that natural resource-based explanations of nineteenth-century tribal warfare in Borneo err if they omit the impact on warfare of the political machinations of the colonial Dutch and English powers.

20. According to the recent global survey by Ruiz-Pérez et al. (2004), the highest-value forest products still tend to be managed most intensively by the most specialized producers.

21. The relationship between rubber cultivation and native rubber gathering is reflected today in the fact that Dayak who do less cash-cropping tend to do more gathering of forest products (Burgers 1993).

22. Compare Wenzlhuemer's (2008) analysis of another major crop transition, from coffee to tea, in Ceylon.

23. The English phrase "tapping rubber" better describes the machete-based "incision" of South America than the knife-based "excision" of Southeast Asia. The common Indonesian/Malay/Ibanic term for tapping rubber, *motong/mutong,* which translates as "to cut," more accurately represents the Southeast Asian technique (Echols and Shadily 1992: 434; Richards 1981: 293; Wilkinson 1959, 2:913–14).

24. See Potter (1997) on intensification of *gutta-percha* gathering in the 1870s following widespread rice crop failures.

25. Williams (1963: 117–18) acknowledges, however, that bark recovery from tapping was not as good with *Dyera* as with *Hevea.*

26. The difference between my figure of 500 trees per hectare and Lawrence, Leighton, and Peart's figure of 1,391 per hectare is likely due to the fact that they counted all trees twenty centimeters or more in diameter at breast height (dbh), whereas I counted trees actually being tapped, whose dbh averaged perhaps twice as great.

27. As Lawrence, Leighton, and Peart (1995: 85) note, the attraction of cultivating rubber and fruit trees—compared with gathering in primary forest—increases with time of settlement and consequent distance to receding forest.

28. Kato (1991: 132) similarly argues that *Hevea* rubber cultivation helped to sedentarize the Malay peasantry.

29. Some other economic trees are planted on the same basis: see Cooke (2002: 204) on Dayak planting of oil palms—which he terms "strategic agriculture"—ahead of expansion into their territories by oil palm companies.

30. Cramer (1956: 264) suggests that a plantation of *Ficus elastica* in Java—established no later than 1864, well before the introduction of *Hevea*—may be the first rubber plantation in the world. Ricklefs (2008: 185) also mentions early *Ficus* plantations on the east coast of Sumatra. The Dutch commitment to *Ficus* helps to explain the tardy development of *Hevea* rubber plantations in Java compared with other parts of the region (Keong 1976: 35–36).

31. See also van Wijk (1941; cited in CAPD 1982: 1344) on planting of *Dyera lowii* and *Dyera borneenis,* the major sources of *jelutong.*

32. In the case of some other forest products, the "hazard" or risk and the consequent ritual focus are yet again different. This is the case in gathering camphor (from *Dryobalanops aromatica* Gaetn. F.), and *gaharu,* or aloes-wood (from *Gonystylus* spp. and *Aquilaria* spp. [especially *A. malaccensis*]): these precious substances are found only in a small minority of their host trees, and so ritual focuses on discerning the valuable trees from the worthless ones (see Andaya and Andaya 1982: 11; Donkin 1999: 176–83; Evans [1923] 1970: 280–87; Gianno 1986: 5; Potter 1997).

33. Cf. Visser's (1989: 31) report of a similar indigenous commentary on agricultural development and pacification on Sahu in eastern Indonesia: Nanga semarang dadi u'u'da. (Our weapon has turned into a hoe.)

34. "Ring" refers to the wide V-shaped cutting pattern developed by Ridley, which nearly circumscribes the tree trunk.

35. The Kantu' and other tribes never used the term *getah* or *gutta* (or *gutta-percha*) for the native rubbers: they used terms from their own languages (e.g., *jangkang* for *Palaquium* spp. among the Kantu' [cf. Richards 1981: 123]), as might be expected for native resources of both economic importance and long history.

36. Some sympathetic observers, however, such as Penot (2004), use the phrase "jungle rubber" with no intentional ironic or negative connotations.

Chapter 4. The Construction of Rubber Knowledge in Southeast Asia

1. Wickham (1908: 63) writes that *Hevea* should "be regarded as a *plantation*—a *cultivated* product rather than as one to be planted with view [*sic*] of being widely disseminated under canopy of an area covered by primitive standing forest."

2. Ridley termed the repeated reopening of the original wound in the tree "calling the rubber" (Wolf and Wolf 1936: 167).

3. According to Dijkman (1961: 68), Ridley's tapping system was as important to the development of the rubber industry as the invention of the pneumatic tire or the process of vulcanization.

4. Dijkman (1961: 40) maintains that the one drawback to natural undergrowth, at least in the estates, was that it encouraged the presence of more game, especially deer, which browsed on the rubber seedlings.

5. Colonial Dutch observers suggested that the involvement of women "is generally not favourable for the plantings" (Cramer 1956: 301).

6. Additional smallholder innovations involved development—in collaboration with downstream traders—of means of monitoring prices, transporting their product to market, marketing it, and managing credit and payment-in-kind in only partially monetized economies.

7. See Bentley (2006) on folk experimentation in agriculture.

8. Schultes (1956: 140–41) writes: "I have never seen a *Hevea* tree growing—either planted or as a survival from felling—in the garden of the house of any primitive Indian anywhere in the Amazon valley, including the northwestern part."

9. Bunker (1984: 1032) additionally notes that grafting can make Amazon rubber trees resistant to the fungus and states, "Peasant communities near Santarém have maintained successful stands of rubber for many decades."

10. Bunker (1984: 1032) similarly argues that it was not plant disease that explained Amazon's failure to compete with Asian rubber plantations, it was lack of rural population.

11. Over one-half of Brazil's domestic demand now is met by rubber from cultivated plantations, albeit located in eastern Brazil, outside of its native range in Amazonia (Browder 1992: 176).

12. As Ellen (1999: 142) writes: "Transfer of new cultigens is not just about the movement of genetic material, but of cultural knowledge as well, knowledge which always carries a social burden."

13. See Wolf and Wolf (1936: 163): "Perhaps as widespread as the legend of Wickham's omnipotence is the conception of the Hevea and the Hevea alone being rushed to the East expressly to replace devastated coffee plants and of an eager army of planters whirling into

action to set out the seedlings and reap 'white money' just as fast as they could tear up other crops and knock over jungle."

14. See Wolf and Wolf (1936: 163–64) for details of all the other latex-yielding plants experimented with.

15. Dijkman (1961: 9) writes: "[T]he methods practiced by the native farmers, when applied to plantation routine, have been responsible for a number of the most startling developments known in the culture of rubber—for example, planting density programs and the hedge-row system of planting were both adapted from native practices."

16. Industry acceptance of clean weeding was hastened by the 1930s depression, as well as the Japanese occupation during World War II, both of which made labor for weeding scarcer and the benefits of non-weeding perforce more apparent (Dijkman 1961: 27).

17. Gouyon, de Foresta, and Levang (1993: 182) write, "No accurate, reliable census of jungle rubber exists to date in Indonesia" (cf. Tomich 1991: 257).

18. Tomich (1991: 259) writes, "The history of rubber development in Southeast Asia provides ample reasons to suspect that research programs would generate technology suited to relatively capital-intensive rubber production." The clonal rubber that has been the focus of so much Indonesian research, for example, is not well suited to the conditions on small-holdings (Gouyon, de Foresta, and Levang 1993: 199–200).

19. As Tomich (1991: 258) writes, "Because smallholders are planting substantial amounts of rubber even though they are excluded from supplies of higher-yielding trees, an important opportunity is missed by restricting improved planting material to projects."

Chapter 5. Depression-Era Responses to Smallholder Rubber Development by Tribesmen and Governments

1. Dayak society uses plant metaphors to express many different types of relationships. As Sather (1990: 37) writes of the Iban: "Virtually, all social groupings and relationships are conceptualised in terms of botanic metaphors, and the ritual language of the Ibans is permeated with plant and forest imagery. Every living human being is represented, not only by a conjunction of body (*tuboh*) and spirit or soul (*semengat*), but by an invisible plant counterpart, the *ayu*, which symbolises human life in its vulnerable, mortal aspect."

2. Tedlock (1992: 2) notes that the Western dichotomization of dreaming and waking has roots in classic Aristotelian philosophy and, more recently, in Cartesian dualism.

3. Durkheim (1953: 25–26) defines "collective representations" as follows: "If one can say that, to a certain extent, collective representations are exterior to individual minds, it means that they do not derive from them as such but from the association of minds, which is a very different thing. No doubt in the making of the whole each contributes his part, but private sentiments do not become social except by combination under the action of the *sui generis* forces developed in association. In such a combination, with the mutual alterations involved, *they become something else*. . . . The resultant surpasses the individual as the whole the part. It is *in* the whole as it is *by* the whole. In this sense it is exterior to the individuals."

4. The Stevenson Restriction Scheme came out of a review commission set up by Winston Churchill, then British Colonial Secretary (Tucker 2007: 124).

5. The Stevenson Restriction Scheme applied, within Borneo, only to Sarawak, Brunei, and Sabah, the western and northern parts of the island that are today included in the independent nations of Malaysia and Brunei, but not to the eastern and southern portions that lay then within the Dutch East Indies and are today part of Indonesia.

6. Under pressure from the British colonial office, the English rajah Vyner Brooke brought Sarawak under the IRRA too (Pringle 1970: 334).

7. As Wolf and Wolf (1936: 231) wrote at the time, "In addition to receiving free land the natives in the Indies had other advantages over the English planters in Malaya. They did not have to stand the cost of roads, permanent buildings, machinery; had no expenditures for managing directors, superintendents and huge staffs; no payrolls to meet, no labor to recruit at distant points. They could in fact make a fine profit at prices below the Englishmen's cost."

8. The Dutch colonial government promised to use the massive revenue from the IRRA duties on smallholder rubber to develop the smallholder industry in particular and the rural economy in general, but it failed to do so (Thomas and Panglaykim 1976: 196).

9. The worst diseases of rubber in Indonesia are caused by fungi affecting the root system (Dijkman 1961: 144).

10. An assumption that native tapping practices are destructive continues to the present day. In contemporary nucleus estates smallholders are provided with high-yielding rubber clones on a credit base, and a chief concern of estate management is the perceived predilection of the smallholders to tap this rubber too intensively. As one estate manager said to me, "Memotong setiap hari tanpa berpikir tentang masa depan." ([Smallholders] tap every day without thinking about the future.) (interview at the nucleus estate PIR VI Sambas, Monterado, Samalantang sub-district, Singkawang district, West Kalimantan, 29 September 1993).

11. Opposition by American consumers to rubber-restriction policies began with the 1922–28 Stevenson Restriction Scheme (Tucker 2007: 125). See also Whitford (1924).

12. Cf. Stoler (1985a, 1985b) on obfuscation of the economic basis of planter-peasant conflict in colonial Indonesia.

13. Marcus and Fischer (1986: 13–15) suggest that irony is especially salient at times when reigning paradigms are threatened, and they identify the 1930s as one such time.

14. The colonial-era poem cited in chapter 3, ends with the line, "Wherein is wrapped in clothes the babe whose future lies / In the price of rubber tapped in a ring." The challenge of the rice-eating rubber dream was for the tribal smallholders to avoid precisely this fate, that is, to manage their children's future so that it did *not* lie in the price of rubber.

15. Similar actions were taken to defend the subsistence rice sector against market-oriented rubber cultivation in other parts of Indonesia. For example, Potter and Badcock (2004: 345) cite Slotemaker (1926, 4:9) to the effect that the Minangkabau in Central Sumatra were not permitted by their traditional leaders to grow rubber on rice fields near the village.

16. These figures are from Creutzberg (1975: 93–94, table 10) and Government of Indonesia (1992: 232, table 5.2.5).

17. Allen and Donnithorne ([1957] 1962: 34) say that the Netherlands East Indies were "one of the chief victims of the depression" given the role of commodities in its economy and the attendant crash in world staple prices.

18. Aspengren (1986) suggests that the impact of the Depression on most Indonesian smallholders was to cause a decrease in cash cropping and an increase in subsistence cultivation (see also Allen and Donnithorne 1962: 123–24).

19. See Touwen's (2000) analysis of the impact of the Depression on indigenous production of rubber and other export commodities.

20. Liging, Kantu' longhouse of Tikul Batu, 9 May 1976.

21. Reed Wadley, personal communication.

22. See Dove (2006) for an analysis of the analogous failure of contemporary Dayak to blame state policy for ethnic competition and conflict.

23. Cf. Nash's (1994: 24) observation: "Workers' awareness of the global dimensions of their conditions is not isometric with the social relations in production. . . ."

24. Compare Li (2002) on the impact of cocoa in Sulawesi.

25. See Suyanto et al. (2001) on the role of rubber in the shift in Sumatra in tenure from lineage to joint family to single family, due to population pressure and low returns from upland rice.

26. Kato (1994: 153) writes that rubber has similarly led to abandonment of irrigated rice cultivation in Peninsular Malaysia.

27. The same conclusion is implicit in Freeman's ([1955] 1970: 286) comment regarding Iban who felled rubber because of the dream: "Today they bewail their stupidity, but because of it, many Iban families in the Baleh region are now without productive rubber plantations."

28. Taussig (1980) may have overdrawn his distinction between peasant agriculture and capitalist mining in South America due to inability to see the coexistence of monetary and nonmonetary spheres (Harris 1989: 251; Sallnow 1989: 217).

29. Cf. Alexander and Alexander's (1995) analysis of the contemporary elaboration of different spheres of exchange by Dayak as an attempt to exert more agency in their evolving relationship with the wider world.

30. Compare to Nugent's (1996) analysis of how perceptions of the market changed in Peru between the 1930s and the 1980s, in accordance with changing views of the market's role—from benign to malign—in national development.

31. The imagery of consumption also applies to other aspects of upland rice production in Borneo. The clearing of forest for swiddens is often called "eating" the forest, with variously the cultivators or their cultigens being characterized as the "eaters." Cf. the title to Condominas's ([1957] 1977) classic work on shifting cultivation in Vietnam, *We Have Eaten the Forest*.

32. Shipton (1995: 181) felicitously calls this "a one-way turnstile" in his work among the Luo of Kenya.

33. Cf. Ferguson (1990: 146–47) on the bovine mystique among the Basutho in Southern Africa: "There exists what one might call a one-way barrier: cash can always be converted into cattle through purchase; cattle, however, cannot be converted to cash through sale, except under certain conditions, conditions usually specified as a great and serious need for money which cannot be raised any other way, a situation arising from an emergency or from poverty." One of the earliest anthropological analyses of this subject was Bohannon's (1959) study of the three separate universes of exchange values—three separate commodity spheres—of the Tiv of West Africa. He discerned a moral hierarchy in the universes of spheres, such that it was morally appropriate to convert upward and shameful to convert downward.

34. Cf. Biersack's (1999: 77) account of a belief from Mount Kare in Papua New Guinea regarding a python whose feces become a source of gold.

35. Cf. Sugishima (1994: 159) on the Lionese of Central Flores: "Witches are also feared as the providers of 'extraordinarily large harvests' (*kesu*), since their souls (*ana wera*) are contained in these. Those who eat of such crops will become incurably ill and die." Cf. Boomgaard (1993) on illicit riches and spirit beliefs in contemporary Java.

36. Murphy (1978) analyzes the progressive domination by rubber of a tribal Amazonian economy and concludes that reciprocal exchange died as a result and the community died with it.

37. Wolf (1982), regards transformation in trade relations—from an activity that supplements the subsistence economy to an activity that supplants it—as a critical turning point in the histories of relations between peripheral societies and the world system.

38. As Murphy and Steward (1956: 336) write: "The process of gradual shift from a subsistence economy to dependence upon trade is evidently irreversible. . . . The culmination point may be said to have been reached when the amount of activity devoted to production for trade grows to such an extent that it interferes with the aboriginal subsistence cycle and associated social organization and makes their continuance impossible."

39. See Drake (1992: 2) on millenarian movements in West Kalimantan.

40. See Gordon's (1993) lament on the failure to seize the opportunity of smallholder rubber cultivation for sustainable resource management today.

41. Compare Kirsch's (2008) analysis of a native, Melanesian critique of capitalism.

42. Cf. Sahlins (1985) study of how the Europeans themselves were absorbed into native mythic structures in different parts of the Pacific, as also noted in my Preface.

Chapter 6. The Dual Economy of Cultivating Rubber and Rice

1. See Cramb (1993) for comparative data on Iban smallholder rubber production in Sarawak from 1979 to 1989.

2. Cf. Eder's (1981) description of a case of arboricultural development in the Philippines, in which tree crops became competitive with swidden food crops.

3. See Dove (1985c), Drake (1982), Freeman ([1955] 1970), and Padoch (1982) on the practice of swidden agriculture, and its labor seasonality, among Ibanic peoples.

4. Compare Perz, Walker, and Caldus's (2006) analysis of household domestic cycles and resource use in the Amazon.

5. Some otherwise astute observers (e.g., Lindblad 1988) have focused on the time that it takes to *grow* a rubber tree — eight to ten years — instead of the time that it takes to bring an existing but dormant tree back into production — two to four days.

6. See Psota's (1992: 46) comment on the temporal complementarity of swidden-rice cultivation and forest-product collection because of their "different cosmologies."

7. Dijkman (1961: 72) reports a drop in latex production of 15 percent from 7:00 to 11:00 AM.

8. In a similar vein, Cramb (2007) writes that swidden-rice cultivation has been completely abandoned in favor of pepper cultivation in parts of Sarawak today.

9. On the use of rubber as a cash reservoir, see Chin (1982: 33), Colfer, Gill, and Agus (1988: 203), Drake (1982: 127), and Geddes (1954: 95).

10. This is calculated by comparing the Kantu' mean of 102 tapping days per year with the estate norm of 160 days per year (Barlow 1978: 71). The attainability of the latter figure for smallholders is indicated by the fact that Collier and Tjakra Werdaya (1972: 85) observed an average tapping intensity of 162 days per year in their survey of Sumatran smallholders.

11. The importance of this independent subsistence base to Dayak political economy is underscored by the fact that the insecurity of rubber tappers in the Amazon was based on their dependence on *patrons* for food (Romanoff 1992: 23). Southeast Asian smallholders who have similarly lacked a subsistence base, like the Chinese immigrants in Sarawak, were also hard put to survive years with low rubber prices (Pringle 1970: 305–6; cf. Pelzer 1945: 24–25).

12. This is a nonparametric measure of statistical significance between two variables, customarily represented by the Greek letter ρ (rho) or as r_s.

13. Siegel (1969) describes a similar history of involvement in pepper cultivation in Aceh which, when pepper went into a long-term decline in the 1930s due to disease and pests, contributed to the rise of Islamic modernism.

Chapter 7. Living Rubber, Dead Land, and Persisting Systems

1. Whereas the Kantu' use the term *tanah mati* (dead land) for rubber gardens, they do not explicitly use the term *tanah idup* (living land) for swidden land. In this opposition, swidden land is the privileged register for comparison: rubber land needs to be differentiated from swidden land, but not the reverse.

2. See Dove (1993) for an analysis of the place of mast fruiting in the ecology and economy of Borneo's forest-dwelling peoples.

3. The *kolak* (basket) is a regional unit of standard measure of volume (Wilkinson 1959, 1:607, 621), which averages 5.9 liters among the Kantu'. Since the human eye has an average volume of 6.37 cubic centimeters (personal communication, J. Scott Kortvelesy, M.D.), one *kolak* could hold approximately 157 eyes or the eyes of 78.5 persons. An alternate version of this belief is that the spirits only demand a "basketful of human eyes" when the mast occurs two years in a row. The principle is the same in either case: unusual bounty is thought to carry a cost commensurate with its benefit. The spirits' demand for human eyes is not an uncommon belief: the Dogon of Mali, for example, fear that spirits of the bush "will exchange eyes with humans, rendering them blind" (van Beek and Banga 1992: 67).

4. The linkage between sacrifice and good harvest reflects a reciprocating or symmetrical relationship with the forest spirits, typical of many tropical forest cultivators like the Kantu', and distinguished by Bird-David (1990) from one-way giving or asymmetrical relationship as held by many hunter-gatherers.

5. Similar notions of the morality of exchange between society and environment are common throughout Southeast Asia. Jorgenson (1989) writes that the Pwo of Thailand periodically thank the forest for the bounty that it provides them by turning over to the forest and forest animals an entire swidden, complete with standing crops. Schneider (1990) suggests that this sort of "equity consciousness" with nature spirits was common in the Western world as well before the advent of capitalist relations of production.

6. The Kantu' say that the offending couple would have been buried in the ground with a bamboo stake driven through them, the subsequent growth of this stake being intended to serve as a warning sign to future would-be transgressors.

7. See Burkill (1966, 2:1305–6) and Richards (1981: 369).

8. Cf. Dobbin (1983: 14) on traditional "wealth-siphoning mechanisms" among the Minangkabau of Central Sumatra, which historically kept individual families or lineages from accumulating too much wealth.

9. The belief that material accumulation, as opposed to distribution, is the work of the devil, is familiar from works such as that of Taussig (1980) on Peruvian mining.

10. Cf. Biersack (1999: 74) on similar beliefs that life is predicated on exchange in Papua New Guinea.

11. This traditional proscription applied to the use of ironwood for *tiang* (longhouse poles), *atap* (roof shingles), *tangga'* (longhouse ladder/stairs), and *perau* (canoe). The Kantu' subgroup with whom I worked honored this proscription in its entirety in the 1890s; by the 1930s, they were honoring it for the longhouse pillars but not for the roof shingles, for which they had started using ironwood; by the 1950s, they were using ironwood for all parts of the longhouse.

12. An analogous system of belief found elsewhere in Indonesia focuses on matching the "directionality" of construction timber to that of the living trees (Domenig 2008).

13. Cf. van Beek and Banga's (1992: 69) analysis of the dichotomy between the fixed village and the moving bush among the Dogon of Mali: "Anything in the bush moves and

changes, in any season—sand dunes, gullies, trees and rocks. Only the village stays put as the only fixed point in the Dogon ethnogeography, inhabited by a series of succeeding populations (Toloy, Tellem, Dogon). They are the areas of stability. However, they also represent stagnation, the places where the forces of the bush whither away: life and death, wisdom and knowledge coming from the bush are applied in the village, but used up and worn down in the process."

14. The principle that long-lived trees should only be associated with long-lived social groups is also found among the Huaorani of the Ecuadorian Amazon, where enduring peach palm groves are associated with long-term local endogamous groups, whereas short-term manioc gardens are associated with ephemeral exogamous marriages and political alliances (Rival 1993: 648-49).

15. The threat to the moral order in the case of the Merina is based on the fact that the forever-enduring trees are individually owned. When trees are owned not by individuals or individual households but by larger groups, they may not undermine but rather support the descent group, as Sather (1990: 20) writes of an Ibanic group in Sarawak: "Thus, tree rights transcend the basic units of everyday social life—the household and longhouse—and in doing so, reflect a sense of deeper historical connection, linking individuals and families through ties of ascent to past generations of household members, regional pioneers and longhouse and household founders, thus reinforcing their membership in a wider regional society encompassing the whole of the upper and middle Paku."

16. I derive the idea of moral ecology, in part, from Scott's (1976) concept of moral economy.

17. On the role of tropical forest ecology in Ibanic systems of meaning, see Davison and Sutlive (1991: 203, 213): "The ritual significance of Iban headhunting, as a cultural institution, is built upon an organic metaphor of frugivorous [viz., vegetative] reproduction, rather than one of phallic procreation. . . . Ultimately, it is the Bornean rain forest, with its endless cycle of vegetative growth, decay and regeneration, which underpins the Iban cult of headhunting and sustains its ritual significance as an agency of fertility."

18. Personal communication, Stepanus Djuweng, Institute of Dayakology Research and Development, Pontianak, West Kalimantan, 28 September 1993.

19. The income from rubber tapping may be used to support the system of reciprocal exchange, most commonly when rubber income is used to purchase commercial *arak* (distilled spirits) for ceremonial feasts, which are part of a wider regional system of exchange (Dove 1988). However, if rubber income is *not* used for this purpose, there are no social sanctions; whereas there *are* sanctions against holding back the surplus produce of the swidden rice system from this system of ceremonial exchange.

20. The Kantu' say that land planted in rubber is still *mati* (dead) even if all of that rubber itself dies.

21. Cf. Scott's (1985: 104) report on the usage in Peninsular Malaysia of the term *sewa hidup* (living rent) for land rents that vary with the harvest, and *sewa mati* (dead rent) for rents that are fixed, unvarying, and rigidly enforced.

22. See Sherman's (1980: 127) critique of Pelzer.

23. In less-narrow terms, however, pepper cultivation differs considerably from a typical system of swidden cultivation. Bartlett (1957-1961, 2:385), who routinely problematized "common-sense" views of traditional systems of resource use, correctly notes, "Pepper might indeed seem to be 'shifting' if abandoned after being found unprofitable, but still pepper [. . .] plantings would probably belong to the village-horticulture aspect of agriculture rather than to shifting cultivation properly so called [. . .]."

24. Pelzer (1945: 31) writes, somewhat ingenuously, of the articulation between teak forestry and indigenous swidden cultivation: "It is ingenious in that it recognizes the habits of the shifting cultivator and fits them into a modern forest economy instead of persecuting the cultivator and forcing him to give up his traditional culture." He does not explicitly address the issue of who benefits from this ingenuity, but his following summary of the *taungya* system implies that it is the government forester: "The taungya forestry system is an excellent way of getting pure stands of commercial timber. The typical forest of the tropics is expensive to exploit because of the large variety of trees which it contains, many of which have little or no commercial value" (ibid.).

25. Even the colonial Dutch Agriculture Department argued that the subsistence rice farmers of Java were "in fact ecologically subsidizing sugar production" of wealthy sugar estates, which insisted that the farmers plant sugarcane in between rice harvests (Moon 2004: 66).

26. A lack of "fit" does not, of course, rule out exploitation. Sundaram (1986: 77-78) argues that since rubber smallholders in post-World War II Malaysia paid a disproportionate amount of export duties and replanting levies, they in effect subsidized the estate sector.

27. Personal communication, Stepanus Djuweng, Institute of Dayakology Research and Development, Pontianak, West Kalimantan, 28 September 1993.

28. See Rival's (1998) global review and Frazer's (1951) classic compendium. For examples from the Indo-Malay region, see Fox (1971) on the Rotinese of eastern Indonesia, Sather (1990) on the Iban of Sarawak, and Sugishima (1994) on the Lionese of Central Flores.

29. De Boeck (1994: 461) relates a similar example from among the Aluund of southwestern Zaire, who say that the people are to the king as animals (frugivores) are to a fruit tree.

30. Plant imagery is often used to refer to human growth and reproduction, and the reverse also occurs: Visser (1989: 82-83, 95-97) describes how the Sahu of Halmahera in eastern Indonesia use metaphors of human reproduction to characterize the cultivation and maturation of rice plants, as do the Kantu' to some extent (cf. Dove 1985c: 317-18).

31. The fact that this status is unchanged by the death of the rubber trees themselves affirms that it is not the life of the trees that is referred to here, but the life of the planters (and their descendants).

32. See Wilkinson (1959, 1:407, 418; 2:1265) for the Malay term *sa-umur hidup* ("as long as one lives," literally "for the age of life").

33. Elsewhere, markedly short-lived plants may be avoided for the same reason. The Kuna Yala of Panama will not use *Tachigalia versicolor*, which dramatically flowers once then dies, for fear they would follow suit (Archibold and Davey 1993: 55).

34. Personal communication, Charles Peters, New York Botanical Garden.

35. The *jingah* tree has been variously identified as either the fig tree (*Ficus benjamina* Linn.) or as what the Malays call the *rengas* tree, which refers to a group of trees (mostly *Anacardiaceae*) with an irritating sap (Ras 1968: 175-76, 176n 5, 543; Wilkinson 1959, 2:964-65).

36. Cf. Lansing's (2006: 135) reference to a 1905 Balinese poem by the Rajah of Badoeng, in which one of the signs that foretold their coming doom at the hands of the Dutch army was "The beautiful beringan tree of Tabanan enveloped in spider's webs so that it turned white, a sign of great danger."

37. Thongmak and Hulse (1993: 162) similarly report that among the Karen of highland Burma and Thailand, after the birth of a child the afterbirth is placed in the crook of a branch of a large tree, and thereafter the health and well-being of the child is linked to this tree.

38. Some Iban groups link the welfare of the human soul with the welfare of a mythical plant. Freeman (1967: 323n) writes, "It is believed by the Iban that every soul has a counter-

part or *ayu*, which takes a plant-like form. These *ayu* grow on a mythical mountain where they are tended by celestial shamans. An *ayu* is said to be in mystical symbiosis with the individual to whom it belongs, and its appearance is supposed to reflect his state of health." Sather (1990: 37) similarly writes of the Iban, "Every living human being is represented, not only by a conjunction of body (*tuboh*) and spirit or soul (*semengat*), but by an invisible plant counterpart, the *ayu*, which symbolizes human life in its vulnerable, mortal aspect."

39. An example is the Javanese shadow puppet called the *gunungan* (literally meaning "mountain-shaped," Horne 1974: 225), which takes the form of a giant tree on which all manner of life is depicted. Another is the Rotinese image of the cosmos as an immense *waringin* tree (*Ficus benjamnia*, Linn.) (Fox 1971).

40. Cf. Gould's (1997) critique of linear versus "bushy" models of human evolution.

41. Bourdieu ([1972] 1977: 38) writes: "The genealogical tree constructed by the anthropologist, a spatial diagram that can be taken in at a glance, *uno intuitu*, and scanned indifferently from any point in any direction, causes the complete network of kinship relations over several generations to exist as only theoretical objects exist, that is, *tota simul*, as a totality present in simultaneity."

42. Cf. Fox's (1971) work on botanical idioms—soft cultigens versus hardwood forest trees—of kinship.

43. The Dayak, in contrast, do anthropomorphize rice.

44. Interview in PT Perkebunan XVIII, 18 February 1984.

45. One of the few partly negative voices is Tucker's (2007), who suggests that although smallholder rubber is good for the smallholders, estate rubber is better for the forest because its yields are higher and therefore (cet. par.) less tropical forest must be cleared to make way for it than in the case of the lower-yielding smallholder trees.

46. Cf. Ellen's (1999) analysis of evolving views of the environment among the Nuaulu in eastern Indonesia.

Chapter 8. Material Wealth and Political Powerlessness

1. See Roth (1896, 2:238–39) for a description of native diamond shafts and workings in North Borneo.

2. The local people assumed that news of diamonds had drawn me to South Kalimantan as well, which made perfect sense (see the preface; compare Walsh 2005).

3. *Pancasila* translates as "five principles": Ketuhanan (belief in God), Kebangsaan (nationalism), Perikemanusiaan (humanitarianism), Keadilan Sosial (social justice), and Demokrasi (democracy).

4. See Forshee's (2002) analysis of narratives of loss of valuable objects on Sumba and Timor in eastern Indonesia.

5. Nagtegaal (1994) entitled a paper on entrepreneurial Javanese rulers in the early modern era, "Diamonds Are a Regent's Best Friend."

6. The concept of valuable minerals "moving" has wider provenance, as in Slater's (1994) report on Amazonian miners' conception of gold as a living, feminine presence that seeks out favored men and then moves on.

7. "Si Misim," alternatively transcribed as "Si Sinim" or Sie Manisim," is difficult to translate, and may have been mistranscribed. As "Si Manisem," it might translate as "The Sweetening One" (Wilkinson 1959, 2:739), which would perhaps be in keeping with its calculating use in interstate relations. On the impact of center-periphery relations on patterns of resource use in Indonesia, see Dove (1985a, 1996) and Dove and Kammen (2001).

8. See Walsh (2010) on native biographies of gemstones in Madagascar; and see Appadurai (1986) and Kopytoff (1986) more generally on biographies of commodities.

9. Cf. Hoskins (1998) on the autobiography of valued objects in Sumba, eastern Indonesia.

10. There is a wider system of folk belief concerning negative reciprocity in center-periphery relations, which is exemplified by the still-widespread belief in Borneo that the state requires human sacrifices for its large-scale construction projects. The symbolic if not literal logic of this belief is sound. As Tsing (1993: 91) notes, "The necessity of human heads for state building projects suggests Meratus [Dayak] appreciation of a relationship between core and periphery, city and frontier, such that the ostentation of the first requires the vulnerability of the latter. These are indeed the conditions of uneven development."

11. Pollan takes this account from Herbert (1993).

12. The throwing away of pearls has older and different literary allusions as well, such as the Moor in Shakespeare's *Othello*, Act V, Scene II ([1604] 1856: 1533):

> . . . Then must you speak.
> . . . of one, whose hand,
> Like the base Júdean, threw a pearl away [Desdemona]
> Richer than all his tribe; . . .

13. See McWilliam (2005) for an analysis of the political-economic dynamics of sandalwood on Timor through the post-colonial era. The response of native Hawaiians to the exploitation of sandalwood by their own monarchy during the second and third decades of the nineteenth century was similarly destructive (Bradley 1942; Kent 1983: 20).

14. See Dove and Kammen (2001) for an analysis of the efficiency of resource flows *out* of peripheral regions in Indonesia and the inefficiency of resource flows *in* to them.

15. Cycles of tropical resource development and degradation have heretofore been explained chiefly in economic, not political, terms (e.g., Homma 1992).

16. Cf. Hecht and Cockburn on the impact of the collapse of the Amazon rubber boom on the tappers as opposed to middlemen (1989: 166): "In a reversal of the usual pattern, where workers suffer most when the industry collapses, the end of the boom toppled the rich in Manaus and Belem from their high estate. The *aviadores* [trading houses] faced slower times, but the *seringueiro* [rubber tapper] could always find a market for his balls of rubber, while in these changing conditions his agriculture, fishing and hunting kept him alive."

17. Cambridge (MA)-based Cultural Survival is different from London-based Survival International, which was an early critic of rain forest marketing (Corry 1993a, 1993b).

18. The international skin-and-hair-care marketing phenomenon known as the Body Shop became closely linked to Cultural Survival Enterprises, Inc.

19. Rainforest Crunch ice cream was made by Ben & Jerry's Homemade, Inc. of South Burlington, Vermont.

20. This cereal was marketed by Rainforest Products Inc. of Mill Valley, California.

21. See Vandermeer and Perfecto (1995) on the "blame-the-victim" premises of rain forest marketing.

22. Even some rubber tappers have recently taken to raising cattle, however (Campos 2006).

23. This marketing flies in the face of the common sense principle, "When the food of the poor reaches the palate of the rich, the food disappears from the poor man's table" (Pope Leo XIII). I am grateful to Yancey Orr for this citation.

24. It has since been updated (de Beer and McDermott 1996).

25. Political calculations also can lead to strategically downplaying the importance of

forest products. Caldecott (1988: 55) claims that the Sarawak government was underestimated by more than 99 percent the importance of feral pigs in the diet of forest dwellers, as part of its effort to downplay the value of the forests for purposes other than commercial logging.

26. Cf. Sider's (1986: 30) observation that in colonial North America, native peoples were permitted to commercially exploit only *diminishing* resources: "they could sell deerskin and beaver pelts, they could sell their bodies as soldiers, and they could sell their land . . . for as the resources diminished . . . so too, it was thought, would the people and their way of life."

27. Ludwig et al. (1993: 17) reach a similar conclusion regarding the inevitability of resource degradation by focusing on the other part of this equation, namely the association of rich resources and *strong* peoples, writing, "The larger and the more immediate are the prospects for gain, the greater the political power that is used to facilitate unlimited exploitation."

28. Cf. the pioneering work outside anthropology by Edelman (1974: 296), who writes, "The most fundamental and long-lasting influences upon political beliefs flow . . . from language that is not perceived as political at all, but nonetheless structures perceptions of status, authority, merit, deviance, and the causes of social problems."

29. Wickham actually gathered and sent to Kew seventy thousand seeds, where just twenty-seven hundred germinated, which became the antecedents of the future rubber industry of Asia. Melby's figure underplays the risk to the seeds in gathering, transporting, planting, at the same time as it makes the theft seem more feasible: removing "several thousand rubber seeds" from Brazil by subterfuge seems more believable than seventy thousand. The citation of the smaller and completely fictitious number de-emphasizes the botanic challenges of this project and exaggerates the political ones.

30. Shiva (1993: 79) misses this critical difference in equating the rubber "theft" with the Dutch clove monopoly in the Moluccas.

Chapter 9. Plantations and Representations in Indonesia

1. Interview on 29 September 1993 at PIR VII Sambas plantation, Monterado, subdistrict Samalantang, district Singkawang, West Kalimantan.

2. Interview on 29 September 1993 with officials in the district-level planning office (BAPPEDA, Tingkat II) in Singkawang, West Kalimantan.

3. Institute of Dayakologi Research and Development, personal communication.

4. The plantation managers who attended the seminar were those experiencing overt resistance from workers, smallholders, and/or local villagers, so our sample of plantations was preselected for those that made such resistance possible in the first place. Such conditions were more likely to be found in nontraditional plantation areas (e.g., Kalimantan vs. Sumatra). Managers from long-established plantations, in which management-worker relations were more authoritarian, were less likely to experience the kind of open resistance that would have brought them to our seminar. I am grateful to George McTurnan Kahin for bringing this point to my attention.

5. Interview with visiting sugar mill team at the Plantation Training Institute headquarters, 30 March 1984.

6. The Dayak are criticized by government officials not just for being backward, but for not realizing that they are backward. Tsing (1993: 154) cites the caption to a photograph from an article on "isolated [tribal] populations" in a publication of the federal government's Social Department (Suhud 1979: 41): "Seringkali mereka tidak mengetahui akan keterasingannya." (Often they are unaware of their own estrangement.)

7. Interview with visiting estate team at the Plantation Training Institute headquarters, 18 June 1984.

8. Stoler (1985a) found that planters on colonial plantations in Sumatra similarly tended to misconstrue conflicts over competing economic interests as conflicts over inferior cultures.

9. Memo from estate team visiting the Plantation Training Institute headquarters, 13 April 1984.

10. Interview with visiting estate team at the Plantation Training Institute headquarters, 18 June 1984.

11. The manager of a rubber nucleus-estate project in West Kalimantan said of the local Dayak (interview at Plantation Training Institute, 18 June 1984), "Masih ada kesenjangan dalam cara berpikir, teknik berladang, cara-cara pengambilan keputusan." (There is still asymmetry in their way of thinking, in their swidden technology, [and] in their ways of reaching decisions.)

12. This manager blamed this misunderstanding on the *kuat tanah ulayat* (strong customary land tenure) of the Dayak. (Interview with visiting estate team at the Plantation Training Institute headquarters, 18 June 1984.)

13. Peluso and Poffenberger (1989: 338) write about the same phenomenon in the Forest Service on Java: "The foresters' conceptualization of rural people as ignorant of 'the meanings and functions of the forest' was deeply ingrained and widespread throughout the agency."

14. Memo from estate team visiting the Plantation Training Institute headquarters, 18 February 1984.

15. See Anderson (1990: 56): "The traditional image of the acquisition of knowledge [in Java] is that of a search for a key that opens the door between ignorance and knowledge, making possible the qualitative leap from one to the other. . . . Bearing it in mind does much to render comprehensible the typical division of the population by the political elite into two radically separate groups, those who are masih bodoh (still stupid, still unenlightened) and those who are insyaf or terpelajar (aware, educated)."

16. Interview at Institute of Dayakology Research and Development, Pontianak, 28 September 1993.

17. Memo from estate team visiting the Plantation Training Institute headquarters, 18 February 1984.

18. Interview with visiting estate team at the Plantation Training Institute headquarters, 18 June 1984. This is a thesis of wide provenance. Hahamovitch (1997: 82) writes that planters in the nineteenth-century U.S. South believed that African-American plantation workers worked less the more they were paid, which she labels the "planters' theory of value."

19. Interview with visiting estate team at the Plantation Training Institute headquarters, 30 March 1984.

20. Cf. Cooke (2002) and Colchester et al. (2007) on the response of Dayak in Sarawak to the oil palm boom there.

21. Interview on 2 July 1982 at Sungai Mayang, near Sanggau, West Kalimantan.

22. Interviews in the provincial planning offices (BAPPEDA, Tingkat I & II) in Pontianak on 28 September 1993 and Singkawang on 29 September 1993.

23. Government planners in Pontianak, West Kalimantan, also said that they try to prevent the construction of any factory for processing rubber or oil palm without the simultaneous development of estates to supply it, to eliminate the alternative marketing possibilities that a produce-starved factory might give to the participants in nearby nucleus-estate projects (interview in BAPPEDA, Tingkat I offices, Pontianak, West Kalimantan, 28 September 1993).

24. White (1999) similarly writes that the smallholders on a coconut nucleus estate in West Java who sell their produce on the open market are accused by the estate managers of thievery.

25. Interview in provincial planning offices (BAPPEDA, Tingkat I), Pontianak, West Kalimantan, 1 October 1993.

26. See Anderson's (1983: 55–57) pioneering work on the effects of these "secular pilgrimages."

27. Interview at Berua', near Sanggau, West Kalimantan, 30 June 1982.

28. Stoler (1985a: 196–97) similarly found that the workers on colonial Sumatran plantations did not perceive their managers as a class. Cf. Anderson's (1983: 139n25) observation of the asymmetry between colonized and colonizers in the production and use of racist argots: that of the colonists is impoverished, that of the colonizers is rich.

29. Interview at Berua', near Sanggau, West Kalimantan, 30 June 1982.

30. Interview at Sungai Tapang, near Sanggau, West Kalimantan, 2 July 1982.

31. McTaggart (1982), in one of the few references to this topic, acknowledges the problem of information flow through the Indonesian government, but he fails to see that it is structurally determined, blaming it instead on a simple overabundance of data. See Dove and Kammen (2001) for an analysis of the institutional forces behind information flows and non-flows in Indonesia.

32. The wider context of this aversion to communication from worker to planter is a tradition of governance in Indonesia that emphasizes communication from the governing to the governed as opposed to the reverse. Suharto's New Order era of governance in Indonesia was colloquially referred to within the country as *jaman pidato* (the age of speeches). A *pidato* (speech) by a government official represents not a two-way dialogue but a one-way communication from state to subject.

33. Memo from estate team visiting the Plantation Training Institute headquarters, 13 April 1984.

34. This principle of hierarchical baffles, although not found among many of the Dayak and other egalitarian tribal groups of the outer islands, is highly important in Javanese culture; and the Javanese are extremely sensitive to deviations from it. Thus, the aboriginal Badui of West Java gained island-wide notoriety in the 1970s when a delegation of them left their mountain forests, walked to Jakarta, and presented a petition *directly* to then-President Suharto.

35. Stoler (1985a: 58, 79) documented the same practice, of inhibiting worker feedback in the colonial plantations of North Sumatra.

36. Cf. Tomich (1991: 261) for another example of resistance to the facts within the estate sector: "Many key people continue to accept the premises that block planting schemes were affecting a significant share of the smallholder rubber subsector and that unassisted planting by smallholders is negligible. They believe this despite the apparent contradiction between these premises and information that is available to almost anyone concerned with smallholder rubber development."

37. I am grateful to Carol Carpenter for this insight.

38. Sider draws this account from Wareham (1975: 19; 1982: 45).

39. Interview at Berua', near Sanggau, West Kalimantan, 30 June 1982.

Chapter 10. Smallholders and Globalization

1. See van Leur's ([1955] 1967: 289) pointed correction of the idea of an East Indies at the margins of history: "It knew a mighty East, a rich fabric of a strong, broad weave with a more fragile Western warp thread inserted in it at broad intervals."

2. Markham, who was responsible for the transplantation of *Cinchona* from the Peru-

vian Andes to southern India before also playing a role in the transplantation of *Hevea,* viewed the global redistribution of plants as "one of the greatest benefits that civilisation has conferred upon mankind" (Philip 1999: 133–34).

3. See Donkin's (1999: 132) observation that the historic place names associated with *Dryobalanops* (camphor) were all exotic, and all coming from customers not suppliers.

4. See Appadurai's (1986: 54) insightful analysis of "the many forms that the fetishism of commodities can take [by consumers and producers alike] when there are sharp discontinuities in the distribution of knowledge concerning their trajectories of circulation."

5. There were exceptions to this rule of non-use by producers: Mintz (1985: 72) writes that sugar consumption in the old sugar colonies was substantial, including by the slaves. On the other hand, when the sugar trade began in the early Middle Ages, it was a spice, less commonly used; but it had become a food item of mass consumption by the modern industrial era.

6. See Cook's (2007: 416) in-depth analysis of the co-development of the spice trade and European science: "The new science did not always simply knock at the door of wisdom and ask to be seated at the table with other manifestations of knowledge. Instead, it sometimes arrived in the form of the very things that were consumed at the meal: new foods and medicines that made the body feel strong or exotic flowers that brought delight to eye and nose." An example of the European obsession to pierce the mystery of not only alluring but frightening Asian plants was the state effort to lay bare the secrets of the famed *upas* tree (*Antiaris toxicaria* [Pers.] Lesch) of the East Indies, from whence native warriors obtained the poison for their darts, arrows, and spears (Dove and Carpenter 2005).

7. See Walsh's (2004) study of speculative imagining of end-uses by producers in long-distance trade (namely, sapphire miners in Madagascar).

8. Nationwide, the area under oil palms in Indonesia reached 7,824,623 hectares in 2010, compared with 3,445,317 hectares under rubber and 192,389 hectares under black pepper (website of Dinas Perkebunan, http://ditjenbun.deptan.go.id, accessed July 2010).

9. An interesting recent example of global commodity imagination is the development of interest in shade-grown coffee among environmentalists and consumers in the industrialized nations (Lyon 2004).

10. I am grateful to Adrian Cerezo for this insight.

11. Cf. the work on collaboration versus contest by Conklin and Graham (1995), Li (2000), and Tsing (2000).

12. I am grateful to David Kneas for his insights on this topic.

13. Cf. Tsing's (2005: 184, 185–86) observation that subsistence activities support collecting forest products for the market in South Kalimantan, just as collecting supports subsistence.

References

Acciaioli, Greg. 2008. Mobilizing against the 'cruel oil': Dilemmas of organizing resistance against oil palm plantations in Central Kalimantan. In *Reflections on the heart of Borneo*, ed. Gerard A. Persoon and Manon Osseweijer, 91–119. Tropenbos 24. Wageningen, The Netherlands: Tropenbos International.

ACIAR (Australian Centre for International Agricultural Research). 1985. Smallholder rubber production and policies: Proceedings of an international workshop held at the University of Adelaide. Canberra: ACIAR.

Adas, Michael. 1981. From avoidance to confrontation: Peasant protest in precolonial and colonial Southeast Asia. *Comparative Studies in Society and History* 23 (3): 217–47.

Agrawal, Arun. 1995. Dismantling the divide between indigenous and scientific knowledge. *Development and Change* 26:413–39.

Ahearn, Laura M. 2001. Language and agency. *Annual Review of Anthropology* 30: 109–38.

Airriess, Christopher A. 2003. The ecologies of Kuala and Muara settlements in the premodern Malay culture world. *Journal of the Malaysian Branch of the Royal Asiatic Society* 76 (1):81–98.

Alatas, Syed Hussain. 1977. *The myth of the lazy native: A study of the Malays, Filipinos, and Javanese from the sixteenth to the twentieth century and its function in the ideology of capitalism.* London: Frank Cass.

Alexander, Jennifer, and Paul Alexander. 1995. Commodification and consumption in a Central Borneo community. *Bijdragen* 151 (2):179–93.

Ali Haji, Raja. 1982. *Tuhfat al-nafis* (The precious gift). Ed. and trans. Virginia Matheson and Barbara Watson Andaya. Kuala Lumpur: Oxford University Press.

Allen, G. C., and Audrey G. Donnithorne. [1957] 1962. *Western enterprises in Indonesia and Malaya: A study in economic development.* Reprint, London: George Allen and Unwin.

Andaya, Barbara Watson. 1993a. Cash cropping and upstream-downstream tensions: The case of Jambi in the seventeenth and eighteenth centuries. In *Southeast Asia in the early modern era: Trade, power, and belief*, ed. Anthony Reid, 91–122. Ithaca, NY: Cornell University Press.

——— 1993b. *To live as brothers: Southeast Sumatra in the seventeenth and eighteenth centuries.* Honolulu: University of Hawaii Press.

———— 1995. Women and economic change: The pepper trade in premodern Southeast Asia. *Journal of the Economic and Social History of the Orient* 38 (2): 165–90.

Andaya, Barbara Watson, and Leonard Y. Andaya. 1982. *A history of Malaysia*. New York: St. Martin's Press.

Anderson, Benedict R. 1983. *Imagined communities: Reflections on the origin and spread of nationalism*. London: Verso.

———— 1990. The idea of power in Javanese culture. In *Language and power: Exploring political cultures in Indonesia*. Ithaca, NY, and London: Cornell University Press. First published 1972 in *Culture and politics in Indonesia*, ed. Claire Holt, 1–69. Ithaca, NY: Cornell University Press.

Angelsen, Arild. 1995. Shifting cultivation and "deforestation": A study from Indonesia. *World Development* 23 (10): 1713–29.

Anonymous. 1935. Rubber-leverende planten in Ned.-Indie. (Latex-producing plants in the Dutch East Indies). *Algemeen Landbouw Weekblad van Nederlandsch-Indie* 11:1186–89.

Appadurai, Arjun. 1986. Introduction: Commodities and the politics of value. In *The social life of things: Commodities in cultural perspective*, ed. Arjun Appadurai, 3–63. Cambridge: Cambridge University Press.

———— 1996. *Modernity at large*. Minneapolis, MN: University of Minnesota Press.

Archibold, Guillermo, and Sheila Davey. 1993. Kuna Yala: Protecting the San Blas of Panama. In *The law of the mother: Protecting indigenous peoples in protected areas*, ed. Elizabeth Kemf, 52–57. San Francisco: Sierra Club.

Ashplant, Herbert. 1940. Wickham not a smuggler. *International Rubber Workers* 99: 52, 55.

Ashton, Peter S., T. J. Givinish, and S. Appanah. 1988. Staggered flowering in the Dipterocarpaceae: New insights into floral induction and the evolution of mast fruiting in the aseasonal tropics. *American Naturalist* 132 (1): 44–66.

Aspengren, Evald. 1986. Java and the world: A study in the relationship between the rice agriculture of Java and the world economy in the 1930s. In *Rice societies: Asian problems and prospects*, ed. Irne Norlund, Sven Cederroth, and Ingela Gerdin, 230–63. London: Curzon Press; Riverdale, MD: Riverdale.

Associated Press. 25 March 1996, cited in *Honolulu Advertiser*, 1996.

Barham, Bradford L., and Oliver T. Coomes. 1994. Reinterpreting the Amazon rubber boom: Investment, the state, and Dutch disease. *Latin American Research Review* 29 (2): 73–109.

Baring-Gould, Sabine, and Charles Asar Bampfylde. 1909. *A history of Sarawak under its two white rajahs, 1839–1908*. London: H. Sotheran.

Barlow, Colin. 1978. *The natural rubber industry: Its development, technology, and economy in Malaysia*. Kuala Lumpur: Oxford University Press.

———— 1990. Changes in the economic position of workers on rubber estates and smallholdings in Peninsular Malaysia, 1910–1985. In *The underside of Malaysian history: Pullers, prostitutes, plantation workers*, ed. P. J. Rummer and L. M. Allen, 25–49. Singapore: Singapore University Press.

———— 1991. Developments in plantation agriculture and smallholder cash-crop production. In *Indonesia: Resources, ecology, and environment*, ed. Joan Hardjono, 85–103. Singapore: Oxford University Press.

Barlow, Colin, and J. H. Drabble. 1990. Government and the emerging rubber industries in Indonesia and Malaya, 1900–40. In *Indonesian economic history in the Dutch colonial era*, ed. Anne Booth, W. J. O'Malley, and Ana Weidemann, 187–209. Monograph Series No. 35. New Haven, CT: Yale University, Southeast Asia Studies Program.

Barlow, Colin, and S. K. Jayasuriya. 1984. Problems of investment for technological advance: The case of Indonesian smallholders. *Journal of Agricultural Economics* 35 (1):85–95.

———— 1986. Stages of development in smallholder tree crop agriculture. *Development and Change* 17 (4): 635–58.

Barlow, Colin, and Muharminto. 1982. The rubber smallholder economy. *Bulletin of Indonesian Economic Studies* 18 (2): 86–119.

Barlow, Colin, and Thomas Tomich. 1991. Indonesian agricultural development: The awkward case of smallholder tree crops. *Bulletin of Indonesian Economic Studies* 27 (3): 29–54.

Barnes, R. H. 1993. Construction sacrifice, kidnapping, and head-hunting rumors on Flores and elsewhere in Indonesia. *Oceania* 64 (2): 146–58.

Barthes, Roland. [1957] 1972. *Mythologies.* Trans. Annette Lavers. Reprint, New York: Hill and Wang.

Bartlett, H. H. 1957–1961. *Fire in relation to primitive agriculture and grazing in the tropics: An annotated bibliography.* 3 vols. Ann Arbor, MI: University of Michigan, Department of Botany.

Bassett, Thomas J. 2006. *The peasant cotton revolution in West Africa: Côte d'Ivoire, 1880–1995.* Cambridge, UK: Cambridge University Press.

Bauer, P. T. 1948. *The rubber industry: A study in competition and monopoly.* London: Longmans, Green.

Beccari, Odoardo. [1904] 1986. *Wanderings in the great forests of Borneo.* Reprint, Singapore: Oxford University Press.

Bechmann, Roland. 1990. *Trees and man: The forest in the Middle Ages.* Trans. Katharyn Dunham. New York: Paragon House.

Bedner, Adriaan, and Stijn van Huis. 2008. The return of the native in Indonesian law: Indigenous communities in Indonesian legislation. *Bijdragen* 164 (2/3): 165–93.

Beeckman, Captain Daniel. [1718] 1973. *A voyage to and from the island of Borneo.* Reprint, Folkestone, UK: Dawson's of Pall Mall.

van Beek, Walter E. A., and Pieteke M. Banga. 1992. The Dogon and their trees. In *Bush base: Forest farm, culture, environment, and development,* ed. Elizabeth Croll and David Parkin, 57–75. London: Routledge.

de Beer, Jenne H., and Melanie J. McDermott. 1989. *The economic value of non-timber forest products in Southeast Asia: With emphasis on Indonesia, Malaysia, and Thailand.* Amsterdam: Netherlands Committee for International Union for the Conservation of Nature/ World Wildlife Fund.

———— 1996. *The economic value of non-timber forest products in Southeast Asia.* 2nd rev. ed. Amsterdam: Netherlands Committee for IUCN/WWF.

Benjamin, Walter. 1969. *Illuminations.* New York: Schocken.

Bentham, Jeremy. 1791. *Panopticon, or, The inspection-house: containing the idea of a new principle of construction applicable to any sort of establishment, in which persons of any description are to be kept under inspection: and in particular to penitentiary-houses, prisons, houses of industry . . . and schools: with a plan of management adapted to the principle: in a series of letters, written in the year 1787.* London: Reprinted and sold by T. Payne, 1791.

Bentley, Jeffery W. 2006. Folk experiments. *Agriculture and Human Values* 23 (4): 451–62.

Bernal, Victor. 1994. Peasants, capitalism, and (ir)rationality. *American Ethnologist* 21 (4): 792–810.

Berry, Sara. 1988. Concentration without privatization? Some consequences of changing patterns of rural land control in Africa. In *Land and society in contemporary Africa,* ed. R. E. Downs and S. P. Reyna, 53–75. Hanover, NH: University Press of New England.

Best, J. R. 1988. Change over time in a farming system based on shifting cultivation of hill rice in Sarawak, Malaysia. *Agricultural Administration and Extension* 29:69–84.

Biersack, Aletta. 1999. The Mount Kare python and his gold: Totemism and ecology in the Papua New Guinea highlands. *American Anthropologist* 101 (1): 68–87.

Bird-David, Nurit. 1990. The giving environment: Another perspective on the economic system of gatherer-hunters. *Current Anthropology* 31 (2): 189–96.

Black, Ian. 1985. The "lastposten": Eastern Kalimantan and the Dutch in the nineteenth and early twentieth centuries. *Journal of Southeast Asian Studies* 16 (2): 281–91.

Blacklock, J. Stewart. 1954. A short study of pepper cultivation with special reference to Sarawak. *Tropical Agriculture* (Trinidad) 31:40–56.

Blicher-Mathiesen, Ulla. 1994. Borneo Illipe, a fat product from different *Shorea* spp. (Dipterocarpaceae). *Economic Botany* 48 (3): 231–42.

Bloch, Maurice. 1989. The symbolism of money in Imerina. In *Money and the morality of exchange*, ed. Jonathan Parry and Maurice Bloch, 165–90. Cambridge, UK: Cambridge University Press.

Bloch, Maurice, and Jonathan Parry. 1989. Introduction: Money and the morality of exchange. In *Money and the morality of exchange*, ed. Jonathan Parry and Maurice Bloch, 1–32. Cambridge, UK: Cambridge University Press.

Bock, Carl. [1881] 1985. *The head-hunters of Borneo: A narrative of travel up the Mahakam and down the Barito; Also, journeyings in Sumatra*. Reprint, Singapore: Oxford University Press.

de Boeck, Filip. 1994. Of trees and kings: Politics and metaphor among the Aluund of southwestern Zaire. *American Ethnologist* 21 (3): 451–73.

Boeke, J. H. 1931. *Economics and economic policy of dual societies*. Inaugural lecture, University of Leiden.

——— 1953. *Economics and economic policy of dual societies: As exemplified by Indonesia*. New York: Institute of Pacific Relations.

Bohannon, Paul. 1959. The impact of money on an African subsistence economy. *Journal of Economic History* 19:491–503.

Bonneuil, Christophe. 2001. Development as experiment: Science and state building in late colonial and postcolonial Africa, 1930–1970. *Osiris* 15:258–81.

Boomgaard, Peter. 1993. Illicit riches: Economic development and changing attitudes towards money and wealth as reflected in Javanese popular belief. In *New challenges in the modern economic history of Indonesia*, ed. J. T. Lindblad, 197–215. The Hague: Cip-Gegenvens Koninklijk Bibliotheek.

——— 2003. In the shadow of rice: Roots and tubers in Indonesia, 1500–1950. *Agricultural History* 77 (4): 582–610.

Booth, Anne. 1988. *Agricultural development in Indonesia*. Asian Studies Association of Australia, Southeast Asia Publications Series No. 16. Sydney: Allen and Unwin.

Borsboom, Ad. 1988. The savage in European thought: A prelude to the conceptualization of the divergent peoples and cultures of Australia and Oceania. *Bijdragen* 144 (4): 420–32.

Bouquet, Mary. 1995. Exhibiting knowledge: The trees of Dubois, Haeckel, Jesse, and Rivers at the *Pithecanthropus* centennial exhibition. In *Shifting contexts: Transformations in anthropological knowledge*, ed. Marilyn Strathern, 31–55. London: Routledge.

Bourdieu, Pierre. [1972] 1977. *Outline of a theory of practice*. Trans. Richard Nice. Cambridge, UK: Cambridge University Press. (Original, *Esquisse dúne théorie de la practique, précédé de trois études d'ethnologie kabyle.*)

Bradley, Harold W. 1942. *The American frontier in Hawaii: The pioneers, 1789–1843*. Stanford, CA: Stanford University Press.

Braginsky, Vladimir, and Ben Murtagh, eds. 2007. *The portrayal of foreigners in Indonesian and Malay literatures: Essays of the ethnic "other."* Lewiston, NY: The Edwin Mellen Press.

Breman, Jan. 1983. *Control of land and labour in colonial Java: A case study of agrarian crisis and reform in the region of Cirebon during the first decades of the twentieth century*. Verhandelingen No. 101. Dordrecht: Foris Publications.

———— 1989. *Taming the coolie beast: Plantation society and the colonial order in Southeast Asia*. New Delhi: Oxford University Press.

Brockway, Lucille H. 1979. *Science and colonial expansion: The role of the British royal botanical garden*. New York: Academic Press.

Brondizio, Eduardo S. 2008. *The Amazonian caboclo and the açai palm: Forest farmers in the global market*. Advances in Economic Botany, Volume 16. Bronx: New York Botanical Garden Press.

Bronson, Bennet. 1977. Exchange at the upstream ends: Notes toward a functional model of the coastal state in Southeast Asia. In *Economic exchange and social integration in Southeast Asia: Perspectives from prehistory, history, and ethnography*, ed. Karl L. Hutterer, 39–52. Michigan Papers on South and Southeast Asian Studies. Ann Arbor, MI: University of Michigan.

Brookfield, Harold, Francis Jana Lian, Low Kwai-Sim, and Lesley Potter. 1990. Borneo and the Malay Peninsula. In *The earth as transformed by human action*, ed. B. L. Turner, William C. Clark, Robert W. Kates, John F. Richards, Jessica T. Mathews, and William B. Meyer, 495–512. Cambridge, UK: Cambridge University Press.

Brosius, J. Peter. 1999a. Analyses and interventions: Anthropological engagements with environmentalism. *Current Anthropology* 40 (3): 277–309.

———— 1999b. Locations and representations: Writing in the political present in Sarawak, East Malaysia. *Identities* 6 (2–3): 345–86.

Browder, John O. 1992. The limits of extractivism: Tropical forest strategies beyond extractive reserves. *BioScience* 42 (3): 174–82.

Brummeler, T. 1883. Getah pertjah en caoutchouc (Gutta percha and India rubber). *Tijdschrift voor Nijverheid & Landbouw in Nederlandsch-Indie* 28:11–46.

Brunig, E. F. 1974. Ecological studies in the *kerangas* forests of Sarawak and Brunei. Kuching, Malaysia: Borneo Literature Bureau (for Sarawak Forest Department). .

Brush, Stephen B. 2004. *Farmers' bounty: Locating crop diversity in the contemporary world*. New Haven, CT: Yale University Press.

Bryant, Raymond L. 1994. Shifting the cultivator: The politics of teak regeneration in colonial Burma. *Modern Asian Studies* 28 (2): 225–50.

Bulbeck, David, Anthony Reid, Lay Cheng Tan, and Yiqi Wu. 1998. *Southeast Asian exports since the fourteenth century: Cloves, pepper, coffee, and sugar*. Singapore: Institute of Southeast Asian Studies.

Bunker, Stephen G. 1984. Modes of extraction, unequal exchange, and the progressive underdevelopment of an extreme periphery: The Brazilian Amazon, 1600–1980. *American Journal of Sociology* 89 (5): 1017–64.

Burbidge, F. W. 1880. *The gardens of the sun: A naturalist's journal of Borneo and the Sulu Archipelago*. London: John Murray.

Burgers, P. P. M. 1993. Rainforest and rural economy in Sarawak. *Sarawak Museum Journal* 65:19–44.

Burkill, I. H. 1966. *A dictionary of the economic products of the Malay Peninsula.* 2 vols. Ministry of Agriculture and Cooperation, Kuala Lumpur.

Cairns, Malcolm, ed. 2007. *Voices from the forest: Integrating indigenous knowledge into sustainable upland farming.* Washington, DC: Resources for the Future.

Caldecott, Julian. 1988. *Hunting and wildlife management in Sarawak.* Gland, Switzerland and Cambridge, UK: International Union for the Conservation of Nature (IUCN).

Campos, Marina T. 2006. *New footprints in the forest: Environmental knowledge, management practices, and social mobilization among colonos from the transamazon region.* Ph.D. dissertation, Yale University School of Forestry and Environmental Studies.

CAPD (Centre for Agricultural Publishing and Documentation). 1982. *Indonesian forestry abstracts: Dutch literature until about 1960.* Wageningen, The Netherlands.

Carpenter, Carol. 1997. Women and livestock, fodder, and uncultivated land in Pakistan. In *Women working in the environment,* ed. Carolyn E. Sachs, 157–71. Washington, DC: Taylor & Francis.

———— 2001. The role of economic invisibility in development: Veiling women's work in rural Pakistan. *Natural Resources Forum* 25: 11–19.

Chhatre, Ashwini, and Arun Agrawal. 2009. Trade-offs and synergies between carbon storage and livelihood benefits from forest commons. *Proceedings of the National Academy of Sciences* 106 (42): 17667–70.

Chin, S. C. 1982. The significance of rubber as a cash crop in a Kenyah swidden village in Sarawak. *Federation Museum Journal* 27:23–38.

———— 1985. Agriculture and resource utilization in a lowland rainforest Kenyah community. *Sarawak Museum Journal,* n.s., 35 (56), Special Monograph No. 4.

Clark, Jeffrey. 1993. Gold, sex, and pollution: Male illness and myth at Mt. Kare, Papua New Guinea. *American Ethnologist* 20 (4): 742–57.

Clay, Jason. 1991. Cultural survival and conservation: Lessons from the past twenty years. In *Biodiversity: Culture, conservation, and ecodevelopment,* ed. Margery L. Oldfield and Janis B. Alcorn, 248–73. Boulder, CO: Westview Press.

———— 1992a. Some general principles and strategies for developing markets in North America and Europe for non-timber forest products. *Advances in Economic Botany* 9: 101–6.

———— 1992b. Why Rainforest Crunch? *Cultural Survival Quarterly* 16 (2): 31–37.

Cleary, Mark, and Peter Eaton. 1992. *Borneo: Change and development.* Singapore: Oxford University Press.

Coates, Austin. 1987. *The commerce in rubber: The first 250 years.* Singapore: Oxford University Press.

Cohn, Bernard S. 1996. *Colonialism and its forms of knowledge.* Princeton, NJ: Princeton University Press.

Colchester, Marcus, et al. 2007. *Land is life: Land rights and oil palm development in Sarawak.* Moreton-in-Marsh: Forest Peoples Programme; Bogor (Indonesia): Perkumpulan Sawit Watch.

Colfer, Carol J. Pierce, Dan W. Gill, and Fahmuddin Agus. 1988. An indigenous agricultural model from West Sumatra: A source of scientific insight. *Agricultural Systems* 26:191–209.

Collier, William L., and Suhud Tjakra Werdaya. 1972. Smallholder rubber production and marketing. *Bulletin of Indonesian Economic Studies* 8 (2): 67–92.

Condominas, Georges. [1957] 1977. *We have eaten the forest: The story of a Montagnard village in the central highlands of Vietnam.* Trans. Adrienne Foulke. New York: Hill and Wang. (Original, *Nous Avons Mangé la Forêt de la Pierre-Génie Gôo.*)

Conklin, Beth A., and Laura R. Graham. 1995. The shifting middle ground: Amazonian Indians and eco-politics. *American Anthropologist* 97 (4): 695–710.

Conklin, Harold C. [1957] 1975. *Hanunóo agriculture: A report on an integral system of shifting cultivation in the Philippines.* Reprint, Northford, CT: Elliot's Books. (Original, published by the Food and Agriculture Organization of the United Nations, Rome.)

Cook, Harold J. 2007. *Matters of exchange: Commerce, medicine, and science in the Dutch golden age.* New Haven: Yale University Press.

Cooke, Fadzilah Majid. 2002. Vulnerability, control and oil palm in Sarawak: Globalization and a new era? *Development and Change* 33 (2): 189–211.

Coomes, Oliver T., and Bradford L. Barham. 1997. Rain forest extraction and conservation in Amazonia. *Geographical Journal* 163 (2): 180–88.

Coppen, J. J. W. 1995. *Gums, resins and latexes of plant origin.* Non-wood forest products 6. Rome: Food and Agriculture Organization of the United Nations.

Corominas, J., and J. A. Pascual. 1980. *Diccionario critico etimologico Castellano e Hispanico (Critical dictionary of the etymology of Castilian and Spanish).* 5 vols. Madrid: Editorial Gredos.

Corry, Stephen. 1993a. *"Harvest moonshine" taking you for a ride.* London: Survival International.

———— 1993b. The rainforest harvest: Who reaps the benefit? *Ecologist* 23 (4): 148–53.

Cowell, A. 1990. *The decade of destruction: The crusade to save the Amazon rain forest.* New York: Henry Holt.

CPIS (Center for Policy and Implementation Studies). 1993. *Towards a planting materials policy for Indonesian rubber smallholdings: Lessons from past projects.* Agriculture Group Working Paper No. 14. Jakarta.

Cramb, R. A. 1988. The commercialization of Iban agriculture. In *Development in Sarawak: Historical and contemporary perspectives,* ed. R. A. Cramb and R. H. W. Reece, 105–34. Monash Paper on Southeast Asia No. 17. Melbourne, Australia: Monash University, Center of Southeast Asian Studies.

———— 1993. Shifting cultivation and sustainable agriculture in East Malaysia: A longitudinal case study. *Agricultural Systems* 42: 209–26.

———— 2007. *Land and longhouse: Agrarian transformation in the uplands of Sarawak.* Copenhagen: Nordic Institute of Asian Studies.

Cramer, P. J. S. 1956. The rubber production in the Dutch East Indies. *Archives of Rubber Cultivation* 33:260–344.

Crawfurd, John. 1820. *History of the Indian archipelago: Containing an account of the manners, arts, languages, religions, institutions, and commerce of its inhabitants.* 3 vols. Edinburgh: Archibald Constable.

———— [1856] 1971. *A descriptive dictionary of the Indian islands and adjacent countries.* Reprint, Kuala Lumpur: Oxford University Press.

———— 1868. On the history and migration of cultivated plants used as condiments. *Transactions of the Ethnological Society of London* 6: 188–206.

Creutzberg, P., ed. 1975. *Indonesia's export crops 1816–1940.* Vol. 1 of *Changing economy in Indonesia: A selection of statistical source material from the early nineteenth century up to early 1940.* The Hague: Martinus Nijhoff.

Davidson, Jamie S. 2008. *From rebellion to riots: Collective violence on Indonesian Borneo.* Madison, WI: University of Wisconsin Press.

Davidson, Jamie S., and David Henley, eds. 2007. *The revival of tradition in Indonesian politics: The deployment of adat from colonialism to indigenism.* London: Routledge.

Davidson, Sir L. 1927. The rubber plantation industry: Pioneer rubber planting in Ceylon and the Straits. *Bulletin of the Rubber Growers' Association* 9: 673–98.

Davies, Douglas. 1988. The evocative symbolism of trees. In *The iconography of landscape: Essays on the symbolic representation, design and use of past environments*, ed. Denis Cosgrove and Stephen Daniels, 32–42. Cambridge, UK: Cambridge University Press.

Davison, Julian, and Vinson H. Sutlive Jr. 1991. The children of Nising: Images of headhunting and male sexuality in Iban ritual and oral literature. In *Female and male in Borneo: Contributions and challenges to gender studies*, ed. Vinson H. Sutlive, 153–230. Borneo Research Council Monograph Series, Vol. 1. Williamsburg, VA: Borneo Research Council.

Day, Tony. 1994. "Landscape" in early Java. In *Recovering the Orient: Artists, scholars, appropriations*, ed. Andrew Gerstle and Anthony Milner, 175–203. Amsterdam: Harwood.

Dean, Warren. 1987. *Brazil and the struggle for rubber: A study in environmental history*. Cambridge, UK: Cambridge University Press.

Deleuze, Giles, and Félix Guattari. [1980] 1987. *A thousand plateaus: Capitalism and schizophrenia*. Trans. Brian Massumi. Minneapolis, MN: University of Minnesota Press. (Original, *Mille plateaux*. Vol. 2 of *Capitalisme et schizophrénie*.)

Dentan, Robert Knox. 1982. A dream of Senoi. *Journal of Asian Affairs* 7 (2): 1–61.

Dijkman, M. J. 1961. *Hevea: Thirty years of research in the Far East*. Coral Gables, FL: University of Miami Press.

Dillon, H. S. 1985. Development of rubber smallholders in North Sumatra. In *Smallholder rubber production and policies: Proceedings of an international workshop held at the University of Adelaide*, 116–26. Canberra: Australian Center for International Agricultural Research (ACIAR).

Dillon, Michael. 1995. Sovereignty and govermentality: From the problematics of the "new world order" to the ethical problematic of the world order. *Alternatives* 20: 323–68.

Dobbin, Christine. 1983. *Islamic revivalism in a changing peasant economy: Central Sumatra, 1784–1847*. London: Curzon Press.

Domenig, Gaudenz. 2008. Timber orientation in the traditional architecture of Indonesia. *Bijdragen* 164 (4): 450–74.

Domhoff, G. William. 1985. *The mystique of dreams: A search for Utopia through Senoi dream theory*. Berkeley, CA: University of California Press.

Donkin, R. A. 1999. *Dragon's brain perfume: An historical geography of camphor*. Leiden: Brill.

Dove, Michael R. 1983. Theories of swidden agriculture and the political economy of ignorance. *Agroforestry Systems* 1:85–99.

——— 1984. The Chayanov slope in a swidden society: Household demography and extensive agriculture in Western Kalimantan. In *Chayanov, peasants and anthropology*, ed. E. Paul Durrenberger, 97–132. New York: Academic Press.

——— 1985a. The agroecological mythology of the Javanese, and the political economy of Indonesia. *Indonesia* 39:1–36.

——— 1985b. The Kantu' system of land tenure: The evolution of tribal land rights in Borneo. *Studies in Third World Societies* 33:159–82.

——— 1985c. *Swidden agriculture in Indonesia: The subsistence strategies of the Kalimantan Kantu'*. Berlin: Mouton.

——— 1986a. Peasant versus government perception and use of the environment: A case study of Banjarese ecology and river basin development in South Kalimantan. *Journal of Southeast Asian Studies* 17 (1): 113–36.

——— 1986b. Plantation development in West Kalimantan II: Perceptions of the indigenous population. *Borneo Research Bulletin* 18 (1): 3–27.

———— 1986c. The practical reason of weeds in Indonesia: Peasant versus state views of *Imperata* and *Chromolaena*. *Human Ecology* 14 (2): 163–90.

———— 1988. The ecology of intoxication among the Kantu' of West Kalimantan. In *The real and imagined role of culture in development: Case studies from Indonesia*, ed. Michael R. Dove, 139–82. Honolulu: University of Hawaii Press.

———— 1993. The responses of Dayak and bearded pig to mast-fruiting in Kalimantan: An analysis of nature-culture analogies. In *Tropical forests, people, and food*, ed. Claude Marcel Hladik, Annette Hladik, Olga F. Linares, Helene Pagezy, Alisa Semple, and Malcolm Hadley, 113–23. Man and the Biosphere Series, Vol. 13. Paris: UNESCO; Carnforth, UK: Parthenon Publishing.

———— 1996. Center, periphery, and biodiversity: A paradox of governance and a developmental challenge. In *Valuing local knowledge: Indigenous people and intellectual property rights*, ed. Stephen B. Brush and Doreen Stabinsky, 41–67. Washington, DC: Island Press.

———— 1999. The agronomy of memory and the memory of agronomy: Ritual conservation of archaic cultigens in contemporary farming systems. In *Ethnoecology: Situated knowledge / located lives*, ed. V. Nazarea, 45–70. Tucson, AZ: University of Arizona Press.

———— 2003. Forest discourses in South and Southeast Asia: A comparison with global discourses. In *Nature in the global South: Environmental projects in South and Southeast Asia*, ed. P. Greenough and A. Tsing, 103–23. Durham, NC: Duke University Press.

———— 2006. "New barbarism" or old agency among the Dayak? Reflections on post-Suharto ethnic violence in Kalimantan. *Social Analysis* 50 (1): 192–202.

———— 2010. The panoptic gaze in a non-western setting: Self-surveillance on Merapi Volcano, Central Java. *Religion* 40: 121–27.

————, ed. 2008. *Southeast Asian grasslands: Understanding a folk landscape*. New York: New York Botanical Garden Press.

Dove, Michael R., and Carol Carpenter. 2005. The "poison tree" and the changing vision of the Indo-Malay realm: Seventeenth to twentieth centuries. In *Histories of the Borneo environment: Economic, political, and social dimensions of change and continuity*, ed. R. L. Wadley, 183–210. Verhandelingen 231. Leiden: Koninklijk Instituut voor Taal-, Land- en Volkenkunde.

Dove, Michael R., and Daniel M. Kammen. 1997. The epistemology of sustainable resource use: Managing forest products, swiddens, and high-yielding variety crops. *Human Organization* 56 (1): 91–101.

———— 2001. Vernacular models of development: An analysis of Indonesia under the "New Order." *World Development* 29 (4): 619–39.

Dove, Michael R., Andrew Mathews, Keely Maxwell, Jonathan Padwe, and Anne Rademacher. 2008. The concept of human agency in contemporary conservation and development. In *Against the grain: The Vayda tradition in human ecology and ecological anthropology*, ed. B. Walters, B. J. McCay, P. West, and S. Lees, 225–53. Lanham, MD: Lexington Books.

Down to Earth. 1990a. Farmer shot in plantation dispute. No. 7 (March): 3.

———— 1990b. Farmers impoverished by World Bank-funded plantation project. No. 11 (November): 10–11.

———— 1990c. Loggers destroy local forest product supplies. No. 7 (March): 10.

Drabble, J. H. 1973. *Rubber in Malaya 1876–1922: The genesis of the industry*. Kuala Lumpur: Oxford University Press.

———— 1979. Peasant smallholders in the Malayan economy: An historical study with special reference to the rubber industry. In *Issues in Malaysian development*, ed. J. C. Jackson and M. Rudner, 69–99. Kuala Lumpur: Heinemann.

Drake, Richard Allen. 1982. *The material provisioning of Mualang society in hinterland Kalimantan Barat, Indonesia*. Ph.D. dissertation, Michigan State University.

——— 1989. Construction sacrifice and kidnapping rumor panics in Borneo. *Oceania* 59:269–79.

——— 1992. The Christian conversion of the Mualang as a phase of a messianic movements cycle. Presented at the Borneo Research Council 2nd Biennial International Conference, 13–17 July, Kota Kinabalu.

Drewes, G. W. J., ed. and trans. 1979. *Hikajat Potjut Muhamat: An Achehnese epic*. Koninklijk Instituut voor Taal-, Land- en Volkenkunde, Bibliotheca Indonesica 19. The Hague: Martinus Nijhoff.

Drijber, B. H. 1912. Djeloetoeng concessie op Borneo (Jelutong concessions in Borneo). *De Indische Gids* 34 (2): 1444–69.

Duke, James A., and Judith L. duCellier. 1993. *CRC handbook of alternative cash crops*. Boca Raton, FL: CRC Press.

Dumas, Alexandre. ca. 1902. *The black tulip*. Trans. Mary D. Frost. New York: Thomas Y. Crowell.

Dunn, F. L. 1975. *Rain-forest collectors and traders: A study of resource utilization in modern and ancient Malaya*. Monograph No. 5. Kuala Lumpur: Malaysian Branch of the Royal Asiatic Society.

Durkheim, Emile. 1953. *Sociology and philosophy*. Trans. D. F. Pocock. Glencoe, IL: Free Press.

Durst, Patrick B., Wulf Killmann, and Chris Brown. 2004. Asia's new woods. *Journal of Forestry*, June: 46–53.

Eaton, B. J. 1952. Wild and plantation rubber plants: Gutta-percha and balata. In *History of the rubber industry*, ed. P. Schidrowitz and T. R. Dawson, 49–63. Cambridge, UK: W. Heffer and Sons for the Institution of the Rubber Industry.

Echols, John M., and Hassan Shadily. 1992. *Kamus Indonesia-Inggris: An Indonesian-English dictionary*. 3rd ed. Jakarta: P. T. Gramedia.

Economist. 1977. The Dutch disease. 26 November: 82–83.

Edelman, Marc, and Angelique Haugerud, eds. 2005. *The anthropology of development and globalization: From classical political economy to contemporary neoliberalism*. Boston: Blackwell.

Edelman, Murray. 1974. The political language of the helping professions. *Politics and Society* 4 (3): 295–310.

Eder, James F. 1981. From grain crops to tree crops in the Cuyunon swidden system. In *Adaptive strategies and change in Philippine swidden-based societies*, ed. Harold C. Olofson, 91–104. Laguna, Philippines: Forest Research Institute. .

Ehrenburg, Ilya. 1976. *The life of the automobile*. Trans. Joachim Neugroschel. New York: Urizen.

Ekwall, Eilert. 1955. Slash-and-burn cultivation: A contribution to anthropological terminology. *Man* 55 (144): 135–36.

Ellen, Roy F. 1979. Sago subsistence and the trade in spices: A provisional model of ecological succession and imbalance in Moluccan history. In *Social and ecological systems*, ed. P. C. Burnham and R. F. Ellen, 43–74. London: Academic Press.

——— 1999. Forest knowledge, forest transformation: Political contingency, historical ecology and the renegotiation of nature in Central Seram. In *Transforming the Indonesian uplands*, ed. Tania M. Li, 131–57. Amsterdam: Harwood.

———— 2003. *On the edge of the Banda Zone: Past and present in the social organization of a Moluccan trading network*. Honolulu: University of Hawaii Press.

Ellen, Roy F., and Holly Harris. 2000. Introduction. In *Indigenous environmental knowledge and its transformations*, ed. R. F. Ellen, A. Bicker, and P. Parkes, 1–33. Amsterdam: Harwood.

Elson, Robert E. 1979. Cane-burning in the Pasuruan area: An expression of social discontent. In *Between people and statistics: Essays on modern Indonesian history*, ed. Francien van Anrooij et al., 219–33. The Hague: Martinus Nijhoff.

———— 1984. *Javanese peasants and the colonial sugar industry: Impact and change in an East Java residency 1830–1940*. Singapore: Oxford University Press.

Errington, Frederick, and Deborah Gewertz. 2004. *Yali's question: Sugar, culture, and history*. Chicago: University of Chicago Press.

Escobar, Arturo. 1994. *Encountering development*. Princeton, NJ: Princeton University Press.

———— 1999. After nature: steps to an antiessentialist political ecology. *Current Anthropology* 40 (1): 1–30.

Evans, Ivor H. N. [1923] 1970. *Studies in religion, folk-lore, & customs in British North Borneo and the Malay peninsula*. Reprint, London: Frank Cass.

Evans-Pritchard, E. E. 1940. *The Nuer: A description of the modes of livelihood and political institutions of a Nilotic people*. New York: Oxford University Press.

Fabian, Johannes. 1983. *Time and the other: How anthropology makes its object*. New York: Columbia University Press.

Fairhead, J. 2001. International dimensions of conflict over natural and environmental resources. In *Violent Environments*, ed. N. L. Peluso and M. Watts, 213–36. Ithaca, NY: Cornell University Press.

FAO (Food and Agriculture Organization of the United Nations). 2001. *Global forest resources assessment 2000*. FAO Forestry Paper No. 140. Rome.

Fasseur, Cornelis. 1992. *The politics of colonial exploitation: Java, the Dutch, and the cultivation system*. Trans. R. E. Elson and Ary Kraal, ed. R. E. Elson. Studies on Southeast Asia. Ithaca, NY: Cornell University, Southeast Asia Program.

FEER (*Far Eastern Economic Review*). 1985. The NES takes root—but will it flourish? 7 February.

Feintrenie, Laurène, Wan Kian Chong, and Patrice Levang. 2010. Why do farmers prefer oil palm? Lessons learnt from Bungo District, Indonesia. *Small-Scale Forestry* 9 (3): 379–96. http://www.springerlink.com/content/at02715653t75704/ (accessed July 1, 2010).

Ferguson, James. 1990. *The anti-politics machine: "Development," depoliticization, and bureaucratic power in Lesotho*. Cambridge, UK: Cambridge University Press.

———— 2006. *Global shadows: Africa in the neoliberal world order*. Durham, NC: Duke University Press.

Fish, Stanley. 1980. *Is there a text in this class?* Cambridge, UK: Cambridge University Press.

Florida, Nancy. 1995. *Writing the past, inscribing the future. History as prophecy in colonial Java*. Durham, NC: Duke University Press.

Flückiger, Friedrich A., and Daniel Hanbury. 1879. *Pharmacographia: A history of the principal drugs of vegetable origin, met with in Great Britain and British India*. 2nd ed. London: Macmillan.

Foley, Kathy. 1987. The tree of life in transition: Images of resource management in Indonesian theatre. *Crossroads* 2–3:66–77.

Forbes, Henry O. [1885] 1989. *A naturalist's wanderings in the eastern archipelago: A narrative of travel and exploration from 1878 to 1883.* Reprint, Singapore: Oxford University Press; New York: Oxford.

de Foresta, Hubert, and Genevieve Michon. 1994. Agroforests in Sumatra—Where ecology meets economy. *Agroforestry Today* 6 (4):12–13.

Forshee, Jill. 2002. Tracing troubled times: Objects of value and narratives of loss from Sumba and Timor islands. *Indonesia* 74: 65–77.

Foucault, M. 1982. Afterword: The subject and power. In *Michel Foucault: Beyond structuralism and hermeneutics,* ed. H. Dreyfus and P. Rabinow, 208–26. Chicago: University of Chicago Press.

——— 1984. Right of death and power over life. In *The Foucault reader,* ed. Paul Rabinow, 258–72. New York: Pantheon Books.

——— 1986. Of other spaces. Trans. Jay Miskowiec. *Diacritics* 16 (1): 22–27.

——— 1991. *The Foucault effect: Studies in governmentality,* ed. G. Burchell, C. Gordon, and P. Miller. Chicago: University of Chicago Press.

——— [1975] 1995. *Discipline and punish: The birth of the prison.* 2nd ed. Trans. Alan Sheridan. New York: Vintage. (Original, *Surveiller et Punir: Naissance de la prison.* Paris: Editions Gallimard.)

Fox, James. 1971. Sister's child as plant: Metaphors in an idiom of consanguinity. In *Rethinking kinship and marriage,* ed. Rodney Needham, 219–52. London: Tavistock.

——— 1988. Origin, descent and precedence in the study of Austronesian societies. Public lecture in connection with De Wisselleerstoel Indonesische Studien, 17 March, Leiden University.

Foxworthy, F. W. 1922. Minor forest products of the Malay Peninsula. *Malayan Forest Records* 2: 151–217.

Frank, Andre Gunder. 1967. *Capitalism and underdevelopment in Latin America: Historical studies of Chile and Brazil.* New York: Monthly Review Press.

Frazer, Sir James George. 1951. *The golden bough: A study in magic and religion.* Abridged ed. New York: Macmillan.

Freedman, Paul. 2008. *Out of the east: Spices and the medieval imagination.* New Haven, CT: Yale University Press.

Freeman, Derek. [1955] 1970. *Report on the Iban.* New ed. New York: Athlone Press.

——— 1960. Iban augury. In *The birds of Borneo,* ed. B. E. Smythies, 73–98. Edinburgh: Oliver and Boyd.

——— 1967. Shaman and incubus. *Psychoanalytic Study of Society* 4:315–43.

Fried, Stephanie Gorson. 2000. Tropical forests forever? A contextual ecology of Bentian rattan agroforestry systems. In *People, plants, and justice: The politics of nature conservation,* ed. Charles Zerner, 204–33. New York: Columbia University Press.

Frossard, D. 1998. "Peasant science": A new paradigm for sustainable development? *Research in Philosophy and Technology* 17:111–26.

Fyfe, A. J. 1949. "Gutta percha." *Malayan Forester* 12:25–27.

Geddes, William R. 1954. *The Land Dayaks of Sarawak.* Colonial Research Study No. 14. London: Her Majesty's Stationery Office.

Geertz, Clifford. 1960. *The religion of Java.* Chicago: University of Chicago Press.

——— [1963] 1971. *Agricultural involution: The processes of ecological change in Indonesia.* Association of Asian Studies Monographs and Papers No. 11. Berkeley, CA: University of California Press.

Ghani, Mohd. Noor A., Ong Seng Huat, and M. Wessel. 1986. *Hevea brasiliensis* (Willd. ex

A. L. Juss.) Muell. Arg. In *Plant resources of South-East Asia*, ed. E. Westphal and P. C. M. Jansen, 152–61. Wageningen, The Netherlands: PUDOC Scientific Publishers.

Ghee, Lim Teck. 1974. Malaysian peasant smallholders and the Stevenson restriction scheme, 1922–1928. *Journal of the Malaysian Branch of the Royal Asiatic Society* 47:105–22.

Gianno, Rosemary. 1986. The exploitation of resinous products in a lowland Malayan forest. *Wallaceana* 43:3–6.

Giddens, Anthony. 1979. *Central problems in social theory: Action, structure, and contradiction in social analysis*. Berkeley, CA: University of California Press.

——— 1984. *The constitution of society: Outline of the theory of structuration*. Berkeley, CA: University of California Press.

Glamann, Kristof. 1958. *Dutch-Asiatic trade, 1629–1740*. Copenhagen: Danish Science Press; The Hague: Martinus Nijhoff.

Godoy, Ricardo, and Tan Ching Feaw. 1989. The profitability of smallholder rattan cultivation in central Borneo. *Human Ecology* 16 (4): 397–420.

Godoy, Ricardo, Victoria Reyes-García, Elizabeth Byron, William R. Leonard, and Vincent Vadez. 2005. The effect of market economies on the well-being of indigenous peoples and on their use of renewable natural resources. *Annual Review of Anthropology* 34:121–38.

Goldammer, J. G. 1990. The impact of drought and forest fires on tropical lowland rain forest of East Kalimantan. In *Fire in the tropical biota: Ecosystem processes and global challenges*, ed. J. G. Goldammer, 11–31. Berlin: Springer-Verlag.

Goldman, Michael. 2005. *Imperial nature: The World Bank and struggles for social justice in the age of globalization*. New Haven, CT: Yale University Press.

Gomes, Edwin H. 1911. *Seventeen years among the Sea Dyaks of Borneo: A record of intimate association with the natives of the Bornean jungles*. London: Seeley.

Gordon, Alec. 1993. Smallholder commercial cultivation and the environment: Rubber in Southeast Asia. In *Asia's environmental crisis*, ed. Michael C. Howard, 135–53. Boulder: Westview Press.

Gould, Stephen J. 1997. Unusual unity. *Natural History* 4:20–23, 69–71.

Gouyon, A., Hubert de Foresta, and P. Levang. 1993. Does "jungle rubber" deserve its name? Analysis of rubber agroforestry systems in Southeast Sumatra. *Agroforestry Systems* 22:181–206.

Government of Indonesia. 1992. *Statistik Indonesia: Statistical yearbook of Indonesia*. Jakarta: Central Bureau of Statistics.

——— 2004. *Statistik karet Indonesia* (Indonesian Rubber Statistics). Jakarta: Central Bureau of Statistics.

Griffiths, T., and F. Martone. 2009. Seeing "REDD"? Forests, climate change mitigation, and the rights of indigenous peoples and local communities. Updated Report. Forests and Peoples Programme.

Groeneveldt, W. P. 1960. *Historical notes on Indonesia and Malaysia: Compiled from Chinese sources*. Jakarta: C. V. Bhratara.

Grossman, Lawrence S. 1998. *The political ecology of bananas: Contract farming, peasants, and agrarian change in the Eastern Caribbean*. Durham, NC: University of North Carolina Press.

Gudeman, Stephen. 1986. *Economics as culture: Models and metaphors of livelihood*. London: Routledge.

Gudeman, Stephen, and Alberto Rivera. 1990. *Conversations in Colombia: The domestic economy in life and text*. Cambridge, UK: Cambridge University Press.

Guerreiro, Antonio. 1988. Cash crops and subsistence strategies. *Sarawak Museum Journal* 39 (60): 15–52.

Gupta, Akhil. 1998. *Postcolonial developments: Agriculture in the making of modern India.* Durham, NC: Duke University Press.

Haenn, Nora. 1999. The power of environmental knowledge: Ethnoecology and environmental conflicts in Mexican conservation. *Human Ecology* 27 (3): 477–91.

Hahamovitch, Cindy. 1997. *The fruits of their labor: Atlantic coast farmworkers and the making of migrant poverty, 1870–1945.* Chapel Hill, NC: University of North Carolina Press.

Haines, W. B. [1934] 1940. *The uses and control of natural undergrowth.* 2nd ed. Kuala Lumpur: Rubber Research Institute of Malaya.

Hall, Kenneth R. 1995. Upstream and downstream networking in seventeenth century Banjarmasin. In *From Buckfast to Borneo: Essays presented to Father Robert Nicholl on the 85th anniversary of his birth,* ed. Victor T. King and A. V. M. Horton, 489–504. Kuching, Sarawak: Sarawak Literary Society.

Hall, Stuart. 1996. *Stuart Hall: Critical dialogues in cultural studies.* Ed. David Morley and Kuan-Hsing Chen. London and New York: Routledge.

Hansen, Gary E. 1973. *The politics and administration of rural development in Indonesia: The case of agriculture.* Research Monograph No. 9. Berkeley, CA: University of California, Center for South and Southeast Asian Studies.

Hapip, Abdul Djebar. 1977. *Kamus Banjar-Indonesia* (Banjar-Indonesian dictionary). Jakarta: Pusat Pembinaan dan Pengembangan Bahasa, Departemen Pendidikan dan Kebudayaan.

Hardin, Rebecca. 2002. Concessionary politics in the Western Congo Basin: History and culture in forest use. Environmental Governance in Africa. Working Paper 6. Washington, DC: World Resources Institute.

Harms, Robert W. 2003. *The diligent: A voyage through the worlds of the slave trade.* New York: Basic Books.

Harris, Marvin. 1966. The cultural ecology of India's sacred cattle. *Current Anthropology* 7:51–59.

Harris, Olivia. 1989. The earth and the state: The sources and meanings of money in northern Potosi, Bolivia. In *Money and the morality of exchange,* ed. Jonathan Parry and Maurice Bloch, 232–68. Cambridge, UK: Cambridge University Press.

Harrisson, Tom, and Stanley J. O'Connor. 1969. *Excavations of the prehistoric iron industry in West Borneo.* Ithaca, NY: Cornell University, Southeast Asia Program.

——— 1970. *Gold and megalithic activity in prehistoric and recent west Borneo.* Ithaca, NY: Cornell University, Southeast Asia Program.

Harwell, Emily. 2000. Remote sensibilities: Discourses of technology and the making of Indonesia's natural disaster. *Development and Change* 31:307–40.

——— 2003. *Without remedy: Human rights abuse and Indonesia's pulp and paper industry.* Human Rights Watch report 15, no. 1 (6 January). http://www.hrw.org/reports/2003/indono103/.

Hecht, S. B., A. B. Anderson, and P. May. 1988. The subsidy from nature: Shifting cultivation, successional palm forests, and rural development. *Human Organization* 47 (1): 25–35.

Hecht, Susanna, and Alexander Cockburn. 1989. *The fate of the forest: Developers, destroyers and defenders of the Amazon.* London: Verso.

Heersink, Christiaan G. 1994. Selayar and the green gold: The development of the coconut trade on an Indonesian island (1820–1950). *Journal of Southeast Asian Studies* 25 (1): 47–69.

Heidhues, Mary F. Somers. 1992. *Bangka tin and Mentok pepper: Chinese settlement on an Indonesian island.* Singapore: Institute of Southeast Asian Studies.

von Heine-Geldern, Robert. 1945. *Prehistoric research in the Netherlands Indies.* New York: Southeast Asia Institute.

Hellwig, Tineke, and Eric Tagliacozzo. 2009. *The Indonesia reader: History, culture, politics.* Durham, NC: Duke University Press.

Henley, David. 2009. Review: John H. McGlynn's "Indonesia in the Soeharto years: Issues, incidents and images." *Bijdragen* 165 (1): 153–55.

Herbert, Zbigniew. 1992. The bitter smell of tulips. In *Still life with a bridge: Essays and apocryphas.* London: Jonathan Cape.

Hirth, Friedrich, and W. W. Rockhill, eds. and trans. 1911. *Chau Ju-kua: His work on the Chinese and Arab trade in the twelfth and thirteenth centuries, entitled "Chu-fan-chï."* St. Petersburg, Russia: Imperial Academy of Sciences.

Hirtz, Frank. 2003. It takes modern means to be traditional: On recognizing indigenous cultural communities in the Philippines. *Development and Change* 34 (5): 887–914.

Hobhouse, Henry. 1985. *Seeds of change: Five plants that transformed mankind.* New York: Harper & Row.

Hobsbawm, Eric. 1994. *The age of extremes: A history of the world, 1914–1991.* New York: Pantheon Books.

Hoffman, Carl. 1988. The "wild Punan" of Borneo: A matter of economics. In *The real and imagined role of culture in development: Case studies from Indonesia,* ed. M. R. Dove, 89–118. Honolulu: University of Hawaii Press.

Homer-Dixon, T. F. 1991. On the threshold: Environmental changes as causes of acute conflict. *International Security* 16 (2): 76–116.

Homma, Alfredo Kingo Oyama. 1992. The dynamics of extraction in Amazonia: A historical perspective. *Advances in Economic Botany* 9:23–31.

Honolulu Advertiser. 1996. Golden Buddha adds twist to Marcos suits. 25 March.

——— 1997. Marcos trial award biggest ever. 19 January.

Hornaday, William T. 1885. *Two years in the jungle: The experiences of a hunter and naturalist in India, Ceylon, the Malay Peninsula, and Borneo.* New York: Charles Scribner's Sons.

Hornborg, Alf. 1996. Ecology as semiotics: Outlines of a contextualist paradigm for human ecology. In *Nature and society: Anthropological perspectives,* ed. Philippe Descola and Gísli Pálsson, 45–62. London: Routledge.

Horne, Elinor Clark. 1974. *Javanese-English dictionary.* New Haven, CT: Yale University Press.

Hose, Charles, and William McDougall. [1912] 1966. *The pagan tribes of Borneo.* 2 vols. London: Frank Cass.

Hoskins, Janet. 1998. *Biographical objects: How things tell the stories of people's lives.* New York and London: Routledge.

Howell, William, and D. J. S. Bailey. 1900. *A Sea Dyak dictionary.* Singapore: American Mission Press.

Hudson, Alfred B. 1967. *Padju Epat: The ethnography and social structure of a Ma'anyan Dayak group in Southeastern Borneo.* Ph.D. dissertation, Cornell University.

Hurgronje, Christiaan Snouck. 1888. Nog iets over de Salasila van Koetai (Another thing regarding the Salasila of Kutai). *Bijdragen* 37:109–20.

Hvalkof, Søren. 2000. Outrage in rubber and oil: Extractivism, indigenous peoples, and justice in the Upper Amazon. In *People, plants, and justice: The politics of nature conservation,* ed. Charles Zerner, 83–116. New York: Columbia University Press.

IDRD (Institute of Dayakology Research and Development). 1994. Konflik antara Masyarakat Adat Dengan Perusahaan HPH dan HTI di Kabupaten Ketapang KalBar (Conflict between traditional communities and timber concessions and plantations in Ketapang District, West Kalimantan). *Kalimantan Review* 9 (3): 22–28.

Imbs, Paul. 1977. *Tresor de la langue Française* (Treasures of the French language). 15 vols. Paris: Centre National de la Recherche Scientifique.

Isaacman, Allen. 2005. *Cotton is the mother of poverty: Peasants, work, and rural struggle in Colonial Mozambique, 1938–1961*. Portsmouth, NH: Heinemann.

IUCN (International Union for the Conservation of Nature). 1993. *Improving the capacity of the Lao PDR for sustainable management of wetlands benefits*. Vientiane, Laos: IUCN.

Izikowitz, K. G. 1951. *Lamet: Hill peasants in French Indochina*. Göteborg, Sweden: Etnografiska Museet.

Jackson, J. C. 1970. *Chinese in the West Borneo goldfields: A study in cultural geography*. Occasional Papers in Geography No. 15. Hull, UK: University of Hull.

Jacobs, Julius. 1894. *Het familie- en kampongleven op Groot-Atjeh. Eene bijdrage tot de ethnographie van Noord-Sumatra* (Family and village life in Greater Aceh. A contribution to the ethnography of North Sumatra). 2 vols. Leiden: E. J. Brill.

de Janvry, Alain. 1981. *The agrarian question and reformism in Latin America*. Baltimore, MD: Johns Hopkins University Press.

Jessup, Timothy C., and Nancy L. Peluso. 1985. Minor forest products as common property resources in East Kalimantan, Indonesia. *Proceedings of the conference on common property resource management 21–26 April*, 505–31. Washington, DC: National Academy Press.

Jessup, Timothy C., and Andrew P. Vayda. 1988. Dayaks and forests of interior Borneo. *Expedition* 30 (1): 5–17.

de Jong, Wil. 1997. Developing swidden agriculture and the threat of biodiversity loss. *Agriculture, Ecosystems & Environment* 62: 187–97.

de Jong, Wil, Brian Belcher, Dede Rohadii, Rita Mustikasari, and Patrice Levang. 2003. The political ecology of forest products in Indonesia: A history of changing adversaries. In *The political ecology of tropical forests in Southeast Asia: Historical perspectives*, ed. Lye Tuck-Po, Wil de Jong, and Abe Ken-ichi, 107–32. Kyoto, Japan: Kyoto University Press; Melbourne, Australia: Trans Pacific Press.

Jongejans, J. 1918. Een en ander over Semangka (A thing or two concerning Semangka). *Tijdschrift voor Indische Taal-, Land- en Volkenkunde* 58:229–300.

Jorgenson, Anders Baltzer. 1989. A natural view: Pwo Karen notions of plants, landscapes, and people. *Folk* 31:21–51.

Joshi, Lawman, Gede Wibawa, Hendrien Beukema, Sandy Williams, and Meine van Noordwijk. 2003. Technological change and biodiversity in the rubber agroecosystem of Sumatra. In *Tropical agroecosystems*, ed. John H. Vandermeer, 133–57. Boca Raton, FL: CRC Press.

Kahn, Joel S. 1982. From peasants to petty commodity production in Southeast Asia. *Bulletin of Concerned Asian Scholars* 14 (1): 3–15.

———— 1984. Peasant political consciousness in West Sumatra: A reanalysis of the Communist uprising of 1927. *Senri Ethnological Studies* 13:293–325.

Kano, Hiroyoshi. 2008. *Indonesian exports, peasant agriculture and the world economy, 1850–2000: Economic structures in a Southeast Asian state*. Singapore: National University of Singapore Press; Athens: Ohio University Press.

Kaplan, R. D. 1994. The coming anarchy: How scarcity, crime, overpopulation, and disease are rapidly destroying the social fabric of our planet. *Atlantic Monthly*, February, 44–76.

Kartodihardjo, H., and A. Supriono. 2000. *The impact of sectoral development on natural forest conversion and degradation: The case of timber and tree crop plantations in Indonesia.* Center for International Forestry Research Occasional Paper No. 26(E). Bogor, Indonesia.

Kathirithamby-Wells, Jeya. 1977. *The British West Sumatran presidency 1760–1785: Problems of early colonial enterprise.* Kuala Lumpur: Penerbit Universiti Malaya.

——— 2011. The implications of plantation agriculture for biodiversity in Peninsular Malaysia: An historical perspective. In *Beyond the Sacred Forest: Complicating Conservation in Southeast Asia,* ed. Michael R. Dove, Percy E. Sajise, and Amity A. Doolittle. Durham, NC: Duke University Press.

Kato, Tsuyoshi. 1991. When rubber came: The Negeri Sembilan experience. *Southeast Asian Studies* 29 (2):109–57.

——— 1994. The emergence of abandoned paddy fields in Negeri Sembilan, Malaysia. *Southeast Asian Studies* 32 (2):145–72.

Keck, Margaret E. 1995. Social equity and environmental politics in Brazil: Lessons from the rubber tappers of Acre. *Comparative Politics* 27 (4): 409–24.

Keller, Eva. 2008. The banana plant and the moon: Conservation and the Malagasy ethos of life in Masoala. *American Ethnologist* 35 (4): 650–64.

Kent, Noel J. 1983. *Hawaii: Islands under the influence.* New York: Monthly Review Press.

Keong, Voon Phin. 1976. *Western planting enterprises in Southeast Asia 1876–1921.* Kuala Lumpur: Penerbit Universiti Malaya.

Kerr, K. 1991. The economic potential of handicraft enterprises in rural development: Focus on Indonesia. *Unasylva* 165 (42): 31–36.

King, Victor T. 1988. Social rank and social change among the Maloh. In *The real and imagined role of culture in development: Case studies from Indonesia,* ed. Michael R. Dove, 219–53. Honolulu: University of Hawaii Press.

——— 1996. Environmental change in Malaysian Borneo: Fire, drought and rain. In *Environmental change in South-East Asia: People, politics and sustainable development,* ed. Michael J. G. Parnwell and Raymond L. Bryant, 165–89. London and New York: Routledge.

Kirsch, Stuart. 2008. Social relations and the green critique of capitalism in Melanesia. *American Anthropologist* 110 (3): 288–98.

Kloppenburg, Jack R., Jr. 1988. *First the seed: The political economy of plant biotechnology, 1492–2000.* Cambridge, UK: Cambridge University Press.

Knapen, Han. 1997. Epidemics, droughts, and other uncertainties on Southeast Borneo during the eighteenth and nineteenth centuries. In *Paper landscapes: Explorations in the environmental history of Indonesia,* ed. P. Boomgaard, F. Colombijn, and D. Henley, 121–52. Verhandelingen 178. Leiden: Koninklijk Instituut voor Taal-, Land- en Volkenkunde.

Knight, G. R. 1980. From plantation to padi-field: The origins of the nineteenth century transformation of Java's sugar industry. *Modern Asian Studies* 14 (2):177–204.

Kopytoff, Igor. 1986. The cultural biography of things: Commoditization as process. In *The social life of things,* ed. Arjun Appadurai, 64–91. Cambridge, UK: Cambridge University Press.

Koster, G. L. 2005. Of treaties and unbelievers: Images of the Dutch in seventeenth- and eighteenth-century Malay historiography. *Journal of the Malay Branch of the Royal Asiatic Society* 78 (1):59–96.

KSPKS (Kantor Statistik Propinsi Kalimantan Selatan). 1992. *Kalimantan Selatan dalam angka (South Kalimantan in figures) 1992.* Banjarmasin, Indonesia.

Lansing, J. Stephen. 2006. *Perfect order: Recognizing complexity in Bali.* Princeton, NJ: Princeton University Press.

Lawrence, Deborah C. 1996. Trade-offs between rubber production and maintenance of diversity: The structure of rubber gardens in West Kalimantan, Indonesia. *Agroforestry Systems* 34 (1): 83–100.

Lawrence, Deborah C., Mark Leighton, and David R. Peart. 1995. Availability and extraction of forest products in managed and primary forest around a Dayak village in West Kalimantan, Indonesia. *Conservation Biology* 9 (1):76–88.

Leach, Edmund R. 1982. *Social anthropology*. Glasgow: Fontana.

Leighton, Mark, and Nengah Wirawan. 1986. Catastrophic drought and fire in Borneo associated with the 1982–1983 El Niño Southern Oscillation event. In *Tropical rainforests and the world atmosphere*, ed. Gilian T. Prance, 75–102. Washington, DC: American Association for the Advancement of Science.

Van Leur, J. C. [1955] 1967. *Indonesian trade and society: Essays in Asian social and economic history*. 2nd ed. The Hague: W. Van Hoeve.

Lévi, S. 1918. Pour l'histoire du *Ramayana* (On the history of the *Ramayana*). *Journal Asiatique*, January–February, 1–160.

Li, Tania Murray. 1996. Images of community: Discourse and strategy in property relations. *Development and Change* 27 (3): 501–27.

——— 1999. Marginality, power and production: Analysing upland transformations. In *Transforming the Indonesian uplands*, ed. Tania Murray Li, 1–44. Amsterdam: Harwood.

——— 2000. Articulating indigenous identity in Indonesia: Resource politics and the tribal slot. *Comparative Studies in Society and History* 42 (1): 149–79.

——— 2002. Local histories, global markets: Cocoa and class in upland Sulawesi. *Development and Change* 33 (3): 415–37.

——— 2006. Neo-liberal strategies of government through community: The social development program of the World Bank in Indonesia. *International Law and Justice Working Paper 2006/2*, Institute for International Law and Justice, New York University, School of Law.

——— 2007. *The will to improve: Governmentality, development, and the practice of politics*. Durham, NC: Duke University Press.

Lian, Francis J. 1988. The economics and ecology of the production of the tropical rainforest resources by tribal groups of Sarawak, Borneo. In *Changing tropical forests: Historical perspectives on today's challenges in Asia, Australasia, and Oceania*, ed. John Dargavel, Kay Dixon, and Noel Semple, 113–25. Canberra: Australian National University, Centre for Resource and Environmental Studies.

Lindblad, J. Thomas. 1988. *Between Dayak and Dutch: The economic history of Southeast Kalimantan, 1880–1942*. Verhandelingen No. 134. Dordrecht, The Netherlands: Foris Publications.

Little, Lester K. 1978. *Religious poverty and the profit economy in medieval Europe*. London: Paul Elek.

Loadman, John. 2005. *Tears of the tree: The story of rubber—a modern marvel*. New York: Oxford University Press.

Logan, J. R. 1848a. Notices of Chinese intercourse with Borneo proper prior to the establishment of Singapore in 1819. *Journal of the Indian Archipelago and Eastern Asia* 2:611–15.

——— 1848b. Notices of European intercourse with Borneo proper prior to the establishment of Singapore in 1819. *Journal of the Indian Archipelago and Eastern Asia* 2:498–512.

Lohmann, Larry. 1991. Who defends biodiversity? Conservation strategies and the case of Thailand. In *Biodiversity: Social and ecological perspectives*, ed. Vandana Shiva, Patrick Anderson, Heffa Schucking, Andrew Gray, Larry Lohmann, and David Cooper, 77–104. London: Zed Books; Penang: World Rainforest Movement.

Low, Hugh. [1848] 1968. *Sarawak, its inhabitants and productions: Being notes during a residence in that country with his excellency Mr. Brooke*. Reprint, London: Frank Cass.

Lowe, Celia. 2006. *Wild profusion: Biodiversity conservation in an Indonesian archipelago*. Princeton, NJ: Princeton University Press.

Ludwig, Donald, Ray Hilborn, and Carl Walters. 1993. Uncertainty, resource exploitation, and conservation: Lessons from history. *Science* 260:17, 36.

Lumholtz, Carl. 1920. *Through central Borneo: An account of two years' travel in the land of the head-hunters between the years 1913 and 1917*. 2 vols. New York: Charles Scribner's Sons.

Luytjes, A. 1925. *De Bevolkingsrubbercultuur in Nederlandsche Indie* (Native rubber cultivation in the Dutch East Indies). Vol. 2 of *Zuider en Ooster Afdeeling van Borneo* (South and West Divisions of Borneo). Weltevreden, Java: Dept van Landbouw, Nijverheid en Handel. Published in cooperation with Native Rubber Investigation Committee, Batavia.

Lye, Tuck-Po. 2004. *Changing pathways: Forest degradation and the Batek of Pahang, Malaysia*. Lanham, MD: Lexington Books.

———— 2005. The meanings of trees: Forest and identity for the Batek of Pahang, Malaysia. *Asia-Pacific Journal of Anthropology* 6 (3): 249–61.

Lyon, Sarah. 2004. Migratory imaginations: The commodification and contradictions of shade grown coffee. *Social Anthropology* 14 (3): 377–90.

Marcus, George E., and Michael M. J. Fischer. 1986. *Anthropology as cultural critique: An experimental moment in the human sciences*. Chicago: University of Chicago Press.

Marsden, Magnus. 2008. Muslim cosmopolitans? Transnational life in Northern Pakistan. *Journal of Asian Studies* 67 (1): 213–48.

Marsden, William. [1811] 1966. *The history of Sumatra*. 3rd ed. Kuala Lumpur: Oxford University Press.

Mary, Fabienne, and Geneviève Michon. 1987. When agroforests drive back natural forests: A socio-economic analysis of a rice-agroforest system in Sumatra. *Agroforestry Systems* 5:27–55.

Maxwell, Allen R. 1992. Balui reconnaissances: The Sihan of the Menamang river. *Sarawak Museum Journal* 43 (64): 1–45.

Mayer, Enrique. 2002. *The articulated peasant: Household economies in the Andes*. Boulder, CO: Westview Press.

Mayer, Judith. 1996. Impacts of the East Kalimantan forest fires of 1982–1983 on village life, forest use, and land use. In *Borneo in transition: People, forests, conservation, and development*, ed. C. Padoch and N. Peluso, 87–218. Kuala Lumpur: Oxford University Press.

McCann, James C. 2005. *Maize and grace: Africa's encounter with a new world crop, 1500–2000*. Cambridge, MA: Harvard University Press.

McGrath, D. G. 1987. The role of biomass in shifting cultivation. *Human Ecology* 15 (2): 221–42.

McTaggart, W. Donald. 1982. Some characteristics of government and quasi-government writings dealing with South Sulawesi. *Indonesian Quarterly* 10 (2): 44–62.

McWilliam, Andrew. 2005. Haumeni, not many: Renewed plunder and mismanagement in the Timorese sandalwood industry. *Modern Asian Studies* 39 (2): 285–320.

———— 2007. Harbouring traditions in East Timor: Marginality in a lowland entrepôt. *Modern Asian Studies* 41 (6): 1113–43.

Medway, Lord. 1977. *Mammals of Borneo*. Monograph No. 7. Kuala Lumpur: Malaysian Branch of the Royal Asiatic Society.

Meilink-Roelofsz, M. A. P. 1962. *Asian trade and European influence in the Indonesian archipelago between 1500 and about 1630*. The Hague: Martinus Nijhoff.

Melby, John F. 1942. Rubber river: The rise and collapse of the Amazon rubber boom. *Hispanic American Historical Review* 22 (3): 452–69.

Mendes, F. 1992. Peasants speak: Chico Mendes—the defense of life. *Journal of Peasant Studies* 20:160–76.

Michon, Geneviève, Hubert de Foresta, Kusworo, and Patrice Levang. 2000. The Damar agroforests of Krui, Indonesia: Justice for forest farmers. In *People, plants, and justice: The politics of nature conservation*, ed. Charles Zerner, 159–203. New York: Columbia University Press.

Mintz, Sidney W. 1959. The plantation as a socio-cultural type. In *Plantation systems of the New World*, 42–49. Social Science Monograph 7. Washington, DC: Pan American Union.

———— 1985. *Sweetness and power: The place of sugar in modern history*. New York: Viking Penguin.

Missen, G. J. 1972. *Viewpoint on Indonesia: A geographical study*. Melbourne, Australia: Thomas Nelson.

Mitchell, T. 1988. *Colonising Egypt*. Cambridge, UK: Cambridge University Press.

Moertono, Soemarsaid. 1981. *State and statecraft in old Java: A study of the later Mataram period, sixteenth to nineteenth century*. Monograph Series No. 43. Rev. ed. Ithaca, NY: Cornell University, Southeast Asia Program.

Monier-Williams, Sir Monier. 1899. *A Sanskrit-English dictionary*. Oxford, UK: Clarendon Press.

Moon, Suzanne. 2004. Empirical knowledge, scientific authority, and native development: The controversy over sugar/rice ecology in the Netherlands East Indies, 1905–1914. *Environment and History* 10:59–81.

Moore, Donald. 2005. *Suffering for territory: Race, place, and power in Zimbabwe*. Durham, NC: Duke University Press.

Morrison, Kathleen D., and Laura L. Junker, eds. 2002. *Forager-traders in south and southeast Asia: Long-term histories*. Cambridge, UK: Cambridge University Press.

Multatuli (Eduard Douwes Dekker). [1859] 1982. *Max Havelaar, or the coffee auctions of the Dutch trading company*. Trans. Roy Edwards. Reprint, Amherst, MA: University of Massachusetts Press.

Murphy, Robert F. 1978. *Headhunter's heritage: Social and economic change among the Mundurucu Indians*. New York: Octagon Books, Farrar, Straus, and Giroux.

Murphy, Robert F., and Julian Steward. 1956. Tappers and trappers: Parallel process in acculturation. *Economic Development and Culture Change* 4:335–55.

Murray, Martin J. 1992. "White gold" or "white blood"? The rubber plantations of colonial Indochina, 1910–40. *Journal of Peasant Studies* 19 (3–4):41–67.

Muzzall, A. H. 1925. Native plantation rubber industry of Sumatra: Palembang district. In *The plantation rubber industry of the Middle East*, ed. D. M. Figart. Trade Promotion Series No. 2. Washington, DC: Department of Commerce.

Nagtegaal, L. W. 1994. Diamonds are a regent's best friend: Javanese Bupati as political entrepreneurs. In *State and Trade in the Indonesian Archipelago*, ed. G. J. Schutte, 77–97. Working Papers 13. Leiden: Koninklijk Instituut voor Taal-, Land- en Volkenkunde.

Nash, June. 1994. Global integration and subsistence insecurity. *American Anthropologist* 96 (1): 7–30.

Netting, Robert McC. 1990. Links and boundaries: Reconsidering the alpine village as ecosystem. In *The ecosystem approach in anthropology*, ed. Emilio F. Moran, 229–45. Ann Arbor, MI: University of Michigan Press.

———— 1993. *Smallholders, householders: Farm families and the ecology of intensive, sustainable agriculture*. Stanford, CA: Stanford University Press.

Nevins, Joseph, and Nancy Lee Peluso, eds. 2008. *Taking Southeast Asia to market: Commodities, nature, and people in the neoliberal age*. Ithaca, NY: Cornell University Press.

New York Times. 1997. Small investors and big money taken by tale of jungle gold. 6 May.

Nonini, Donald. 1992. *British colonial rule and the resistance of the Malay peasantry, 1990–1957*. Monograph Series 38. New Haven, CT: Yale University, Southeast Asia Studies Program.

Noorlander, J. C. 1935. *Bandjarmasin en de compagnie in tweede helft der 18de eeuw* (Banjarmasin and the company in the second half of the 18th century). Leiden: M. Dubbeldeman.

Nugent, David. 1996. From devil pacts to drug deals: Commerce, unnatural accumulation, and moral community in "modern" Peru. *American Ethnologist* 23 (2):258–90.

Obeyesekere, Gananath. 1992. *The apotheosis of Captain Cook: European mythmaking in the Pacific*. Princeton, NJ: Princeton University Press; Honolulu: Bishop Museum Press.

O'Brien, Donal B. Cruise. 1975. *Saints and politicians: Essays in the organisation of a Senegalese peasant society*. Cambridge, UK: Cambridge University Press.

Ohlsson, Bo. 1990. *Socio-economic aspects of forestry development*. Indonesia Forestry Studies VIII-3. Jakarta: Indonesian Ministry of Forestry and UN Food and Agriculture Organization.

Ong, Aihwa, and Stephen J. Collier. 2005. *Global assemblages: Technology, politics, and ethics as anthropological problems*. Malden, MA: Blackwell.

Ooi, Jin-Bee. 1959. Rural development in tropical areas, with special reference to Malaya. *Malayan Journal of Tropical Geography* 12: 1–222.

Ormeling, F. J. 1957. *The Timor problem: A geographical interpretation of an underdeveloped island*. Groningen and Jakarta: J. B. Wolters; The Hague: Martinus Nijhoff.

Ortiz, Fernando. [1947] 1995. Cuban counterpoint: Tobacco and sugar. Durham, NC: Duke University Press.

Ortner, Sherry. 1984. Anthropological theory since the sixties. *Comparative Studies in Society and History* 26 (1): 126–66.

Osche, Jacob Jonas (with Reinier Cornelis Bakhuizen van den Brink). [1931] 1980. *Vegetables of the Dutch East Indies: Survey of the indigenous and foreign plants serving as pot-herbs and side-dishes*. Reprint, Amsterdam: A. Asher.

Oxford English Dictionary. 1999. CD-ROM version. New York: Oxford University Press.

Oxley, Thomas. 1847. Gutta Percha. *Journal of the Indian Archipelago and Eastern Asia* 1:22–29.

Padoch, Christine. 1980. The environmental and demographic effects of alternative cash-producing activities among shifting cultivators in Sarawak. In *Tropical ecology and development*, ed. J. I. Furtado, 475–81. Kuala Lumpur: International Society of Tropical Ecology.

———— 1982. *Migration and its alternatives among the Iban of Sarawak*. Verhandelingen No. 98. The Hague: Martinus Nijhoff.

———— 1988a. Agriculture in interior Borneo: Shifting cultivation and alternatives. *Expedition* 30 (1): 18–28.

———— 1988b. People of the floodplain and forest. In *People of the tropical rain forest*, ed. Julie Sloan Denslow and Christine Padoch, 127–42. Berkeley, CA: University of California Press; Washington, DC: Smithsonian Institution Traveling Exhibition Service.

Paige, Jeffery M. 1975. *Agrarian revolution: Social movements and export agriculture in the underdeveloped world*. London: Free Press.

Parry, Jonathan, and Maurice Bloch, eds. 1989. *Money and the morality of exchange*. Cambridge, UK: Cambridge University Press.

Peluso, Nancy P. 1983a. *Markets and merchants: The forest product trade of East Kalimantan in historical perspective.* M.S. thesis, Cornell University.

――― 1983b. Networking in the commons: A tragedy for rattan? *Indonesia* 35:95–108.

Peluso, Nancy P., and Mark Poffenberger. 1989. Social forestry in Java: Reorienting management systems. *Human Organization* 48 (4): 333–44.

Pelzer, Karl J. 1945. *Pioneer settlement in the Asiatic tropics: Studies in land utilization and agricultural colonization in Southeast Asia.* Special Publication No. 29. New York: American Geographical Society.

――― 1978a. *Planter and peasant: Colonial policy and the agrarian struggle in East Sumatra, 1863–1947.* Verhandelingen No. 84. The Hague: Martinus Nijhoff.

――― 1978b. Swidden cultivation in Southeast Asia: Historical, ecological, and economic perspectives. In *Farmers in the forest: Economic development and marginal agriculture in Northern Thailand,* ed. Peter Kunstadter, E. C. Chapman, and S. Sabhasri, 271–86. Honolulu: East-West Center.

Peluso, Nancy Lee. 2009. Rubber erasures, rubber producing rights: Making racialized territories in West Kalimantan, Indonesia. *Development and Change* 40 (1): 47–80.

Penot, Eric. 2004. Improved rubber agroforestry systems. In *From slash-and-burn to replanting: Green revolutions in the Indonesian uplands?,* ed. François Ruf and Frederic Lançon, 129–46. Washington, DC: World Bank.

――― 2007. From shifting cultivation to sustainable jungle rubber: A history of innovations in Indonesia. In *Voices from the forest: Integrating indigenous knowledge into sustainable upland farming,* ed. Malcolm Cairns, 577–99. Washington, DC: Resources for the Future.

Perz, Stephen G., Robert T. Walker, and Marcellus M. Caldus. 2006. Beyond population and environment: Household demographic life cycles and land use allocation among small farms in the Amazon. Human Ecology 34: 829–49.

Peters, Charles M., Alwyn H. Gentry, and Robert O. Mendelsohn. 1989. Valuation of an Amazonian rainforest. *Nature* 339:655–56.

Philip, Kavita. 1999. Global botanical networks, environmentalist discourses, and the political economy of cinchona transplantation to British India. *Revue Francaise d'Histoire d'Outre Mer* 322–23 (April): 119–42.

Pierce, Jennifer. 1995. Reflections on fieldwork in a complex organization: Lawyers, ethnographic authority, and lethal weapons. In *Studying elites using qualitative methods,* ed. Rosanna Herz and Jonathan B. Imber, 94–110. Thousand Oaks, CA: Sage Publications.

Pires, Tomé. 1944. *The Suma Oriental of Tomé Pires, and the book of Francisco Rodrigues.* Trans. Armando Cortesão. London: Hakluyt Society.

Polanyi, Karl. 1957. *The great transformation: The political and economic origins of our time.* Boston: Beacon Press.

Pollan, Michael. 2001. *The botany of desire: A plant's-eye view of the world.* New York: Random House.

Polo, Marco. [1298] 1969. *The travels of Marco Polo.* New York: Airmont.

Potter, Lesley. 1988. Indigenes and colonisers: Dutch forest policy in South and East Borneo (Kalimantan), 1900 to 1950. In *Changing tropical forests: Historical perspectives on today's challenges in Asia, Australasia, and Oceania,* ed. John Dargavel, Kay Dixon, and Noel Semple, 127–49. Canberra: Australian National University, Centre for Resource and Environmental Studies.

――― 1997. A forest product out of control: Gutta percha in Indonesia and the wider Malay world, 1845–1915. In *Paper landscapes: Explorations in the environmental history of Indonesia,* ed. Peter Boomgaard, Freek Colombijn, and David Henley, 281–308. Verhandelingen 178. Leiden: Koninklijk Instituut voor Taal-, Land- en Volkenkunde.

———— 2008. The oil palm question in Borneo. In *Reflections on the heart of Borneo*, ed. Gerard A. Persoon and Manon Osseweijer, 69–90. Tropenbos 24. Wageningen, The Netherlands: Tropenbos International.

Potter, Lesley, and Simon Badcock. 2004. Tree crop smallholders, capitalism, and *adat*: Studies in Riau Province, Indonesia. *Asia Pacific Viewpoint* 45 (3): 341–56.

———— 2007. Can Indonesia's complex agroforests survive globalisation and decentralisation? Sanggau District, West Kalimantan. In *Environment, development, and change in rural Asia-Pacific: Between local and global*, ed. John Connell and Eric Waddell, 167–85. London and New York: Routledge.

Potter, Lesley, and J. Lee. 1998. *Tree planting in Indonesia: Trends, impacts and directions (West Kalimantan case study)*. Center for International Forestry Research. Occasional Paper No. 18. Bogor, Indonesia.

Powell, J. M. 1976. Ethnobotany. In *New Guinea vegetation*, ed. K. Paijams, 106–213. Amsterdam: Elsevier.

Prawiroatmodjo, S. 1981. *Bausastra Jawa-Indonesia* (Java-Indonesian dictionary). 2nd ed. 2 vols. Jakarta: Gunung Agung.

Pringle, Robert. 1970. *Rajahs and rebels: The Ibans of Sarawak under Brooke rule, 1841–1941*. Ithaca, NY: Cornell University Press.

Psota, Thomas M. 1992. "Forest souls and rice deities": Rituals in hill rice cultivation and forest product collection. In *The Rejang of Southern Sumatra*, ed. Victor T. King, 30–51. Occasional Paper No. 19. Hull, UK: University of Hull, Centre for Southeast Asian Studies.

Ptak, Roderick. 1993. China and the trade in cloves, circa 960–1435. *Journal of the American Oriental Society* 113 (1):1–13.

Purseglove, J. W. 1956. Ridley and rubber. *Malayan Shell* 1:15–19.

———— 1957. History and functions of botanic gardens with special reference to Singapore. *Tropical Agriculture* 34 (3): 125–54.

———— 1968. *Tropical crops: Dicotyledons*. Harlow, UK: Longman.

Purseglove, J. W., E. G. Brown, C. L. Green, and S. R. J. Robbins. 1981. *Spices*. London: Longman.

Rabinow, Paul. 1986. Representations are social facts: Modernity and post-modernity in anthropology. In *Writing culture: The poetics and politics of ethnography*, ed. J. Clifford and G. E. Marcus, 234–61. Berkeley, CA: University of California Press.

Raffles, Thomas Stafford. [1817] 1978. *The history of Java*. 2 vols. Reprint, Kuala Lumpur: Oxford University Press.

Rambo, A. Terry. 1980. Fire and the energy efficiency of swidden agriculture. *Asian Perspectives* 23 (2): 309–16.

———— 1982. Orang Asli adaptive strategies: Implications for Malaysian natural resource development planning. In *Too rapid rural development*, ed. Colin MacAndrews and Lucas S. Chin, 251–99. Athens, OH: Ohio University Press.

Rappaport, Roy A. 1979. *Ecology, meaning, and religion*. Richmond, CA: North Atlantic Books.

Ras, J. J. 1968. *Hikajat Bandjar: A study in Malay historiography*. Koninklijk Instituut voor Taal-, Land- en Volkenkunde, Bibliotheca Indonesica 1. The Hague: Martinus Nijhoff.

Reece, R. H. W. 1988. Economic development under the Brookes. In *Development in Sarawak: Historical and contemporary perspectives*, ed. R. A. Cramb and R. H. W. Reece, 21–34. Monash Paper on Southeast Asia No. 17. Melbourne, Australia: Center of Southeast Asian Studies, Monash University.

Reid, Anthony. 1993. *Southeast Asia in the age of commerce 1450–1680.* Vol. 2 of *Expansion and crisis.* New Haven, CT: Yale University Press.

———. 1995. Humans and forests in pre-colonial Southeast Asia. *Environment and History* 1:93–110.

Richards, Anthony. 1972. Iban augury. *Sarawak Museum Journal* 2:63–81.

———. 1981. *An Iban-English dictionary.* Oxford, UK: Clarendon Press.

Richards, Paul. 1992. Saving the rain forest! Contested futures in conservation. In *Contemporary futures: Perspectives from social anthropology,* ed. Sandra Wallman, 138–53. London: Routledge.

———. 1996. *Fighting for the rain forest: War, youth and resources in Sierra Leone.* Oxford, UK: International African Institute.

Ricklefs, M. S. 2008. *A history of modern Indonesia since c. 1200.* 4th ed. Stanford, CA: Stanford University Press.

Rival, Laura. 1993. The growth of family trees: Understanding Huaorani perceptions of the forest. *Man* 28 (4): 635–52.

———, ed. 1998. *The social life of trees: Anthropological perspectives on tree symbolism.* Oxford, UK: Berg.

Robbins, Joel. 1995. Dispossessing the spirits: Christian transformations of desire and ecology among the Urapmin of Papua New Guinea. *Ethnology* 34 (3): 211–24.

Robequain, Charles. [1946] 1955. *Malaya, Indonesia, Borneo, and the Philippines: A geographical, economic, and political description of Malaya, the East Indies, and the Philippines.* Trans. E. D. Laborde. London: Longmans, Green. (Original, *Le Monde Malais.* Paris: Editions Payot.)

Romanoff, Steve. 1992. Food and debt among rubber tappers in the Bolivian Amazon. *Human Organization* 51 (2):122–35.

van Romburgh, P. 1897. Getah Pertja, hare eigenschappen, haar voorkomen en de wijze, waarop zij gewonnen wordt (Gutta-percha, its properties, its wise development, for gaining profit). *Teysmannia* 7:37–44, 134–42.

Rosaldo, Renato. 1978. The rhetoric of control: Ilongots viewed as natural bandits and wild Indians. In *The reversible world: Symbolic inversion in nature and society,* ed. Barbara A. Babcock, 240–57. Ithaca, NY: Cornell University Press.

Roseberry, William. 1991. *Anthropologies and histories: Essays in culture, history, and political economy.* New Brunswick, NJ: Rutgers University Press.

Roseman, Marina. 1991. *Healing sounds from the Malaysian rainforest: Temiar music and medicine.* Berkeley, CA: University of California Press.

Ross, Michael L. 2001. Does oil hinder democracy? *World Politics* 53 (April): 325–61.

Roth, Henry Ling. 1896. *The natives of Sarawak and British North Borneo.* 2 vols. London: Truslove and Hanson.

Rudner, Martin. 1976. Malayan rubber policy: Development and anti-development during the 1950s. *Journal of Southeast Asian Studies* 7:235–59.

Ruiz-Pérez, Manuel et al. 2004. Markets drive the specialization strategies of forest peoples. *Ecology and Society* 9 (2): 4. http://www.ecologyandsociety.org/vol9/iss2/art4 (accessed July 2010).

Safran, Elizabeth A., and Ricardo A. Godoy. 1993. Effects of government policies on smallholder palm cultivation: An example from Borneo. *Human Organization* 52 (3): 294–98.

Sahlins, Marshall. 1972. *Stone age economics.* Chicago: Aldine.

———. 1985. *Islands of history.* Chicago: University of Chicago Press.

Said, Edward. 1978. *Orientalism.* London: Routledge and Kegan Paul.

Salafsky, Nick. 1994. Drought in the rain forest: Effects of the 1991 El Niño-Southern Oscillation event on a rural economy in West Kalimantan, Indonesia. *Climatic Change* 27: 373-96.

Salafsky, Nick, Barbara L. Dugelby, and John W. Terborgh. 1993. Can extractive reserves save the rain forest? *Conservation Biology* 7 (1): 39-53.

Saleh, M. Idwar. 1976. Pepper trade and the ruling class of Banjarmasin in the seventeenth century. In *Proceedings of the Dutch-Indonesian historical conference, held at Noordwijkerhout, 19-22 May, The Netherlands*, 203-21. Leiden and Jakarta: Bureau of Indonesian Studies.

Sallnow, M. J. 1989. Precious metals in the Andean moral economy. In *Money and the morality of exchange*, ed. Jonathan Parry and Maurice Bloch, 209-31. Cambridge, UK: Cambridge University Press.

Sandin, Benedict. 1980. *Iban adat and augury*. Penang: Universiti Sains Malaysia.

———— 1994. Sources of Iban traditional history. Special Monograph. *Sarawak Museum Journal* 46 (67): 1-78.

Sandker, Marieke, Aritta Suwarno, and Bruce M. Campbell. 2007. Will forests remain in the face of oil palm expansion? Simulating change in Malinau, Indonesia. *Ecology and Society* 12 (2):37 (online).

Sarawak Gazette. 1925. A Dayak house, no. 859 (1 April).

———— 1938a. Rubber in Sarawak, no. 1016 (2 May): 64-65.

———— 1938b. Correspondence, no. 1017 (1 June): 96.

Sather, Clifford. 1990. Trees and tree tenure in Paku Iban society. *Borneo Review* 1 (1): 16-40.

van Schaik, Carel P., John W. Terborgh, and S. Joseph Wright. 1993. The phenology of tropical forests: Adaptive significance and consequences for primary consumers. *Annual Review of Ecology and Systematics* 24:353-77.

Schärer, Hans. 1963. *Ngaju religion: The conception of God among a South Borneo people*. Trans. Rodney Needham. Koninklijk Instituut voor Taal-, Land- en Volkenkunde, Translation Series 6. The Hague: Martinus Nijhoff.

Schmidgall-Tellings, A. Ed., and Alan M. Stevens. 1981. *A contemporary Indonesian-English dictionary*. Athens, OH: Ohio University Press.

Schneider, Jane. 1990. Spirits and the spirit of capitalism. In *Religious orthodoxy and popular faith in European society*, ed. Ellen Badone, 24-53. Princeton, NJ: Princeton University Press.

Schneider, Jürg. 1995. *From upland to irrigated rice: The development of wet-rice agriculture in Rejang Musi Southwest Sumatra*. Berlin: Reimer.

Schrieke, B. [1955] 1966. *Indonesian sociological studies: Selected writings of B. Schrieke*. 2nd ed., pt. 1. Trans. Ann de Leeuw, J. T. Brookway, James S. Holmes, and A. van Marle. The Hague: W. van Hoeve.

Schultes, Richard Evans. 1956. The Amazon Indian and evolution in Hevea and related genera. *Journal of the Arnold Arboretum* 37:123-47.

———— 1984. The tree that changed the world. *Arnoldia* 44 (2): 3-16.

———— 1987. Members of Euphorbiaceae in primitive and advanced societies. *Botanical Journal of the Linnaean Society* 94: 79-95.

Schwartzman, S., and P. Moutinho. 2008. Compensated reductions: Rewarding developing countries for protecting forest carbon. In *Climate change and forests: Emerging policy and market opportunities*, ed. Charlotte Streck, Robert O'Sullivan, and Toby Janson-Smith 227-36. Washington, DC: Brookings Institution Press.

Scott, James C. 1976. *The moral economy of the peasant: Rebellion and subsistence in Southeast Asia*. New Haven, CT: Yale University Press.

———— 1984. History according to winners and losers. In *History and peasant consciousness in*

South East Asia, ed. Andrew Turton and Shigeharu Tanabe, 161–210. Senri Ethnological Studies 13. Osaka, Japan: National Museum of Ethnology.

———. 1985. *Weapons of the weak: Everyday forms of peasant resistance*. New Haven, CT: Yale University Press.

———. 1998. *Seeing like a state*. New Haven, CT: Yale University Press.

———. 2009. *The art of not being governed: An anarchist history of upland Southeast Asia*. New Haven: Yale University Press.

Sellato, Bernard. 1994. *Nomads of the Borneo rainforest: The economics, politics, and ideology of settling down*. Honolulu: University of Hawaii Press.

Shakespeare, William. 1856. *The complete works of Shakespeare: Tragedies*. New York: Johnson, Fry.

Sheil, Douglas, Anne Casson, Erik Meijaard, Meine van Noordwijk, Joanne Gaskell, Jacqui Sunderland-Groves, Karah Wertz, and Markku Kanninen. 2009. The impacts and opportunities of oil palm in Southeast Asia: What do we know and what do we need to know? Occasional Paper No. 51. Bogor, Indonesia: Center for International Forestry Research.

Sherman, George. 1980. What "green desert"? The ecology of Batak grassland farming. *Indonesia* 29:113–48.

———. 1990. *Rice, rupees, and ritual: Economy and society among the Samosir Batak of Sumatra*. Stanford, CA: Stanford University Press.

Shipton, Parker. 1989. *Bitter money: Cultural economy and some African meanings of forbidden commodities*. Washington, DC: American Anthropological Association.

———. 1995. Luo entrustment: Foreign finance and the soil of the spirits in Kenya. *Africa* 65 (2): 165–96.

Shiva, Vandana. 1993. *Monocultures of the mind: Perspectives on biodiversity and biotechnology*. Dehra Dun, India: Natraj Publishers.

Sider, Gerald M. 1986. *Culture and class in anthropology and history: A Newfoundland illustration*. Cambridge, UK: Cambridge University Press.

Siegel, James T. 1969. *The rope of God*. Berkeley: University of California Press.

Sinar Harapan (newspaper). 1984. A. M. Nasution lebih suka memilih kelapa sawit (A. M. Nasution prefers to choose oil palm), 11 July.

Sivaramakrishnan, K. 2002. Situating the subalterns: History and anthropology in subaltern studies project. In *Reading subaltern studies*, ed. David Ludden, 212–55. London: Anthem Press.

Skeat, Walter William. [1900] 1967. *Malay magic: Being an introduction to the folklore and popular religion of the Malay Pensinula*. Reprint, New York: Dover.

Slater, Candace. 1994. "All that glitters": Contemporary Amazonian miners' tales. *Comparative Studies in Society and History* 36 (4): 720–42.

Soesaptono, B.J. 1993. Studi banding: Sengkuang (Comparative study: Sengkuang). Mimeograph, 2 July.

Sonius, H. W. J. 1981. Introduction. In *Van Vollenhoven on Indonesian adat law: Selections from "Het adatrecht von Nederlandsch-Indië." (Vol. 1, 1918; Vol. 2, 1931)*, ed. J. F. Holleman, xxix–lxvii. Translation Series 20. Leiden, Netherlands: Koninklijk Instituut voor Taal-, Land- en Volkenkunde.

Speelman, Cornelis. [1670] 1983. De handelsrelaties van het Makassaarse rijk volgens de notitie van Cornelis Speelman uit 1670 (The trade relations of the Makassarese state according to notes of Cornelis Speelman from 1670). In vol. 3 of *Nederlands historische bronnen* (Historical sources of the Netherlands), ed. J. Noorduyn, 96–121. Amsterdam: Verloren.

Stearman, Allyn M. 1994. "Only slaves climb trees": Revisiting the myth of the ecologically noble savage in Amazonia. *Human Nature* 5 (4): 339–57.

Steinbeck, John. [1945] 1974. *The pearl*. New York: Bantam Books.

Steward, Julian H. 1977. The foundations of basin-plateau Shoshonean society. In *Evolution and ecology: Essays on social transformation by Julian H. Steward*, ed. Jane C. Steward and Robert F. Murphy, 366–406. Urbana, IL: University of Illinois Press.

St. John, Spenser. [1862] 1974. *Life in the forests of the Far East*. 2 vols. Reprint, Kuala Lampur: Oxford University Press.

Stoler, Ann. 1985a. *Capitalism and confrontation in Sumatra's plantation belt, 1870–1979*. New Haven, CT: Yale University Press.

——— 1985b. Perceptions of protest: Defining the dangerous in colonial Sumatra. *American Ethnologist* 12 (4): 642–58.

Stoll, Steven. 2006. The smallholder's dilemma. *Technology and Culture* 47:808–13.

Sturgeon, Janet C. 2005. *Border landscapes: The politics of Akha land use in China and Thailand*. Seattle, WA: University of Washington Press.

Sugishima, Takashi. 1994. Double descent, alliance, and botanical metaphors among the Lionese of Central Flores. *Bijdragen* 150 (1): 146–70.

Suhud, Pribadi. 1979. Fungsi pembinaan masyarakat terasing dalam rangka membina kelestarian tanah dan hutan (The purpose of developing indigenous peoples in the course of conserving land and forests). *Penyuluh Sosial* 43:37–41.

Sulistyawati. 2011. The historical demography of resource use and abuse in a swidden community in West Kalimantan. In *Beyond the sacred forest: Complicating conservation in Southeast Asia*, ed. Michael R. Dove, Percy E. Sajise, and Amity A. Doolittle. Durham, NC: Duke University Press.

Sundaram, Jomo Kwame. 1986. *A question of class: Capital, the state, and uneven development in Malaya*. Singapore: Oxford University Press.

Suntharalingam, R. 1963. The British in Banjarmasin: An abortive attempt at settlement 1700–1707. *Journal of Southeast Asian History* 4 (2): 33–50.

Survival International. 2009. *The most inconvenient truth of all: Climate change and indigenous people*. London.

Sutlive, Vinson H., Jr. 1978. *The Iban of Sarawak*. Arlington Heights, IL: AHM Publishing.

——— 1992. *Tun Jugah of Sarawak: Colonialism and Iban response*. Kuala Lumpur: Penerbit Fajar Bakti.

Suyanto, S., T. P. Tomich, and K. Otsuka. 2001. Land tenure and farm management efficiency: The case of smallholder rubber production in customary land areas of Sumatra. *Agroforestry Systems* 52:145–60.

Tagliacozzo, Eric. 2005. Onto the coast and into the forest: Ramifications of the China trade on the history of Northwest Borneo, 900–1900. In *Histories of the Borneo environment*, ed. Reed Wadley, 25–60. Leiden: Koninklijk Instituut voor Taal-, Land- en Volkenkunde.

Taussig, Michael T. 1980. *The devil and commodity fetishism in South America*. Chapel Hill, NC: University of North Carolina Press.

Tedlock, Barbara. 1992. Dreaming and dream research. In *Dreaming: Anthropological and psychological interpretations*, ed. Barbara Tedlock, 1–30. Santa Fe, NM: School of American Research Press.

Thee, Kian-wie. 1977. *Plantation agriculture and export growth: An economic history of east Sumatra, 1863–1942*. Jakarta: LEKNAS-LIPI.

Thomas, Kenneth D. 1965. Shifting cultivation and production of smallholder rubber in a south Sumatran village. *Malayan Economics Review* 10:100–115.

Thomas, Kenneth D., and J. Panglaykim. 1976. The Chinese in the south Sumatran rubber industry: A case study in economic nationalism. In *The Chinese in Indonesia: Five essays*, ed. J. A. C. Mackie, 139–98. Honolulu: University Press of Hawaii, in association with the Australian Institute of International Affairs.

Thongmak, Seri, and David L. Hulse. 1993. The winds of change: Karen people in harmony with world heritage. In *The law of the mother: Protecting indigenous peoples in protected areas*, ed. Elizabeth Kemf, 161–68. San Francisco: Sierra Club.

Tomich, Thomas P. 1991. Smallholder rubber development in Indonesia. In *Reforming economic systems in developing countries*, ed. D. H. Perkins and M. Roehmer, 249–70. Cambridge, MA: Harvard University Press.

Torquebiau, E. F. 1984. Man-made dipterocarp forest in Sumatra. *Agroforestry Systems* 2 (2): 103–27.

Touwen, Jeroen. 2000. Entrepreneurial strategies in indigenous export agriculture in the outer islands of colonial Indonesia, 1925–1938. In *Weathering the storm: The economies of Southeast Asia in the 1930s depression*, ed. Peter Boomgaard and Ian Brown, 143–70. Leiden: Koninklijk Instituut voor Taal-, Land- en Volkenkunde; Singapore: Institute of Southeast Asian Studies.

Tremeer, R. E. 1964. The early history of rubber planting in Sarawak, 1880–1910. *Sarawak Gazette* 90:50–52.

Tsing, Anna L. 1984. *Politics and culture in the Meratus mountains*. Ph.D. dissertation, Stanford University.

——— 1993. *In the realm of the diamond queen: Marginality in an out-of-the-way place*. Princeton, NJ: Princeton University Press.

——— 1999. Becoming a tribal elder and other green development fantasies. In *Transforming the Indonesian uplands: Marginality, power and production*, ed. Tania M. Li, 159–202. London: Berg.

——— 2000. Inside the economy of appearance. *Public Culture* 12 (1): 115–44.

——— 2005. *Friction: An ethnography of global connection*. Princeton, NJ: Princeton University Press.

Tucker, Richard P. 2007. *Insatiable appetite: The United States and the ecological degradation of the tropical world*. Rev. ed. Lanham, MD: Rowman and Littlefield.

Uchibori, Motomitsu. 1984. Transformations of Iban social consciousness. *Senri Ethnological Studies* 13:211–34.

Uljee, G. L. 1925. *Handboek voor de Residentie Westerafdeling van Borneo* (Manual for the residency of the Western Division of Borneo). Weltevreden, Java: Visser.

Vandermeer, John, and Ivette Perfecto. 1995. *Breakfast of biodiversity: The truth about rain forest destruction*. Oakland, CA: Food First Books.

Vayda, Andrew P. 1961. Expansion and warfare among swidden agriculturalists. *American Anthropologist* 63 (2): 346–58.

——— 1976. *War in ecological perspective: Persistence, change, and adaptive processes in three Oceanian societies*. New York: Plenum Press.

——— 2009. *Explaining human actions and environmental change*. Lanham, MD: Altamira Press.

Vayda, Andrew P., and Bradley B. Walters. 1999. Against political ecology. *Human Ecology* 27 (1): 167–79.

Visser, Leontine E. 1989. *My rice field is my child: Social and territorial aspects of swidden cultivation in Sahu, Eastern Indonesia*. Trans. Rita DeCoursey. Verhandelingen 136. Dordrecht, The Netherlands: Foris Publications.

Vlekke, Bernard H. M. 1961. *Nusantara: A history of Indonesia*. Rev. ed. Bruxelles: Les Editions A. Manteau S. A.; Jakarta: P. T. Soeroengan.

van Vollenhoven, Cornelis. [1919] 1932. *De Indonesier en Zijn Grond: Onveranderde herdruk* (The Indonesian and his land: Unabridged reprint). 2nd ed. Leiden: Brill.

———— 1981. *Van Vollenhoven on Indonesian adat law: Selections from "Het adatrecht von Nederlandsch-Indië." (Vol. 1, 1918; Vol. 2, 1931)*, ed. J. F. Holleman. Translation Series 20. Leiden, Netherlands: Koninklijk Instituut voor Taal-, Land- en Volkenkunde.

de Vries, Jan. 1976. *Economy of Europe in an age of crisis, 1600–1750*. Cambridge: Cambridge University Press.

de Waard, P. W. F. 1964. Pepper cultivation in Sarawak. *World Crops* 16 (3): 24–30.

———— 1989. *Piper nigrum* L. In *Plant resources of South-East Asia: A selection*, ed. E. Westphal and P. C. M. Jansen, 225–30. Wageningen, The Netherlands: PUDOC Scientific Publishers.

Wadley, Reed L. 2004. Punitive expeditions and divine revenge: Oral and colonial histories of rebellion and pacification in western Borneo, 1886–1902. *Ethnohistory* 51 (3): 609–36.

———— 2007. Slashed and burned: War, environment, and resource insecurity in West Borneo during the late-nineteenth and early twentieth centuries. *Journal of the Royal Anthropological Institute* 13 (1):109–28.

Wadley, Reed L., and Ole Mertz. 2005. Pepper in a time of crisis: Smallholder buffering strategies in Sarawak, Malaysia and West Kalimantan, Indonesia. *Agricultural Systems* 85: 289–305.

Wallace, Alfred R. 1869. *The Malay archipelago: The land of the orang-utan, and the bird of paradise. A narrative of travel, with studies of man and nature*. New York: Harper.

Wallerstein, Immanuel. 1974. *Capitalist agriculture and the origins of the European world economy in the sixteenth century*. The Modern World System, Vol. 1. New York: Academic Press.

———— 1980. *Mercantilism and the consolidation of the European world economy, 1600–1750*. The Modern World System, Vol. 2. New York: Academic Press.

Walsh, Andrew. 2004. In the wake of things: Speculating in and about sapphires in northern Madagascar. *American Anthropologist* 106 (2): 225–37.

———— 2005. The obvious aspects of ecological underprivilege in Ankarana, northern Madagascar. *American Anthropologist* 107 (4): 654–65.

———— 2010. The commodification of fetishes: Telling the difference between natural and synthetic sapphires. *American Ethnologist* 37 (1): 98–114.

Ward, Arthur Bartlett. 1966. *Rajah's servant*. Cornell Southeast Asia Program Data Paper 61. Ithaca, NY: Cornell University, Department of Asian Studies.

Ward, Marion W., and R. Gerard Ward. 1974. An economic survey of West Kalimantan. *Bulletin of Indonesian Economic Studies* 10 (3): 26–53.

Wareham, Wilfred William, ed. 1975. *The little nord easter: Reminiscences of a Placentia Bayman*. Community Studies Series 1. St. John's, Newfoundland: Memorial University of Newfoundland.

———— 1982. *Toward an ethnography of "times": Newfoundland party traditions, past and present*. Ph.D. dissertation in Folklore and Folklife, University of Pennsylvania.

Watt, George. [1889–1896] 1972. *A dictionary of the economic products of India*. 7 vols. in 10. Reprint, Delhi: Gordhan.

te Wechel, P. 1911. Iets over z.g.n. Djeloetoeng (Something concerning the so-called jelutong). *Teysmannia* 22:588–97.

Weinstein, Barbara. 1983. *The Amazon rubber boom 1850–1920*. Stanford, CA: Stanford University Press.

Weinstock, Joseph A. 1983. Rattan: Ecological balance in a Borneo rainforest swidden. *Economic Botany* 37 (1): 58–68.

Wenzlhuemer, Roland. 2008. *From coffee to tea cultivation in Ceylon, 1880–1900: An economic and social history.* Leiden (Netherlands): Brill.

West, Paige. 2005. Translation, value, and space: Theorizing an ethnographic and engaged environmental anthropology. *American Anthropologist* 107 (4): 632–42.

——— 2006. *Conservation is our government now: The politics of ecology in Papua New Guinea.* Durham, NC: Duke University Press.

Wheatley, Paul. 1959. Geographical notes on some commodities involved in Sung maritime trade. *Journal of the Royal Asiatic Society* 32 (2): 1–140.

White, Ben. 1999. Nucleus and plasma: Contract farming and the exercise of power in upland West Java. In *Transforming the Indonesian uplands,* ed. Tania Li, 229–55. Amsterdam: Harwood Academic Publishers.

Whitford, Harry N. 1924. The crude rubber supply: An international problem. *Foreign Affairs* 2 (4):613–21.

Wibawa, Gede, Sinung Hendratno, and Meine van Noordwijk. 2005. Permanent smallholder rubber agroforestry systems in Sumatra, Indonesia. In *Slash-and-burn agriculture: The search for alternatives,* ed. Cheryl A. Palm, Stephen A. Vosti, Pedro A. Sanchez, and Polly J. Ericksen, 222–32. New York: Columbia University Press.

Wickham, Henry A. 1908. *On the plantation, cultivation, and curing of Parà Indian rubber.* London: Kegan Paul, Trench, Trübner.

van Wijk, C. L. 1941. Enkele aantekeningen over de verjonging van de Pantoeng (*Dyera lowii* en *D. borneensis*) (Notes on the regeneration of the pantung [*Dyera lowii* and *D. borneensis*]). Unpublished.

de Wilde, A. Neytzell, and J. Th. Moll. 1936. *The Netherlands Indies during the depression: A brief economic survey.* Amsterdam: J. M. Meulenhoff.

Wilkinson, R. J. 1959. *A Malay-English dictionary.* 2 vols. New York: Macmillan.

Williams, Llewelyn. 1963. Laticiferous plants of economic importance IV: Jelutong (*Dyera* spp.). *Economic Botany* 17:110–26.

Williams, Raymond. 1980. *Problems in materialism and culture: Selected essays.* London: New Left Books.

Wolf, Eric R. 1982. *Europe and the people without history.* Berkeley, CA: University of California Press.

Wolf, Howard, and Ralph Wolf. 1936. *Rubber: A story of glory and greed.* New York: Covici Friede.

Wolters, O. W. 1967. *Early Indonesian commerce: A study of the origins of Srivijaya.* Ithaca, NY: Cornell University Press.

——— 2008. *Early Southeast Asia: Selected essays.* Ithaca, NY: Cornell University, Southeast Asia Program.

Woodside, Alexander. 1976. *Community and revolution in modern Vietnam,* Boston: Houghton Mifflin.

Worster, Donald. 1995. Nature and the disorder of history. In *Reinventing nature: Responses to postmodern deconstruction,* ed. Michael E. Soule and Gary Lease, 65–85. Washington, DC: Island Press.

Wycherley, P. R. 1968. Introduction of *Hevea* to the Orient. *Planter* 44:1–11, 127–37.

Zoetmulder, P. J. 1982. *Old Javanese-English dictionary.* 2 vols. The Hague: Martinus Nijhoff.

General Index

Page numbers in italics refer to figures.

weaving and pepper cultivation, 68–69; rubber production involvement, 94, 107, *159*, 271n5; swidden labor of, 152–53, *153*
World Bank, 28, 209, 214
world system, 18, 54, 252–53, 256, 275n37; *Hikayat Banjar* and, 71, 72; teleology of, 99.

See also capitalism; globalization; markets, global
World War II, 10, 12, 150
Wycherley, P. R., 216

Zimbabwe, 18, 253–54

Index of Plant Names